The Question of Integration

The Question of Integration:
Immigration, Exclusion
and the Danish Welfare State

Edited by

Karen Fog Olwig and Karsten Paerregaard

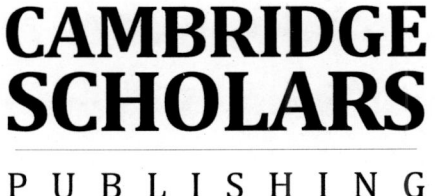

The Question of Integration: Immigration, Exclusion and the Danish Welfare State,
Edited by Karen Fog Olwig and Karsten Paerregaard

This book first published 2011. The present binding first published 2011.

Cambridge Scholars Publishing

12 Back Chapman Street, Newcastle upon Tyne, NE6 2XX, UK

British Library Cataloguing in Publication Data
A catalogue record for this book is available from the British Library

Copyright © 2011 by Karen Fog Olwig and Karsten Paerregaard and contributors

All rights for this book reserved. No part of this book may be reproduced, stored in a retrieval system, or transmitted, in any form or by any means, electronic, mechanical, photocopying, recording or otherwise, without the prior permission of the copyright owner.

ISBN (10): 1-4438-2635-9, ISBN (13): 978-1-4438-2635-8

TABLE OF CONTENTS

Preface vii

Introduction 1
"Strangers" in the Nation
Karen Fog Olwig and Karsten Paerregaard

Part I: The Cultural Construction of Danish Society

Chapter One 30
Integrating Denmark: The Welfare State as a National(ist) Accomplishment
Steffen Jöhncke

Chapter Two 54
"The Family of Denmark" and "the Aliens": Kinship Images in Danish Integration Politics
Mikkel Rytter

Chapter Three 77
The Paradox of Integration: Excluding while Claiming to Integrate into Danish Society
Inger Sjørslev

Chapter Four 94
Religion and Integration: Three Danish Models for the Relationship between Religion and Society
Cecilie Rubow

Chapter Five 112
To be Danish and Muslim: Internalizing the Stranger?
Tina Gudrun Jensen

Chapter Six 129
Contesting Danish Civility: The Cartoon Crisis as Transitional Drama
Heiko Henkel

Part II: Inclusion and Exclusion in the Welfare Society

Chapter Seven 150
Day-Care in Denmark: The Key to Social Integration
Helle Bundgaard

Chapter Eight 168
Psychiatric Patients with a Non-Danish Ethnic Background:
Categorization in a Danish Welfare Institution
Katrine Schepelern Johansen

Chapter Nine 187
Suffering for Benefits? Integration and Social Exchange between
Iraqi Refugees and Danish Welfare Institutions
Sofie Danneskiold-Samsoe

Chapter Ten 207
Caught in the Grid of Difference and Gratitude: HIV Positive
Africans Facing the Challenges of Danish Sociality
Hanne Overgaard Mogensen

Chapter Eleven 230
The Obligation to Participate: Micro-integrative Processes of Civil
Sociality
Sally Anderson

Part III: Epilogues

Integration, of the *Folk* and by the *Folk*... 256
Richard Jenkins

Danes and Others 266
Ralph Grillo

The Multiple Registers of Immigrant Reception: Comparative
Mythologies 277
Vered Amit

Contributors 282

Index 287

PREFACE

For several years Denmark has attracted the attention of the world because of its strict policy toward its immigrant population. Formerly known for its liberal lifestyle and generous welfare society, this Scandinavian country has now gained an international reputation of being one of the most anti-Islamic and anti-immigrant nations in Europe. Why is it that a country, until recently considered a role model by the rest of the world in terms of granting its citizens equal opportunities and respecting the cultural and religious differences of minority groups, now stands out as an example of how the prosperous societies of the Global North exclude and discriminate immigrants and refugees from the Global South? This book, by anthropologists who live and work in Denmark, seeks to find some answers to this question by exploring, through in depth ethnographic analysis, the encounter between the Danish welfare society and its population of immigrants and refugees.

The book is a revised, translated version of a previous Danish publication, *Integration: Antropologiske perspektiver* (Copenhagen: Museum Tusculanum, 2007). Written in the wake of the Mohammad cartoon crisis that erupted in 2006 (see the introductory chapter and the chapter by Heiko Henkel), it attempted to account ethnographically for the many questions and concerns that the cartoon crisis triggered. With this English language edition of the book we wish to show how ethnographic analysis can shed light on burning issues of globalization, immigration and integration in a small European country that has been subject to relatively little anthropological investigation. We also hope that the larger international community of migration and integration scholars will engage in the debate and help give the many questions and topics that the book brings up new perspectives. A key question is to what extent – and how – Denmark is exceptional in its reception of immigrants and refugees. Does Denmark stand apart or is it merely a representative of a more general trend of excluding and discriminating minorities in Europe and North America? To start the conversation we have invited three distinguished colleagues (from Britain and Canada) to write epilogues to the book discussing the Danish case from their particular scholarly and national vantage point. The broader, comparative framework suggests that the Danish case may be understood as both part of a general European response to the growing globalization that seems to undermine the autonomy of the nation-state and as a more particular example of the development of the welfare state and the integration of its citizens in a time of uncertainty and crisis.

Two chapters (by Heiko Henkel and Helle Bundgaard) have been added to the English edition, whereas two chapters (by Katja Kvaale and Marianne Holm Pedersen) are not included in this volume, but published in other international venues. We wish to thank Zachary Whyte and Robert Parkin for editing the English language chapters, and the Migration Initiative and the Department of Anthropology, both at the University of Copenhagen, for their financial assistance. We also want to thank Marianne Alenius, the director of Museum Tusculanum Press, for supporting our ambition to publish an English edition of the Danish book. Finally, we would like to thank Kirsten Gelting, of the Migration Initiative, for her invaluable assistance with the lay-out of the book.

Copenhagen, September 1, 2010.
Karen Fog Olwig and Karsten Paerregaard

Introduction

"Strangers" in the Nation

Karen Fog Olwig
and Karsten Paerregaard

In 2006 Denmark made headlines in the media across the world as Muslims reacted to a Danish newspaper's publication of satirical cartoons depicting the Islamic prophet Muhammad by boycotting Danish goods, burning the Danish flag and even attacking Danish embassies in the Middle East. Danes, who consider their country to be a respected, peaceful, freedom-loving country, reacted with shock and disbelief at this outburst of anger towards Denmark. For most ethnic Danes, the newspaper's right to publish the cartoons, which violated Muslim prohibitions on graven images of the Prophet and in one case suggested he was a terrorist, could not be disputed due to the principle of freedom of expression, whether or not they agreed with the wisdom of publishing these particular cartoons. For many Muslims in Denmark and abroad, however, the publication of the cartoons was yet another example of the disrespect that is shown to Muslims – and the Islamic faith in general – in Denmark and other Western countries.

This book does not concern the global "cartoon crisis" per se, but rather the Danish society that provided the nexus for it. In some respects, Denmark may be considered a microcosm of a more general European situation in which identities based on notions of national development grounded in the land are being confronted with a new globalized world in which increasing migration and ethnic diversity have become the norm. In other respects, however, Denmark, like the other nations of Europe, has also developed a particular national version of the cultural anxiety that has swept the continent in recent decades in response to the arrival of growing numbers of immigrants and refugees (Grillo 2003: Hervik 2006). Concretely, since the 1960s, this north European country of 43,094 square kilometers and almost 5.5 million people has seen the development of a population of immigrants, refugees and their offspring (usually referred to as second-generation immigrants) amounting to eight percent[1] of the total population. While the size of the immigrant population in Denmark is modest by international standards, it has called into question the country's self-understanding as a culturally homogeneous, egalitarian welfare society with deep historical roots in the Danish landscape. This immigration therefore presents a lens through which to examine how a close-knit north European society has responded to contemporary forces of globalization and the social and economic changes that they have brought about.

A key issue in the Danes' response to globalization has been how to incorporate, or "integrate," a foreign population with cultural values and social norms that Danes widely perceive as backward and oppressive into what Danes believe is a modern, liberal, egalitarian and democratic welfare society grounded in the culture and history of the land. Part one of the book therefore focuses on the public debates among politicians, journalists, the clergy and researchers concerning how best to integrate foreign immigrants and refugees into Danish society without jeopardizing the social and cultural cohesion of the welfare state. It begins with a chapter on the development of the Danish welfare state and the challenges that contemporary immigration and integration are seen as posing for Danish society. This is followed by chapters analysing the political rhetoric concerning Danish society as a "tribe" or a "family," the public debate and policy on immigration and integration, religious discussions concerning the ability of the hitherto virtually mono-religious state to accommodate a plurality of religious practices and beliefs, and the particular position of Muslim immigrants in Denmark and their reaction to the publication of "the Muhammad cartoons." It is a central argument of the book that "integration" is not a neutral concept denoting the joining together of different population groups. It is rather an ideologically loaded concept, linked to Danish ideas of equality and belonging, which in turn are related to notions of cultural similarity closely associated with the Danish welfare state.

The second part of the book examines how Danish understandings of integration translate into everyday life for immigrants and refugees in Denmark. This section of the book presents a number of ethnographic case studies of immigrants in Denmark and their encounters with the Danish welfare state and ethnically Danish staff in such places as educational institutions, social welfare offices, psychiatric hospitals, health clinics and exercise clubs. They scrutinize how these encounters have shaped immigrants' perceptions of Denmark and their experiences of social inclusion and exclusion. The studies show that, while the welfare state has extended considerable social and economic assistance to immigrants and refugees, thus helping them settle in Denmark, Danish perceptions of these people as culturally different – and therefore as foreign elements in the country – have presented a serious obstacle to their social acceptance in Danish society. The Danish classification of immigrants and refugees as different has led to a strong focus on the need to integrate them culturally into Danish society, which has had the ironic consequence that a substantial part of the immigrant population, despite having lived in Denmark for years, even generations, has become permanently categorized as not (yet) belonging in the country. This reluctance to recognize immigrants and their descendants as Danish is reflected in the use of expressions such as "second-generation immigrant" or "person of other ethnic origin."

Denmark: a culturally homogeneous society?

During the 1960s and early 1970s, Denmark received thousands of immigrants from the Balkans, the Middle East, Pakistan and North Africa who came to work as unskilled workers in Danish factories in need of labour at the time.[2] In 1973, when oil prices rose sharply, Denmark experienced an economic recession that created increased unemployment. Further immigration into Denmark was stopped immediately, but most of the foreign workers, who by then had obtained permanent visas in Denmark, opted to stay, and many who lost their jobs started their own retail or taxi businesses. The immigrant population continued to rise, as the immigrants sent for their spouses and children, or married and brought over people from their country of origin. By 1983 the immigrant population from non-Western countries had grown to approximately 50,000, or almost 60,000 if their descendants are included (Udlændingeservice 2008: 15). From the mid-1970s, when labour migration ceased, Denmark began to receive a considerable number of refugees from Vietnam, Sri Lanka, Iraq, the Balkans, Iran, Lebanon, Somalia and other politically unstable areas of the world. As a result of these population movements, Denmark had acquired a foreign-born population of non-Western origin of close to 240,000 in 2008. The descendants of this immigrant population accounted for more than 100,000 inhabitants in Denmark (Udlændingeservice 2008).

To many Danes, what began as the arrival of a few thousand labour migrants in the 1960s has turned into the large-scale influx of people from distant parts of the world with entirely different ways of life. Though the scale of this immigration is modest in the light of the much more extensive immigration that has taken place in other parts of the world in recent decades, it is nevertheless common today to hear Danes remark that, whereas Denmark used to be a culturally homogeneous society, this is no longer the case because of the growing number of immigrants and refugees who have brought foreign cultures and religions into the country.

Interestingly, a close scrutiny of the culturally homogeneous Danish community that is supposed to be the foundation of modern Danish society will show that it was characterized by considerable cultural diversity. An important aspect of this diversity is related to the social and economic differences and the regional variations that characterized Denmark well into the twentieth century. This is described well in two novels from the early twentieth century, *The fishermen* by Hans Kirk, published in 1928,[3] and the first volume of *Pelle the conquerer* by Martin Andersen Nexø, which appeared in 1906.[4] Kirk's book focuses on a community of fishermen on the west coast of Jutland who made a precarious living on the rough North Sea, finding personal and moral strength in their fundamentalist interpretation of the Lutheran faith and their pious, ascetic way of life. They are depicted as significantly different from the nearby community of inland farmers, who made a relatively comfortable living from agriculture, practiced a rather liberal version of Lutheranism and enjoyed a more outgoing, this-worldly social life. These two communities had few social encounters, and when they did, they disagreed squarely on most moral, religious and social issues. Martin Andersen Nexø's volume describes another, though very different rural community located on the island of Bornholm in the easternmost part of Denmark. Whereas the Jutland communities were divided sharply along religious and occupational lines, Bornholm society was strongly class-stratified, ranging from wealthy owners of large farms to poor day-labourers, who barely eked out a living on the paltry wages they received for their work on the farms. The dialect spoken by the islanders would have differed so much from that spoken by the West Jutlanders that the two population groups would have found it difficult to communicate.

From a contemporary perspective, this diversity may be viewed as only variations within the single, overriding Danish cultural tradition that has shaped the country since time immemorial. Nonetheless for the Danish population at the turn of the twentieth century, these cultural differences were real enough and associated with significant social barriers. If the Danish society of the 1960s, before the late twentieth-century migrations into Denmark began, can be described as culturally homogeneous, we suggest that this is not so much because of the shared Danish ethnic roots of the population or because of a Danish heritage of shared cultural traditions and social norms. It is rather due to several important social and economic developments that took place from the mid-eighteenth to the mid-twentieth centuries.[5]

The first development concerns the emergence of a Danish democratic society believed to be based on an ethnically Danish population. Historically speaking, contemporary Danish democracy is usually contrasted with the strongly hierarchical absolute monarchy that ruled in Denmark until the middle of the nineteenth century. In this system, the upper class was dominated by foreigners, notably Germans who played a highly influential role during the eighteenth century. While these foreigners were responsible for introducing a number of progressive reforms,[6] they lost their influential position with the rise of a national, democratic movement in the late eighteenth century supported largely by the emerging, ethnically Danish middle class, which eventually led to the downfall of the absolute monarchy (Feldbæk 1992). The emergence of a democratic nation state is therefore intimately related to the rejection of a dominant foreign population within the country.

It is rarely acknowledged that Denmark, in fact, experienced considerable immigration in the period from the late nineteenth to the early twentieth century. Thousands of poor Polish and Swedish farm labourers immigrated to Denmark (Nellemann 1981; Willerslev 1983).[7] Their plight as a low-paid and badly treated underclass is depicted in *Pelle the conqueror*, which describes how Pelle arrives on Bornholm as a child with his father, a Swedish farm labourer, who seeks employment on a large farm.[8] The present-day tendency for Danes to regard themselves as having a culturally homogenous society that has only recently come under threat is thus based on a form of historical amnesia that blocks out the history of Swedish and Polish immigration to the country and the earlier diversity that was characteristic of pre-industrial Danish society.[9] These immigrant groups now appear to have become appropriated within the Danish notion of cultural homogeneity, and today the Swedish and Polish surnames that have been passed down through the generations are the only obvious trace of this immigration into Denmark.

Another important development during the nineteenth century, which shaped the notion of Denmark as a culturally homogeneous society, concerns the devolution of the multi-cultural Danish empire. In 1800 Denmark was a minor imperial power that included a number of small tropical colonies (in India, West Africa and the West Indies), several North Atlantic possessions (Norway, Iceland, the Faroe Islands and Greenland) and suzerainty over the duchies of Schleswig and Holstein. A number of these territories were lost in the course of the nineteenth and early twentieth centuries, several of them due to humiliating military defeats at the hands of the neighbouring countries of Sweden and Germany, and today only the Faroe Islands, Greenland and the northern part of Schleswig remain part of Denmark.[10] The down-sizing of the Danish empire led Danish society to focus on the internal social and economic development of the country, largely through rural cooperative movements that helped modernize farms and formed the basis of an agricultural industry (Østergaard 1992). In the historical consciousness of the Danish population, the development of the modern country is therefore closely associated with the emergence of an ethnically Danish, egalitarian nation state concerned with internal social and economic progress (Olwig 2003).

The modernization of the agricultural sector and its accompanying industrialization resulted in large-scale population movements, as the excess rural population sought economic opportunities in the industrializing urban centres. In 1840, 80% of the Danish population lived in rural areas. The 20% who resided in urban areas lived in small towns of less than 10,000 people, the single exception being the capital, Copenhagen, which had a population of about 120,000. By 1960, the rural-urban ratio had reversed completely. Seventy-four percent of the population now lived in urban areas, several of which had more than 50,000 inhabitants. Copenhagen remained the largest city, and with a population of 1.2 million the greater Copenhagen area had grown tenfold (Thøgersen 2007: 8). As most of the population adopted a modern, urban way of life, and as farming communities became increasingly depopulated and dependent on modern technology, many of the local cultural, religious and social distinctions disappeared.

If Danes today can maintain that Denmark was once a culturally homogeneous society, this past is only a fairly brief interlude in a long history of social, economic and cultural diversity. Nevertheless, the idea of Denmark as a formerly culturally homogeneous society is very strong. We suggest that the main reason for this is that it has become linked to perceptions of the contemporary welfare society as grounded in a community of people who, through a long shared culture and history, together built a modern, egalitarian and just society. The national welfare system has its ideological roots in the old village communities of cooperating and self-sufficient farmers (Østergård 1992), as well as in the more recent urban labour movement's notion of solidarity within the workers' collectivity (see Jöhncke, this volume). It therefore combines the traditional and modern virtues of extending help to those in need, associated respectively with the village and the labour unions, but now extended to society at large in the form of welfare services organized through national agencies that are closely integrated into the public sector and funded by general taxation (Andersen 1984: 115-188).[11] This welfare system has reduced the social and economic inequality of nineteenth-century Danish society, and today Denmark is the country with the lowest Gini-coefficient in the world (UNDP 2009).[12]

The Danish welfare society has a well-established, progressive tradition of encouraging – and supporting with generous state support – groups of citizens who wish to form a range of political, cultural or social organizations or establish independent schools based on different educational principles or religious beliefs associated with particular religious congregations. In recent decades, a large number of ethnic organizations and Muslim schools have benefited from this tradition. As a welfare state Denmark also, of course, offers cradle-to-grave medical services and hospital treatment, care for the elderly and disabled, up to one year's largely paid maternity leave that can be shared by the parents, free education at all levels and subsidized care or after-school programmes for children from the age of six months. The extensive care programme for children has made it possible for both parents of young children to take up employment. With 73.2% of Danish women aged 15-64 employed in 2007, Denmark had the highest female employment rate in Europe (Eurostat Newsrelease 2008). Finally, Danish society has been very open to modern life-styles. The right to abortion has not been seriously questioned since it was established by law in 1973, pregnancy out of wedlock raises few eyebrows, but rather sets in motion a number of welfare measures intended to support the new family, and same-sex marriages have been legal – and socially accepted – since 1989.

With this general public support for differing educational, religious and cultural institutions serving varying ways of life, it may seem strange that Danes bemoan the loss of cultural homogeneity. In the eyes of the Danes, however, notions of cultural homogeneity do not imply a regime of social conformity, but rather one insisting on individual freedom, personal choice and social engagement. These are values that Danes believe are generally shared by the ethnically Danish population, but which they see as being challenged by immigrants and refugees. Thus in the eyes of many Danes, immigrants and refugees often adhere to religious (Islamic) beliefs that they view as fundamentalist and oppressive, practice arranged (often understood as forced) marriages and are unduly loyal to their families. Indeed, in the minds of many Danes, the welfare system depends on the existence of a national community of people who value a modern European way of life based on respect for individual choice and autonomy as well as a sense of social solidarity. Because this welfare system has become so closely linked to what are perceived to be Danish core values, the question of how to integrate immigrants and refugees has come to revolve around how to turn them into "proper" members of society who adhere to these values, the assumption being that they do not share them.

From assimilation to integration

While many Danes, like many other Europeans, view the recent influx of immigrants and refugees as a threat to the national community, in many other parts of the world, such as the Americas, immigration has long been regarded as an important basis of the modern nation state. The contrasting migration experiences of the new and the old worlds help explain the different ways in which American and European scholars have theorized migration and their use of the terms "assimilation" and "integration". Whereas North American scholars have traditionally employed "assimilation" to account for the processes by which immigrants become part of, and achieve social mobility in, the receiving society, Danish (and increasingly also other European scholars) often use the notion of "integration" to examine the challenges that immigration poses to the cohesion of the nation state.

In a review of American migration research, anthropologist Nancy Foner notes that a great deal of "the scholarship concerning the earlier immigration emphasized the way immigrants were assimilating and becoming American; ties to the home society were often interpreted as 'evidence for, or against, Americanization' and, in many accounts, were seen as impeding the assimilation process" (2000: 183). The underlying assumption in this research, according to the historian Charles Tilly (1990), is the idea that immigration and social and economic mobility are intricately linked and that the latter automatically follows from the former. Thus immigration was imagined as taking place in the form of a long queue of people of different nationalities waiting their turn to be assimilated, so that they might gain access to the many possibilities that the country offered newcomers (1990: 81).

The concept of assimilation was coined by the Chicago School of sociology, which was concerned with the many poor European immigrants who came to work in the meat industry of Chicago at the beginning of the twentieth century, and the poverty and need for social reforms that this immigration generated.[13] Anthropologist Jonathan Schwartz observes that many of the sociologists associated with the Chicago School believed that the rural communities that these immigrants came from in Europe had more or less disintegrated due to heavy outmigration and that what was left of village culture was therefore of little use in American society. At best it was regarded as a possible resource to draw on as the immigrants adapted; at worst, "the peasant-immigrant culture appeared a useless and heavy obstacle to effective integration, assimilation and Americanization" (Schwartz 1985: 131).[14] In this understanding of immigration, then, the immigrants' abilities to become part of American society and thus acquire social and economic mobility were contingent on their readiness to abandon their cultural traditions and "assimilate" into the receiving society.

This notion of American assimilation was subject early on to critical scrutiny, and in the 1940s W. Lloyd Warner and Leo Srole presented a new model suggesting that the adaptation of immigrants took place in a three-generational process that ended when the immigrants' grandchildren assumed an ethnic identity based on their grandparents' cultural traditions and thus found their particular place in the United States' multi-ethnic society (Waters 1999a: 194-5). The model, in other words, conceptualized immigration as a process that not only lasted several generations, but also involved the development of a multicultural society that recognized the cultural traditions that immigrants had brought into the country. It also viewed immigrants' adaptation to the United States as a process that constituted an essential aspect of the receiving society, rather than as something that takes place on its margins. This concept of immigration and adaptation is closely linked to the idea of the United States as an immigrant society consisting of people from different parts of the world who have come to create a new society on the North American continent (Tilly 1990: 83).

In recent decades this model of generational adaptation has been criticised, as the increasing focus on equal rights in the United States has created an awareness that racial barriers prevent many immigrants from enjoying the sort of improvement to which they should be entitled in the land of freedom and opportunities. This has led American migration scholars to examine the obstacles that prevent immigrants from achieving the expected economic and social mobility and to explore how they cope with this problem (see, for example, Portes 1995; Portes, Halle and Guarnizo 2002). There has been particular interest in the role of immigrants' continued relationships and connections to their countries of origin and the ways in which these ties may help immigrants increase the "possibility of survival in the places full of uncertainty" (Foner 2000: 184). Furthermore, there has been an increasing interest in multi-cultural identities, as American society has developed "an official commitment to cultural pluralism and cultural diversity" (ibid.: 183). Thus, today "the maintenance of multiple identities and loyalties is viewed as a normal feature of immigrant life; ties to the home society complement – rather than detract from – commitments in this country" (ibid.).

In the United States, immigration is associated with the creation of a modern North American society, which means that the vast majority of North Americans are the descendants of immigrants and that most North Americans expect that contemporary immigrants will become Americans. Indeed, according to Schwartz, the "immigrant who becomes an American in the 'melting pot' is one of the distinctive heroes of Modern Times" (1985: 131). In the United States, immigration studies have therefore become a research area of critical importance for everybody in North American society, and they have always played a crucial role in the social sciences (see Waters 1999b: 1264). The heroic status given to successful American immigrants does not mean that all immigrants have been well-received, as many undocumented Mexicans have learned. Nor have all immigrants found a better life in America. Indeed, immigrants are generally expected to fend for themselves, often under difficult conditions.

In Denmark and most other Western European countries, by contrast, immigrants and refugees have not achieved the heroic status that they have historically enjoyed in North America. Rather, they have been regarded as a marginal population associated with inexpensive labour and flight from problem areas suffering political or religious persecution or outright war. Similarly, migration research has tended to be a relatively peripheral area of study concerned with social problems in the welfare society, which reflects the general conception of immigration as a burden for the welfare state. The American ideal of the United States as a harmonious land of immigrants is in some ways just as unfounded in reality as is the Danish ideal of Denmark as the traditionally cohesive country of a culturally homogenous people. Thus Foner notes that "debates about incorporation on both sides of the Atlantic are imprisoned within divergent mythic constructions – endogenous nations of Europe, on the one hand, and...the United States as a nation that has always celebrated immigrants, on the other" (2005: 212). In a globalizing era of increasing population movements, however, the American insistence on emphasizing the contribution that immigrants make to the receiving society may seem more timely than the Danish persistence in viewing immigration as a force that threatens the cohesion of society and that should therefore be avoided as far as possible.

When examining immigrants' adaption to the receiving society, migration researchers in Denmark and other European countries often make use of the notion of "integration" (Koopmans 2010; Phillips 2010).

In the Danish context the term is both new and old. According to the Danish Language Committee, an institution that records the vernacular use of words in Danish newspapers and other public media, "integration" has been part of the Danish language since the nineteenth century.[15] However, early references to the word indicate that the majority of the population did not know its meaning, and therefore it needed to be defined. Common definitions of "to integrate" included to "incorporate," "absorb," "assimilate," or "adapt" something or somebody into "a larger whole."

By the mid-twentieth century, "integration" had become more common in Danish. For the past fifty years it has been used increasingly in public debates, but often with different meanings reflecting the general development of Danish society and its growing complexity. In the 1950s "integration" referred to the economic, political and military integration of Europe, while in the 1960s it became an important term in public debates on the European Common Market, as Danes began to discuss how joining the Common Market would influence Danish society.[16] During the 1970s it began to be used within the field of pre-school pedagogy. Here "integration" was, and still is, used to refer to the need to incorporate children of varying mental and physical capacities (e.g. due to age or possible forms of disability) within the public pre-school institutions.

By the 1990s politicians, journalists and social scientists had begun to employ the concept to discuss the social and cultural challenges of incorporating immigrants and refugees into the Danish welfare society. Around the turn of the millennium, accordingly, the meaning of "integration" gradually changed from referring to more general problems of integration within Danish welfare institutions to the specific problem of integrating immigrants and political refugees into Danish society. When a new Ministry of Integration was created in 2001 by the newly elected right-of-centre government, nobody had any doubts about the target group of this Ministry.[17] The issue of integration no longer had to do with Denmark's position in the EU or how to create a well-functioning group of children with various abilities – it concerned how to deal with the immigrants and refugees in Danish society.

From an anthropological perspective, integration concerns not only the particular processes of adaptation that migrants experience when they adjust to life in a new society. Integration also refers to the more general processes of adaptation that all individuals must go through if they are to become part of a functioning society. A society cannot exist through time if it only consists of individuals or groups who insist on doing everything their own way without regard for the welfare of the larger collectivity. Members of a society must come to some sort of agreement regarding how they are going to live together if a society is to function. This agreement does not necessarily imply cultural conformity, but rather some sort of mutual understanding concerning what sort of cultural differences can be accommodated and how. Furthermore, this understanding will change through time in response to the changing historical contexts of life. Analytically, this means that we must see social communities and cultural ideas of belonging as constructions that are constantly challenged, contested and attributed with new meanings. While it is possible for social scientists to discuss at a more abstract level different models and systems of integration, at a concrete empirical level they must investigate how specific notions of community and belonging are constructed and negotiated in particular societies and historical eras, as well as the ways in which this leads to the inclusion and exclusion of certain kinds of people.

Immigration and integration in Denmark

From a Danish historical perspective, it cannot be taken for granted that immigrants or refugees will be regarded as strangers who must be subjected to various measures of integration before they can be accepted into Danish society. As already noted, well into the eighteenth century, Germans were regarded as resourceful citizens who could make a useful contribution to the country. Similarly, in the seventeenth century the Danish king allowed European Jews to establish a community in Copenhagen, and during the eighteenth century Denmark welcomed French Huguenots. Whether or not a receiving society sees the need for immigrants to undergo processes of integration – and if so, what kinds of integration it will call for – depends on what social and cultural distinctions the members of a given society make in relation to foreigners, the value that they attach to these distinctions and the ways in which they apply them to specific people. This will become clearer through an examination of the ways in which immigrants and refugees have been received in Denmark since the 1960s.

The growing focus in popular and political debates on the integration of refugees and immigrants into Danish society occurred in the aftermath of the foreign labour migration that took place in the late 1960s and early 1970s. Up to the middle of the latter decade, many Danes considered these labour migrants to be "guest workers" who were in Denmark only temporarily. This impression may very well have corresponded with the migrants' own plans, since returning to one's country of origin is often the final goal of labour migrants (see, for example, Foner 2000). The Danish media, according to Jonathan Schwartz, described the labour migrant as a "guest worker" who was "thankful" because he (the vast majority of the immigrants in the late 1960s and early 1970s were males) was allowed to take up work in Denmark (Schwartz 1990). The media also published stories about the guest worker who brought presents to his Danish employers to express his gratitude when he returned to Denmark after his summer vacation in his home country. The Turkish immigrants, who apparently arrived with little hope of receiving a warm welcome in Denmark, fit this image of guest workers well. Greek immigrants, however, who had greater expectations of Danish society and therefore showed signs of disappointment when they were not treated on equal terms with their Danish co-workers, were regarded as more troublesome. In this period the presence of immigrant workers in Denmark was expected to be temporary, and most Danes simply assumed that they would all return to their home countries once their labour was no longer required. Hence, their stay in Denmark and their continued ties to the country of origin were not regarded as a problem, and there was little interest in developing a policy of integration to facilitate their adaptation to Danish society (Schwartz 1990: 45-7).

The notion of immigrant workers as temporary guest workers changed when unemployment rates increased rapidly after the oil crisis in 1973 and the immigrants did not leave the country, but rather decided to establish themselves in Denmark by bringing their wives, children and other close relatives into the country. As it gradually became apparent that the temporary guest workers were becoming permanent immigrants, integration became an issue of public concern. The growing numbers of political refugees who arrived during the 1980s and 1990s added fuel to the integration debate. Statistics were produced showing that immigrants and refugees had a rate of unemployment three to four times higher than the ethnically Danish population (Thomsen and Moes 2002: 2) and that they lived in ethnic ghettos and married within their ethnic groups (see Rytter, this volume). By the early 2000s, it had apparently become the general view that most immigrants and refugees "have their origins in countries that are very different from Denmark with respect to understandings of democracy, the labour market and participation in the labour market, family structure, etc." and further that their "education, experiences, values and norms cannot be regarded as immediately useful in Danish society" (Emerek 2003: 2-3, our translation). Little attention was paid to the ways in which the economic and social environment of the receiving Danish society might have influenced the position of immigrants and refugees in Denmark and their continued attachment to religious practices and cultural traditions connected with these countries of origin.

Out of the debate emerged a general public attitude that the immigrants' and refugees' great cultural difference from Danes prevented them from becoming properly integrated into Danish society (for critical discussion of this view, see Steen 1993; Preis 1996; Schierup 1993; Schwartz 1998).[18]

As can be seen from this brief review of Danish attitudes towards immigrants and refugees, it was only in the 1990s that Danes really began to become concerned with the perceived existence of irreconcilable cultural differences between immigrants and refugees on the one hand and Danes on the other (Hervik 2004). This happened at a time when Danes were becoming aware of the increasing impact of globalization, whether in the form of the export of Danish jobs to foreign countries with a cheaper labour force, the substantial migration to Denmark through family reunification or flight, or the growing difficulty of controlling Danish borders and maintaining Danish sovereignty as the European Common Market evolved into a European Union that assumed greater political and legal power. In this climate of national anxiety – which finds parallels in many other European countries, as the British anthropologist Ralph Grillo (2003) has shown – the perceived cultural differences of immigrants and refugees have become a symbol of the social difficulties being experienced by the Danish population today. The debate has therefore come to focus almost entirely on the problem of the immigrants and refugees, rather than on the problem of Denmark as a receiving society (Hervik 1999).

In their efforts to define integration as a problem that concerns only immigrants and refugees, and not ethnic Danes, the media and the politicians often prefer to ignore the growing discrimination against non-ethnic Danes (ENAR 2008) as well as the underlying racism that fuels the xenophobic rhetoric against cultural and religious minorities such as Muslims (Quraishy and O'Connor 1991). At the same time, in the public debate on integration in Denmark, offensive and condescending terms are increasingly being used, as immigrants and refugees are blamed for their failure to become integrated. The negative tone of the debate paved the way for the Muhammad cartoons in 2005 and the crisis they generated (Berg and Hervik 2007). Indeed, the crisis that followed the publication of the cartoons was not just triggered by the images themselves, but just as much by the apparent inability of the political establishment and of Danish society at large to recognize the devastating effect of the derogatory vocabulary employed in the public debate on immigrants and refugees.

Although some Danish scholars have publicly questioned the ways in which the media and the politicians discuss immigration and integration, the Danish preoccupation with culturally problematic immigrants and refugees is reflected in much Danish migration research. According to Schwartz (1990, 1998), Danish researchers have generally viewed immigrants and refugees as outsiders who resist adaptation because of their cultural differences. They have therefore tended to focus on the cultural differences that are believed to underlie the most problematic aspects of immigration to Denmark. This approach has led one migration researcher to criticize her colleagues for viewing immigrants as problem cases for the welfare state (Mørck 1998: 35), and another to note that immigrants and refugees are increasingly being regarded as a serious burden on the welfare system (Emerek 2003: 4). For the British migration scholar Karen Wren (2001), such views are evidence of what she calls a cultural racism among Danish scholars studying immigration and integration. She argues that this cultural racism is caused by "the culturalist bias of academic research, which has been very closely connected with public policy" (Wren 2001: 152), and she claims that it has led Danish scholars to neglect the social structure of Danish society.

The aim of this book

The aim of this book is to analyse critically how cultural categories are employed in Danish society to differentiate immigrants and refugees socially from the ethnically Danish population and the ways in which this has shaped social perceptions of people with foreign backgrounds and their encounters with the welfare state. It is not the goal of this book to judge either Danish society or the architects of Danish immigration policy. Rather, using anthropological perspectives, we wish to describe and analyse how a society that has long prided itself on being progressive, enlightened and egalitarian can end up being regarded as intolerant and xenophobic in many of the countries with which the Danes like to compare themselves (Hedetoft 2006). We suggest that, by defining Denmark as a modern welfare society based on cultural values and social norms that are linked to the ethnically Danish population, Danes have erected considerable barriers to the inclusion of immigrants and refugees into Danish society. This barrier-building cannot be explained by facile reference to racist or xenophobic tendencies in Danish society. Rather, it must be analyzed as a response to the difficulties Danes are experiencing in redefining their understanding of Denmark as a welfare state within a globalizing world that is increasingly interconnected and interdependent. This is the topic of the first section of the book.

Another major concern is to analyse, using ethnographic case studies, the role of the welfare society in the reception of immigrants and refugees in Denmark and how they have experienced this political project. The studies show that the Danish perception of immigrants and refugees as a "social problem" has resulted in a lack of recognition of the positive qualities that these people possess. Within the context of a welfare society, however, a focus on social problems can be regarded as a proactive strategy deployed in order to designate a segment of the population as a particular category of people in need of help. This is an approach that has worked with other "problem" groups, such as the destitute, the seriously ill and the fragile elderly. By categorizing them in this way, the welfare system can give them the economic support, medical treatment or physical care they need. The case studies in this book show that immigrants and refugees *have* been provided with significant social and economic assistance through the welfare system, and that this has helped them settle in Denmark. Indeed, some groups of immigrants and refugees have done extremely well in Denmark. Thus, within one generation, the free system of education in Denmark has enabled the descendants of Pakistani immigrants to reach the educational level of the ethnically Danish population, whereas the descendants of Vietnamese refugees have actually outperformed the ethnically Danish population educationally.

The historical background of Danish society discussed in this introductory chapter and the analyses of the contemporary welfare state in a globalizing world presented in the two following sections of this book show that "Danishness" and "the welfare state" are inseparable. Thus despite the fact that "Danishness" and "the welfare state" at times seem to have completely conflicting goals, they are so intertwined that they have to be understood as interconnected. As long as this is the case, the tremendous efforts of the welfare system to "integrate" immigrants and refugees will only have the result of drawing attention to a category of people who can then be perceived as not belonging to this society. The book therefore raises questions concerning how to preserve, and further develop, a social welfare society, based on a system of social solidarity that is closely connected with shared cultural values, in a globalizing world of increasingly interconnectivity and mobility.

Part I: The cultural construction of Danish society

The first part of the book examines dominant ideas of Danish society and Danishness and the ways in which they shape the reception of immigrants and refugees in Denmark. The second part explores how immigrants and refugees experience their encounter with Danish society. The chapters therefore move from a general analytical level that examines how Danish national society is both imagined and practised to a more specific empirical-analytical level. The ethnographic case studies examine the different forms of social relations and kinds of communities that emerge when people interact and communicate in specific situations and particular circumstances.

In his contribution, Steffen Jöhncke shows that there is a close link between the ways in which contemporary Danish society is conceived, structured and practised and its development as a welfare state. The idea that the goods of a society must be distributed in order to create welfare and equality for all is based on the belief that, although people may have different needs and capabilities, these differences are relatively minor and will disappear if everyone contributes to the commonweal because people are, fundamentally, alike. In popular understanding, however, this idea of equality and equivalence is closely associated with the notion of Denmark as a culturally homogeneous society, and it therefore tends to be applied only to people who are ethnically Danish. Thus it is a common perception that only the ethnically Danish population understands and appreciates the rights and obligations associated with being part of the Danish welfare system. If immigrants and refugees are categorized as so different – in terms, for example, of culture, economic resources or educational background – that they cannot participate properly in the system of redistribution upon which the welfare society rests, then they become stigmatized as a group of people who sponge off the system without contributing to it, whether or not this can be documented.[19]

The perception of immigrants and refugees as a problem group is underscored by the prevalent perception of Denmark as a culturally homogeneous national community. Mikkel Rytter shows how this conception is supported by the common use of kin images, such as "the family of Denmark," to refer to Danish society. In using such images, Danes are essentially stating that shared blood ties and biological descent are necessary preconditions for the legitimate claim to a Danish national identity and full membership in society. The idea that immigrants and refugees need to become part of the family of Denmark, through marital and kin ties grounded in Denmark, has been influential in the passing of bills in the Danish parliament imposing increasing restrictions on the right to marry a spouse from the country of origin. Because the bills are couched in a "neutral" language concerning immigrants' and refugees' years of residence in Denmark and their national affiliation, their discriminatory effect is concealed.

In her discussion of the grammatical structures behind the public debate on immigrants and refugees in Denmark, Inger Sjørslev suggests that categories of social inequality and cultural difference have become so imbedded in the contemporary Danish language that they appear "natural" in everyday life. With reference to the German society of the 1930s, she argues that the current public debate on immigrants and refugees employs a comparable vocabulary that makes possible social exclusion not only in speech but also in practice. This leads her to reject integration as an analytical term and to suggest that researchers adopt concepts of a higher level of abstraction that allow a bird's eye analysis of the many political implications of the notion of integration and the social and political contexts in which this notion unfolds.

These studies show that cultural constructions not only reflect the existing world but also contribute to the creation of particular social orders. The specific ways in which these constructions are interpreted and practised, however, may vary considerably. Thus, it is possible for most Danes to concur that Denmark is culturally homogeneous because the exact meaning of cultural homogeneity is rarely articulated except for relatively vague references to the Danes' shared ethnic background. The power of a strong consensus model becomes apparent in Cecilie Rubow's analysis of the Danish National Church. She shows that the Church is dominated by such a model, even though the clergy disagree on important issues and carry out their work according to different perceptions of the Church as a public institution. Thus, the emphasis on consensus within the Church can be seen to gloss over a wish to conceal internal differences and create a community that is so resilient that it can include everybody. This suggests that the notions of homogeneity and consensus can only be maintained as long as the majority agrees to highlight their similarities and downplay their differences.

The ongoing debate on homogeneity and difference, consensus and conflict, social inclusion and exclusion, and the social practices with which this debate is connected, define to a great extent the conditions under which integration in Danish society can take place, be maintained and be contested. This debate has acquired an increasingly Islamophobic tone, and a common view today is that Danish culture is incommensurable with Muslim culture. As Sjørslev shows, Muslim immigrants are described in the media as representing the antithesis of Danish democratic, open-minded and civilized values. This has had the paradoxical result, as Tina Jensen describes in her article, that Danes who convert to Islam are believed to have "undergone [such] fundamental and radical processes of transformation" that their conversion basically entails "abdicating their Danishness" or "emigrating from Danish society."

This refusal to recognize Muslims as part of Danish society provides the most important key to understanding why the publication of the cartoons of Muhammad in a Danish newspaper developed into a serious crisis. In his analysis of the "cartoon crisis," Heiko Henkel argues that the complicated turn of events must basically be viewed as a "transitional drama" involving "an ongoing struggle for recognition". This struggle concerned not only the terms through which Muslims in Denmark can be "recognized as legitimate citizens/residents of Danish society – and on which Muslims may recognize the demands of Danish society as legitimate," but also, at a more general level, "the forms of identity that can mutually be recognized as 'Danish.'" He concludes that a solution to the ethno-religious conflict can only be found in a new framework of mutual understanding and recognition.

By subjecting the political project of integration to critical inquiry, we do not wish to disregard the impact of immigration on Danish society, nor the many challenges it may entail for either the Danish welfare state or the immigrants and refugees arriving in it. On the contrary, it is precisely because the political project of integration intervenes so directly in the lives of a large number of people that it needs to be subjected to critical analysis. Critically, these analyses must not content themselves with observations on the macro-level, that is, at the level of the general society and its many institutions, but must also engage with the micro-level of integration, that is, in the myriad of informal and face-to-face relations that unfold in daily life as immigrants and refugees seek to create a life for themselves in Danish society. This is the subject of Part II of the book, which focuses on the specific social contexts in which processes of integration become visible.

Part II: Inclusion and exclusion in the welfare society

The ethnographic studies presented in this book show that welfare institutions play a central role in the encounters of refugees and immigrants with Danish society. As soon as asylum-seekers achieve refugee status, together with other recent arrivals they are enrolled in introduction programmes that are intended to prepare them for their new lives in Danish society. As legal Danish residents, they can obtain job training at educational institutions; their children are expected to attend day-care centres so that they can become socialized the Danish way together with Danish children; those who suffer from various ailments are treated at clinics and hospitals; and those who need to improve their general well-being are offered a variety of exercise programmes. Welfare

Denmark clearly invests considerable resources in preparing immigrants and refugees for life in the country.

While these welfare institutions do offer a range of services that are intended to ease immigrants and refugees into Danish society, they have the unfortunate effect of emphasizing what these people lack, rather than what they have to offer.[20] In the current political climate, this lack is often viewed as a cultural lack caused by non-Danish backgrounds. In many instances, as the ethnographic cases make clear, a foreign cultural background therefore becomes equated with problems. When, as Helle Bundgaard shows, the child of an immigrant or refugee experiences difficulties adjusting to a pre-school, the teachers are quick to look for the cause of this problem in problematic child-rearing practices in a home where the parents have a different cultural background. When, as Katrine Schepelern Johansen points out, doctors and nurses find that an immigrant patient at a psychiatric ward is difficult to treat, they attribute this to his or her non-Danish ethnic background.

The problem with these ways of perceiving and treating people is that they never go beyond cultural stereotypes about immigrants and refugees in Denmark. The professional staff essentially rely on commonsense categories such as "minority parents" or "patients with a non-Danish ethnic background" that reinforce notions of cultural others. An important reason for this is that the staff lack the resources to invest the time and effort needed to develop a more informed approach. The cases also show, however, that some staff members react instinctively to immigrants and refugees in terms of ethnic stereotypes.

While some professionals inadvertently create cultural barriers between themselves and the people they are supposed to help, others disregard the significance of individuals' cultural background entirely and treat them solely in terms of problems they can diagnose on the basis of their particular training. When Iraqi refugees describe their suffering, as Sofie Danneskiold-Samsoe shows, they crave recognition of their heroic resistance against an oppressive political regime so that they can be shown the sort of respect to which they think this entitles them. In the Danish welfare system, however, they are either diagnosed as torture victims who need to be rehabilitated through psychiatric treatment, or as suffering from various physical ailments that can be treated with pharmaceutical products. Hence, their narratives of suffering are only acknowledged as documentation for their ruined health that entitles them to obtain various welfare benefits.

The torture victims' outrage at being reduced to damaged bodies and psyches points to the limits of the welfare system: it can attempt to find solutions for practical problems related to education, health, housing, income, etc., but it cannot create the social and emotional conditions that make life worth living. Hanne Overgaard Mogensen's study of HIV-infected Ugandan women exemplifies this. While they were very grateful for the medical treatment they received, they experienced their lives in Denmark as extremely lonely. They had largely lost contact with their Danish husbands and their families after being diagnosed with HIV, and they tended to avoid fellow Ugandans, fearing that the knowledge of their HIV status in the African community would subject them to further negative stereotyping. The women therefore longed for close personal relations, not just a formal relationship with a Danish professional in the health system – something the national health system could not offer them.

While the national welfare system has made great efforts to provide education, health services and various social benefits to immigrants and refugees in order to ensure that they can function on a par with the native-born population, the ethnographic studies in this collection thus show that the results have been mixed. The welfare system may have succeeded in creating an acceptable social and economic standard of living for the new Danes, but it has failed to recognize the resources they possess. Being an immigrant and refugee with a non-Danish ethnic background has often been tantamount to being a problem case for the welfare system.

Fortunately, a somewhat different picture emerges from the ethnographic studies that go beyond investigating the formal relations generated by the welfare system to look at the more informal ties created through personal interactions within the various social settings. This is perhaps most clearly brought out by Sally Anderson's analysis of a group of women participating in exercise classes. In a detailed study of their interactions over the year they exercised together, she shows that they increasingly developed verbal and non-verbal contact and gradually created a community across ethnic and religious boundaries in which they engaged in social, economic and cultural exchanges on an equal basis. Anderson suggests calling such physical accommodation and social exchange, involving strangers interacting at particular times and spaces, *micro-integration*. Through this micro-integration categorical identities are bridged and negated, and personal resources can come to the forefront. Similar processes of micro-integration can be seen as having taken place in some of the other social contexts discussed here, such as the pre-school. However, the ethnographic studies also show that crosscutting ties are most easily sustained within more intimate spaces of closely knit personal relations. As Mogensen points out, such spaces tend to be closed off to strangers in Denmark. In the public domain, however, which is characterized by more fragile consociate relations, categories such as Danes, immigrants and Muslims tend to take over, allowing the divisive ethnic and religious boundaries to re-emerge.

The chapters in this book show that, while the Danish welfare system has succeeded to a great extent in eradicating poverty and reducing class differences, contemporary globalization processes and, in particular, the influx of immigrants and refugees from countries outside the Western world have posed a challenge to the ideology of equality and equivalence on which it rests. They also demonstrate that the welfare society tends to experience serious difficulties in seeing migration and the cultural diversity to which it may lead as positive forces that can contribute to Danish society. Rather, the Danish welfare system and public discourses in Denmark regard people with a non-Danish ethnic background as particularly problematic and difficult to integrate, and therefore in need of special attention and means of intervention. Instead of addressing the challenges that contemporary globalization poses to Danish society the categories of cultural difference and the public discourses (and cartoons) that convey (and picture) them generate and sustain the idea that equality and cohesion are incompatible with immigration and heterogeneity. Future generations of Danes will therefore be faced with the challenge of inventing new ways of promoting welfare that build on notions of equality as well as engagement in the global world.

International Perspectives

To discuss the perspectives on immigration and integration presented here, we have asked three international scholars to write an epilogue in which they engage in a critical dialogue with the chapters in this book and offer an external view on the issues raised. In the first epilogue Richard Jenkins identifies the idea of integration as a general challenge for all citizens in modern society, rather than as one that primarily involves immigrants and refugees. In a thought-provoking discussion of educational institutions and processes of enculturation in contemporary Danish society he compares the integration of foreigners to the socialization of children, thus reminding us of the many implicit assumptions and expectations that are glossed over by "the problem of integration". Jenkins lines up several possible scenarios for the future relationship between Danes and immigrants and concludes that even though the formers' increasing demands on the latter to "integrate" have complicated their co-existence and created a regrettable "us-them" conflict, there is hope that the pragmatics of Danish everyday life over time will teach both sides to live together.

The following two epilogues examine the Danish focus on the "problem" of integration from a comparative perspective. Ralph Grillo discusses the notions of integration and multiculturalism within a broader European context, arguing that ideas of integrating both citizens and foreigners into society are as vague and fuzzy in other countries, such as Britain, as they are in Denmark. He recognizes, however, that the concept of integration attains a particular societal significance in Scandinavia because of the close link between ideas of sameness and equality in this part of Europe. Eventually, Grillo locates the Danish experience as a particular version of a more general European pattern of responding to globalization and transnationalism through a strengthening of nationalist feelings.

In the last epilogue, written from a Canadian vantage point, Vered Amit also underscores that the Danish insistence on categorizing immigrants and refugees as integration problems is not exceptional. She points to a similar case in Canadian multi-cultural society involving an attempt in Quebec to make respect for certain local values and practices a precondition for integration and acceptance in a local community. Amit uses the example to demonstrate that issues of immigration or immigrant integration may be used as "a cipher for anxiety about a much wider range of social cleavages and historical transformations." Thus, immigrants and refugees are not alone in experiencing various difficulties of integration. Yet, as in Denmark, the majority population comfortably constructs integration issues in terms of an "us/them" opposition, caused by immigration and globalization, that allows it to ignore other and sometimes more problematic cleavages in the nation state.

Notes

1. This is based on figures obtained on the home page of the Danish Ministry of Refugees, Immigrants and Integration, 5 September 2008, http://www.nyidanmark.dk/da-dk/spoergsmaal_og_svar/indvandrere-_og_efterkommere/test.htm)
2. The statistics from the early period of immigration are rather uncertain. In 1971 4,591 Yugoslavs, 6,073 Turks and 1,898 Africans had work permits in Denmark (Sane 2000: 291). In 1974, there were almost 40,000 immigrants and descendants from non-Western countries in Denmark. Of these, 8,138 were from Turkey, 6,779 from the former Yugoslavia and 3,733 from Pakistan (Mikkelsen 2008: 37).
3. The book, entitled *Fiskerne* in Danish, was translated into English in 1999 by Marc Linder.

4. The first volume, *Barndom*, of the series *Pelle Erobreren* has been translated into English by Jessie Muir as *Boyhood*, Volume 1 of *Pelle the conqueror*.
5. This is a very brief and simplified summary of the complex historical changes that took place in Denmark from the middle of the eighteenth to the middle of the twentieth centuries. For more extensive treatment of this history, see, for example, Jespersen (2004).
6. For example, the law to abolish the transatlantic slave trade, which Denmark passed in 1792 as the first country in the world to do so, was to a great extent the work of Ernst Schimmelmann, who, as Minister of Finance in Denmark, was one of the main forces behind the establishment of a commission to investigate the trade. Schimmelmann was of German origin and strongly oriented toward German culture, and the report of the commission was written in German (Green-Pedersen 1970-1; see also Olwig 2003).
7. In certain parts of Denmark they had a very strong presence: thus in one area of Bornholm, Swedish farm laborers comprised a third of the population around 1900 (Willerslev 1983: 7).
8. The exact number of these immigrant laborers is rather uncertain because some worked seasonally in Denmark, and many opted to return to their country of origin or were involuntarily deported. At the same time as Denmark experienced considerable immigration, a large number of Danes emigrated to the United States. A total of approximately 360,000 Danes are estimated to have emigrated from Denmark between 1870 and 1930, close to 15 percent of the 2.5 million population of Denmark in 1900 (Helmer Pedersen 1984; Hvidt 1975).
9. When Richard Willerslev published his book on Swedish immigration into Denmark in 1983, he gave it the title *The forgotten immigration*.
10. Greenland and the Faroe Islands have home rule. The northern part of Schleswig has been a fully integrated part of Denmark since 1920, when a plebiscite was held in Schleswig to determine whether the population wished to be affiliated with Germany or Denmark. As a result, the southern half of Schleswig remained in Germany, whereas the northern half joined Denmark.
11. Called the "Nordic model", this is found in somewhat different versions in all the Scandinavian countries.
12. The Gini co-efficient is a statistical measure of dispersion. It is commonly used to measure inequalities of wealth and income.
13. The Chicago School of sociology emerged during the 1920s and 1930s and specialized in urban sociology and research on the urban environment by combining theory and ethnographic fieldwork.
14. Among the most important studies are W. I. Thomas and F. Znaniecki's *The Polish peasant in Europe and America*, which was published for the first time in 1918, and Lewis Wirth's *In the ghetto* from 1928 (Schwartz 1985: 136-8).
15. This information was provided by the Danish Language Committee (*Det Danske Sprognævn*) on 12 January 2006.
16. Denmark joined the European Common Market in 1973.
17. This government, consisting of the Venstre Party (a right of center neo-liberal party) and the Conservative Party, is dependent upon the support of an ultra-nationalist party, The Danish People's Party. The necessity to please this party

helps explain the present Danish government's hard line with regard to immigrants, which, in turn helped to fuel the cartoon crisis.

18. For discussions of immigrants' changing position in Danish society since the 1960s, see Schierup and Ålund (1986); Rytter (2011); Juul (2011).

19. For an analysis of immigrants and refugees in the Norwegian welfare society along these lines, see *Generous betrayal* by Unni Wikan (2002); for a critique, see Gullestad (2002, 2006).

20. This is a general problem for Scandinavian welfare societies. See the forthcoming special issue of *Journal of Ethnic and Migration Studies* (Olwig, Larsen, and Rytter 2011).

References

Andersen, Bent Rold. 1984. Rationality and Irrationality of the Nordic Welfare State. *Dædalus* 113 (1): 109-39.

Berg, Clarissa and Peter Hervik. 2007. "Muhammedkrisen": en politisk magtkamp i dansk jounalistik. Aalborg: *AMID Working Paper Series* 62.

Danish Ministry of Refugees, Immigrants and Integration. 2008. http://www.nyidanmark.dk/da-dk/spoergsmaal_og_svar/indvandrere-_og_efterkommere/test.htm), accessed September 5, 2008.

Emerek, Ruth. 2003. Integration – eller inklusion? Den danske diskussion om integration. Aalborg, *AMID Working Paper Series* 31/2003.

ENAR (European network against racism). 2008. *Racism in Denmark*. Shadow Report (by Bashy Quraishy). Copenhagen: Ethnic Debate Forum.

Eurostat Newsrelease. 2008. *Labour Force Survey 2007*, 104/2008 - 22 July. http://ec.europa.eu/eurostat

Feldbæk, Ole. 1992. Clash of Cultures in a Conglomerate State: Danes and Germans in 18th Century Denmark. In *Clashes of Cultures: Essays in Honour of Niels Steensgaard*, ed. J. C. V. Johansen, E. K. Petersen and H. Stevnsborg, 80-93. Odense: Odense University Press.

Foner, Nancy. 2000. *From Ellis Island to JFK: New York's Two Great Waves of Immigration*. New Haven: Yale University Press.

—. 2005. *In a New Land: A Comparative View of Immigration*. New York: New York University Press.

Green-Pedersen, S. E. 1970-71. Danmarks ophævelse af negerslavehandelen. *Arkiv* 3: 19-37.

Grillo, Ralph D. 2003. Cultural Essentialism and Cultural Anxiety. *Anthropological Theory* 3 (2): 157-74.

Gullestad, Marianne. 2002. *Det norske sett med nye øyne*. Oslo: Universitetsforlaget.

—. 2006. *Plausible Prejudice: Everyday Experiences and Social Images of Nation, Culture and Race*. Oslo: Universitetsforlaget.
Hedetoft, Ulf. 2006. Divergens eller konvergens. In *Bortom Stereotyperna? Invandrare och Integration i Danmark och Sverige*, ed. Ulf Hedetoft, Bo Petersson and Lina Sturfeldt, 390-407. Gothenburg: Makadam.
Helmer Pedersen, Erik. 1984. *Drømmen om Amerika*. Copenhagen: Nationalmuseet.
Hervik, Peter. 1999. *Den generende forskellighed*. Copenhagen: Hans Reitzels Forlag.
—. 2004. The Danish Cultural World of Unbridgeable Differences. *Ethnos* 69 (2): 247-267.
—. 2006. The Emergence of Neo-nationalism in Denmark, 1992-2001. In *Neo-nationalism in Europe and Beyond: Perspectives from Social Anthropology*, ed. Andre Gingrich and Marcus Banks, 136-161. Oxford: Berghahn Books.
Hvidt, Kristian. 1975. *Flight to America: The Social Background of 300,000 Danish Emigrants*. New York: Academic Press.
Jespersen, Knud J.C. 2004. *A History of Denmark*. New York: Palgrave/Macmillan.
Juul, Kristine. 2011. From Danish Yugoslavs to Danish Serbs: national affiliation stuck between visibility and invisibility. *Journal of Ethnic and Migration Studies*.
Kirk, Hans. 1999[1928]. *The Fishermen*, translated by Marc Linder, Iowa City: Fanpihua.
Koopmans, Ruud. 2010. Trade-Offs between Equality and Difference: Immigrant Integration, Multiculturalism and the Welfare State in Cross-National Perspective. *Journal of Ethnic and Migration Studies* 36 (1):1-126.
Mikkelsen, Flemming. 2008. *Indvandring og Integration*. Copenhagen: Akademisk Forlag.
Mørck, Yvonne. 1998. *Bindestregsdanskere: fortællinger om køn, generationer og etnicitet*. Frederiksberg: Forlaget Sociologi.
Nellemann, George. 1981. *Polske landarbejdere i Danmark og deres efterkommere: et studie af landarbejderindvandringen 1893-1929 og indvandringens integration i det danske samfund i to generationer*. Copenhagen: Nationalmuseets Forlag.
Nexø, Martin Andersen. 2006[1906]. *Boyhood*, Volume 1 of *Pelle the Conqueror*, translated by Jessie Muir, New York: Mondial Books.
Østergård, Uffe. 1992. Peasants and Danes: The Danish National Identity and Political Culture. *Comparative Studies in Society and History* 34 (1): 3-27.

Olwig, Karen Fog. 2003. Narrating deglobalization: Danish perceptions of a lost empire. *Global Networks* 3 (3):207-222.

Olwig, Karen Fog, Birgitte Romme Larsen and Mikkel Rytter, eds. 2011. 'Integration': Migrants and Refugees between Scandinavian Welfare Societies and Family Relations, Special Issue of *Journal of Ethnic and Migration Studies*.

Phillips, Deborah. 2010. Minority Ethnic Segregation, Integration and Citizenship: A European Perspective. *Journal of Ethnic and Migration Studies* 36 (1): 209-225.

Portes, Alejandro. 1995. Children of Immigrants: Segmented Assimilation and its Determinants. In *The Economic Sociology of Immigration: Essays on Networks, Ethnicity and Entrepreneurship*, ed. A. Portes, 248-79. New York: Russel Sage Foundation.

Portes, Alejandro, W.J. Haller and L.E. Guarnizo. 2002. Transnational Entrepreneurs: An Alternative Form of Immigrant Adaptation. *American Sociological Review* 67: 278-98.

Preis, Ann-Belinda. 1996. *Flygtninge, sandheden og andre gåder*. Copenhagen: Rosinante.

Rytter, Mikkel. 2011. Money or education? Strategies of improvement among Pakistani families in Denmark. *Journal of Ethnic and Migration Studies*.

Quraishy, Bashy and O'Connor, Tim. 1991. Denmark: No Racism by Definition. *Race and Class* 32 (3): 114-119.

Sane, Henrik Zip. 2000. *Billige og villige? Fremmedarbejdere i Fædrelandet ca. 1800-1970*. Farum: Farums Arkiver and Museer.

Schierup, Carl Ulrich. 1993. *På kulturens slagmark: mindretal og størretal taler om Danmark*. Esbjerg: Sydjysk Universitetsforlag.

Schierup, Carl Ulrich and Alexandra Ålund. 1986. *Will they still be dancing? Integration and ethnic transformation among Yugoslav immigrants in Scandinavia*. Umeå: Department of Sociology.

Schwartz, Jonathan. 1985. *Reluctant Hosts: Denmark's Reception of Guest Workers*. Kultursociologiske Skrifter 21. Copenhagen: Akademisk Forlag.

—. 1990. On the Representation of Immigrants in Denmark: A Retrospective. In *Every Cloud has a Silver Lining*, ed. Flemming Røgilds. Studies in Cultural Sociology no. 28, 42-52. Copenhagen: Akademisk Forlag.

—. ed. 1998. *Et midlertidigt liv: Bosniske flygtninge i de nordiske lande*. Copenhagen: Nordisk Ministerråd.

Steen, Ann-Belinda. 1993. *Varieties of the Tamil Refugee Experience in Denmark and England*. Copenhagen: Minority Studies, University of Copenhagen, and The Danish Centre for Human Rights.

Thøgersen, Mette Ladegaard. 2007. *Landdistrikternes urbanisering: en analyse af de rurale byers opståen, udvikling og karakteristika ca. 1840-1960*. Ph.D. Thesis, University of Southern Denmark.

Thomsen, Margit Helle and Mette Moes. 2002. Kompetencer mellem kulturalisering og mangfoldighed: om brugen og bedømmelsen af etniske minoriteters kompetencer og ressourcer på det danske arbejdsmarked. Aalborg: *AMID Working Paper Series* 9/2002.

Tilly, Charles. 1990. Transplanted Networks. In *Immigration Reconsidered: History, Sociology, and Politics*, ed. Virginia Yans-McLaughlin, 79-95. New York: Oxford University Press.

Udlændingeservice. 2008. *Tal og fakta: befolkningsstatistik om udlændinge*. Copenhagen: Ministeriet for Flygtninge, Indvandrere og Integration.

UNDP (United Nations Development Programme). 2009. *Human Development Report*. New York: Palgrave MacMillan.

Waters, Mary C. 1999a. *Black Identities: West Indian Immigrant Dreams and American Realities*. Cambridge, Mass.: Harvard University Press.

—. 1999b. Sociology and the Study of Immigration. *American Behavioral Scientist* 42 (9): 1264-67.

Wikan, Unni. 2002. *Generous Betrayal*. Chicago: The University of Chicago Press.

Willerslev, Richard. 1983. *Den glemte indvandring: den svenske indvandring til Danmark 1850-1914*. Copenhagen: Gyldendal.

Wren, Karen. 2001. Cultural Racism: Something Rotten in the State of Denmark. *Social and Cultural Geography* 2 (2): 141-161.

PART I

THE CULTURAL CONSTRUCTION OF DANISH SOCIETY

CHAPTER ONE

INTEGRATING DENMARK: THE WELFARE STATE AS A NATIONAL(IST) ACCOMPLISHMENT

STEFFEN JÖHNCKE

This chapter explores how the challenge of "integrating" ethnic minorities in Denmark must be seen in the context of the more general question of how "Denmark" became integrated as a social unit in the first place. The discussion is concerned with certain important aspects of Danish culture and history that have contributed to the formation of the welfare state. By necessity, the discussion here is also concerned with the definition of integration, as this definition is integral to what needs to be questioned and explained. In her discussion of the uses of the concept of integration in Danish social research, the social scientist Ruth Emerek (2003) draws attention to the lack of disagreement across disciplines, so that economists, political scientists and anthropologists seem to be referring to widely different ideas about and criteria for what it means to be integrated. Referring to the political scientist Charlotte Hamburger (1997), she therefore suggests a distinction between systemic and social integration, in which the "systemic" refers to aspects such as formal rights and economic participation, the "social" to popular processes of mutual recognition between minority and majority groups. The anthropologist Carl-Ulrik Schierup (1993) makes a somewhat parallel distinction between "structural" integration – the equal participation of minority groups in politics, employment and education – and "cultural" integration, which implies the mutual recognition of cultural differences, including in terms of religion, norms and morality. However useful these distinctions may be in many contexts, this chapter will argue conversely that a crucial, structural element of the Danish economy and politics, namely the universalist welfare state, is simultaneously eminently *cultural*, in the sense of being both an expression of widely held values and ideals, and an explicit part of the Danish self-image. The historical roots of this situation are discussed, as are its current and future implications for the integration of ethnic minorities.

Anthropologists, of course, are not alone in arguing that economy and politics are also cultural phenomena. In a comment on the differences and similarities between American and Scandinavian models of social policy, the political scientist Eric S. Einhorn (2000: 9) reminds us that modern welfare states like those in the Nordic countries are an ideological as well as a bureaucratic project. Americans are astounded that across the European political spectrum there are no real foes of the basic premises of the welfare state.

Einhorn connects this observation to a general difference between the US and Europe as to the political meaning and interrelatedness of such notions as solidarity, equality and national unity: In times of crisis – such as during the Great Depression of the 1930s and World War II – Americans too tend to support the government's initiation of nation-wide schemes for the common good, including health and welfare programmes. But in general, "solidarity" applies to the family or the local community rather than to the US nation as a whole, and "equality" is taken as referring to "equal opportunity" rather than to "equal outcomes" and a (more) equal distribution of the national wealth. In Europe, on the other hand, the redistributive social policies of the welfare state have gathered support from various political parties, building on a common understanding that it would be in the interests of the well-being and security of all social groups – as well as of the nation as a whole – if the forces of the (labour) market were supplemented by political measures to protect a basic quality of life for the population.

Nowhere has this line of political and ideological reasoning in favour of the welfare state been more dominant than in the Scandinavian countries, of which Denmark is one. Even though homogenizing forces such as European Union integration and global competition tend to propel countries towards greater similarity in terms of economic structure and policy, the Scandinavian model of welfare still stands out as the most extensive in terms of policies that regard the national population as "a whole" towards which the state has obligations. Yet such a notion of unity presupposes a remarkable degree of consensus, and it makes an appeal to a particular kind of communality that calls for closer inspection.

It is a standard observation that until a few decades ago the population of Denmark was unusually homogeneous in terms of language, religion and ethnic origins, and that this situation has changed somewhat due to increased immigration and international mobility. Be that as it may, the "unity" of Denmark in the pre-immigration era should not be treated as a natural given, but as a result of social and political processes to which immigration flows pose new challenges. Minority ethnic communities have become a part of Scandinavian societies since the 1960s, and in Denmark in particular political debate has been rife with the combined concern over immigration and the state of welfare, as that "whole population" to whom social policy applies changes (Einhorn and Logue 2003: 174ff.). The small but politically influential Danish People's Party has won international attention for its ill-masked xenophobic rhetoric; it is less well known that the party's pro-welfare state rhetoric is equally marked. Usually classified as a right-wing party due to its appeal to populist nationalism, it also claims a role as a fierce defender of public spending on "weak groups", not least on its alleged core electorate of old-age pensioners, while it encourages cuts elsewhere, for example, on child benefits for large families (which are wrongly assumed to be mostly of immigrant background). The Danish People's Party is thus an expression of the enduring but evolving character of the welfare system as a tool for nationalist policies.

This chapter addresses the issue of the mutually reinforcing relationship between, on the one hand, national identity and ideology in Denmark and, on the other, the character and position of the welfare state in the economic and cultural construction of the country. It is argued that the advent of religious and ethnic minorities poses actual challenges for a re-conceptualization of Denmark, not merely on the superficial level of "Danes' attitudes towards immigrants," but much more broadly in terms of the social and ideological fabric of the country. Across diverse political opinions, including even the Danish People's Party, there is a consensus that immigrants and ethnic minorities need to be *integrated* into Danish society. Disagreements rather concern what this means, how it may be achieved and who should be blamed for its alleged failure. The keen attention to *integration* may in itself be seen as an expression of a cultural propensity of Danes to stress likeness, unity and agreement as indispensable for social interaction, a theme to which we shall return. The apparent obsession with the "integration" of immigrants in contemporary Denmark could also be interpreted as an attempt to maintain the achievements and socially integrative effects of the welfare state. This chapter is an attempt to explain how this may be so.

The concept of integration

In Danish politics and public debates, the term "integration" has come to mean the cumbersome and slow process of integrating immigrants and their descendants – particularly those from "non-Western countries" – *into* Danish society at large. This is a question of how immigrants "become part of Denmark" and "participate in Danish social life on an equal footing with everybody else," as typical phrases have it, whatever this may mean in practice. This understanding of integration as the absorption of new parts into a pre-existing whole is quite different from the classical meaning of integration in the social sciences, in which it refers to the fundamental theoretical question of how a society is held together – how "the whole" exists in the first place, and what the social forces and functions are that make a society possible and durable.

The question of integration has received particular attention in relation to studies and theories of early state formation (Cohen and Service 1978), in which an interest in processes of gradual and functional integration represents one line of thinking, as opposed to an understanding that states are mainly formed through domination, exploitation and conflict. But taken in an even more general sense, the question of integration goes back to the foundation of "society" as the object or problem of social science (Simmel 1983 [1917]; Spencer 1967[1885]; Weber 1984[1921]), and it was particularly crucial to the sociological perspective of Émile Durkheim, as expressed here in the words of Talcott Parsons:

> He was the theorist par excellence of the problem area of social integration.... Durkheim's central problem, the solution of which he pursued with rare persistence, was to determine the major axes around which the integrative functions and processes of a society are organized. (Parsons 1964[1960]: 150)

For the sake of brevity and argument, the two meanings of integration mentioned above – the first pertaining to the integration of immigrants "into society", the second to the question of the integration of society as a whole – may be labelled the "political" and the "analytical" versions respectively, and the differences between them may be explored. The argument here will be that the current political use and understanding of integration in Denmark as a question of how to absorb immigrants may be understood better if it is placed in a longer historical view and analyzed in the context of how the current form of "Denmark" as a specific society – a certain "social whole" in the world – came into being.

The two meanings of integration, the political and the analytical respectively, differ in important ways, but it is worth noting that they are also similar in certain respects. One similarity concerns how both meanings refer to a process of *integrating* as well as to the result of this process – a state of *integratedness*, however this may be identified.

Moreover, integration may refer to the *mechanisms* of (improved) integrating in order to achieve integratedness; this function of the term seems particularly obvious in current political use – for example, supposedly this is what the Danish Ministry for Integration is busy organizing – but it is also implied in the analytical version of integration.[1]

Another similarity between the political and analytical uses of the term "integration" is their *normative* element: integration is invariably a good thing, something socially desirable connoting harmony, balance and concord. Likewise, the concern for integration is generally linked to a deeper, underlying concern about *disintegration* – the spectre of "society falling apart" or becoming less coherent than it supposedly used to be, as modern times encroach on us with social mobility, the diversification of lifestyles and morals, and the straining of traditional social ties. Apart from Herbert Spencer (1967: 216), who had a vision of society becoming *more* coherent concurrently with the increased heterogeneity and diversification of social roles, social theorists seem to have been consistently concerned with the possible disintegration of modern society. Émile Durkheim, for example, was worried that too much diversification could be the potential cause of disintegration: "The division of labour cannot therefore be pushed too far without becoming a source of disintegration" (Durkheim 1960[1893]: 348, my transl.). While for Durkheim disintegration was a matter of the division of labour in society going too far, in today's political debate in Denmark it has become a question of ethnic diversification going beyond the manageable, thus causing a loss of a sense of unity. Clearly the threat of disintegration contains powerful political imagery, and as such it plays a crucial role in current Danish debates over immigration and the changing social landscape of the nation. Critics of immigration – and of some (read: Muslim) immigrants' alleged inability to integrate – refer to the Danes' supposedly unique sense of social cohesion and mutual trust in order to argue what is at stake (Jespersen and Pittelkow 2005). Conversely their opponents argue that the Danish welfare state ensures social cohesion irrespective of ethnic background (Schultz Jørgensen 2005).

So, what both political and analytical uses of the concept of integration also seem to have in common is the implicit and simultaneous reference to *coherence* and *cohesion*. Whereas coherence may be defined as the building blocks of society, the (sum of) complex social relations between individuals, cohesion is what gives social relations their meaning, validity and weight, the forces that both enable and fulfil social relations. In contemporary Western societies we have become used to defining cohesion in strongly emotional terms, so that the validity of social relations – in intimate relationships, in the family, in the work place, in religious matters, towards the nation state – all depend on the presence of deep and authentic feelings (of love, faith, conviction, patriotism). However, such an insistence on emotional fervour is a cultural peculiarity that easily ignores the arguably equally strong effects of such forces as obligation, tradition, convention, convenience, opportunity and an interest in social relations. Actually, such outer-worldly concerns are equally important for the interpretation of coherence and cohesion in social integration – in this case the analysis of the Danish welfare state. What I will argue is that Denmark is held together not just by the mutual identification and trust of the inhabitants of the country, but also by culturally defined mutual interests in certain economic and practical arrangements, and that the two sides are closely linked. For immigrants this means that, in order to become accepted as integrated, they must not only "feel Danish," they must also "do Danish" in close accordance with a whole range of particular social and cultural demands of the welfare state.

This line of thinking may suggest that "integration" is too vague and imprecise a concept for analytical purposes (Emerek 2003). What exactly does it mean in practice to be integrated? Society is too complex for integration to be a simple question of either-or. The German sociologist Niklas Luhmann has suggested that we abandon the concept of integration altogether and replace it with a more useful distinction between inclusion and exclusion (1997: 619-21). According to Luhmann, there is no single "society" into which one may be integrated or not, but rather a whole range of social systems (of education, housing, the labour market, political life, criminal justice, etc.), each with their specific forms of communication and exchange. For the analyst, the task then becomes to identify how inclusion and exclusion – which are simultaneous and mutually dependent processes – happen in practice, how individuals and groups are included into or excluded from participation in the exchanges of a specific social system. This approach seems to provide an analytical framework for studying integration politics, showing how intentionally "integrative" policies and practices may produce as much exclusion as they do inclusion simply by framing "integration problems" and their solutions in particular ways.

In this section, I have discussed certain similarities between the political and analytical uses of the term "integration", and among other things I have noted its inherently positive connotations, which it seems to instil in us. However, more critical perspectives on integration are also possible, for instance, if it is considered to be an example of an ideology of harmony, such as those Laura Nader (1990, 1997) has alerted us to. Nader describes how a cultural emphasis on consensus, agreement and harmony in diverse settings – from the handling of legal cases in the justice system to relations between workers and employers in the modern workplace – works as a mechanism of power that makes controversial issues of justice and equal rights secondary. If, with Nader, the Danish consensus over and within social integration is regarded as an ideology of harmony, one may ask which conflicts of interest and which differences of status and opportunity are glossed over by appeals to integration, consensus and social unity. This is highly relevant in the analysis of Danish welfare state ideology, as we shall see.

Yet, as one becomes more analytically sceptical of the injustices that the ideology of integration may give rise to, one may also ask – without being naïve about the ideological character of the phenomenon – which elements and functions that are beneficial for social justice may be equally enabled by the lure of "integration." After all, as cultural constructions the notions and practices of "integration" and of "the welfare state" should not necessarily be regarded as harmful distortions of reality – they may also be considered prime examples of human ingenuity.

To sum up, in both the "political" and the "analytical" version, the concept of integration implies multiple meanings of the process, result and mechanisms of integration – it refers to social coherence as well as to social cohesion, and (*pace* Nader) it has a distinct positive value. However, there are also important differences between the political and analytical versions. The attention paid in political debates in Denmark to the integration of immigrants *into* Danish society reflects the perceived need for political action on the matter, the obligation of politics to intervene in society to solve problems. The political approach reflects the dominant part-into-whole understanding of integration, with its associated tendency to problematize the part (in this case the immigrants), at the expense of a broader understanding of the character of the whole (in this case Danish society), which is – or was – the traditional focus of analysis in social science. By contrast, a purely analytical, deconstructive approach to social integration issues implies the privilege of detachment from intervention, which may easily grant the analyst the comfortable role of a mere commentator.[2] What I would argue is that there are important advantages to be gained from maintaining an interest in those ideas and practices of "the whole" that may exist in a given society, and that this interest may provide a better basis for understanding how and why the ethnically identified problems and policies of integration in Denmark appear and develop as they do. This, in turn, may have both political and practical relevance.

The creation of modern Denmark as a welfare state project

So, in order to understand problems of ethnic integration in Denmark, we need to understand better what "Denmark" is currently all about. In this, we should steer clear of certain essentialist depictions of the Danes that are already abundant in political debates and even in some scholarly writing, including anthropology. One side of the debate argues that the Danish mindset is unusually democratic, Christian, secular, liberal, egalitarian and anti-authoritarian – which is why the integration of immigrants from very different cultural and religious backgrounds is impossible. The other side argues that Danes are unusually racist, prejudiced, self-sufficient, parochial and brainwashed by a manipulative press into hating foreigners (Hervik 1999) – which is why the integration of immigrants and the acceptance of a multicultural society become impossible. Both approaches take opinions and attitudes among the Danes to be both the cause and effect of integration problems, and ignore the ways in which changing social and economic conditions impinge on the matter.

An entirely different way of looking at the situation is therefore to consider how current ideas about Denmark are intimately linked to the establishment of the Danish welfare state, or more precisely, the development and character of the Danish welfare state, at least since the Social Reform Act of 1933. The reform had been underway for some time and was put forward by K.K. Steincke, Minister of Social Affairs and Member of Parliament for the Social Democratic Party. It was adopted as part of a large political horse-trade known as the Kanslergade compromise, named after the small Copenhagen street where the prime minister had his apartment at that time. The agreement was made between the ruling Social Democratic and Radical Liberal parties and the opposition Agrarian Liberalists.[3] Certainly the roots of the Danish welfare state may be traced much further back than 1933 (Petersen 2003; Plough et al. 2004), from poor relief in the Middle Ages through philanthropic and mutual assistance societies to the first public-sector programs in the late nineteenth century for the elderly poor and children in need. And certainly the Social Reform Act of 1933 may be regarded as just one instance in the continuous re-organization of Danish social policy (Christensen 2004). Nevertheless, whether for its symbolic more than its practical effects alone, for generations of working Danes the 1933 Act has remained a dividing line between the social injustices of the past and the promise of a fair, modern and prosperous nation in the present and future.

The timing of the Social Reform Act was essential. The Act was agreed on the very day that Adolf Hitler was appointed Chancellor of Germany – though the symbolism of this coincidence was probably not known until later. Still, at the time there were strong political concerns over the precarious situation of Denmark, a small unaligned nation in a time of growing and aggressive totalitarian ideologies in Europe: Nazism and Fascism to the south, Communism to the east, and strong anti-democratic sentiments in many countries. This condition furthered the idea of creating a solid and solidary society on the basis of economic and social policies that were in the common interest of national survival and independence (Lidegaard 2003). A small country such as Denmark could not allow very strong, internal social tensions to exist, and all parties seemed to agree to a common, economic interest in compromise. Usually the Scandinavian model of the social welfare state is regarded as the product of a Social Democratic agenda, but even though this party has been dominant for long periods of time, welfare policies have usually been rooted in broad political compromises between workers' and farmers' representatives, and later between working-class and middle-class interests (Esping-Andersen 1990: 32).

Since 1933 the general trend has been towards a coordination of policies in terms of national economy, employment and social welfare, as well as the creation of universal schemes covering the entire population, run by the public sector and financed out of general taxation. The principle of universality is a crucial characteristic of the Scandinavian model. It is based on the commonly accepted assumption that "the entire population" forms a natural unity, not simply in terms of compelling mutual interests in a compromise, but in terms of a people of remarkable ethnic, linguistic and social homogeneity. The nationalist imagery of "being of one kind" has served as an important argument in favour of the establishment of the welfare state as a politically and economically legitimate project of integration.

In his pioneering book *The Three Worlds of Welfare Capitalism*, the economist Esping-Andersen (1990) sets out three ideal types of welfare state models in the Western world. They should not be regarded as stages in a development, but as different paths along which welfare states have evolved, even though in practice they have also borrowed ideas and policies from each other. First, there is the liberal and rather limited welfare state, of which the United States and to a certain degree the United Kingdom are usually taken as examples, which focuses on incentives to work, self-help schemes and only limited benefits provided against certain forms of social problems, such as (extreme) poverty. Secondly, there is the conservative, corporatist model – Germany and Austria are usually taken as examples – which focuses on the responsibilities of the family, as well as on a range of parallel, insurance-based and usually private schemes for various social groups, often related to employment. Thirdly, there is the universalist model – with Scandinavia as the standard example – in which the emphasis is on common and rather comprehensive public sector schemes. In this model, all residents – not just citizens – receive certain benefits to which they are entitled: child benefits for all and sickness benefits for wage-earners, for instance, or old-age pensions in proportion to the number of years the recipient has lived in Denmark. Other benefits are provided according to assessed need: early retirement benefit, for instance, or medical treatment. Health services in Denmark are almost entirely free of charge and form part of the public sector.[4]

According to Esping-Andersen (ibid.), different historical circumstances – political, economic, demographic, social – in different countries have given rise to different developments and characteristics of contemporary welfare state models. These circumstances have not "created" the models, but they have enabled different forms of political arguments, decisions and compromises. Once established, welfare state institutions have had a reinforcing feedback effect on society – the economy, the labour market, the demands and expectations of citizens – and the characteristics of the welfare state model in question have been maintained and even elaborated.

When considered in this light, it is important to stress that the relationship between the idea of the homogeneous, social unity of the Danish population and the universalist characteristics of the Danish welfare state is not a simple, unilateral one of cause and effect. Rather, it is a complex and mutually reinforcing relationship that develops and changes over time (see the introductory chapter by Olwig and Paerregaard for a discussion of the historical construction of "the homogeneous Denmark"). Homogeneity and universalism are both cultural constructions on the basis of prevailing opportunities, neither merely fact nor merely fiction, but the result of social processes, some of which express conscious, political choices. The idea of the homogeneous people drew on existing experiences of unity – for instance, that the entire population spoke (variants of) Danish – while equally obvious experiences of heterogeneity, such as differences between rural and urban living conditions, and differences of class and economic interest, had to be played down.

Cultural constructions are not fictions (Hacking 1999), they are manners in which human beings relate to complex realities by emphasizing certain aspects and downplaying others. Cultural constructions exist and work, some of them even as someone once intended.

In Scandinavia it was possible to claim with some credibility that the inhabitants were alike, of one kind, but in other countries this would have been a less obvious line of argument. The values of alikeness and equality figure prominently in anthropological studies of Scandinavian culture (Gullestad 1991): in social relations, there is a cultural preference for a performance of alikeness, of similarity between people, as it underpins the notion that everyone is equal – a crucial cultural ideal. The possibility of equality between differences – social, ethnic, economic – tends to be regarded with distrust, at least as a possibility around here. Likewise, the existence of hierarchies and authorities, which are as common in Scandinavia as everywhere else, may be ignored or denied.[5] Alikeness is a powerful cultural assumption, and it appears prominently in indigenous ideas about Denmark, as well as in their material construction of society. It has been possible to mobilize these notions in support of a universalist welfare state, but in the current global, post-immigration era, Danes are confronted with the downside of their ideals. The values they once held dear seem less obviously suited to handling and maintaining a multiethnic and multicultural everyday reality. What is a stake is not just a matter of mere "attitudes to foreigners": the fate of the welfare state has become a matter of what Denmark is all about.

The welfare state in national identity

The Danes are on welfare. Not welfare in the limited American sense of meagre economic benefits for the poor, but welfare as a form of distributed social wealth. Even though members of the Danish middle and upper classes may sometimes think they are beyond the mercy of the welfare state, they usually only need to be reminded of some of the services they themselves expect to receive in return for the extortionate taxes[6] they claim to be paying: free education from primary school through to university, six years of non-repayable student grants, paid maternity and paternity leave for a total of one year per child, heavily subsidized child-care facilities, free and comprehensive health services, pensions and home help for the elderly, sickness benefits, free or subsidized cultural activities in the form of public libraries, theatres, radio, television. And the list goes on.

The welfare state has become a public good that no political voices – except the odd anti-statist radical (Olesen 2007) – want to challenge. In 2005 the so-called Welfare Commission, set up by the current centre-right government, produced a catalogue of ideas for the reduction or reorganization of a number of welfare state schemes, only to be rejected across the political spectrum, and not least by the government itself. Even though changes obviously do occur from time to time – regarded as improvements or deteriorations, depending on one's political position – the point is that in Scandinavia it has become all but impossible to speak out against the welfare state as such (Christiansen and Åmark 2006: 354).

This popular support of the welfare state may be regarded as an expression of the degree to which the ideal of social solidarity – that "we are all in the same boat" – is accepted at face value. Or one may, with historian Søren Mørch (2003: 74-5), reject "the fraudulent talk about all of us being in the same boat," as some are always expected to row more than others. Mørch dryly remarks: "The welfare state has not been set up to be kind to the poor, but in order to avoid social unrest, class struggle, and civil war" (ibid.). Nevertheless, the welfare state has developed to become part of the national self-image, a crucial part of what the idea of Denmark is all about to its inhabitants. It has become difficult to imagine Denmark without the welfare state, and the Danes are fond and proud of it. In a report from SFI, the Danish National Centre for Social Research, the matter is put as follows:

> There is widespread support for the welfare state, as all opinion polls show. The welfare state has become part of the everyday life and identity of the Danes. In the self-perception of the Danes, the welfare state principles of solidarity and help for the socially weak are part of what separates them from other nations. When in the middle of the 1990s SFI published a study that showed the existence of comprehensive welfare systems in a number of other European countries, one of the reactions was that this could not be true. We know well that the Swedes have a welfare system, but that the same is true of the Germans, the French and the English is not quite believable. To a great extent welfare must be something particularly Danish, and therefore a section of the Danes are worried that the development of the EU and the immigration of foreigners into the country will threaten the welfare state. (Plough et al. 2004: 15; my translation)

The welfare state has had a considerable effect in terms of national integration, and remarkably the same is true of the other Nordic countries. Based on a comparison of the Nordic welfare states, a group of historians has concluded that

> since the inter-war period, the national cohesion has been a dominant orientation, especially promoted by the welfare policies and, in the second half of the 20th century, the very understanding of the Nordic countries as highly developed welfare states has become an integrated element in the national identities. (Christiansen and Markkola 2006: 11)

The Danish version of the welfare state is a social construction and a political achievement that, according to general sentiment, has benefitted the people of Denmark in numerous ways, and that has both drawn on and contributed to the notion of Denmark as a society and as an integrated whole – the Danish version of the nation as an imagined community (Anderson 1983). Whether they recognize it or not, the welfare state is a framework for the daily life of all Danes and what they have in common, whereby it contributes to the creation and maintenance of a "we": *our* schools, *our* hospitals, etc.

It is exactly the identity of this "we", closely related to welfare state provisions, that is the focus in immigration and integration discourses in Scandinavia, as Gullestad (2002: 53) has noted in discussing the situation in Norway. The Nordic welfare states are simultaneously inclusive of all (of the right ones) and exclusive of all others.

The system therefore homogenizes within. It is one of the hallmarks of a universalist welfare state model that there should be nothing stigmatizing about the receipt of benefits such as pensions, child allowances and free medical care, precisely because it is something everybody else receives too. Even services such as the "health visitor" (Buus 2001), which was invented to cope with high infant mortality rates among the poor, has gradually been extended to cover the whole population, and today it is a service that middle-class families in particular demand and take advantage of. Some welfare programs have achieved the status of civic rights, something to which one is entitled as a tax-paying citizen, not just by virtue of being particularly frail or victimized. For instance, to the concern of some, public home help for the elderly has begun to move in the direction of being regarded as a common entitlement. It is generally accepted that universal measures (such as old-age pensions) increase the legitimacy of the welfare state with the population because their value is experienced by all. This legitimacy then tends to be extended to other benefits (such as cash relief) that are only awarded to a few. However, this is not automatically the case. It has been widespread in Denmark to consider the receipt of public benefits and the inability to provide for oneself as shameful and embarrassing, just as the contempt for "welfare scroungers" – whether ethnically identified or not – can still be found in the press. The gradual reduction of the stigma associated with welfare programs is the result of a historical development that has increased acceptance of the welfare state as a whole – it is not solely the effect of the universalist model per se.

Today the economic redistribution effected by welfare state schemes enjoys a high level of political legitimacy with the Danish population. It seems fair to them that there is a certain degree of economic equalization between social groups, so that some receive more than they themselves are (at least currently) paying for through their taxes. This redistribution of wealth in itself has an integrative effect, as it induces the Danes to consider the economy of society as a whole, just as it represents a guarantee that you will be provided for yourself if need be. The state functions as a single, gigantic mutual insurance scheme. Paying taxes becomes the definitive proof of one's participation in and real contribution to the community, that is, to the working of the whole of society, and not just to the maintenance of an anonymous state bureaucracy. Paying some of the highest taxes in the world may then be taken as the expression of a systematized social conscience without the need to involve oneself personally in the problems of other people. Danes are not necessarily *happy* to pay their taxes – tax evasion and unreported moonlighting are national pastimes – but it is remarkable that studies show time and again that the Danes prefer better welfare schemes to tax reductions. Taxes are members' subscription fees to the co-operative society called Denmark.

The denial and re-emergence of class

Even though the welfare state has both been built on and contributed to the notions of equality and alikeness in the Danish people, the effect of the welfare state is not the creation of an actually egalitarian society. As Esping-Andersen says:

> The welfare state is not just a mechanism that intervenes in, and possibly corrects, the structure of inequality; it is, in its own right, a system of stratification. It is an active force in the ordering of social relations. (1990: 23)

The universalist welfare state has ordered – and re-ordered – social relations in Denmark, but it has not created universal equality and classlessness.

The Danish welfare state structure is rather a reflection of a particular class structure. As Esping-Andersen explains further:

> the system is meant to cultivate cross-class solidarity, a solidarity of the nation. But the solidarity of flat-rate universalism presumes a historically peculiar class structure, one in which the vast majority of the population are the "little people" for whom a modest, albeit egalitarian, benefit may be considered adequate. (1990: 25)

Roughly speaking, the Danish class structure has been characterized by a large proportion of lower middle-class people – typically of skilled workers, smallholding farmers and public employees – whose interests have been well covered by the universalist welfare state, which has reflected and not overcome this social structure of stratification.

Even though it has certainly helped improve general living conditions for all, class is still a fact of Danish life – albeit a different one than a hundred years ago. First of all, of course, there is a limit to redistribution, and Denmark too has its share of both extremely rich and alarmingly poor people, even if deaths by outright starvation or medical neglect are rare. Moreover, as the Danes and their social engineers are perhaps beginning to accept, social and economic inequality is not just an aberration that will disappear once the welfare state has been fully developed to cover all corners of capitalist society. Contrary to the original promises of social and economic policy, the poor and the marginal are still with us, social inequalities and problems are being reproduced, and social mobility – through the educational system, for instance – is poor in Denmark. Class differences, that spectre of social conflict that the welfare state was supposed to have overcome, have re-emerged. This is not in the classical Marxist form of the destitute masses in opposition to a small and wealthy ruling class, but in the form of a massive middle class that has benefitted enormously from the welfare state, and which is socially and culturally – and increasingly geographically too – separated from a marginalized class of people with complex social problems, a disproportionally large part of whom belong to ethnic minorities. If the relevance of class could once be denied as a soon-to-be-gone phenomenon, it has re-emerged with a vengeance as a fact of daily life in Denmark (whether it is admitted or not), and ethnicity is part of the equation.

The welfare state, Danish-style, is built on an ideal of "Denmark for the people," as the title of a famous Social Democratic battle song goes (Hansen 1934).[7] This means Denmark for the *whole* people, not just for the rich, the powerful and the learned – a nation with "room for all of us at the table of society", as one line in the song has it. "Denmark for the people" is not really a patriotic song, but the musical emblem of a party that claims that class differences may be subordinated to a popular community through a (certain) redistribution of wealth: class may be denied as the governing principle of social structure if people want it. And apparently they did, even if different classes obviously wanted it for different reasons.

What is new to the Danish image of society, social strata, social problems and (in)equality is the growing presence of ethnic differences among the inhabitants of the country. The homogeneity of the population, which for seven decades has been presented as an obvious and unproblematic fact in support of the universalist welfare state, re-appears as a new form of political argument with a new line of consequences: Who is it really that the welfare state is supposed to provide for? What is this "same boat" that "we" are all in anyway? With the advent of ethnic minorities with legitimate claims to the benefits of the Danish welfare state, the notion of "the people" changes; how may it be defined now?

This development may be seen in the broader context of what Schierup et al. (2006) refer to as the "dual crisis" of European welfare states: changing economic structures and policies create increased social exclusion, which, combined with changing notions of the nation and of citizenship, gives rise to racialized exclusion.

Even so, this exclusion takes on different forms in different countries. It should be noted that even though Denmark only has a small immigrant population by international standards, ethnic minorities have not settled equally over the country. In terms of housing patterns, school attendance and labour market involvement, lower-class Danes have experienced the influx of immigrants in their daily lives to a much higher degree than upper-class Danes have. Social mechanisms of exclusion – from economic disincentives to overt racism[8] – have virtually barred immigrants from entering large parts of the job and housing markets, so that better-off Danes may never actually be in contact with people from the large immigrant communities at all (except, perhaps, as the cleaning staff of their offices). At the other end of society, so to speak, through the same mechanisms, it is the lower-class Danes who have witnessed the changing ethnic composition of people in housing projects and working-class jobs. And with various degrees of success, they are the ones who have had to figure out what this thing called integration might be about.

Moreover, the universalist welfare state has had a strong tendency to try and solve integration issues as a particular kind of social policy (Preis 1998). In the past few decades, a large proportion of immigrants to Denmark have been refugees from the Middle East, Somalia and Sri Lanka, rather than, as was the case earlier, labour migrants, who were expected to be integrated through the labour market. The welfare system has regarded the very status of being a refugee or immigrant, particularly from non-Western countries, as a social problem in itself. This has led to a focus on people's problems and incapacities, turning people into clients of the welfare bureaucracy rather than considering other options (Preis 1996). Even though this line of thinking has been substantially challenged in later years, the fact remains that large sections of the welfare state bureaucracy, not least in the local municipalities, have been expected to devote a considerable amount of time, money and effort to dealing with the "integration problems" of immigrants, on top of the benefits that were paid.

Given these changes, more Danes have begun to express their concerns over the future of the welfare state: why are immigrants entitled to the benefits of a Danish welfare system they have not (yet) contributed to? Some move this question further and take "Denmark for the people" to mean "Denmark for the Danes." It might well be argued that this is a complete distortion, as these two slogans connote antithetical values of inclusive solidarity versus exclusive and racist self-sufficiency. Yet it should also be remembered that not long ago there was no large nominal difference between the two statements, as it was accepted that the people consisted of self-identified, Danish-speaking, nationalist Danes, and that the welfare state ideology, and the political and administrative practices associated with it, used the reference to the (whole) people as an important part of its legitimacy. "Denmark for the people" meant "welfare and justice for *all* Danes," not just for the few. But it only takes a slight shift of emphasis to have the line read "welfare and justice for all *Danes,*" which aligns Scandinavian welfare policy with entirely different political potentials.

It probably does not need much arguing at this point to claim that Laura Nader's critical analysis of "ideologies of harmony" applies well to the case of the Danish welfare state. The trust in consensus, which characterized the construction and operation of the welfare state in most of the twentieth century, successfully glossed over the continued existence of class differences, as the vast majority of the population experienced the benefits of the redistributive welfare system. The combined cultural ideals of equality and alikeness veil rather than remove class as a structural principle. But today the harmony is shattered. As has been argued, the welfare state as such is not being challenged; the question is rather who should have access to it.

The general elections of 2001 brought in a new centre-right minority government that enjoys the loyal parliamentary support of the anti-immigration Danish People's Party. This party happily refers to the election and change of government as "the System Change," as the Social Democrats were ousted, and strict immigration laws and fierce anti-Muslim rhetoric became the political order of the day (see the chapters by Sjørslev and Rytter in this volume). Convincing political analyses of the 2001 and subsequent elections have been few, the general interpretation being that the Danes were simply tired of the idealist centre-left parties and their inability to take the real problems of immigration and integration seriously. Or maybe the Danes simply revealed their ugly racist face. Only recently, the journalist and literary critic Rune Lykkeberg (2008) has presented a broad analysis of changes in Danish society before and after the 2001 elections. Lykkeberg suggests that the country has come to the end of the illusion that the modern welfare state may produce a classless community of common values under the moral guidance of progressive intellectuals and visionary politicians. Instead, Denmark has been revealed as a society divided by class along cultural (which does not mean ethnic) rather than merely economic lines, and the 2001 election signalled a protest against the know-all attitude of the cultural upper class (urban, intellectual, liberal and cosmopolitan). Resistance to immigration is only one element in this upheaval. From a different angle, in a series of books the journalist Lars Olsen (2005, 2007, 2009, 2010) has focused on persistent and new social inequalities in Danish society, reproduced not least though the educational system and increased segregation in housing, leaving one sixth of the population with large and combined social problems. Olsen stresses how ethnicity plays into this picture, arguing that Denmark is in danger of producing and maintaining a permanent underclass, partly ethnically identified. Class has become a more complex issue, but we cannot understand Danish society without it.

National(ist) welfare in a global(ist) world?

Do universalist welfare states of the Scandinavian type stand a chance of surviving the changing population and migration patterns of the global world? Some argue that ethnic diversification seriously shatters the legitimacy of welfare systems of the universalist kind:

> it is clearly harder for many Scandinavians to support their "foreign" neighbors than their native fellow citizens. ... This cultural conflict has undermined some of the support that universal welfare provisions have otherwise enjoyed. Solidarity rested, after all, on the small group cohesion of the workplace or the village extended, first, to your class and, then, to your nation. The sudden appearance of significant groups with very different cultural norms in the midst of your neighborhood ... strains social bonds. (Einhorn and Logue 2003: 312)

Against this view, other commentators (e.g. Goul Andersen 2006) maintain that general public support for the welfare state is not declining, and – as Esping-Andersen also argued – once particular systems of welfare provision have been put in place, the population tends to be unwilling to relinquish them. It is generally true that welfare schemes that benefit people similar to oneself enjoy the most support in Denmark (ibid.: 6), and there is a certain scepticism towards the rights of immigrants to public assistance. But there is also a continued popular support for the redistributive mechanisms of the state and for solidarity with the poor, "even when they are foreigners" (ibid.).

Nevertheless, the Danish parliament has in fact passed social policy legislation that explicitly aims to reduce the social benefit opportunities of certain immigrant individuals and families in order to make Denmark less attractive for non-working immigrants. For instance, "introduction benefit" and "start assistance" are the names given to cash relief on a severely reduced level in comparison with benefits for Danes. The first of them may be awarded for three years to new immigrants with no other means of subsistence, provided that they participate in a so-called "introductory programme" set up by the local municipality. The second may be awarded to immigrants who have spent less than seven years of the past eight years in Denmark, and who have no other means of providing for themselves. Both benefits are below official levels of minimum subsistence and below the official EU poverty level, yet they are defended for giving incentives to immigrants to start working and become integrated into Danish society. Apparently poor immigrants need greater incentives than poor Danes to work! Other welfare provisions are less explicit in their targeting of immigrant families, for instance, the so-called "300 hours rule" that requires married spouses who are unemployed and receive cash relief to find 300 hours of paid work within a two year period if they want to maintain their benefits. It is well known (and intended) that this rule affects minority ethnic families to a much greater extent than other Danish families – yet, of course, the provision itself is technical and objective.

What all of these examples show is the general shift in Danish social policy, in close accordance with international trends, from welfare to "workfare" – i.e. an increased attention to self-maintenance and incentives to work as the primary function of welfare provisions. Moreover, the whole debate about the relationship between ethnic minorities and the Danish welfare state has exposed the implicit cultural assumption of the present welfare system that all people (women as well as men) take up paid employment outside the home, pay a lot of taxes, and leave the care of the children, the sick, the disabled and the elderly to professionals in public institutions. Not all Danes are necessarily perfectly happy with this arrangement as it is, but clearly it forms a strict cultural guideline for the normal life course of a Danish person and has a considerable impact on the daily lives of families. The character of the welfare system in itself requires immigrants to adjust their personal and family lives in order to "integrate" into this narrow cultural and economic logic – to "do Danish", to use a phrase from earlier in this chapter.

The welfare system is only financially and practically viable if everyone provides for themselves most of the time through work and only take advantage of those benefits that they need. Yet employment rates among ethnic minorities with a non-Western family background are lower than among other Danes (Dahl 2005: 29-33), which turns this whole section of the population into net receivers of welfare benefits seen over a life-time perspective (Gerdes and Wadensjö 2006). This may seem like a petty form of accounting, but it has very real social and political implications as it affects the core of the universalist welfare state logic, even with its redistributive intentions. The problem may not be so much about differences in the take-up rates of benefits alone, but lies rather in the potential for a political response in the form of a differentiation of welfare provisions and benefit levels along the lines discussed above. At the same time, the universalist welfare state is also under attack from within in another sense, as the Danish parliament has allowed the establishment of private luxury hospitals and given tax relief for private health-insurance schemes, thus effectively creating a fast track to health services for the rich. If the welfare state for "the people as a whole" is disintegrating in this manner, what may be at stake is the incipient dismantling of Denmark as a social unit as we know it. The Danish welfare state is not just a piece of social and economic engineering, it is inherently a project of cultural construction, a building site of social relations and values. The current challenge for the universalist welfare state ideology seems to be to find ways to demonstrate that a functional "Denmark for the inhabitants" ultimately remains for the benefit of everyone.

Notes

1. For instance, in Durkheim (1960: 28), where he asks how solidarity, developed through the division of labour, contributes to "the general integration of society."
2. Unlike academic commentators, applied anthropologists working in policy and practice in this field have to confront and handle integration issues pragmatically through personal and professional involvement (Feldman 2009).
3. The compromise included assistance for agricultural exports through a devaluation of the Danish currency, an extension of existing labour-market agreements to prevent industrial unrest, and the Social Reform, which created or reorganized a range of schemes of interest particularly to the urban working class (unemployment benefits, employment programs, industrial injury insurance) and to the population as a whole, including the rural poor (sick-benefit associations,

public poor relief, and public old-age pensions). On the Kanslergade compromise, Einhorn and Logue (2003: 225) note that "this consensus set a pattern for governmental activism in managing the economy that would hold sway throughout Scandinavia for the rest of the century. The Social Democratic governments sought new policy tools that would stimulate economic growth, reduce unemployment, and improve national economic security."

4. Health services in primary care and hospitals are entirely free for all inhabitants with legal residence in Denmark, a fact sometimes regarded as the jewel of the Danish welfare state. Other health services are only partly state-subsidized, such as services and products from the pharmacy, the dentist and the optician.

5. One of the more bizarre expressions of this denial of hierarchy is the continued existence and popularity of the monarchy in all three Scandinavian countries. The extended royal families are heavily subsidized by the public purse and treated with reverence, even by the gutter press, yet it is quite common to hear Scandinavians claim that the royals are popular because "really, they are ordinary people like you and me."

6. By comparative standards, Danish taxes are very high – roughly a 40% income tax plus a 25% sales tax. However, it should be noted that this covers all social and health insurance, and employers are not liable to pay such benefits. Wage policies are generally more egalitarian in Denmark than in the US.

7. "Denmark for the people" was also the name of a political program for the Social Democratic party from 1934, signalling a change of self-perception from a class-based to a broader popular party.

8. Interestingly, studies show that unemployed immigrants have a higher level of education than unemployed native Danes (Hald Andersen 2006). Issues of health and language may account for some of this situation, but a lack of recognition of foreign qualifications and plain racism in the job market are also part of the picture.

References

Anderson, Benedict. 1983. *Imagined Communities. Reflections on the Origin and Spread of Nationalism.* London: Verso.

Buus, Henriette. 2001. *Sundhedsplejerskeinstitutionens dannelse. En kulturteoretisk og kulturhistorisk analyse af velfærdsstatens embedsværk.* Copenhagen: Museum Tusculanums Forlag.

Christensen, Jacob. 2004. Socialreformen 1933: Principiel reform eller administrativ omlægning? In *Den danske velfærdsstats historie,* ed. N. Plough, I. Henriksen and N. Kærgård. Report no. 04:18. Copenhagen: Socialforskningsinstituttet.

Christiansen, Niels Finn and Pirjo Markkola. 2006. Introduction. In *The Nordic Model of Welfare. A Historical Reappraisal*, ed. N. F. Christiansen, K. Petersen, N. Edling and P. Haave. Copenhagen: Museum Tusculanum Press.

Christiansen, Niels Finn and Klas Åmark. 2006. Conclusions. In *The Nordic Model of Welfare. A Historical Reappraisal*, ed. N. F. Christiansen, K. Petersen, N. Edling and P. Haave. Copenhagen: Museum Tusculanum Press.
Cohen, Ronald and Elman R. Service, eds. 1978. *Origins of the State. The Anthropology of Political Evolution.* Philadelphia: ISHI.
Dahl, Karen Margrethe. 2005. *Etniske minoriteter i tal.* Copenhagen: Socialforskningsinstituttet.
Durkheim, Émile. 1960[1893]. *De la division du travail social.* Paris: Presses Universitaires de France.
Einhorn, Eric S. 2000. *Nordic Welfare States: A Perspective from the American Sonderweg.* Working Paper. Copenhagen: Socialforskningsinstituttet.
Einhorn, Eric S. and John Logue. 2003. *Modern Welfare States. Scandinavian Politics and Policy in the Global Age.* Second edition. Westport: Praeger.
Emerek, Ruth. 2003. Integration – eller inklusion? Den danske diskussion om integration. *AMID Working Paper Series* 31. Aalborg: Aalborg University.
Esping-Andersen, Gøsta. 1990. *The Three Worlds of Welfare Capitalism.* Cambridge: Polity Press.
Feldman, Maia. 2009. Vejledning fra et antropologisk synspunkt. In *Hverdagspraksis i socialt arbejde – antropologiske perspektiver*, ed. Katrine Schepelern Johansen et al. Copenhagen: Akademisk Forlag.
Gerdes, Christer and Eskil Wadensjö. 2006. Immigration and the Welfare State: Some Danish Experiences. *AMID Working Paper Series* 60. Aalborg: Aalborg University.
Goul Andersen, Jørgen. 2006. Immigration and the Legitimacy of the Scandinavian Welfare State: Some Preliminary Danish Findings. *AMID Working Paper Series* 53. Aalborg: Aalborg University.
Gullestad, Marianne. 1991. The Scandinavian Version of Egalitarian Individualism. *Ethnologia Scandinavica* 21: 3-18.
—. 2002. Invisible Fences: Egalitarianism, Nationalism and Racism. *Journal of the Royal Anthropological Institute* 8: 45-63.
Hacking, Ian. 1999. *The Social Construction of What?* Cambridge: Harvard University Press.
Hald Andersen, Signe. 2006. Hjælper uddannelse indvandrere i beskæftigelse? *AKF Nyt* 2: 10-11.
Hamburger, Charlotte. 1997. Etniske minoriteter og social integration. In *Social Integration*, ed. Lilli Zeuner. Copenhagen: Socialforskningsinstituttet.

Hansen, Oskar. 1934. *Danmark for folket*. Copenhagen: Fremad.
Hervik, Peter. 1999. *Den generende forskellighed: Danske svar på den stigende multikulturalisme*. Copenhagen: Hans Reitzels Forlag.
Jespersen, Karen og Ralf Pittelkow. 2005. *De lykkelige danskere – en bog om sammenhængskraft*. Copenhagen: Gyldendal.
Lidegaard, Bo. 2003. Velfærdsstaten som dansk overlevelsesstrategi. In *13 historier om den danske velfærdsstat*, ed. Klaus Petersen. Odense: Syddansk Universitetsforlag.
Luhmann, Niklas. 1997. *Die Gesellschaft der Gesellschaft*. Vol. 2. Frankfurt am Main: Suhrkamp.
Lykkeberg, Rune. 2008. *Kampen om sandhederne. Om det kulturelle borgerskabs storhed og fald*. Copenhagen: Gyldendal.
Mørch, Søren. 2003. Velfærdsstaten – en moderne spøgelseshistorie. In *13 historier om den danske velfærdsstat*, ed. K. Petersen. Odense: Syddansk Universitetsforlag.
Nader, Laura. 1990. *Harmony ideology: Justice and control in a mountain Zapotec village*. Stanford: Stanford University Press.
—. 1997. Controlling Processes. Tracing the Dynamic Components of Power. *Current Anthropology,* 38 (5): 711-737.
Olesen, Ole Birk. 2007. *Taberfabrikken*. Copenhagen: People's Press.
Olsen, Lars. 2005. *Det delte Danmark*. Copenhagen: Gyldendal.
—. 2007. *Den nye ulighed*. Copenhagen: Gyldendal.
—. 2009. *Den sociale smeltedigel*. Copenhagen: Forlaget Sohn.
—. 2010. *Eliternes triumf. Da de uddannede klasser tog magten*. Copenhagen: Forlaget Sohn.
Parsons, Talcott. 1964[1960]. Durkheim's Contribution to the Theory of Integration of Social Systems. In *Essays on Sociology and Philosophy* by Emile Durkheim et al., ed. Kurt H. Wolff. New York: Harper and Row.
Petersen, Klaus, ed. 2003. *13 historier om den danske velfærdsstat*. Odense: Syddansk Universitetsforlag.
Plough, Niels, Ingrid Henriksen and Niels Kærgård, eds. 2004. *Den danske velfærdsstats historie*. Copenhagen: Socialforskningsinstituttet. Report no. 04:18.
Preis, Ann-Belinda S. 1996. The vagaries of refugee resettlement: power, knowledge and narrativity. *Anthropology in Action* 3 (1): 4-8.
—., ed. 1998. *Kan vi leve sammen? Integration mellem politik og praksis*. Copenhagen: Munksgaard.
Schierup, Carl-Ulrik. 1993. *På kulturens slagmark. Mindretal og størretal taler on Danmark*. Esbjerg: Sydjysk Universitetsforlag.

Schierup, Carl-Ulrik, Peo Hansen and Stephen Castles. 2006. Understanding the Dual Crisis. In *Migration, Citizenship, and the European Welfare State. A European Dilemma*. Oxford: Oxford University Press.
Schultz Jørgensen, Per. 2005. Sammenhængskraft er velfærd – og det økonomiske grundlag for den. *Socialpolitik*, special issue: 20-27.
Simmel, Georg. 1983[1917]. Das Gebiet der Soziologie. In *Schriften zur Soziologie. Eine Auswahl.* Frankfurt am Main: Suhrkamp.
Spencer, Herbert. 1967[1885]. *The Evolution of Society. Selections from Herbert Spencer's* Principles of Sociology. ed. R. L. Carneiro. Chicago: The University of Chicago Press.
Weber, Max. 1984[1921]. *Soziologische Grundbegriffe*. Tübingen: Mohr.

CHAPTER TWO

"THE FAMILY OF DENMARK" AND "THE ALIENS": KINSHIP IMAGES IN DANISH INTEGRATION POLITICS

MIKKEL RYTTER

In recent years, there has been a growing scholarly interest in transnational marriages as a path to migration (Ballard 1990; Shaw 2001; Constable 2004; Kofman 2004; Strassburger 2004; Charsley 2006; Charsley and Shaw 2006; Beck-Gernsheim 2007; Rytter 2007, 2012). Marriage migration has in many respects become the last legal entry point into "Fortress Europe" for non-European immigrants, and many European countries have altered their rules on family reunification, in order to protect their national interests against an uncontrolled inflow of foreign spouses. Denmark took a leading position in this endeavour when in 2002 the *Folketing* (Parliament) adopted new legislation on family reunification, which was proudly presented by the Liberal-Conservative (*Venstre-Konservative*) government as the strictest in the world (Schmidt 2011). The immigration regime makes it difficult not only for foreigners but also for Danish citizens – and in particular the 8% of the population with immigrant backgrounds[1] – to obtain family reunification with non-European spouses.

The new legislation had three overall purposes. First, it was meant to hamper the practices of transnational arranged marriages documented among Turkish and Pakistani immigrants where more than 80% of all marriages were contracted with spouses from Turkey and Pakistan (Schmidt and Jakobsen 2000:144). In a broader historical perspective, the new legislation was the culmination of a moral panic concerning the marriage patterns of immigrants in Denmark, and was thus presented as a necessary means to rescue young, second generation immigrants (especially women) from being forced into marriages with spouses from their countries of origin (Rytter 2003a:43). Second, the legislation was an aspect of the general securitization of migration following "11 September 2001", adopted to secure the borders and protect the nation from further transgressions by non-European immigrants – especially those from countries dominated by Muslim populations. Finally, it was believed that the combination of these two objectives would provide fertile ground for a new and improved strategy for the national integration of immigrants and refugees already resident in Denmark.

To comply with these three related political objectives five requirements of age (*24-års-reglen*), accommodation (*boligkravet*), financial assistance (*forsørgelseskravet*), collateral (*sikkerhedsstillelsen*) and national attachment (*tilknytningskravet*) for obtaining family reunification were introduced[2]. The new legislation had an immediate effect on marriage-related immigration. Whereas 6499 spouses came to Denmark through family reunification in 2001, the number was reduced to 2619 by 2008. The most frequent reason for a newly wed couple to be denied reunification is that their combined national attachment to Denmark is considered insufficient. The requirement of national attachment is based on a calculation made by the immigration authorities in order to decide whether the total national attachment of a married couple consisting of a Dane and a foreign spouse is greater to Denmark than to any other country.

This article applies insights from anthropological studies of kinship to discuss common ideas of national community, identity, and relatedness in Denmark and explain why it has become widely accepted to base citizens' right to family reunification on a notion of national attachment.

The five requirements dictate certain standards regarding where marriages should be contracted and how family life should be organized in Denmark. But whereas the requirements of age, accommodation, financial assistance and collateral could be called "democratic", as they affect everyone equally, the requirement of national attachment targets specific groups of Danes as it distinguishes within the pool of national citizens, between the majority of "real" Danes and the minority of "not-quite-real" Danes. The latter group comprises the growing number of immigrants, refugees, and their descendants who have settled in the country and obtained Danish citizenship in the last 50 years.

I will argue that the persistent distinction between "real" and "not-quite-real" Danes is not only made possible, but also perceived as legitimate, by the widespread use of what could be called "kinship images". Kinship images constitute an indigenous theory of how Danes are related to each other (Carsten 2000, 2004) and are a specific way to talk and think about the nation that continuously marks out who belongs to it and who does not. Bertel Haarder, the former Minister of Integration representing the Liberal party (*Venstre*), utilized just such an image of kinship when he wrote about the Danes in 2003 in one of the major Danish newspapers:

> We [the Danes] have a job, because we care about what our family and neighbours think about us, and because we want to set a good example for our children. But foreigners do not feel these inhibitions in the same way. They live in a subculture outside the Danish tribe. That is why they so quickly learn about the possibilities for getting money [out of the welfare system] without making an effort. (Berlingske-Tidende, September 20, 2003)

Here the Minister not only offered a generalized, derogatory description of foreigners in Denmark, he also introduced an explanation for the differences between Danes and foreigners: the latter live "outside the Danish tribe", and the ways "they" live and think are radically different from the ways "we" (the Danes) do. However, Haarder's depiction of the Danish tribe is in no way exceptional, but rather an example of how kinship images are used to delimit the national community. Even though it may not necessarily be done to harm or exclude anyone, kinship images nevertheless produce and reproduce "symbolic fences" (Gullestad 2002, 2006) between different segments of the population.

This article discusses the basic conditions for integration in the current historical situation where both Danish national legislation and popular kinship images tend to distinguish between different types of citizens and in the same process to question the legitimate rights and attachments that some groups have in relation to the nation and the welfare state. The first part of the article explores how ideas of national relatedness are embedded in the requirement of national attachment. The second part analyses the notions of integration implied in the current immigration regime and discuss how people categorized as "not-quite-real" can aspire to become "real" Danes.

The National Order

The nation-state is the basic unit for developments in politics, economy, art, language and knowledge, which in turn has fostered the idea that every human being belongs to one (Wimmer and Glick Schiller 2003). This has resulted in the creation of a global "national order" of separate peoples and nation-states (Malkki 1992)[3]. National belonging is manifested through citizenship. Anyone with a passport can literally document which location in the world he or she supposedly belongs to. However, the national order is challenged by flows of globalization, with people crossing national borders on an unforeseen scale and frequency, and by the fact that many people change their nationality. Furthermore several sovereign nation-states, such as Sweden, Pakistan and the USA, actually allow dual citizenship. These examples all contradict the logic of "the national order".

The geographical territory of the Danish nation state has changed in recent centuries. It was not until the cession of Norway in 1814, the military loss of Schleswig-Holstein in 1864 and the plebiscite deciding the southern borders in 1920 that Denmark ended up with the territory we recognize today[4]. However, since the nineteenth century periods of extensive nation-building have utilized language, public schools, the mass media and national history as ways of fostering the idea of a more or less coherent national community and identity. Today Denmark is often described as an old nation-state with a very homogenous population (Gundelach 2002:58), despite the fact that approximately 8% of the population has a different ethnic background than Danish.

Since 1950, the distribution of Danish citizenship, that is, the process of naturalizing aliens as Danish subjects, has been granted twice a year to foreigners who meet specific, politically defined criteria. Currently, all applicants have to comply with the laws passed in 2002 by the parliamentary majority consisting of the Liberal-Conservative government and the right-wing "Danish People's Party" (Ersbøl 2004:96). The parliamentary body responsible for these matters is a specific "citizenship committee" (*indfødsretsudvalg*). So historically, Danish citizenship has been granted on varying legal and moral principles, depending on contemporary politicians and international trends (Hansen and Jelstrup 2005:89). However, the key point in relation to my argument is the fact that so far Danish citizens have been equals before the law (Ersbøl 2004:92). Danish citizenship used to be based on an exclusive status and a set of legal rights that gave national subjects certain privileges and obligations in relation to the national community and the welfare state. This basic principle has been broken by the introduction of the requirement of national attachment.

Notions of National Attachment

When the requirement of national attachments was first introduced in 2000, it was only applied to foreigners living in Denmark who requested family reunification. Then, the total national attachment of the married couple should be *at least as great* to Denmark as to any other country. When the new legislation was introduced in 2002, the requirement was changed in two ways. First it was also applied to Danish citizens who married foreigners, and second the total national attachment of the married couple now had to *be greater* to Denmark than to any other country in the world (Dilou Jacobsen 2004:104). These apparently minor changes had a major impact.

When the Danish Immigration Service has to decide the total national attachment of a newly wed transnational couple applying for family reunification, it does so on the basis of various predefined parameters. These parameters have been adjusted several times since 2002 and constitute a flexible political tool when it comes to regulating which foreigners are to be allowed family reunification. In 2008, the parameters for deciding the total national attachment of a married couple were as follows[5]:

- How long you and your spouse/partner have lived in Denmark.
- Whether one or both of you have family or other acquaintances in Denmark.
- Whether one or both of you have custody of or visiting rights to a child under the age of 18 living in Denmark.
- Whether one or both of you have completed an educational program in Denmark, or have a solid connection to the Danish labour market.
- How well you and your spouse/partner speak Danish.
- The extent of the ties of both of you to any other country, including whether any or both of you have made extended visits to that country.
- Whether you have children or other family members in any other country.

The evaluation procedure amounts to a calculation, the purpose of which is to decide whether or not a married couple fulfils the requirement of national attachment, and should be given permission to live together in Denmark. The following example of Sohail and Nadia, a newly wed Danish-Pakistani couple, is a real case taken from a report published by the Danish Institute for Human Rights (Olsen *et al.* 2004), where it was used to exemplify how the Immigration Service evaluates the total national attachment of a newly wed couple:

Sohail is twenty-five years of age, born and raised in Denmark by parents originating from Pakistan. He is a Danish citizen and his parents and siblings all live in Denmark. At the time of handing in the application, Sohail has worked continuously as a salesperson for almost six years and is furthermore representing Denmark on the national team in an unnamed sport. Nadia is a Pakistani citizen. She is twenty-four years of age and has never visited Denmark before. Nadia has a sister who is already living in Denmark, but this is not considered to be a circumstance that enhances the national attachment of Nadia herself. The married couple met during Sohail's holiday in Pakistan, and were soon after married. The couple communicates in Urdu. The report does not say whether or not Sohail has been on a longer holiday in Pakistan or whether he has been there frequently. In their final decision, the Immigration Service denied them family reunification because their total national attachment to Denmark was not seen as greater than their total national attachment to Pakistan. In the decision the Immigration Service emphasized that Nadia had no independent attachment to Denmark. (Case reproduced from Liisberg 2004:32).

The case of Sohail and Nadia shows how Danish citizens with parents originating in another country have a hard time fulfilling the requirement of national attachment, because they lack a long family history and genealogy related to Denmark. In this case, it was not enough that Sohail was a Danish citizen and had his entire family in the country, that he had worked steadily since he was nineteen and that he represented Denmark at international sport events. Despite these circumstances, Nadia's and Sohail's total national attachment to Denmark was not considered great enough.

In an ideal "national order" there is an absolute correlation between the territorial boundaries of a nation-state and the nationality of those living there. To some extent this was the case in Denmark half a century ago, but recently the picture has become more blurred. Groups of immigrants, refugees and spouses and relatives who have entered the country from non-western countries and in time obtained citizenship embody the disparity between the Danish nation and Danish citizens. Despite their achieved legal status they are not regarded as "real" Danes.

In a broader perspective the recent developments in Denmark are far from unique but are part of the more general rise in "neo-nationalism" (Gullestad 2002; Hervik 2004; Gingrich and Banks 2006) and "cultural fundamentalism" (Stolcke 1995) that is documented all over Europe. In fact, the Danish situation has many similarities with Norwegian "ethno-nationalism", defined by Gullestad as (2006):

An imaginary geography where "foreign" appearance and family name work as markers of cultural difference and social distance. Ethnonationalism is a close-knit set of specific understandings about geography, history, culture, religion and perceptions about skin colour and descent, a close-knit set of ideas that has only recently been re-invented. (p. 302)

What is notable about the specific Danish case is that by introducing the requirement of national attachment, exclusionist kinship images have been elevated to a legal principle, which again legitimizes the idea that some citizens have more rights to and ownership of the benefits of the welfare state than others due to their "natural" relatedness to the Danish nation.

The Family of Denmark

The force of kinship images is their ability to construct and characterize the national community through metaphors. In *Metaphors we live by*, Lakoff and Johnson (1980) emphasize that metaphors are embedded in language and therefore in the very ways in which we comprehend the world. A metaphor is not a single arbitrary, more or less poetic, construction, but an element in a broader structure of concepts and meanings. As an example, the nation itself is a concept we can *love, build up, nurse* or *defend* in meaningful speech-acts. Metaphors are also grounded in bodily experiences of the physical and cultural environment. When we cope with abstract phenomena, such as the nation, we use a *Gestalt* from one domain of experience to structure another domain (Lakoff and Johnson 1980:230). In this respect, the nation has been described metaphorically as a biological organism, for instance a body (Eriksen 1997), or as grounded in local idioms of solidarity within family and kin groups (Herzfeld 1997:75; Gullestad 2006). The nation is also represented as complementary parental figures. On the one hand, the nation is the caring mother who protects and nurtures the children of the nation (mother's milk, mother tongue). On the other hand, the nation is described as the vigilant father, the fatherland, ready to defend the territory and the children of the nation against external aggressions (Hage 2003:31ff.; Carsten 2004:158). These examples show how we use tangible experiences from the primary sphere of the family to grasp the abstract imagined community of the nation.

In the Danish socio-political context, the notion of "the family of Denmark" (*familien Danmark*) is one such significant and productive kinship image. As the social anthropologist, Anne Knudsen poetically observes: "the family of Denmark has a beautiful ring to it" (Knudsen 1996:64; translation mine). This beauty is embedded in the condensed figure signalling coherence, solidarity and security, but it is also associated with peacefulness, cosiness and happiness – all values found in the ideal family. Evoking the notion of "the family of Denmark" in public discourses is a way in which to speak of average people such as Jensen, Hansen or Olsen without differentiating among them or accentuating one over the others. In that respect, "the family of Denmark" also sometimes signals mediocrity and may be used with a touch of sarcasm. It also represents the envious side of Scandinavian egalitarianism, where no one is supposed to stand out from fellow kinsmen, friends, colleagues or neighbours. The notion of "the family of Denmark" combines real experiences (or idealized fantasies) of family life with the more abstract national community.

"The family of Denmark" has been discussed in ethnographic studies in and of Denmark. Anne Knudsen provides a polemical discussion of the Danish welfare state and illustrates through numerous examples how the family is the general model for social organization at different levels. Relations between caseworkers and clients, teachers and pupils, medical staff and patients (and one might add Danes and foreigners or majorities and minorities) are all modelled on the structures of authority and intimacy found in the family (Knudsen 1996:56–7). In particular, the relationship between mother and child is to be found everywhere in the Danish welfare system (Knudsen 1996:73). Similarly, the American-born anthropologist Jonathan Schwartz, who has lived and worked for decades in Denmark, notes how immigrants and refugees are often reduced to symbolic children when they are represented by the majority:

> One of the obvious differences between our [immigrants'] situation in Denmark and [those] of France and Britain is that voices of the settlers in the two large countries are audible. They may not be listened to, but at least they can be heard [. . .] Danish journalists, politicians, social workers and social scientists talk about us sometimes as if we were not even present – something like the way children are talked about when they misbehave or are "so cute". (Schwartz 1990:43)

A number of studies conducted in Denmark are preoccupied with the same power mechanism and point out how dominant ideas of national "selves" and "others" are structured as relations between "hosts" and "guests" (Schwartz 1985; Hervik 1999, 2004; Rytter 2003b). The logic is straightforward: the aliens have come to Denmark and settled in "our" country. We invited guest workers from the European periphery in the 1960s and 1970s, and more or less voluntarily accepted groups of refugees and their spouses who have entered through family reunification. To reciprocate this gesture, the newcomers should submit to the explicit and implicit rules of the country.

There are several examples of how the Danes and the Danish nation are constructed as an imagined form of kinship, and how basic ideas of what it means to be a family, structure the relations between majorities and minorities. Kinship images are often taken for granted which only serves to conceal their impact. It is even difficult for the people exercising the power of "familism" to see and understand what they are doing. They have no evil intentions, but act as they do for the common good, as they see it (Knudsen 1996:61).

I now go on to test the range and validity of these kinship images against some of the findings in recent anthropological studies of kinship.

Euro-American Kinship

In *American Kinship*, Schneider (1980[1968]) explores dominant understandings of family and kinship in North America. According to Schneider, a core element of American and European kinship is the idea that "blood is thicker than water". Schneider finds two distinct types of family relations defined within the *order of nature* and *the order of law*, respectively.

Family and kinship relations of *the order of nature* are divided into two categories of family and kin which are both considered variations of natural connections. First there are relations based on substance, referring to the idea that each parent provides one-half of the child's biogenetic constitution. In this respect, people are said to contain a part of their mother and of their father and therefore also parts of their grandparents, and so on. The second type of natural bond is that understood as a relation of blood. Common blood relates ego to his or her siblings, aunts, uncles, cousins, etc. Even though these are two different ideas of relatedness, they are both considered to be part of what Schneider calls the order of nature and contain categories of relatives that cannot be terminated or changed, because it is never possible to have an ex-mother, ex-child or ex-brother (Schneider 1980:23ff). By contrast, family and kin belonging to *the order of law* are created through marriage such as spouses, in-laws, the children of a spouse's previous marriage, and so on. These relations are not seen as natural but rather as purely juridical and constituted by laws on marriage, divorce, divisions of property, inheritance and so on. These family and kinship relations can in both theory and practice be changed and substituted with similar ones (Schneider 1980:25ff).

Generally, Schneider claims that family and kinship are integrated and work over time due to a "diffuse, enduring solidarity" (Schneider 1980:97): "diffuse" because the relations are not necessarily directed at any specific goal; "enduring" because they last and are often irrevocable; "solidarity" because they are based on mutual trust and imply – and often demand – help, support and cooperation (Smedal 2001:13).

In the history of anthropology, David Schneider's analytical approach to family and kinship was groundbreaking and marked the transition from studying kin and family as biology and functional units, to conceptualizing them as cultural and symbolic domains. In an article published in 1977, 9 years after the first edition of *American Kinship*, Schneider suggests that his findings on family and kinship could also be applied to other domains such as religion or nationalism (Schneider 1977). I will try to follow this suggestion and apply his analytical vocabulary to the Danish national community and the logic behind the legislation on family reunification. The Danish people, the "real" Danes, are part of a coherent national community based on common history and cultural heritage. The national community can be characterized as an enduring, diffuse solidarity. We are Danes and we belong to the land like our parents, grandparents and ancestors did before us. Our presence within the national territory and our national citizenship (*indfødsret*) are of *the order of nature* and comply with the global "national order" of people and nation-states.

It is a totally different situation when we talk about the immigrants and refugees who have entered and settled in Denmark since the 1950s. They are in the country because they have been granted permission through work permits, residence permits, asylum, etc. People from this group have, over the years, obtained Danish citizenship, but only by abandoning their original citizenship. Also the so-called second-generation immigrants, who have been born and raised in Denmark and may never have had any other citizenship than Danish, are regarded as abnormal in relation to *the order of nature*, because even though they live in Denmark, they are supposed to live in another country in another part of the world. The presence of this expanding group of people is the result of *the order of law*. They are only in Denmark due to labour migration, family reunification, wars, or oppressive regimes elsewhere. Since they cannot refer to a specific national birthplace, a local place of origin, a family business or a family farm that substantiates their natural and legitimate belonging and attachment to Denmark, they are structurally excluded from being part of "the family of Denmark". Just as the domain of family and kinship contains different kinds of relatives, so too, the national community is constituted by different kinds of citizens (Schneider 1977:68). In this respect, Schneider's analysis not only explains how and why it has been legitimate to distinguish between "real" and "not-quite-real" Danes in the legislation on family reunification by expanding the requirement of national attachment, it also captures the new tendencies in Danish public and political discourses towards a more hierarchical and exclusive "ethnic nationalism" in contrast to the previously egalitarian and inclusive "civic nationalism" (Ignatieff 1993) that used to characterize the national community and welfare state system.

The distinction between the two categories of national citizens was further stressed in 2003, when the Danish Parliament introduced law no. 1204 in order to remove some of the unintended consequences of the new immigration regime. In the summer of 2002, it became clear that the rules of family reunification not only affected arranged and forced marriages but every transnational marriage. Expatriates, who for years had served Danish interests in the diplomatic corps, employees of NGOs or international companies all over the world, were no longer allowed to bring their foreign spouses back home. Their situation was reported in the media and soon put on the political agenda. As a result, the requirement of national attachment was supplemented by the so-called "28-year rule" (*28-års-regel*) that exempted everyone who had held Danish citizenship for at least 28 years from the requirement of national attachment. As a result of this adjustment, Danes by *the order of nature* were relieved of the requirement of national attachment when they turned 28. By contrast, Danes by *the order of law*, who had often obtained Danish citizenship later in life, had to wait 28 years before the requirement of national attachment was removed[6].

The *Folketing* introduced law no. 1204 as a necessary adjustment, so that the strict rules on family reunification would not affect the "wrong" groups of citizens (Dilou Jacobsen 2004:115–18). However, in making this legal adjustment they once again used national legislation to emphasize and expand the distinction between "real" and "not-quite-real" Danes.

Changing Identities

The rest of this article discusses the ideas of immigrant integration that are implied in dominant kinship images and affirmed by the requirement of national attachment. I discuss some of the strategies that "not-quite-real" Danes can utilize in order to become "real" Danes.

So far, Schneider has provided an analytical perspective that explains why the division of the national community, emblematized by the requirement of national attachment, is widely considered legitimate. On the other hand, his model does not allow much room for contestation or local creativity in response to the mechanisms of differentiation and submission. In this respect, a recent study conducted by Howell (2001, 2003) on childless Norwegians and their ideas and practices, concerning adoption of children from Asia, Latin America and eastern Europe is much more instructive. Howell shows how newly arrived children are soon given a position within the family that adopts them and in Norwegian society as a whole, despite the fact that the adopted children and their new parents do not share any biological substance. These adopted children are included in their adoptive families by Norwegian law, but the families also adopt symbolic gestures themselves, such as narratives and social practices, to transform the children into "real" family members. Howell (2001:207) calls this process of social and cultural becoming "kinning".

In a critical discussion of the concept of integration, Abdelmalek Sayad makes a very similar observation in suggesting that the discourse on integration is about identity. When politicians and policy-makers speak of integration they imagine a movement "from the most radical alterity to the most *total* identity" (Sayad 2004:216; italics in original). This new total identity is bound to be a national identity as the concept of integration is part of the "identitarian" vocabulary of the nation-state (Sayad 2004) that distinguishes between "the children of the nation" and the aliens.

Uniting the insights of Howell and Sayad, there are resemblances between the changes a subject will have to go through when it comes to the processes of "kinning" and "integration", respectively. Both imply an ontological change in the subject involved. They constitute specific locally recognized ways of including aliens in the community of the family or the nation, and, by that same process, of granting them obligations, responsibilities and ownership of the common good.

In the Danish case, there are at least two processes of kinning in which citizens categorized as "not-quite-real" Danes engage in attempts to become "real" Danes. The first is the long-term strategy of intermarriage. The second strategy relies on various technologies of self, which, paradoxically, take place in Sweden.

Intermarriage as a Strategy of Kinning

The explicit political agenda of the new immigration regime was to reduce the flow of newcomers by preventing transnational marriages. Immigrants with a tradition of transnational arranged marriages are urged to redirect their marriage preferences in favour of inter-ethnic and inter-religious marriages with spouses found in Denmark (Rytter 2010:101ff.). The ambitions of national politicians to govern the marriage market and alter existing marriage patterns in many respects resemble a state-defined preference for marriage endogamy within Danish territory, the Danish nation and – following Bertel Haarder, (the former) Minister of Integration, quoted above – the Danish tribe. The current legislation on family reunification assumes that the intermarriage of immigrants already residing in Denmark with ethnic Danes together with their subsequent biological reproduction within the national territory will inevitably make them and their offspring more Danish. It is generally assumed that, during the process of kinning, immigrants will abandon their cultural idiosyncrasies within a generation or two and start to become "real" Danes[7].

In a study of transnational belonging among Somalis in Denmark, sociologist Nauja Kleist (2006) presents a case that illustrates how marriage and biological reproduction are meant to relate people gradually to "the family of Denmark". Saphia, a Somali woman, fled Somalia in the 1990s and went through a long transit period in an institution for asylum-seekers before she managed to establish a meaningful life in Denmark. She has, among other things, married a "real" Danish man and given birth to their daughter. Nevertheless, the reactions her daughter meets depend on whether she is accompanied by her father or her mother. When she is with Saphia, the girl is often treated as an unwanted immigrant, whereas, in the company of her father, she is seen and treated as a lovely little girl with beautiful hair and radiant skin (Kleist 2006:124). Following my line of argument, one could say that in the company of Saphia the daughter is regarded as an alien. In the company of her father, however, she is perceived as a person undergoing transformation, moving away from her embodied radical alterity. She is a girl who through the practice of kinning, is gradually being recognized as a "real" Dane by her surroundings.

The case of Saphia illustrates how it is widely accepted in the Danish social imaginary that biological reproduction within the territory and nation initiates the process of kinning and gives citizens categorized as "not-quite-real" Danes partial rights over national places and spaces. Danish history contains several examples of how aliens have been absorbed into the local as well as the national community. The many French, Dutch and German surnames in the population bear witness to the fact that if one goes back a sufficient number of generations in family genealogies, many forefathers of "real" Danes are actually immigrants.

Kinning as a Technology of the Self

In the work of Signe Howell, kinning is an ontological change that adoptive parents can initiate in favour of their newly arrived children, but Howell does not discuss how the newly arrived children themselves can contribute to this transformation. This is actually possible in the Danish case. As the Immigration Service applies relatively few parameters in deciding the national attachment of newlyweds, it becomes possible for transnational couples to initiate and stimulate the process of kinning themselves. In this way, a couple who were first denied family reunification because their attachment to Denmark was considered insufficient can in time actually improve their record of national belonging and make the evaluation tip over in favour of Denmark. Paradoxically, this mainly happens abroad, in Sweden.

Since the new legislation was introduced, the number of family reunifications has been drastically reduced. Many of the Danish citizens who are – or know beforehand that they will be – denied family reunification move to the region of Scania in southern Sweden, only thirty minutes away from Copenhagen since the building of the Öresund Bridge that connects the two countries. In Sweden, Danish citizens are entitled to family reunification with non-European spouses due to their status as citizens of the European Union. In this way, the current legislation means that Danish citizens have more legal rights when it comes to family reunification in Sweden than they do in Denmark (see Rytter 2007, 2012). In 2005, almost 600 applications for family reunification with a foreign spouse were submitted by Danes in southern Sweden, of which 64 % were men and more than half of the applicants were under the age of 24 (Rapport 2006:9). As a result of this, an estimated 2-3000 Danes have moved to Sweden (or Germany) since 2002 in order to obtain family reunification. In 2007, no less than 12% of Danish-Pakistanis aged 25 had emigrated to Sweden (Schmidt *et al.* 2009:99).

Many of these transnational couples continue to work or study in Denmark where they also have their friends and family, and see life in Sweden as a temporary "necessary evil" before they can return legally to Denmark. During this transition period, it is possible for transnational couples to start the process of kinning and improve their attachment to Denmark. In order to explain how this process takes place, I return to the case of Nadia and Sohail, who were denied family reunification because their total national attachment was considered to be greater to Pakistan than to Denmark. I use Nadia and Sohail to set up a hypothetical scenario of how national attachment and belonging can be acquired, based on my interviews with transnational couples settled in Sweden (see Rytter 2007, 2012). I present it to expose the logics of kinship images and kinning that are inherent in the legislation.

> After his application for family reunification to Denmark is denied, Sohail decides to move to Malmö in Sweden in order to utilize his status as a European citizen to bring Nadia to Europe. He buys an apartment and leaves home. Four months later Nadia is granted permission to go to Sweden and they start living together as man and wife in Malmö. Sohail continues to work in Denmark, commuting across the Öresund Bridge. After a while Nadia begins to attend the local language school, where she starts to learn Swedish. Every evening she voluntarily studies the social conditions and history of Denmark, partly through talking with Sohail and partly from books, TV and the Internet. They spend almost every weekend in Denmark, where they typically spend the night in the house of Sohail's parents. Nadia soon establishes a network of female friends centred around her sister, who is already living in Denmark, and around her sisters-in-law and their friends. In time Nadia learns to speak both Swedish and Danish, and she gets a job at a shopping mall in Malmö. However, she quits her job when she becomes pregnant. After living together for two years, Nadia and Sohail are blessed with a daughter, whom they decide should become a Danish citizen, just like her father.

If the Immigration Service were asked to re-evaluate the total national attachment of Nadia and Sohail after their stay in Sweden, they *might* end up deciding that they now have become much more attached to Denmark than they were 2 years earlier[8]. This change has happened because they spend every weekend in Denmark, Sohail commutes to work in Denmark every day, Nadia has learned to speak Danish and they now have a daughter with Danish citizenship. The parameters for deciding national attachment give priority to certain practices, such as command of language, level of education, work, transnational mobility and reproduction, through which transnational couples in Sweden can increase their national attachment and belonging. These practices constitute a number of "technologies of self" (Foucault 1988) that married couples must subject themselves to in order to continue the process of kinning and increase their degree of relatedness to Denmark.

As I mentioned, the case of Nadia and Sohail is fictitious. In real life, it is not so easy to have a decision on national attachment re-evaluated. The Danish authorities will only deal with applicants living in Denmark, so before a re-evaluation can take place the Danish spouse, in this case Sohail, must move back to Denmark. This also means that the foreign spouse must go back to his or her country of origin, which in this case means that Nadia must return to Pakistan. From there they can reapply for family reunification in Denmark – but there are no guarantees. The Immigration Service may decide once again to reject the application and the foreign spouse furthermore may risk having a difficult time returning to Europe. In fact, I have not heard of any married couples willing to jeopardize their possibilities of building a future together in this way.

Conclusion: Integration of the New Danes

Analysing the Danish legislation on family reunification, I have suggested that kinship images and dominant ideas about the constitution of the national community, obstruct the process of integration. Kinship images mobilized in public discourses not only delimit and characterize the national community, but also at the same time disqualify a large number of people on the basis of their family histories.

I have given two examples of how Danes categorized as "not-quite-real" can attempt to change their position and status. In doing so, I present a relatively unproblematic scenario which neglects the fact that the cultural system itself changes over time. What today constitutes a "real" Dane will change as more and more people with an immigrant background obtain Danish citizenship, get married, and start making claims for recognition as "real" Danes and for ownership of the nation and welfare state. Even though these groups will, in time, become part of what Schneider called *the order of nature*, they will continue to have black hair, coloured skin, names associated with other parts of the world, and not least other religious practices and affiliations than standard Danish Protestantism – all features that are not compatible with the title and status of being a "real" Dane. Contemporary Danish politics has in many respects turned into a battle of identity politics in which the criteria used to define which citizens should be recognized as "real" Danes are contested and redefined.

However, the kinship images themselves are also changing. The notion of "the family of Denmark" is powerful because it is capable of presenting the abstract national community as one big happy family, but due to current divorce rates the nuclear family is just one among numerous ways to organize family life. Single parents, couples "sharing" children, the experience of having "weekend siblings", alternative collective families, long-distance relationships of transnational families, the legal possibility of gay-marriages and the right of lesbians to artificial insemination all urge indigenous Danes to rethink the concept of family fundamentally. This will probably also have effects on the kinship images of the future. The upcoming generations of Danish society might not have the same kind of experiences and sentimental feelings attached to the family as those dominant today, and they will therefore probably develop new images and ideas of the abstract national community. Only time will tell whether this redefinition will make the national community more open or more restricted than it is today when it comes to distributing recognition, ownership and identity.

What we do know is that in late 2009, the strict rules of family reunification were supported by all political parties represented in the Danish *Folketing* except the Social-Liberals (*Det Radikale Venstre*) and the Red-Green Alliance (*Enhedslisten*), a fusion-party consisting of different left-wing organizations, but neither of them currently have any influence on the national policies of immigration or integration. According to frequent opinion polls, the legislation on family reunification is supported by the vast majority of Danes and understood as a fair and reasonable way to deal with the forces of globalization confronting the Danish nation and welfare state. However, in the summer of 2008, the European Court of Justice laid down a verdict in the so-called Metock-case which challenged the Danish immigration regime. The fundamental right to the free movement of labour within the European Union, a corner stone of the European common market, was violated by the restrictive Danish legislation on family reunification. The verdict may very well undermine the protective Danish immigration regime in the future.

On a more general level, this article emphasizes that words and categories are never innocent. Verbal communications are never "just talk", but rather reflect more basic common understandings. Kinship images have a long history in the Danish language and imaginary, but it was not until the introduction of the requirement of national attachment in 2002 that these kinship images became tangible. Elevating specific ideas of national relatedness to a principle of the national law has had a direct impact on the lives of thousands of Danish citizens, who have been forced to rearrange their family lives after marrying spouses from non-European countries.

Words are also important in other ways. In his discussion of the contemporary rise of nationalism in western Europe, Herzfeld (1977:83) points out that the language of blood has returned and with it also the risk of literal bloodshed. Such a far-reaching conclusion cannot be made on the basis of this article, but it is important to emphasize the problematic – and potentially dangerous – situation we face, when it becomes legitimate and commonsensical to mobilize ideas of the order of nature, the unbreakable bonds of blood, or to present the national community as "a Danish tribe" in public and political discourses.

Acknowledgement

This article is a reprint of "'The Family of Denmark' and 'The Aliens': Kinship Images in Danish Integration Politics" by Mikkel Rytter, published in *Ethnos. A Jounal of Anthropology*, vol. 75:3, 2010, pp.301-322. It is reprinted by permission of the publisher Taylor & Francis Ltd, http://www.informaworld.com. The article has benefited a great deal from the readings and suggestions of several discussants. Once again, I want to express my gratitude to Jonathan Schwartz, Peter Hervik, Maria Ventegodt Liisberg, Line Bøgsted, Marianne Holm Pedersen, Helene Bech, Zachary Whyte, Robert Parkin, Karsten Paerregaard and Karen Fog Olwig. I am also grateful for the comments and suggestions provided by the anonymous *Ethnos* reviewers and Editor Mark Graham who helped me improve upon earlier versions.

Notes

1. NYT– fra *Danmarks Statistik*, nr. 37, februar 2005.
2. In order to obtain family reunification, these five requirements have to be fulfilled: (1) Both partners must be above the age of 24 (*24-års-reglen*). (2) The partner residing in Denmark must have "adequate accommodation of reasonable size" at his or her disposal (*boligkravet*). (3) The partner residing in Denmark must be able to provide for his or her partner and must not have received public financial assistance for a year prior to submitting the application (*forsørgelseskravet*). (4) The partner living in Denmark must post a specified sum of money (in 2008 DKK 58,207) as a collateral in the form of a bank guarantee to cover any possible public assistance paid by the municipality after the foreign spouse has moved to Denmark (*sikkerhedsstillelsen*). (5) Finally, the existing requirement of "national attachment" (*tilknytningskravet*), that so far had been significant only for foreign citizens living in Denmark, was increased so that it also became necessary for Danish citizens to comply with the requirement of national attachment when applying for reunification with foreign spouses. For more about the requirements and how they are administrated in practice, see http://www.nyidanmark.dk/en-us/coming_to_dk/-familyreunification/spouses/. See also two reports published by the Danish Institute for Human Rights (Olsen et al. 2004) and (Olsen and Liisberg 2005).
3. It is no coincidence that there is an etymological connection between the concepts of nation and nature. These concepts are related through the Latin concept of nation, meaning birth (Herzfeld 1997:41).
4. This statement neglects parts of Danish colonial history. The national border changed with the relative independence of Iceland in 1903–1918, the Faroe Islands in 1948 and Greenland in 1979, along with the disposal of Tranquebar in Southern India in 1885 and the Caribbean Virgin Islands in 1917.

5. See the Danish Immigration Service, http://www.nyidanmark.dk/en-us/coming_to_dk/familyreunification/spouses/attachment_requirement.htm
6. An example could be the hypothetical Danish-born son of immigrants from Pakistan, who changed his citizenship from Pakistani to Danish at the age of 12. He will have to wait until he is 40 before the requirement of national attachment is annulled. Similarly, a Palestinian refugee, who was granted Danish citizenship at the age of 25, would have to wait until she is 53 before the requirement of national attachment was withdrawn.
7. Seeing national intermarriage as a strategy of kinning echoes former discourses of racial supremacy. In 1921, the cultural anthropologist Franz Boas advocated that intermarriage was the solution to the race question in the USA (Sanjek 1996:104). Later commentators have remarked that the suggestion of the "paling out of blacks as the ultimate solution" denied "equality for the black male" and "ruled out blackness as a firm and rich experience"; basically it remained "unconsciously bent on genocide" (Sanjek 1996:105).
8. I write *"might"* because we do not know for sure. Every decision of national attachment is made individually – which makes the whole procedure blurred and arbitrary. However, legal experts from the Danish Institute for Human Rights and the NGO, Dokumentation og Rådgivningscenteret om Racediskrimination, which works with this legislation and its consequences confirm that a couple with a story resembling that of Nadia and Sohail would probably be said to have greater national attachment to Denmark than to any other country.

References

Ballard, Roger. 1990. Migration and Kinship: The Differential Effect of Marriage Rule on the Processes of Punjabi Migration to Britain. In *South Asians Overseas*, ed. Clarke Colin, Ceri Peach and Steven Vertovec, 219–49. Cambridge: Cambridge University Press.

Beck-Gernsheim, Elisabeth. 2007. Transnational Lives, Transnational Marriages: A Review of the Evidence from Migrant Communities in Europe. *Global Networks* 7(3):271–88.

Carsten, Janet. 2000. Introduction: Cultures of Relatedness. In *Cultures of Relatedness. New Approaches to the Study of Kinship*, ed. Janet Carsten, 1–37. Cambridge: University Press.

—. 2004. *After Kinship*. Cambridge: Cambridge University Press.

Charsley, Katharine. 2006. Risk and Ritual: The Protection of British Pakistani Women in Transnational Marriage. *Journal of Ethnic and Migration Studies* 32(7):1169–87.

Charsley, Katharine and Alison Shaw, eds. 2006. Special issue on 'South Asian Transnational Marriages', *Global Networks*, 6(4).

Constable, Nicole. 2004. *Cross-Border Marriages: Gender and Mobility in Transnational Asia*. Philadelphia: University of Pennsylvania Press.

Dilou Jacobsen, Bjørn. 2004. Tilknytningskravet og forbuddet mod racediskrimination. In *Ægtefællesammenføring i Danmark*, ed. Birgitte Olsen, Maria Ventegodt Liisberg and Morten Kjærum. Udredning no. 1, 104–25. Copenhagen: Institut for Menneskerettigheder.

Eriksen, Thomas Hylland. 1997. The Nation as a Human Being – a Metaphor in a Midlife Crisis? Notes on the Imminent Collapse of Norwegian National Identity. In *Siting Culture. The Shifting Anthropological Object*, ed. Karen Fog Olwig and Kirsten Hastrup, 103–22. London: Routledge.

Ersbøl, Eva. 2004. Statborgerskabets betydning ved ægtefællesammenføring. In *Ægtefællesammenføring i Danmark*, ed. Birgitte Olsen, Maria Ventegodt Liisberg and Morten Kjærum. Udredning no. 1, 82–103. Copenhagen: Institut for Menneskerettigheder.

Foucault, Michel. 1988. *Technologies of the Self. A Seminar with Michel Foucault*, ed. Martin, Luther H., Huck Gutman and Patrick H. Hutton. Amherst: The University of Masachussets Press.

Gingrich, André and Marcus Banks. 2006. *Neo-Nationalism in Europe and Beyond: Perspectives from Social Anthropology*. Oxford: Berghahn.

Gullestad, Marianne. 2002. *Det Norske – sett med nye øyne*. Oslo: Universitetsforlaget.

—. 2006. *Plausible Prejudice*. Olso: Universitetsforlaget.

Gundelach, Peter. 2002. *Det er Dansk*. Copenhagen: Hans ReitzelsForlag.

Hage, Ghassan. 2003. *Against Paranoid Nationalism. Searching for Hope in a Shrinking World*. Australia: Pluto Press.

Hansen, Simon, Kjær and Thomas Jelstrup. 2005. En dansk model? Statsborgerskabets udvikling i Danmark 1776-1990. *Tidsskriftet Politik* 2(8):84–93.

Hervik, Peter, ed. 1999. *Den Generende Forskellighed – danske svar på den stigende multikulturalisme*. Copenhagen: Hans Reitzels Forlag.

—. 2004. The Danish Cultural World of Unbridgeable Differences. *Ethnos* 69(2):247–67.

Herzfeld, Michael. 1997. *Cultural Intimacy. Social Poetics in the Nation-State*. New York: Routledge.

Howell, Signe. 2001. Self-conscious Kinship: Some Contested Values in Norwegian Transnational Adoption. In *Relative Values: Rethinking Kinship*, ed. Sarah Franklin and Susan McKinnon, 203–23. Durham: Duke University Press.

—. 2003. Kinning: The Creation of Life Trajectories in Transnational Adoptive Families. *Journal of Royal Anthropological Institute* (N.S.) 9:465–84.

Ignatieff, Michael. 1993. *Blood and Belonging. Journeys into the New Nationalism*. London: BBC Books.
Kleist, Nauja. 2006. Danmark to ansigter. Somali-danskeres oplevelser af stille integration og diskrimination. In *Den Stille Integration. Nye fortællinger om at høre til i Danmark*, ed. Marianne Holm Pedersen and Mikkel Rytter, 118–42. Copenhagen: C. A. Reitzels Forlag.
Knudsen, Anne. 1996. *Her går det godt – send flere penge*. Copenhagen: Gyldendal.
Kofman, Eleonore. 2004. Family-related Migration: A critical Review of European Studies. *The Journal of Ethnic and Migration Studies* 30(2):243–62.
Lakoff, George and Mark Johnson. 1980. *Metaphors We Live By*. Chicago: The University of Chicago Press.
Liisberg, Maria Vendtegodt. 2004. Regler og administrative praksis for ægtefællesammenføring. In *Ægtefællesammenføring i Danmark*, ed. Birgitte Olsen, Maria Ventegodt Liisberg and Morten Kjærum. Udredning no. 1, 16–45. Institut for Menneskerettigheder.
Malkki, Lisa. 1992. National Geographic: The Rooting of Peoples and the Territorialization of National Identity among Scholars and Refugees. *Cultural Anthropology* 7(1):24–44.
Olsen, Birgitte, Liisberg, Maria Vendtegodt and Morten Kjærum, eds. 2004. *Ægtefællesammenføring i Danmark*. Udredning no. 1. Copenhagen: Institut for Menneskerettigheder.
Olsen, Birgitte and Maria Vendtegodt Liisberg. 2005. *Hvidbog om ægtefællesammenføring i Danmark*, Foreløbig udgave. Institut for Menneskerettigheder.
Rapport. 2006. *Bro, Bostad, Bil and Kärlek*. Udfærdiget i samarbejde mellem Malmö stad, Migrationsverket, Skåneregion, Skatteverket og Öresundskommiteen.
Rytter, Mikkel. 2003a. *Lige Gift – en antropologisk undersøgelse af arrangerede ægteskaber blandt pakistanere i Danmark*. Specialerækken no. 261. Department of Anthropology, University of Copenhagen.
—. 2003b. Islam i Bevægelser. In *Islam i Bevægelse*, ed. Mona Sheikh, Fatih Alev, Babar Baig and Noman Malik, 137–59. Copenhagen: Akademisk forlag.
—. 2007. Giftermål over grænser: arrangerede ægteskaber blandt dansk-pakistanere i Malmö. In *Globala familjer: Transnationell migration ochsläktskap*, ed. Lisa Åkesson and Marita Eastmond, 175–204. Gothenburg: Gidlunds forlag

—. 2010. *Family Upheaval: Generation, Mobility and Relatedness among Pakistani Migrants in Denmark*, PhD thesis no. 57, Department of Anthropology, University of Copenhagen.
—. 2012. The Semi-legal Family Life: Pakistani Couples in the Borderlands of Denmark and Sweden. *Global Networks*.
Sanjek, Roger. 1996. Intermarriage and the Future of Races in the United States. In *Race*, ed. Steven Gregory and Roger Sanjek, 103–30. New Brunswick, NJ: Rutgers University Press.
Sayad, Abdemalek. 2004. *The Suffering of the Immigrant*. Cambridge: Polity Press.
Schmidt, Garbi. 2011. Law and Identity: Transnational Arranged Marriages and the Boundaries of Danishness. *Journal of Ethnic and Migration Studies*.
Schmidt, Garbi and Vibeke Jakobsen. 2000. *20 år i Danmark – en undersøgelse af nydanskeres situation og erfaringer*. Copenhagen: Socialforskningsinstituttet.
Schmidt, Garbi, Annika Liversage, Brian Graversen, Tina Jensen and Vibeke Jakobsen. 2009. *Ændrede familiesammenføringsregler. Hvad har de nye regler betydet for pardannelsesmønstret blandt etniske minoriteter?* Copenhagen: SFI – Det nationale forskningscenter for velfærd, 09:28.
Schneider, David. 1980[1968]. *American Kinship. A Cultural Account*. Chicago and London: University of Chicago Press.
—. 1977. Kinship, Nationality and Religion in American Culture. Toward a Definition of Kinship. In *Symbolic Anthropology: A Reader in the Study of Symbols and Meaning*, ed. Janet Dolgin, David Kemnitzer and David Schneider, 63–71. New York: Colombia University Press.
Schwartz, Jonathan. 1985. *Reluctant Hosts. Denmark's Reception of Guest Workers*. Kultursociologiskeskrifter, no. 21. Copenhagen: Akademisk Forlag.
—. 1990. On the Representation of Immigrants in Denmark: A Retrospective. In *Every Cloud has a Silver Lining*, ed. Flemming Røgilds, 42–52. Copenhagen: Akademisk forlag.
Shaw, Allison. 2001. Kinship, Cultural Preference and Immigration: Consanguineous Marriage among British Pakistanis. *Journal of Royal Anthropological Institute* (N.S.) 7:315–34.
Stolcke, Verena. 1995. Talking Culture. New Boundaries, New Rethorics of Exclusion in Europe. *Current Anthropology* 36(1):1–24.
Strassburger, Gaby. 2004. Transnatinational Ties of the Second Generation: Marriages of Turks in Germany. In *Transnational Social*

Spaces: Agents, Networks and Institutions, ed. Thomas Faist and Eyup Özveren, 211–31. Gateshead: Atheneaum Press.

Smedal, Olaf H. 2001. Innledning: Modeller, fenomenerogrealiteter. In *Blod tykkere enn vann? Betydninger af slektskap i Norge*, ed. Signe Howell and Marit Melhuus, 9–44. Bergen: Fagbokforlaget.

Wimmer, Andreas and Nina Glick Schiller. 2003. Methodological Nationalism, the Social Sciences, and the Study of Migration: An Essay in Historical Epistemology. *International Migration Review* 37(3):576–610.

CHAPTER THREE

THE PARADOX OF INTEGRATION:
EXCLUDING WHILE CLAMING TO INTEGRATE
INTO DANISH SOCIETY

INGER SJØRSLEV

The "tone" in political and general public debates in Denmark concerning the integration of immigrants and refugees into Danish society has been a significant issue for discussion in the Danish media since 2005, culminating in the cartoon crisis of early 2006. Questions have been asked about what is "behind the tone". Accusations have been made that the tone reveals xenophobia and racism, while others have claimed that those who criticize the way Muslim immigrants in particular are spoken about in public are arrogant and see themselves as superior to "the ordinary Dane". A related debate about "the problem of integration" in general has been going on alongside all this. Indeed, integration in general has been another heavily debated theme in Danish public discourse for many years.[1]

This preoccupation with immigrants and integration in public debates in Denmark, and especially the discussions surrounding the tone of and climate in those debates at the time of the cartoon crisis, have inspired my thoughts in the chapter about the concept of integration and its use and meaning in present-day Denmark. In brief, it seems that all the good intentions to integrate immigrants and refugees, expressed from left to right across the political spectrum, do not prevent mechanisms of exclusion from working, nor have they prevented discrimination and abrasive xenophobic talk. There even seems to be a paradoxical correlation between the amount of talk about integration and the number of cases of xenophobic expression. If this is indeed so, what does it reveal about culture and social practices in present-day Danish society, and how can it be conceptualized analytically?

I do not claim to deal with these questions on the basis of thorough empirical research, nor to give a linguistic analysis of the discourses of the

Danish media. My thoughts reflect the sentiments of an engaged reader of newspapers, who is in the possession of useful interpretative anthropological tools. As such, I hope to contribute to an understanding of the extraordinarily harsh public debate concerning immigration in Denmark and the muddle that often seems to surround discourses on integration in the country.

Integration is not a neutral concept. Danish public debates in the last decades of the twentieth century reveal a highly politicized field surrounding the ideas and actions covered by the term. In this chapter, I explore whether there are particular cultural values in Denmark that shape the ways in which integration is conceptualized and practised. In order to illuminate the issue of the tone of the debate in Denmark, the chapter starts with a comparative example that shows how words and concepts may "slide" in meaning under specific circumstances. Words used to characterize immigrants as well as a concept like "integration" gain meanings according to changing attitudes and intentions. It is important to pay attention to such changed meanings, and at the same time it is necessary to get a firmer grip on the meaning behind the widespread talk about integration and try and see what it reveals about more deeply grounded cultural ideas.

The power of language and "heavy" culture

In his autobiography, the German writer Victor Klemperer described the developments that took place in the German city of Dresden in the 1930s. Being of Jewish descent he barely escaped the concentration camp, yet until he finally had to flee from Dresden he was able to follow developments towards the genocide that peaked during the Second World War. He described the smaller and later more dramatic incidents in his diaries, which were published many years later.[2] Klemperer had converted to Protestantism and married a woman not of Jewish descent, but he and his family still became the victims of persecution, though persecution of a more indirect and subtle kind than that experienced by other Jews. Klemperer was able to maintain a reflexive and analytical attitude towards what happened to himself, his family and other citizens. As a writer and journalist who had studied language, his attention was devoted particularly towards small and at first glance insignificant shifts in language. Words like "parasites" and "enemies" slid into the rhetoric of everyday life, along with an increasingly sharp dichotomization between Germans and Jews, the latter becoming more and more excluded as "the others". In her analysis of Klemperer's diaries, the German anthropologist Anne

Friederike Müller shows how they reveal examples of the fact that destructive forces in society are grounded in language (Müller 2004: 74-6) and that the development of a dichotomous us-them "grammar" can be the first step towards destruction.

In choosing to start with Klemperer's diaries, probably the work in European literature that most clearly and revealingly illustrates how persecution can begin in language, I am not comparing the contemporary situation in Denmark with what took place in other parts of Europe during the Second World War. Rather, I am pointing out that concepts, including a concept like integration, may slide into new meanings by becoming politicized, which may be related to their being more or less consciously ingrained in particular cultural ideas. I suggest this may have happened to the concept of integration in Denmark, in particular in discourses concerning Muslim immigrants.[3]

Klemperer showed how everyday language can become a tool for exclusion and how the persecution of certain groups may have a dangerous beginning in language. Language slides with different consequences; although, when theoretical and analytical concepts are adopted into everyday language and political discourse, the consequences may not be directly dangerous, they may certainly have negative side effects. A change in the meaning of central concepts may disguise intentions and create a discourse in which the real meanings and intentions are difficult to detect. If a paradox of integration can be revealed in the sense that the notion has positive connotations but exclusionist effects, what are the Danish cultural values that cause this? I suggest that these cultural values have to do with what I call "heavy culture," that is, cultural models that heavily influence thinking and values in largely unrecognized ways. Heavy culture is not recognized as "culture" but points towards self-evident positive moral values. For instance, the right to bear arms in the American constitution is not in itself heavy culture since it is an explicit, formal right, but the values behind it, which concern the moral right and obligation to protect one's family, are heavy culture. Not everybody agrees with it, but it is ingrained in most moral debates and lies behind much political discourse that implies values, mostly in incontestable and self-evident ways.

In Scandinavia, the idea that equality connotes sameness has been shown to predominate (Gullestad 2006). Historically, ideas about the superiority of content and inner being over form and outer manners, originating in Germany, have also been shown to influence conceptions about identity and values in Scandinavia (Müller 2004: 69). I suggest that these ideas are reflected in Danish notions of an inner, more authentic core of being as the locus of those democratic and egalitarian values that connote Danishness, and that this constitutes some kind of "substance" into which immigrants have to be integrated. Such more or less explicit ideas are what might be considered heavy culture in Denmark. In the following I shall try to show how they contribute to creating a paradox of integration.

Denmark, 2006

Is it possible to exclude by way of an ideology of integration? This is a key question. Can the efforts towards the integration of citizens of non-Danish ethnic descent, particularly Muslims, have the consequence of actually excluding them? Can the ideal of integration become a way of legitimizing a different type of praxis from that which the positive meaning of integration suggests? In other words, if the ideology of integration has become a mechanism for exclusion, how does this work?

There is no doubt that, as a concept, integration has played a significant role in contemporary Danish politics. The need to integrate immigrants who live in Denmark was used in the election programme of the *Venstre*[4] party as an argument for strengthening policies towards foreigners. This was duly implemented when the party came into power in November 2001 in a coalition with the Conservatives and crucially supported by the *Dansk Folkeparti* or Danish People's Party.[5] It is the latter that has set the standard for the immigration policy that has been implemented since. At the same time, attention towards "the problem of integration", as it is so often called in public and media discourses, has been sharpened, becoming focused particularly on the approximately 200,000 Muslim immigrants in Denmark,[6] and being accompanied by a sharpening of the tone in public debate. This debate, particularly in 2005, was characterized by a strong anti-Islamic rhetoric in certain media, including descriptions of the Muslim immigrants as "belonging to the dark Middle Ages", "barbarians", "being on a lower step in the development of civilizations" "a plague over Europe", "irreconcilable with Danish values", "religious fanatics" and "people with an undemocratic way of thinking."[7]

It is an explicit assumption of the government's immigration policy that integration takes place through participation in the labour market. In 2003, the then Minister for Integration, Bertel Haarder, expressed the opinion that a precondition for integration is that refugees who have come to Denmark seeking asylum should learn to get up early in the morning and agree to work at any kind of job:

> Refugees [those who have recently gained asylum] have difficulties getting up in the morning. They simulate illness and get the doctors to make false certificates. They are not at the disposal of the labour market. They should be put to work like skinning mink or looking after pigs, they don't mind that. They must take the dirty, routine and poorly paid jobs. No work is too bad.[8]

Statements like these not only reveal a dichotomous "us-them" way of thinking, but also voice suspicions of fraud among immigrants and obvious disrespect for Muslim values concerning food and animals.

In a book by the journalist Rune Engelbrecht Larsen and the editor-in-chief of the major Danish newspaper *Politiken*, Tøger Seidenfaden, published shortly after the cartoon crisis, the authors describe Denmark – quoting the former Secretary General of the United Nations, Kofi Annan – as

> a country which has within a relatively short period of time obtained a Muslim minority, but which has not yet adapted to this situation as a society, a situation which demands adaptation and the development of new norms by both the minority and the majority (Larsen and Seidenfaden 2006: 15).

As in other European countries, the reaction to this challenge has been the formation of a strong nationalist political party (in Denmark, the Danish People's Party), which is characterized by "an open islamophobic attitude and occasional racism" (ibid.: 16).[9] In Denmark, unlike other European countries, a party representing such attitudes has provided parliamentary support for the government, a fact

> which both mirrors and strongly reinforces the tendency towards the excluding and intolerant ways of tackling integration that this party advocates, which has influenced the conduct of politics, as well as the use of language in public debates (ibid.).[10]

Larsen and Seidenfaden's book minutely details the public debates that took place in the months before the crisis sparked by the publication of the Muhammad cartoons in the newspaper *Jyllands-Posten,* which came to a head in February 2006.

This public discourse recalls the linguistic sliding documented by Klemperer, and it supports the idea that a strong us-them way of thinking is at work. This negative attitude towards immigrants among a great part of the Danish population goes back further than the present government's policies,[11] however, and the xenophobic tone in public debates was present long before the publication of the cartoons of the Prophet Muhammad in *Jyllands-Posten* in September 2005. In June 2000, *The European Commission against Racism and Intolerance* (ECRI) published its second report on Denmark. Commenting on the climate of debate in the country, which was seen as promoting negative attitudes to Muslim immigrants and refugees in particular, the report noted that "Typically these people are portrayed as a threat to Danish identity and accused of different problems, from the Danish economy to street crimes."[12] In November 2004 the UNHCR wrote a press release concerning a proposal by the Danish government that it would not select refugees whom it considered difficult to integrate from among the so-called quota refugees:[13] "The expression *integration potential* seems to emphasize immigration criteria instead of the need to protect when refugees are selected" (*Politiken,* 10 November 2004, quoted in Larsen and Seidenfaden 2006: 37, my emphasis).

I suggest that there is a connection between the xenophobic attitudes expressed in public debates, with the accompanying slides in language – "plague," "barbarians" etc. – and the status and values attached to the concept of "integration" in both actual politics and the ordinary consciousness of part of the Danish population. The tone in public debates is often accompanied by the "little everyday racism", which has been continuously documented through several reports by, among others, the ECRI. In the autumn of 2006, this found an extreme form in the social games of the youth group of the Danish People's Party, who amused themselves by making derogatory new drawings of the Prophet. However, it also reveals itself in more everyday forms in fears of immigration outside the more extreme parts of this political party. To take one example, in the news on 18 October 2006, it was reported that estate agents had received complaints from neighbours of houses that were to be sold to immigrant families. In this respect, the situation in Denmark 2006 brings to mind the situation in the US more than fifty years ago, when the civil rights movement began.

In the book about the debates that were going on before the cartoon crisis, the question is asked whether Danish immigration and integration policies were the key issue during this crisis. Whatever the answer to this question might be, there is not much doubt that the national prehistory of the cartoon crisis was characterized by "a long series of legal restrictions, obviously directed towards ethnic minorities, who experience an increasing deficit of rights in relation to other citizens in the country and at the same time an increasingly islamophobic language in public debates" (Larsen and Seidenfaden 2006: 313-14). This is strong fuel for the contention that "integration" must be regarded as a heavily politicized concept, the present meaning of which cannot be understood without taking into consideration the values and attitudes behind its use. It is thus necessary to go behind the different attitudes and practices in society to try and identify deeper cultural models, which might support the significance of the integration concept and its connection to its negative opposition as voiced in the shape of the many expressions of xenophobia.

As Foucault has shown by way of his concept of discourse, knowledge is constituted through social praxis, forms of subjectivity and power relations. Discourses are forms of power that circulate in a social field (Foucault 2001). In this sense, the concept of integration must be regarded as an extremely "heavy" concept. The way in which it has entered public debates and political discourses in Denmark has significant implications in reality. "Integration" refers to both the goal and the precondition of social incorporation. Immigrants and refugees should be integrated, but in order for them to become integrated, certain requirements have to be met. The use of the concept of integration in public discourses suggests that those who seek integration face a dilemma that brings to mind the situation of double bind (Bateson 1972): "You are not ready to become integrated until you are like us, and you will not prove that you are like us until you are integrated." At the same time, the concept of integration is embedded in current, everyday discourse as a positive word. Integration is good, a beneficial goal for society. Or in other words, and more negatively, without integration, society is in danger. However the implicit meanings are interpreted, there does not seem to be much doubt that this concept is strongly loaded with values. The question is therefore how to analyse and understand what lies "behind the tone" in ways that do not set out from the idea of "integration" as a neutral concept.

Using the notion of structural grammars developed by Gerd Bauman and André Gingrich[14] may be a good way of digging more deeply into mechanisms of inclusion and exclusion, as well as into ways of dealing with identity and alterity in the Danish context. Of the three grammars that Baumann and Gingrich have identified, it is particularly those they call the grammar of encompassment and the dichotomous grammar that seem to be at work here. In the encompassing grammar, one group bases its relations to another group on the idea that they are basically "like us," only they have not yet quite become so. The dichotomous grammar, on the other hand, corresponds more directly to the well-known "us-them" way of thinking (Baumann and Gingrich 2004). The question is whether there is some cultural inertia, or what I call heavy culture, in how present-day Denmark is thought about when it comes to identity and alterity, which codetermines the meanings of integration and the status of the concept in political and public debates.

Heavy culture and the grammar of encompassment

What do political debates in Denmark reveal about the meaning of integration? What is "behind the tone"? *Venstre,* the party of the current Danish Prime Minister, states that its policy towards immigrants is based on "work, teaching of the Danish language and consequence". Immigrants must work and be able to speak Danish, and if those requirements are not fulfilled, there will be consequences. What those consequences might be are not explicitly expressed, but several cases and many political statements suggest that they are likely to take the form of negative sanctions and ultimately expulsion from the country. It is openly stated that one important goal of this policy is to avoid the misuse of public services by immigrants.[15] The policy can therefore be interpreted as an ultimatum: integration or exclusion. In another version, convincingly analysed as regards Sweden by the philosopher Michael Azar, the ultimatum of integration is expressed as "become Swedish or disappear" (Azar 2001: 57). Even though a similar kind of ultimatum may be at work in Danish politics, this is not the whole story. When one seeks to uncover the heavy cultural ideas behind the "tone" expressing the ideology of integration, the picture appears to become more complex. However, it may still be useful to take a closer look at Azar's analysis of the logic at work here.

Azar asks how it is possible to become a *real* Swede after formally becoming a Swedish citizen.[16] It is necessary to ask such a question, he says, because people, including immigrants, are not judged according to how they act, but according to what, deep down, they *are* (Azar 2001: 62). What immigrants "are" within the logic identified by Azar can be described metaphorically in terms of the relationship between adults and children. Just as children are people who have not yet become adults, so immigrants are people who have not yet become real Swedes (or Danes). Azar calls this the guardian metaphor. Using the vocabulary of the structural grammars developed by Bauman and Gingrich (2004), it can also be interpreted as a grammar of encompassment. Immigrants "are" deep down like the rest of us – "us" being "we the majority" – but they have not yet *fully* become so, and *when* that happens is a decision made by "us." The grammar of encompassment is based upon a hierarchically defined relation in which one category – "children" or in other contexts "women", or "low castes" – is subsumed within another, like "adults", or in other contexts "men/rational human beings" or "high castes." The second category comes above the first in the hierarchical order. The category of "immigrants" is subsumed under, or encompassed within, the category "Danes" or "Swedes" or whoever in a given context constitutes a "we."[17]

Azar calls the discourse on *real* Swedishness a kind of metaracism or a metaculturalism, since the point when immigrants have learned all that it takes to become one of "us" and thus become fully integrated can never be determined by the immigrant, but only by the majority into which he or she is seeking to be integrated. It thus seems as if two grammars are at work here, not only the grammar of encompassment, but also a dichotomous grammar that presupposes a split between them, the immigrants, and us, the majority. The point in Azar's analysis is that this split is relative. It can be changed, and the position of the boundary between the immigrants and the majority population is indeed often changed at the moment when the immigrant tries to cross it. There is therefore no way the immigrant can win, as the decision concerning where to draw the line between us and them is always taken by someone else, namely the majority. This gives the very concept of the immigrant a paradoxical status (Azar 2001: 69).

In the same vein, it has been suggested that a new form of racism has arisen in Europe through a revitalization of differences between cultures. While old-fashioned racist thinking had biology as its foundations, it has been argued that what is at work today should rather be called cultural fundamentalism (Stolcke 1995). In cultural fundamentalism, cultures are placed in a hierarchical order. While it is conceded that it might be possible for those lower in the hierarchy to become absorbed into the dominant culture above them, the how and when of this process can only be determined by those in power.

The ideology of immigration in Denmark is based upon two implicit ideas, which I see as related to heavy culture. One concerns integration's connotations of *substance*: there is something *into which* the immigrant must be integrated. Those who are in the process of integration share some of that substance, but not sufficiently to be fully integrated. The second is that a boundary is drawn between "them" and "us." In Denmark, this ideology of immigration has gained such a strong foothold in public debates that it has become self-evident.

In the Danish context, the concept of integration can be analysed as corresponding to a grammar of encompassment, which sustains a good part of the Danish official ideology concerning immigrants and refugees who are already living in or seeking asylum in the country. But if immigrants are to become part of an "us, which is understood as some kind of substance, what is this substance by which immigrants are to be encompassed? I suggest that it is conceived in terms of ideas about equality as sameness, which the Norwegian anthropologist Marianne Gullestad has shown to be a strong cultural idea in all Scandinavian countries.

Sameness and substance

It has been argued that Denmark is characterized by a strong consensus culture that does not tolerate conflicts or even disagreement. Thus, when disagreements emerge within a voluntary association, the general rule seems to be that those who disagree break away and form another association of their own. In this way, it is possible to maintain the ideal that social life is characterized by basic agreement. This is reflected in a phrase that is often used to close a discussion that is becoming a bit heated: "basically we are in agreement" (*I grunden er vi jo enige*), as Karen Lisa Salamon has shown in her astute analysis of the sophisticated dynamics of this consensus culture (Salamon 1992). Scandinavian consensus culture can be interpreted in terms of a grammar of encompassment, the consequences of which are both the demarcation of borders (in relation to others) and homogenization (of those within the borders). This consensus culture is accompanied by the "closed sociality" analysed by Marianne Gullestad in her demonstration of the Scandinavian ideology of sameness. The grammar of encompassment can be regarded as a structural framework for practising the ideology of sameness. The ideology says that "we" ("adults") are more than ready to integrate the others ("children") as soon as they have proved that they are fully the same as "us." While in a country like Brazil cultural processes of inclusion take place by way of the performance and celebration of alterity, in the sense of what creates a multi-coloured and charming mixed culture (Sjørslev 2004), in Scandinavia, including Denmark, it is rather sameness that is celebrated. Here associations ruled by consensus build upon ideas of sameness within the collectivity by way of a conflict-free promotion of cosiness (*hygge*).

The close association between sameness and a kind of substance and inner core finds resonance in the work of Hal Koch (1904-63), a well-known Danish theologian and educator.[18] In 1946, Koch wrote a small book which had an impact beyond Denmark's national borders, but which at the same time seems to reveal a particularly Danish conception of democracy, with ideas that still distinguish a good part of political culture in Denmark. In this conception, democracy is conceived as much more than a particular political system; it is rather a whole way of life involving common values. In Koch's perspective, it is even characterized by a kind of *awakening* and thus imbued with religious (Christian) overtones. Democracy must be sustained by a public awakening, and people must be socialized and educated into democratic thinking. Democracy can thus *not* be reduced to a legal system where it is possible to maintain this view: "we do not care what you believe and think and how you live, as long as you keep to the rules of the country; we are indifferent to how you act in your private life, and we are not preoccupied with your inner life or any kind of substance or deeper values, as long as the rules of good behaviour in public space are maintained and the laws of the country observed." This sounds pretty much like the classic liberal attitude which was being promoted by another political thinker and lawyer of the time of Koch, Alfred Ross.[19]

There is a strong emphasis on dialogue in Koch's conception of democracy, and even today there are many elements in his thinking with which it is difficult to disagree from a normative point of view – at least if one has been raised with these heavy cultural ideas. At the same time, however, the suggested dialogue is more or less implicitly intended to create a common set of values having to do with people's *inner* constitution. The grammar of encompassment at work in Denmark rests upon a strong inner orientation, building as it does on the predominant doctrine which says that the genuine, the real, the true, the authentic are located in (inner) substance rather than in (outer) form.

Recent anthropological theory has challenged dichotomous thinking and taken a critical look at sharp distinctions between form and content where the superficial and artificial are associated with form, the real and genuine with content or inner substance. Webb Keane has used the materiality of clothes as the springboard for a discussion of the relationship between the "inner" and the "outer". He maintains that there is a Western tradition of ontological thinking (stemming from Heidegger, but also prominent in literary works like Thoreau's *Walden*), which deeply influences present ways of thinking about the inner and the outer (Keane 2005: 184). The point is that, in order to understand cultural ways of thinking in connection with ideas about integration, it is necessary to take a closer look at the specific ontological thinking implied in Western cultural models. The ideas of separation between form and substance, with the substance localized in an inner core as ontological being and the real and authentic being related to this, is described in another way through the grammar of encompassment, which implies that real integration takes place in "being," in *becoming* Danish (or Swedish). Integration is conceived as involving *being* rather than *acting*.

The inertia of such heavy cultural ideas about an inner core of real being seems to influence the way immigrants are perceived and the whole ideology of integration. Again, inspiration may be found in parallel ideas as they reveal themselves in other contexts. In her historical analysis of German identity/alterity grammars, Anne Friederike Müller thus says: "True Germans valued being (*Sein*) over illusion (*Schein*), content over form, morality over manners" (Müller 2004: 69). Such values are still praised in historical contexts different from those Müller deals with, and I think they are predominant also in Danish thinking about values and authenticity. Going back to the tone of language in the public debates of recent years on immigrants and refugees in Denmark, there seem to be strong conceptions of what it means to *be* Danish behind much that is expressed in terms of real Danish culture and the threats to it. This makes the criteria for integration a question of inner values rather than simple "outer" compliance with the laws of the land.

Integration politicized

Politics is culturalized and culture politicized, not just in Denmark, but everywhere, although in different ways (Alvarez et al. 1998). Culture is strategically employed in the legitimization of political praxis, and political praxis is influenced by heavy culture and cultural inertia. When dealing with the human and social issues that are meant to be encompassed by the concept of integration, the task must be to become wiser about the ways in which it goes on in praxis, both when conscious strategies are implied and when praxis is sustained by undisclosed ideas of self-evidence.

I have aimed to show that the analytical apparatus for disclosing what lies behind the "tone" and thus the political and cultural use of the concept of integration in Denmark cannot be based upon the concept of integration itself. "Integration" has become politicized and carries heavy connotations pointing to largely unrecognized ideas and values. At the same time, it is important to include the local (or *emic*) meaning of integration in public, political and everyday discourses in the overall analysis of what is going on in present-day Danish society. Gaining a better understanding of the hidden values and meanings attached to integration will help to identify mechanisms of inclusion and exclusion, as well as reveal some of the hidden scripts behind what is expressed both politically and by the general public. There may appear to be more at work than what has been identified here, namely that in present-day Danish society it is possible to exclude while intending to integrate.

Notes

1. This is to some extent different from Sweden, where integration and immigration have never been such large issues for debate. In Sweden attention was paid early on to the integration of immigrants, which has been a relatively smooth process backed by parties from left to right. Only about three percent support the party that has some resemblance to the Danish People's Party, the strongest promoter of an anti-immigration policy in Denmark. In the 2007 elections, 13.8% of the electorate voted for it, giving it 25 seats out of 179 in Parliament. Source: The Ministry of Interior and Health, http://im.dk/imEverest/Publications/imdk%20x2D%20dansk/Valg/2007111916313 3/CurrentVersion/Meddelelse%20om%20det%20endelige%20resultat.pdf and Wikipedia http://da.wikipedia.org/wiki/Folketingsvalg_2007#Valgresultatet
2. Klemperer's diaries from the period 1930-1959 were published in English in 1995 with the titles *I will bear witness* (1933 to 1941), *To the bitter end* (1942 to 1945) and *The lesser evil* (1945 to 1959). The present reading is based on the Danish version, published in 2003 under the title *Jeg vil aflægge vidnesbyrd til det sidste – Dagbøger 1933-41. Dagbøger 1942-45*. Copehagen, Gyldendal.
3. A comprehensive report on the image of Muslims in the Danish media came out in Danish in 2002. It concluded that the Muslims did not recognize themselves in media representations, and that public debates had already polarized Danes and Muslim immigrants into a rigid division between 'us' and 'them' (Hervik 2002).
4. Venstre, though meaning "left", is actually a centre-right rather than a leftist party. The full name is *Venstre – Danmarks Liberale Parti* (The Liberal Party of Denmark). It is the largest political party in Denmark and was founded on the ideology of free market liberalism. It has criticized the welfare state as expressed in a book, *Fra socialstat til minimalstat* ("From social state to minimal state") by its former leader and the former Prime Minster Anders Fog Rasmussen. In the last decade the party's politics has moved considerably towards the centre, and the government now advocates preserving the welfare state.
5. The Danish People's Party (Dansk Folkeparti) http://www.danskfolkeparti.dk/Home.asp is a right-wing party, whose leader Pia Kjærsgård has been a prominent voice in articulating Danish protectionism towards immigration in the last decade. The connection between better integration and restrictions in the admission of immigrants and asylum-seekers is also a strong element in the political programme of the governing party, Venstre (Liberal) http://www.venstre.dk/index.php?id=4620
6. Statistics on Muslims in Denmark are found at 'Factsheet Denmark' from the Ministry of Foreign Affairs in Denmark, http://www.um.dk/um_files/publikationer/um/english/factsheetdenmark/integration/integrationindenmark06.pdf

7. Thorough documentation, with many revealing quotes and precise references to sources in Danish newspapers, political speeches and international reports, can be found in *Karikaturkrisen* ("the cartoon crisis") by Rune Engelbrecht Larsen and Tøger Seidenfaden. See also Rothstein 2006.
8. "Flygtningene har svært ved at komme op om morgenen. De simulerer sygdom og får lægerne til at lave falske lægeerklæringer. De står ikke til rådighed for arbejdsmarkedet. De skal sættes til at flå mink. Til at arbejde med svin, det har de ikke noget imod. De skal tage det beskidte, rutinemæssige og dårligt betalte arbejde. Intet arbejde er for dårligt." From the major newspaper Politiken, 7 October 2003, quoted in Larsen and Seidenfaden 2006: 34.
9. In Danish: "som er præget af åbenlys islamofobi og lejlighedsvis racisme"
10. The quote in Danish says, "hvilket både afspejler og kraftigt forstærker tendensen til, at partiets ekskluderende og intolerante måde at tackle integrationen på har sat et stadig stærkere præg på både den førte politik og på sprogbrugen i den offentlige debat"
11. Already in 1985 the fear of immigration in Denmark had been expressed metaphorically as like a collision between a truck and a Volkswagen (Schwartz 1985: 50-1).
12. See ECRI Report at http://files.secureid.org/sos/PDFCBC2Danemark-danish.pdf. The Report further says that "The predominant attitude to people of foreign descent and the significance and use of propaganda with a xenophobic content in politics is deeply disturbing. Discrimination, particularly in the labour market, but also within other areas such as for instance the housing market and the access to public spaces is cause for special concern." In 2006 ECRI published another report on Denmark, concluding that there are still a number of problems. This report caused much public debate and a strong political reaction.
13. Every year Denmark selects about five hundred "quota refugees" from UNHCR camps around the world. Until recently, they were selected purely on the basis of perceived need. These refugees bypass the usual Danish asylum determination system and are immediately brought to Denmark and started on the state-mandated three-year integration programme.
14. Baumann and Gingrich (2004) operate with three structural grammars which they develop on the basis of a free and to some extent metaphorical use of three key works in the classical anthropological literature. The first is Edward Said's Orientalism (1978), with its revelation of the basic dichotomous thinking of the West in relation to the Orient. The second is Evans-Pritchard's theory of segmentary solidarity among the Nuer (Evans-Pritchard 1940), and the third is Louis Dumont's work Homo Hierarchicus, with its theory of structural encompassment in Indian caste society (Dumont 1980). Baumann humbly ask these ancestors from the anthropological canon for forgiveness for his free use of their works and the reinterpretation of certain points within them. In his grammars he uses them completely independently of the empirical contexts within which they were conceived, with the explicit intention of creating conceptual tools for analyzing mechanisms of formations of identity and alterity. I have used the theoretical-analytical tools of structural grammars developed by Baumann and

Gingrich in an earlier comparison of identity-alterity mechanisms in Denmark and Brazil (Sjørslev 2004). The ideas presented here are inspired by these tools.
15. On the home page of "Venstre" (http://www.venstre.dk/index.php?id=498), integration is explicitly linked to the prevention of dependency and of the misuse of public services.
16. In Denmark 2008 there was a public debate about the legitimacy of the requirements for acquiring Danish citizenship (*Indfødsretsprøven*), which implies rather strict requirements regarding knowledge and language skills. See the newspaper Information, December 20, 2008.
17. As an almost satirical illustration of the patronizing metaphor contained in this, which can also be seen as an illustration of the grammar of encompassment, Azar quotes a passage in Stanley Kubric's film Full Metal Jacket, from 1987. In the film, an American general replies to a question about what a real American is doing in Vietnam by saying, "We are convinced that within anyone of the yellow there is an American; our task is to get him out" (Azar 2001: 64-5).
18. This discussion is based on Nielsen and Sjørslev 2002.
19. The debate has been included in the Danish "democracy canon": see http://pub.uvm.dk/2008/democracycanon/kap30.html in which democracy is significantly characterized as "an intimate ritual."

References*

Alvarez, Sonia E., Evelina Dagnino and Arturo Escobar, eds. 1998. *Cultures of Politics – Politics of Cultures. Re-visioning Latin American Social Movements*. Boulder, Westview Press.

Azar, Michael. 2001. Den äkta svenskheten och begärets dunkla objekt. In *Identitetens omvandlingar – black metal, magdans och hemlöshet*, ed. Ove Sernhede and Thomas Johansson, 57-93. Uddevalla: Daidalos.

Bateson, Gregory. 1972. *Steps to an Ecology of Mind*. New York, Doubleday.

Baumann, Gerd and André Gingrich, eds. 2004. *Grammars of Identity/Alterity: A Structural Approach*. Berghahn Books.

Dansk Folkeparti http://www.danskfolkeparti.dk/Home.asp

Dumont, Louis. 1980[1966]. *Homo Hierarchicus*. The University of Chicago Press.

Evans-Pritchard, E.E. 1940. *The Nuer. A Description of the Modes of Livelihood and Political Institutions of a Nilotic People*. Oxford University Press.

ECRI Report. 2001. European Commission against Racism and Intolerance. *Anden Rapport om Danmark, Vedtaget den 16. Juni 2000*. http://files.secureid.org/sos/PDFCBC2Danemarkdanish.pdf

Factsheet Denmark. The Ministry of Foreign Affairs of Denmark.

http://www.um.dk/um_files/publikationer/um/english/factsheetdenmark/integration/integrationindenmark06.pdf

Foucault, Michel. 2001[1970]). *Talens forfatning*. København, Hans Reitzels Forlag.

Gullestad, Marianne. 2006. *Plausible Prejudice: Everyday Experiences and Social Images of Nation, Culture and Race*. Oslo, Scandinavian University Press.

Hervik, Peter. 2002. *Mediernes muslimer: En antropologisk undersøgelse af mediernes dækning af religioner i Danmark*. Copenhagen: Nævnet for Etnisk Ligestilling.

Keane, Webb. 2005. "Signs Are Not the Garb of Meaning: On the Social Analysis of Material Things". In *Materiality*, ed. Daniel Miller, 182-205. London: Durham University Press.

Klemperer, Victor. 2003. *Jeg vil aflægge vidnesbyrd til det sidste. Dagbøger 1933-41. Dagbøger 1942-45*. Copenhagen, Gyldendal. (English version: *The Lesser Evil. The Diaries of Victor Klemperer*. Orion Publishers, paperback 2004).

Koch Hal and Alf Ross. *Debate on Democracy*. http://pub.uvm.dk/2008/democracycanon/kap30.html

Larsen, Rune Engelbrecht and Tøger Seidenfaden. 2006. *Karikaturkrisen. En undersøgelse af baggrund and ansvar*. København, Gyldendal.

Ministry of Interior and Health, http://im.dk/imEverest/Publications/imdk%20x2D%20dansk/Valg/20071119163133/CurrentVersion/Meddelelse%20om%20det%20endelige%20resultat.pdf

Müller, Anne Friederike. 2004. German Grammars of Identity/Alterity: A Diachronic View. In *Grammars of Identity/Alterity: A Structural Approach*, ed. Gerd Baumann and André Gingrich, 63-78. Berghahn Books.

Nielsen, Finn Sivert and Inger Sjørslev. 2002. *Folkets repræsentanter: Et antropologisk blik på Folketinget*. Århus Universitetsforlag, Magtudredningen.

Rothstein, Klaus and Michael Rothstein. 2006. *Bomben i turbanen*. København, Tidernes Skifter.

Said, Edvard. 1994[1978]. *Orientalism*. New York, Vintage Books.

Salamon, Karen Lisa. 1992. I grunden er vi enige. En ekskurs i skandinavisk foreningsliv. *Tidsskriftet Antropologi* 25: 105-16.

Schwartz, Jonathan. 1985. On the Representation of Immigrants in Denmark. In *Every cloud has a silver lining*, ed. Flemming Røgilds, København: Akademisk Forlag.

Sjørslev, Inger. 2004. Alterity as Celebration, Alterity as Threat: A Comparison of Grammars between Brazil and Denmark. In *Grammars of Identity/Alterity: A Structural Approach*, ed. Gerd Baumann and André Gingrich, 79-100. Oxford: Berghahn Books.

Stolcke, Verena. 1995. Talking Culture: New Boundaries, New Rhetorics of Exclusion in Europe. *Current Anthropolandy* 36 (1): 1-13.

Venstre (The Liberal Party of Denmark).
 http://www.venstre.dk/index.php?id=4620

* All websites referred to were active July, 2010.

CHAPTER FOUR

RELIGION AND INTEGRATION:
THREE DANISH MODELS
FOR THE RELATIONSHIP BETWEEN
RELIGION AND SOCIETY

CECILIE RUBOW

An American observer, the sociologist Phil Zuckerman (2008) has asserted that the Danes and Swedes are the most non-religious peoples in the world. Considering the general American understanding that a "society without God" leads to moral decay and societal collapse, Scandinavians seem an immense counterexample to Zuckerman. Here religion is *not* a precondition for a more well-functioning society than the United States.

The question, however, is what we should understand by religion, and here Zuckerman has a very narrow understanding in the form of "belief in a set of supernatural ideas". This understanding is very effective for comparison through available statistics, but as this chapter will show, it is also overly simplistic. Analyses of supernatural ideas often neglect the fact that religion is a much broader societal phenomenon. If the sociologist Émile Durkheim was correct, God and society simply are the same thing. In its elementary forms, religion is the act of making society itself sacred, i.e., society is the genuine force, which its members invoke when they pray to their god. In this sense, there is no society without religiosity (1965 [1915]). Religion is what integrates and creates the power of social cohesion. Hence the question is: What integrates the Danes in daily life? What makes Danish society sacred? In this chapter the Danish National Church (*folkekirken*[2]) is analyzed to find part of the answer. More specifically, the question addressed is: How do Danes understand the relationship between religion and society, and how do they discuss the ability of a virtually mono-religious nation-state to accommodate changes in religious beliefs and practices?

With the vast majority of the population as members, a middle-of-the-road policy, and a comparatively liberal theology by international comparison, the Danish National Church certainly demonstrates an undisputed degree of homogeneity, not least by American standards. If one examines it more closely, however, the Danish church reveals itself to be full of surprising differences, sharp controversies, and profound disagreements in connection with issues such as belief in God, life after death, the church's role in society, and the nature of reality. In the next sections I will outline the organization of the church and show the fundamentally different understandings of religion inside and outside the *folkekirke* conceived as three different models. Furthermore, I show how these models envision the role of Christianity and other religions in Danish society, and I discuss the possibilities and limitations of the different models by drawing parallels to social science understandings of religion.

The inclusive Danish Lutheran Church

For the Danish population, the Danish Evangelical Lutheran Church is normally connected with a historical taken-for-grantedness and a number of important family ritual traditions. The Danish Lutheran Church has a history that goes back a thousand years, the church buildings are scattered throughout Danish towns and villages, and they are today best known in connection with christenings, confirmations, weddings, and funerals. In the ecclesiastical self-understanding, the desire to be a broadly inclusive (*rummelig*, lit. "spacious") cultural institution is a key value. With such inclusiveness comes a certain ambiguity, as the connection between Danish culture and Christianity can result in many variations.

Officially and legally, the Evangelical-Lutheran people's church is supported by the Danish state with a constitution, which is regulated by law (cf. The Constitutional Act of Denmark, §4 and §66). In several laws, regulations, and circulars the Danish parliament has laid down the frameworks for the operation of the church, which is administered by a minister for ecclesiastical affairs and a number of locally elected organs (parish councils, deaneries, etc.). The church includes 2121 parishes grouped into 111 deaneries and ten dioceses. On 1 January 2008, the Danish National Church had nearly 4.5 million members, corresponding to 82% of all Danish inhabitants. The annual budget was about DKK 6,000 million (ca. $1 billion), of which 12% was subsidies provided by the state, and 81% was revenue from the church tax paid by the members. There were about 2000 ministers, a half million seats in churches, and 90,000 fewer members than in 1990. In the same period, the population of

Denmark increased by 340,000 (Kirkeministeriet [The Ministry of Ecclisiastical Affairs] 2008). Statistics indicate that about 60% of Danes declare that they believe in God, and that 30% believe in a life after death (Lüchau 2005). Nine of ten funerals, and just under half of all weddings are conducted by a clergyman or woman; 70% of youth between 13 and 15 years of age are confirmed (Kirkeministeriet 2008).

Christianity arrived in Denmark with the missionary activities of the German Archbishop Ansgar in the 820's. However, as the official homepage of the Ministry of Ecclesiastical Affairs states, "Scandinavian heathendom died hard and the words on the large Jelling stone to the effect that King Harald [Bluetooth] "made the Danes Christian' must be taken with a pinch of salt" (Kirkeministeriet 2008). In the Middle Ages, the church established a close union with the monarchy and a large number of churches and monasteries were built. The Lutheran reformation in 1536 ended the power of the Catholic bishops, and the Crown took over the property of the Church. Until the Constitution of 1849 Lutheranism was the only permitted religion. The Constitution introduced the principle of religious freedom, but not of religious equality, as the state was given responsibility for supporting the Evangelical Lutheran Church as the Danish National Church. Moreover, the Constitution promised a representative, synodal church constitution, though the "promise" has never been fulfilled.

The present organization of the church has had a life of over 150 years and revisions have been discussed almost continuously. What is new are the ways the relationships between state, church, and people enter into discussions on the integration of the larger religious minorities, and especially the significance of Islam in the political world. Ten years ago, the first significant voices were heard within the church regarding the importance of Muslims' presence in Denmark. If it was possible to ignore these voices in the early years, the issue has since been confirmed as one of the great controversial debate topics, and with Islam's growing international importance, the controversy reached its peak in early 2006 with the Muhammad cartoon crisis. In the sphere of the Danish National Church, Islam is viewed on the one hand as a potential or actual danger in relation to the status quo. On the other hand the presence of Islam has been viewed as a challenge or, as it is put in ecclesiastical circles, "an occasion for reflection," meaning that the times and the culture must be reassessed, the signs read to figure out what the church is, and how it can move forward. "Being Christian" these days means belonging to a broader category of identification than ten years ago, when it more typically signaled a specific form of belonging to the church and the special piety of a religious minority. Similarly, it was a novelty when a small group of Danish bishops took the initiative to conduct a mediation visit to the Middle East during the Muhammad cartoon crisis. Indeed the mere fact of their involvement in a political conflict was new.

The three dominant understandings I will discuss in this chapter are all at once models of the present and normative models for future action. The three models, which I term "traditional," "secular," and "poly-religious," can all be contained in the common understanding of the inclusive Danish National Church. However, they also compete with each other in their diverse officializing strategies (cf. Bourdieu 1991). All three attempt to appear to be working for the common good, representing collective selfless interests. The three models can certainly appear in different combinations and are expressed in different degrees and clarities. Combinations of the traditional and the secular model are the most widespread, while combinations of the secular and poly-religious model are the serious challengers.

Insofar as the Danish National Church order still functions, and inasmuch as there is no prospect of radical changes, the relationship between church and state, religion and society, must be said to be an expression of a very stable mediation between individual and society, and between tradition and renewal. This does not change the fact that there are also significant tensions, "a span of ambiguity" (cf. Buckser 1997), which only with great difficulty and many incantations can get things to function in practice. Classical theological questions about understanding the scriptures, views of the church, female pastors, and the blessing of homosexual partnerships divide the church field, and precisely as in the other political fields, immigration and Islam have also become central questions which both actualize the classical questions and pose new ones: Should the bonds between state and church be severed, and if so what would that mean for the church and for religious minorities? What are the similarities and differences between Islam and Christianity, e.g. in the view of the scriptures. What is the history of the two religions? What is religion at all? Are there grounds to speak only of two distinct religions? And how do we envision a plurality of religious traditions evolving in the future?

The traditional model

The traditional model views Christianity as the historical foundation for the development of Danish society. The church and Christianity form a thousand-year-old spiritual, moral and social history, and an even longer

Western European tradition, out of which present-day society has grown and upon which it is built. According to this model, it does not matter where one looks – be it in art, science, or landscape – and it does not matter where one digs – in the earth or into history; everywhere one finds references to Christianity. In the traditional model, Christianity is the primary religious horizon, a basic narrative and a cultural and spiritual foundation for the values on which Danish society builds, i.e. the modern project with democracy, human rights, equality before the law, welfare, the market, and a constitutional monarchy.

This position can be deciphered in many texts and positions. Here I consider a debate book by Erik Bjerager, the editor-in-chief of the national daily newspaper *Kristeligt Dagblad* (literally, "The Christian Daily"), whose statement of purpose establishes that it should be "managed and written in a Christian spirit." In the book, *Gud bevare Danmark (*God save Denmark) from 2006, Erik Bjerager asserts that Christianity has created Western civilization: capitalism, new technologies, the individual, the idea of human equality, and secularization itself (ibid.: 20, 25-26). The public school is "a child of the church" (ibid.: 37; all translations mine), democracy and human rights are "a fruit of the Christian cultural influence" (ibid., 61). The cross sits on the nation's flag, the Queen is the head of both state and church, the calendar is organized according to the birth of Christ, the laws on Sunday closing of shops are inspired by Christianity (ibid.: 241-42), and "the church as organization and Christianity as an idea have played an important role in forming the welfare state" (ibid.: 178).

In this traditional understanding, Christianity is an inseparable part of Danish culture, which also gives the Church and Christianity a preferential right to be supported by the state. The motto "God, King, and Fatherland" is the overarching symbol of the Danish national community. If society is viewed as a square, the traditional model places Danish society into an even bigger square, a transcendent layer of both material and spiritual meaning. In this sense, Christianity is an integral part of the foundational myth Danes live by, blossoming from time immemorial, the earth, and from the generations. The most passionate advocates of the traditional model have typically had a political orientation toward the Right in the Danish national parliament, *Folketinget*. The model is especially prominent in the program of the Danish People's Party (*Dansk Folkeparti*), a nationalist party established in 1995 which links together Danish culture and Christian faith. The party program reads:

> Christianity has a centuries-old established right in Denmark and is inseparable from the life of the people. The importance that Christianity

has and has had is immense and affects the life paths of the Danes. Through the ages, it has been a guide and road map for the people (Dansk Folkeparti; translation mine).

This model also identifies various threats to "Christian Denmark", both internal and external. Bjerager, whom I quoted above, emphasizes the internal threat, namely "secularization, which will deprive Christianity of its critical significance in the Danish and European societies" (2006:16). It is therefore the insight in Christianity as a historical force and the "legacy from Jerusalem, Rome, Constantinople, and Wittenberg" that must be primarily understood if one wants to preserve basic cultural values. The construction of an external threat and a more confrontational attitude toward Islam in the Danish church context may be found in the Islam Critical Network (*Islamkritisk Netværk*). The Network, formed in 2006, includes about 120 ministers and theologians and sees its task as that of studying and criticizing Islam. According to the founders of the Network, "Islam has now arrived in force into the country. Islam agitates and missionizes. The Danish Lutheran Church should respond to it and without hesitation oppose Islam's religious robbery and preach the freedom of the gospels" (Holm and Rasmussen 2006; translation mine). Inasmuch as Islam is understood as a totalitarian ideology, the network sees mission and confrontation as the necessary defense for the survival of Christian Denmark.

In other debates about the integration of immigrants, Christianity is also a decisive symbol of the definition of Denmark as the home of "the Danes," effectively casting immigrants, especially those with other religions, in the role as guests no matter the length of their stay. This understanding of the relationship between Danes and foreign Muslims has been especially visible in the debate about the extent to which Muslims should be allowed to have separate Muslim burial grounds and build mosques, and so set their architectural mark on the landscape and take over the public space, "our" space. In 2006 the first Muslim cemetery was opened in the southern part of Copenhagen, and other cemeteries are currently being prepared throughout the country.

The secular model

The secular model distinguishes itself from the traditional model by setting a state border as the outside framework for Danish society and allocating to Christianity a place within this, alongside other institutions which Danes finance through taxation: the public school, the health system, the libraries, and even the Zoo! Here it is emphasized that while religion is certainly within the state order, it is voluntary matter whether or not the individual will enter into it. The Danish Lutheran Church is thus the state-supported religious institution, a tradition-bound, voluntary offer extended to the citizens, allowing them to enter an ordered and authorized, private, religious space. The spokesmen for understanding the church order as a civic order emphasize that the relatively secularly-based state in this way sets sensible limits on religion, so that it does not degenerate into being sectarian, fanatical or fundamentalist. A warning from this position is typically given against the traditionalist position's romanticizing of the relationship between Christianity and existing societal principles, inasmuch as the church's influence has never been unambiguously beneficial. Thus, the historian Uffe Østergard warns against romanticizing the contribution of Lutheranism to the welfare state, as the break with Catholicism also entailed religious fanaticism, witch-hunting trials and:

> a catastrophic decline in the level of higher education, inasmuch as the universities in Copenhagen and Uppsala were transformed into primitive seminaries, where literal, orthodox Lutheranism was indoctrinated (2003:28; translation mine).

In this model, religiosity is to a great extent viewed as a personal and private affair. In the aftermath of the Muhammad cartoon crisis, Danish Prime Minister Anders Fogh Rasmussen repeatedly underscored the importance of this view when he addressed the question of the relationship between the state and religion. In a longer article in the national daily *Politiken* (Rasmussen 2006; all translations mine) on the occasion of the Danish Constitution Day, Fogh Rasmussen argued that religion "will always be a part of human life and thereby of our society," but that religion, faith, and the religious commands remain primarily a personal matter for the individual; therefore, religion must not occupy too much of the public sphere, including the political. Religiosity threatens our national cohesiveness (*sammenhængskraften*[3]). "Generally speaking, it could contribute to religious peace in the public sphere if we were much less preoccupied by religious symbols" (Ibid.) In accordance with this, Fogh Rasmussen, in an interview in the newspaper *Kristeligt Dagblad*, emphasizes his view of the Church and of Christianity as marked by regular church attendance, a rational view of the world, and a pragmatic and moderate view of religion (30 June 2006). In this way, "God, King and Fatherland" can still be a cultural reference point, while citizenship is the primary contractual framework of belonging. The state itself does not have any religion; it should only ensure freedom of religion and its own freedom from religion (cf. Rasmussen 2006).

Other expressions of the civic organization of the relationship between religion and society that are widespread within the framework of the Church can be seen in a special emphasis on the Sunday worship services and on the pragmatic framework for the relationship to God. Thus, in the secular model Sunday worship may be considered a high point of the week, after which one lives one's life like everyone else in civil society for the remainder of the week. A powerful tendency towards secularization in the theology of the 20th century has emphasized a certain separation of society and church and has favored Christianity not leaving an exclusively Christian mark on the life of society. This tendency has occurred at a time with well-established connections between the state and society, to which the traditional model attributes a decisive symbolic significance, but which the secular model takes for granted as a practical order. The Church thus has a tradition of having been supported by the state, and instruction in Christianity in the public school system was of the evangelical (preaching) type until 1975.

There are various combinations of the traditional model and the secular model. It is also here that the middle range of Danish politics typically finds itself. In the church context, one of the influential bishops, Jan Lindhardt, has been a prominent spokesman for this combination approach. He recognizes the Danish Church as a state and national body, but does not view it as a special sector. In a book on the Danish Church and its relationship to society, Lindhardt emphasizes the close relationship between state and church by speaking about the National Church as a state church, calling Denmark a "church-state" (2005:48). For Lindhardt, the dialectic between state and church is critical: the church provides the foundation of ideas, values, and ethics; society provides the rest, without which the church would be a small private space outside "the good society, with institutions such as the parliament, government, public schools, defense, justice and much else" (ibid., p. 102; all translations mine). Lindhardt assumes that the cohesive power (*sammenhængskraft*) of a society is largely religious and ideological, and if the church cannot provide this foundation, he fears the worst (ibid.: 25, 117).

> [I]t is thus a case of a double movement: the National Church forms the church, but the church has simultaneously forged the national [Danish: *folkelig*], in its forms. The two have therefore had a long marriage with each other (ibid.: 126).

The poly-religious model

The poly-religious model emphasizes a third view of Danish society. This view argues that while it is possible that Denmark was once a Christian country, this is no longer the case. Christianity is no more than the individual's faith or the faith of a special group. The National Church certainly has a great majority of the population as members, but there are growing groups outside it, who do not accept the church's favored position. In this view, Denmark is understood to be a multicultural society, or a society, which is becoming multicultural, with about 170,000 Muslims, 35,000 Catholics, 15,000 Jehovah's Witness, 5,500 Baptists and 2,000 Jews. The figures come from the book *Limits to God* (*Grænser for Gud*) (2005:28), in which two journalists, Michael Jarlner and Anders Jerichow, argue for a complete separation between state and religion and a religiously neutral state (ibid.: 9). For Jarlner and Jerichow, it is the state that has the duty to ensure society's cohesive forces, and the institution with a special responsibility here is the public school system, which should create a common, democratic foundation (ibid.: 9, 141). In the poly-religious model, priority is given to the freedom to cultivate (or not) one's own beliefs; religion does not occupy a privileged position over other spheres of life (ibid.: 73).

The poly-religious model typically appeals to politically left-wing views, and the model is most prominent in the public debate about teaching religion in the public schools. What should the children be taught? What should they learn? And what is the role of Christianity/ religion in Denmark in the future? In the existing regulations for teaching the school subject called "Knowledge of Christianity" in the Danish primary schools, the point of departure is Christianity as it appears in its present and historical form. Other religions *can* be included in the lowest grade levels, but it is only in the upper grades where there are requirements to teach of other religions. In recent years, increasing attention has been paid to inserting Islam into the curriculum, with frequent reference to the idea that it would help promote integration of Muslim minorities in Danish society. In the same way, the public school system has made efforts to strengthen the "culturally sustaining" (*kulturbærende*) subjects and this includes instruction in Christianity with increased focus on the Biblical narratives. In the 2006/2007 school year, Christianity also became a subject for compulsory examinations. Critics of the poly-cultural perspective have argued that if the goal is understanding and respect between adherents of different faiths, the subject "Knowledge of Christianity" should change its name to "Religion," and focus to a far greater extent on diversity and on the encounters and conflicts between religions. After some years as one of the marginal subjects in the primary school, the political interest in Christianity instruction has increased, and with it, the public debate has become more strident.

Social science versions of the traditional and secular model

The three models are not only competing political and theological schools of thought. They also express dominant modes of the religion that have been conceptualized and debated by the cultural and social sciences in the latter half of the 20th century. The traditional model, for example, has strong points of similarity with the anthropologist Clifford Geertz' classic definition of religion from 1966, where religion is understood as a symbolic universe which interprets the world of human beings in a holistic format. Geertz' definition emphasizes that the religious perspective is a special way of viewing the world, which unites a worldview and a mode of being. This is significantly articulated in ritual, where a people's spiritual consciousnesses and understanding of reality are created (1966). Religious faith thereby functions as the putty which binds together a people, its spirit, and its understanding of reality. The religious condition, in other words, is a naturalized form of cohesive power, as in the traditional model, regardless of whether or not it is expressed through a clear ideology.

Within each model, there are variations, as I have mentioned, but in the Danish scholarly version of the traditional model, there is an emphasis on the historical synthesis between the Danish people, the Lutheran religion, and Danish institutions. These, woven together by history, are the roots and the tree of Danish society, and small twigs and outlying branches must bend for the rights historically won by the majority. This model thereby also contains a traditional understanding of culture, which identifies culture as a unity, with stable properties, rules, and traditions. That the traditional model is widespread and presumably sustainable in broad circles in the near future is reflected in the book, *In the heart of Denmark* (*I hjertet af Danmark*) in which a sociologist, a sociologist of religion, and a theologian have written a Danish version of Robert Bellah's *Habits of the Heart* from 1985 (Gundelach et al 2008). The book focuses on "Danishness" as it relates to common institutions and mental patterns in Denmark. On the basis of statistical data and interviews with 34 Danes, the authors identify seven institutions and seven mental patterns. Religion is one of the seven institutions, and the book's invocation of religion is a textbook example of the traditional model, combined with certain features of the two other models: Denmark is primarily a Christian country, and then secularized with a variety of religious denominations.

In cultural analyses, the secular model shows itself most clearly in mainstream, quantitative sociology of religion and in certain approaches from the history of religion, where religion is conceived primarily as a special symbolic system, and people's connections to religion are conceived in terms of beliefs and practical participation in rituals. Here, religion is a special sector, which one can join or leave, and which to various extents is seen in connection with the rest of the world, all according to the degree of secularization and fundamentalism. It is an understanding, which can be easily combined with a multicultural perspective: the concept simply adds additional conglomerates of religion within the cultural and societal framework.

As mentioned in the introduction, the American sociologist Zuckerman has suggested that Danes are the most non-religious people in the world. He bases his conclusion on an explicit comparison with the relationship between religion and society in the United States, and he does not hide his enthusiasm for the Danish situation, a society he describes as healthy, peaceful, prosperous and filled with a deep goodness – all without God. The Danes, except for a small minority of true believers, do not believe in the "literal, vengeful or forgiving god which the Bible depicts" (2008:19), says Zuckerman. He mentions that this is the belief of most Americans and of many of their popular talk radio hosts, television personalities, and authors. Zuckerman thus understands religion as a belief in the supernatural combined with frequent church attendance, and by this definition, he is presumably correct that the Danes are not as religious as, for examples, the Americans. However, it is fair to ask whether Zuckerman has understood what many Danes understand by religion and their membership in the Danish Evangelical Lutheran Church. Reviewers and commentators thus mention that Zuckerman has overlooked the fact that Danish Lutheran Christianity is based on a shared cultural horizon, which is neither especially verbalized nor visible in the form of frequent church attendance or other obvious indicators. On the contrary, this kind of Christianity is about "securely going out into general human life and doing what we can for our loved ones and for those closest to us" (Holm 2008; translation mine). The foundation of the well-functioning welfare society that Zuckerman describes is, in other words, Christian. The argument is that the Christian faith has certainly been partially secularized in the form of a liberal theology that does not emphasize the supernatural, but this does not necessarily make Danish Evangelical Lutheranism any less religious, less Christian, or less meaningful.

A phenomenological alternative to the poly-religious model

If we turn toward the poly-religious model, it has completely abandoned the idea of cultural foundations and the idea that the church or any other religious institutions should be seen as representatives of religion. Before returning to the Danish situation, I will briefly show how the poly-religious model can be expanded using the unconventional analytical understandings of religion developed by the sociologist of religion Thomas Luckmann. The key concept for Luckmann's understanding of religion is "transcendence"; that people transcend themselves in their relation to the world and connect themselves to a collective understanding of "the good life." In other words, religion is about the social and moral life (2003:276). I introduced this chapter by referring to Durkheim, and Luckmann places himself in clear extension of Durkheim, when he maintains that religion is about the social fact that individuals become persons, i.e. obtain an identity, by growing up in a society (1979:122).

In his later work, Luckmann has presented a more substantial qualification of the social forms of religion by distinguishing between three different degrees of transcendence, which are all part of being human. The "small" transcendences, says Luckmann, concern the fact that we are aware that the world is larger than the "here and now" that we experience here and now. We know and relate ourselves to something before and after, something in front of us and behind us. In this way we frequently, almost constantly, transcend the "here and now" in multiple ways in thoughts (in e.g. memories and planning), feelings (in e.g. longings and hopes), and actions (in e.g. reaching out, creating new things, and in long distance communication). The "intermediate" transcendences are defined by the fact that we relate to other people, and that we form groups, ideas, and societies. In this way, we transcend our own bodies and other individual conditions. These two first transcendences lie within the boundaries of everyday life, whereas the third level, the "great transcendences" grow out of dreams, ecstasy, extreme pain, and wisdom about the limits of death. They thus mark the very boundaries of everyday life (2003:277). Conventional understandings of religion are often linked to the great transcendences (cf. Zuckerman's "belief in a set of supernatural ideas" such as a life after death and a theistically conceived God), but Luckmann argues that this is a much too narrow framework of understanding. Precisely as Durkheim showed, religion in its elementary forms concerns transcendence between the "profane" and the "sacred," and this process of making things, ideas, and people sacred does not exclusively take place within the institutions and symbolic systems which modern understanding constructs as religion.

The three forms of transcendence give Luckmann the tools to draw an unconventional picture of the poly-religious society with several forms of transcendence, operating simultaneously and in different combinations. The intermediate transcendences manifest themselves in "political religion," i.e. the political ideologies which focus on transcending class, race, and nation as well as in more recent religious forms, largely disseminated by the mass media (2003). Sport, both national and international, is a candidate here, mentioned by many others, though not Luckmann (e.g. Birrell 1981). The music and entertainment industries and the Danish practice of virtually uncontrolled praise of the Danish flag in official, commercial, and private contexts are also symbols, which create communities and shared identity. In line with this, the Swedish political scientist Catarina Kinvall (2004) has argued that religious nationalism provides narratives and ideas of belief (discourses) that can create a feeling of security, identity, and "domesticity," i.e. frameworks for the human being's possibilities to act in relation to "the good life." Luckmann cites the family as an essential institution for the investigation of transcendence and a meaningful life (Luckmann 1967, 2003). These and other social forms also include the small transcendences. According to Luckmann, the cultivation of immediate feelings and sensations in the poly-religious society is expressed in forms which lie far from the old religious orthodoxies in content, but not necessarily in form. In this sense, there is an abundance of religious cohesive power, but it is more differentiated and open than in the secular or traditional models of religion.

The tripartite church

In the remainder of this chapter, I return to a more classical church sociological perspective in order to examine how the three models of the relationship between church and state, outlined above, express themselves in the field of the Danish National Church. The question is how the Danish National Church succeeds in remaining a single, unified church, despite the presence of several opposing attitudes to what it is and what keeps it together. Here I shall refer to illustrative examples from the various periods of fieldwork I have undertaken in the Danish National Church from 1992 to 2005.

As mentioned, the Constitution does not include a single governing organ which can articulate Church policies. Rather, there are many parties who can speak for themselves and create a picture of a common church. The Danish Church thereby seems to be defined by a social and symbolic structure, which with a minimum of dogma and shared rituals can contain within it opposing interpretations of key existential or political questions. This observation is not new and does not apply exclusively to the Danish Church. It was a postulate of sociology as early as the 19th century, when the theologian and historian Ernst Troeltsch concluded that it is difficult to find a solid, common foundation in Christian ethics. This observation was also used by Durkheim (1965) and decades later by Bourdieu (1991) in their reflections on the existential conditions of the church community.

A description of the Danish People's Church, in all its institutional breadth, should therefore also include traditional, secular, and poly-religious elements. The Church obviously involves itself in the *traditional* "Denmark of God, King and Fatherland" when its bishops and provosts are on the obligatory list of those being awarded royal orders, and when the church celebrates the royal family at weddings, christenings, and funerals. These royal events often develop into popular celebrations with thousands of people in the streets waving the Danish flag and with the mass media as active participants and disseminators of the ritual liturgy and the genealogy of the participants and ritual objects. On these occasions, the royal family functions as the sacred family that symbolizes the national, good, God-given, and privileged life.

The church and the royal family are also involved in the *secular* state's maintenance and celebration of itself, e.g. in the Church's participation in the annual opening of parliament, where there is a religious service for the members of the Parliament. Another sign is found in the Danish passport imprinted with an image of the Jelling stone, the Viking-era runic-inscribed stone often called "Denmark's baptism certificate." The connection between the state and the church is also visible in the fact that the Church administers the civil birth registrations on behalf of the state, which in return collects the church tax. The clergy are public civil servants, guaranteed economic and symbolic privileges including a pastoral residence.

Insofar as 18% of the Danish population are not members of the Danish Evangelical Lutheran Church, and inasmuch as statistical studies show that many members of the Church also orient themselves toward other religions, the *poly-religious* model is also a part of the Church's own conditions. Numerous theologians have discussed how pure Lutheran Christianity has mixed with popular religion, cultural Christianity, and recent Eastern spirituality. Other indicators of a plural situation are the numerous experiments by the Church in trying to reach non-believers and potential church-goers in different institutional settings (hospitals, prisons, universities, pubs, and so forth) and the efforts to renew the Christian ritual tradition in new forms of performances (new prayers, new psalms, new forms of service, and so forth).

Generally speaking, the Danish Evangelical Lutheran Church succeeds in maintaining its broadly integrative function between individual and community insofar as it succeeds in mediating between the three different models of the church. The church thereby contributes to the idea of "a sacred Denmark," a consolidated nation, which transcends and thereby survives despite differences. There are many specific examples of how the tripartite church functions. I have already mentioned the officializing strategies, which all the groups utilize, whereby the church one fights for is depicted as a collective good. The partisans of a conservative theology, for example, can assert that even though they must refuse to carry out certain Church initiatives (such as blessing of same-sex registered partners) and may in fact be close to leaving the church, it is especially important to remain within the Church while it is fragile. Conversely, the liberal positions assert that the Danish Church must move itself in the direction of the surrounding society's norms and lifestyles in order to survive at all and in order to be able to preach the gospel. Both parties, in other words, see themselves as guarantors of the Church's survival.

It is especially in crisis situations that an observer can gain insight into the kind of tensions that exist, and how they escalate and are minimized. With a gradually more visible Muslim minority, there are more historical Danish-Christian constructions, which become visible and are problematized. Thus, the cemeteries are administered by the Church, and only a few municipalities can offer more neutral burial grounds, let alone specific ones allocated exclusively to the growing minorities. Likewise, it has been the object of ongoing critique that the obligatory birth registrations are managed by the parish office. It is regularly proposed that birth registrations ought to be the task of the official state population register. Today the tax office is in charge of collecting the church tax, but wouldn't it be more in keeping with the times that the state administer a form of religion tax and distribute the revenue to the different religious denominations? The traditional position sees the Danish People's Church as a bulwark against immigration and globalization, the more liberal position appoints the Church as a potential agent in an integration process, which could be promoted by renouncing tradition-bound institutions and participating in a religious encounter based on dialogue.

A diplomatic veil of secrecy is routinely drawn over the ministers' daily work in the parishes, not least sustained by theologians' and ministers' expertise at exploiting the Christian symbolic language in order to create "double meanings" (cf. Bourdieu 1991:20). Using the same linguistic expressions, they create the possibilities for several simultaneous understandings of the same phenomenon. The great theological differences concerning the relationship between politics and religion, between mythic-poetic and literal understandings of the Bible, and other such issues, can invariably be transcended using appropriate texts from the Bible, Luther, or other church fathers. The texts chosen are deliberately open or ahistorical so that they can embrace several possible positions.

As long as the integrative, inclusive conceptions of the Danish National Church continue to be so strong, there remains considerable space to enforce relatively radical views within relatively closed circles, while at the same time underplaying these same views in the public, consensus-seeking church. The mediating forces are without doubt stronger than the radical forces in the National Church, which manifests itself in a very large, middle-of-the-road church containing a relatively loosely organized network of ministers, theologians, and especially clerically interested parties along with a large number of very radical positions and unique standpoints (Rubow 2005: 207ff, 2006: 222ff). Periodically, the church field is stirred, but only momentarily, before the mediating networks, with a minimum of changes, succeed in restoring tranquility. In sum, this mix of intended and unintended consequences of the repertoire of available bureaucratic tools creates a community that is so resilient that it can include the overwhelming majority of the Danish population.

The three models of the relationship between religion and society exist side by side, in both politicized and social science versions. There are at least three understandings, which cite history, the state, or the citizen as the primary agent in the creation of cohesion. In connection with the question of the relationship between religion and integration, there are strong grounds to consider all three models. They are all active in the political debate, and they each struggle for a place. If Durkheim and Luckmann are correct, we must consider religion without restricting it to the confines of church attitudes. When Zuckerman declares that the Danes are the most irreligious people in the world, this is perhaps true in a narrow comparison with the United States, but it would be a mistake to overlook the broad religious processes in the creation of a "sacred" Denmark. These processes involve and challenge the church, but also – as other chapters in this book show – the welfare system, the Danish language, as well as Danish ideas of equality and belonging.

Notes

This article was translated by Steven Sampson.

1. The Danish term "folk" has connotations of both ethnicity and the popular; in this article I will refer to Folkekirken as the Danish National Church.
2. The word sammenhængskraft, literally "power to hold together" or "cohesiveness", is a composite neologism recently inserted into the debate about immigrants and the welfare state, as a Danish synonym for social capital. The term has been invoked in a variety of political debates in Denmark, largely by the Right, in which threats to the nation and the welfare state are debated.

References

Birrell, Susan. 1981. Sport as ritual: interpretations from Durkheim to Goffman. *Social Forces* 60: 354-76.

Bjerager, Erik. 2006. *Gud bevare Danmark. Et opgør med sekularismen.* Copenhagen: Gyldendal.

Bjerager, Erik and Henrik Hoffmann-Hansen. 2006. Religionen i Foghs private rum. *Kristeligt Dagblad* 13 July.

Bourdieu, Pierre. 1991. Genesis and Structure of the Religious Field. In *Comparative Social Research* Vol. 13, ed. C. Calhoun. London: Jai Press.

Buckser, Andrew. 1997. Religion and Spans of Ambiguity on a Danish Island. *Sociology of Religion* 58 (3): 261-275.

Constitutional Act of Denmark of June 5 1953. 1999. Copenhagen: The Folketing.

Dansk Folkeparti [Danish People's Party]. 2002. *Principprogram.* (http://www.danskfolkeparti.dk/Principprogram.asp), accessed July 6, 2010)

Durkheim, Émile. 1965 [1915]. *The Elementary Forms of the Religious Life.* New York: The Free Press.

Geertz, Clifford. 1966. Religion as a Cultural System. In *Anthropological Approaches to the Study of Religion*, ed. M. Banton, 1-46 London: Tavistock.

Gundelach, Peter; Hans Raun Iversen and Margit Warburg. 2008. *I hjertet af Danmark.* Copenhagen: Hans Reitzels Forlag.

Holm, Katrine Winkel and Thomas Reinholdt Rasmussen. 2006. Kristne og muslimer tror ikke på samme Gud. *Kristeligt Dagblad*, 15 May.

Holm, Preben. 2008. Danskerne er det mest religiøse folk i verden. *Kristeligt Dagblad*, 24 August.

Jarlner, Michael and Anders Jerichow. 2005. *Grænser for Gud – giv det verdslige samfund en chance.* Copenhagen: Gyldendal.

Lindhardt, Jan. 2005. *Folkekirke? Kirken i det danske samfund.* Højbjerg: Forlaget Hovedland.

Lüchau, Peter. 2005. Danskernes gudstro siden 1940'erne. In *Gudstro i Danmark,* ed. M. T. Højsgaard and H. R. Iversen. Copenhagen: Forlaget Anis.

Kinnwall, Catarina. 2004. Globalization and religious nationalism: self, identity, and the search for ontological security. *Political Psychology* 25:741-67.

Kirkeministeriet. 2008. Folkekirken. (http://www.km.dk/folkekirken.html, accessed June 28, 23, 2010)

Luckmann, Thomas.1967. *The Invisible Religion. The Problem of Religion in Modern Society.* London: Collier Macmillan Publ.

Luckmann, Thomas. 1979. The Structural Conditions of Religious Consciousness in Modern Societies. *Japanese Journal of Religious Studies* 6: 121-37.

Luckmann, Thomas. 2003. Transformations of Religion and Morality in Modern Europe. *Social Compass* 50: 275-85.

Østergaard, Uffe. 2003. Lutheranismen, danskheden og velfærdsstaten. In *13 historier om den danske velfærdsstat,* ed. K. Petersen. Odense: Syddansk Universitetsforlag.

Rasmussen, Anders Fogh. 2006. Hold religionen indendørs. *Politiken* 20 May.

Rubow, Cecilie. 2005. Medieringer af gudstro i pastoral praksis i Den Danske Folkekirke. In *Gudstro i Danmark,* ed. M. T. Højsgaard and Hans Raun Iversen. Copenhagen: Forlaget Anis.

—. 2006. *Fem præster og antropologiske perspektiver på identitet og autoritet.* Copenhagen: Forlaget Anis.

Zuckerman, Phil. 2008. *Society Without God.* New York: New York University Press.

CHAPTER FIVE

TO BE DANISH AND MUSLIM: INTERNALIZING THE STRANGER?

TINA GUDRUN JENSEN

In the last four decades, about 3000 Danes have converted to Islam. The changes that have taken place in Danish society as a result of the immigration of non-Western Muslims (starting in the late 1960s) are the key to understanding these conversions. They are also complicated by public debates in Denmark that formulate immigration and cultural pluralism as problems for the country's cohesion and welfare. "Muslim culture," and Islam in particular, are considered obstacles to immigrants' integration in Danish society, and the public debates have a conspicuously anti-Islamic rhetoric. Over the years, Danish politicians and other public figures have depicted Islam as "the dark Middle Ages," associating Islam with oppression, religious fanaticism, anti-secularism and (lately) terrorism. They have contrasted Islam with what they by contrast formulate as genuinely Danish core values, such as liberalism, individualism, secularism and democracy. Consequently, public debates generate an opposition between Danish and Muslim identities, categorizing Islam and Muslim immigrants as incompatible with Danishness and Danish identity.

Anti-Islamic rhetoric in Denmark predates September 11, 2001 and the global war on terror. International surveys show that Danes are more negative towards religion than most other Europeans (Goul Andersen and Tobiasen 2002). Danes view Islam in particular as being opposed to Danish liberal values, and their attitudes towards Islam intermesh with xenophobic perceptions of immigration as a threat to Danish national culture (Tobiasen 2003: 361). The xenophobic discourse against Muslims represents a form of power that is manifested in language and has consequences in real life (Sjørslev, see this volume). In Denmark, colloquial ways of talking about immigrants use the term "Muslim" (rather than "immigrant") as a category for anyone foreign to Danish identity and society. Being "Muslim" thus implies not being "Danish." This contrast also appears in language about "us" (Danes) versus "them" (Muslims). This clear dichotomy suggests a social order in which the categories "Dane" and "Muslim" are mutually exclusive, thereby precluding any interrelationship between the two.

The watertight shutters between the two categories also imply that a person cannot be considered both Danish and Muslim. This implication affects not only Muslims who have been born and raised in Denmark, yet are still perceived as strangers, but also Danes who become Muslims by converting to Islam. According to the interpretations offered by the public, politicized discourses that unfold at this macro level, Danes who convert to Islam are people who have undergone fundamental and radical processes of transformation, abdicating their Danishness. Consequently, as victims of the dominant dichotomy between Danes and Muslims, they are ostracized from mainstream Danish society. In this way, the public debates about Danish converts illustrate not only the cultural processes at stake in constructing and maintaining the categories that make up the social order, but also the difficult multicultural co-existence of the two groups.

However, by transgressing cultural borders and categories, converts to Islam also illustrate the "quiet integration" (Pedersen and Rytter 2006) and micro-level integration that take place in everyday interactions in Denmark (Anderson, see this volume), along with the complexities of Danish society. The purpose of the chapter is to show the differences between the public and personal understandings of Danes' conversions to Islam. The chapter focuses on how on the one hand converts relate to the external categorizations that construct Danish and Muslim identities as oppositional, incompatible and mutually exclusive, while on the other hand continuing to engage in relationships and practices that predate their conversion. The analytical focus is on social identity, that is, on identity understood as fundamentally social because it includes both internal and external perceptions and categorizations of identity and community (Jenkins 1996). The chapter illustrates this process by following the stories of three converts who represent different ways of being Muslim and interacting with both ethnic Danes and Muslim immigrants. These stories reveal multifarious identifications, continuities and relationships between Danish and Muslim identities that contrast strongly with the external xenophobic categorisations that portray converts as people who abdicated their Danishness when they became Muslim.

This chapter is based on fieldwork conducted from January 2004 to April 2005 among converts to Islam in the cities of Copenhagen and Århus. The fieldwork consisted of participant observation in different Muslim milieus, ranging from mosques to Muslim associations to private homes. It included interviews with 30 female and male converts between 13 and 58 years of age, along with a survey of 122 converts (Jensen and Østergaard 2007).

Conversion to Islam in Denmark

In 1979, one of the first reports on Danes' conversion to Islam enumerated 150 converts, primarily women who had married immigrant men (*Islamisk Udsyn* 1979). Since then, this number has grown to about 2500-3000 (Jensen and Østergaard 2007). Today, most Danish converts are young, having converted in their teens and twenties. While a majority of them are women, an increasing number of men are also embracing Islam. Danish converts represent different people with different social backgrounds from different regions in Denmark. Like the majority of the Danish population, they were members of the Danish national Lutheran church at the time of their conversion, and some still are. Like other Muslims, they represent very different forms of religious expression and ways of being Muslim. What qualifies a person as a Muslim is the fulfillment of the act of conversion, that is, the pronouncing of the *shahada* or "profession of faith." This act consists of stating in Arabic in the presence of an *imam* and other Muslim witnesses that there is no God but God (*Allah*) and that Muhammad is his Prophet.

Conversion to Islam reflects a condition of cultural complexity as characterized by the interplay between different actors and cultural traditions in which new identities emerge. The conversion thus exemplifies the existence of the multiculturalism that is often denied in public debates on immigration in Denmark. The issue of multiculturalism is something towards which converts generally have very positive attitudes; for example, they say that different ethnic groups enrich each other by mixing cultures (Jensen and Østergaard 2007: 181). Many Danish converts had contacts with Muslims before their conversion, either as schoolmates, friends, boyfriends, girlfriends or spouses. Socialization with Muslim immigrants and a fascination with their cultures are significant factors in the conversion. Another motivation for conversion is that of being a religious seeker for truth and finding that one's truth lies in Islam. Both social relationships and spiritual quests are at stake in the conversions (Allievi 2006), and both are related to the increasing co-existence with Muslims.

When interviewed for the first time, converts nevertheless often hesitate to talk about their relationships with Muslims. The avoidance of talking about one's often intimate interactions with people who belong to immigrant minorities seems to be related to the converts' reproduction of a public discourse that associates Islam with alienation from Danish society and sees it as a threat to it (Hervik 2003). Issues like love and marriage with Muslim immigrants thus appear to constitute a "filth zone" in which intimate relations with "others" on the margins of Danish society and the "risk" of mixture threaten to "pollute" Danishness. Converts tend to keep these issues secret and thereby express an awareness of being categorized as "dangerous," as national traitors, as representing people who have left the Danish community.

Common stereotypes of the incompatibility between Muslim and Danish identities affect the way that converts perceive themselves as having become "different." Converting to Islam is framed in the same language as that of committing the crime of becoming "un-Danish." The newly converted often explain their conversion to Islam as partly motivated by the sensation of being different from other Danes, with statements such as "I have always felt that I was different." This self-image, however, is strongly affected by how other Danes categorize them.

Categorizations and positionings: rupture and continuity

As the term "conversion" generally indicates a transformation of identity, it is perceived as an internal or private matter. Yet this process also involves the external categorizations of the ways in which others perceive the conversion and their ideas about who the convert has become. Signs such as physical appearance and language use are vital for making identifications and categorizations (Jenkins 1996). Converts have different opinions about whether they should wear visible signs of their conversion to Islam, such as the *hijab* (veil) and *jilbab* (dress) for women or a beard and *sunna* clothes (coat and headgear) for men. Those converts who assume Muslim dress experience the power of external categorization more profoundly because other Danes often mistake them for immigrants, categorizing them as "Muslim immigrants." This mistake manifests in ostensibly positive and negative remarks from other Danes, such as "you speak Danish well," "black pig" and "go home." Many converts (often women who wear the *hijab*) have been harassed on the street by other Danes, who have called them "traitor" and even assaulted them. Such incidents suggest that converts are more than victims of the general xenophobia directed toward Muslims. The abusive term "traitor" indicates that they are assaulted because, in contrast to those who are born Muslims, and in the eyes of other Danes, they have consciously chosen to alienate themselves voluntarily from Danish identity.

Because of the prevalent opposition between Danish and Muslim identities, and the notion that Muslims represent strangers, Danish converts tend to be categorized as people who have undergone a transformation from a Danish "us" to a Muslim "them." In this way, conversion to Islam is often seen as a break with Danish identity. Consequently, the issues of "rupture" and "continuity" are at stake in different ways for Danish converts. Among Muslims, a common joke is that the recently converted suffer from an illness referred to as "convertitis" – both an allusion to the generally assumed pathological nature of the conversion and a partial affirmation of its nature (Roald 2004). The newly converted often exhibit a fervour for their new religion, a strict observance expressed in very ritualized behaviour, such as only wearing Islamic dress, changing their name to a Muslim one, or being preoccupied with the Islamic rules of what is *haram* ("forbidden") and *halal* ("allowed"), that is, doing Muslim things "right." The phenomenon of "convertitis" expresses the convert's awareness that, in the eyes of the Danish surroundings, he or she has undergone an identity transformation into the polemicized "other."

Convertitis is an example of the influence of the public image on the individual self-image, where the converts' performance of their Muslim identity appears to result from the stigmatization of external categorizations. The convert's Muslim dress, signs and behaviour are strong indicators that he or she has changed identity by embodying the stereotypic "Muslim other." The performance of Muslim identity thus also takes place *for* the surroundings and is a direct translation from a nominal identification to a factual identification that sends a provocative signal – "I am a Muslim" – indicating a radical change and a rupture with other identities. Whereas this marking of "rupture" confirms the external categorizations of converts as people who break with their Danish identities, it does not necessarily indicate that the same meaning of "rupture" is at stake in converts' self-images.

For some converts, the conversion process appears to take an opposite turn in the sense that the newly converted hesitate to show off their conversion and seek to emphasize continuity with their "former" identities and lifestyles, for example, by not showing any visible signs of their conversion through dress or name change, etc. This behaviour, by contrast, appears as a masking of their Muslim identities and constitutes an emphasis on continuity in relation to prior identities. The underplaying of visible signs also signals a negation of the external categorization.

The two different ways of staging Muslim identity represent positions that communicate either rupture or continuity with identities that pre-date the conversion (Jensen 2008). Both patterns of behaviour are different ways of reacting to being externally categorized as Danes who have alienated themselves from Danish culture and society. Rupture and continuity are thus also recurrent themes in converts' narrations and practices, representing different positions between which converts tend to oscillate. Generally, while the newly converted tend to emphasize "rupture," over time they will lean toward emphasizing "continuity," thereby expressing an integration of identities (Roald 2004).

Danish culture: exclusion and inclusion

For converts, the issues of rupture and continuity also involve their relationship to Danish culture, society, and "Danishness" in general. From the very start of my fieldwork, converts spontaneously discussed whether being both Danish and Muslim was possible. Consequently, Danish identity, culture and society became important topics in the interviews. Converts talk about Danish culture in two main ways, both of which relate differently to the Danish public discourse on the homogeneity of Danish culture. One way expresses an essentialized, reified image of a homogenous Danish culture, understood largely as Danish "customs," such as beer-drinking, in which converts no longer take part. The other way in which converts speak about culture is as a political, hegemonic concept defined by those in power, who relate nationalism to the project of homogenization. Converts' two ways of speaking about Danish culture respectively affirm and reject the notion of cultural homogeneity, and thus represent positions of exclusion and inclusion in relation to Danish culture.

Some express self-exclusion from Danish society, perceiving themselves as having "emigrated" from Danishness. Leila, a 36-year-old woman who had been a Muslim for nine years, said that one of her converted friends described herself in those terms:

> She had emigrated from Danish society because she had become a Muslim, because she was like ... really she was not a Dane any longer, but she was not a foreigner. She described herself.... I thought it was so funny. She had *emigrated* from Danish society, not *immigrated*. In fact, I thought it was very telling because that's an issue, one differs, and one is not accepted by the Danes like that, right away....

This statement indicates how the converts think of themselves as Muslims as opposed to Danes. While some see themselves as having "emigrated" from Danish society as a result of their conversion, others designate themselves as "immigrants." The ironic consequence is that these converts, all of whom were born and raised in Denmark, end up categorizing themselves as "strangers" and thus as people who do not belong (Simmel 1950).

Others, however, insist on their Danishness. They seek to be conscious of the political definitions of the concept of culture and reject the discriminatory discourse on difference, a discourse that indicates an incompatibility between being Danish and being Muslim. Above all, they seek to separate culture from religion, pointing to their Danish identity as a national identity and to their Muslim identity as a religious identity. By doing so, they seek to universalize Muslim religious identity by defining Muslim identity as a religious identity (like being Christian) that anybody can practice, no matter what his or her national belonging. This way of universalizing Muslim identity serves as a strategy to include Islam in a Danish context. Furthermore, they maintain that since diversity already characterizes Danish culture and society, they reject any homogenous and exclusionary definition of "Danishness." One example is 38-year-old Yousef, who had been a Muslim for four years and who insisted on the heterogeneity of Danish identity:

> Well, of course I am still who I am. I have opted out of some things and chosen other things. But I still feel as Danish as I was before – except that there are things that I don't participate in, like some of the Danish Christian traditions. But that does not make me feel less Danish. I could just as well have become a Buddhist, I could have become a shaman sitting there and drumming my drum.... I am Danish and Muslim. Because my entire life is Denmark, I have just chosen another religion. I could also have become something else: a Hindu-Dane....

Converts' discourses about Danish culture express their position as the victims of a homogeneous and xenophobic discourse on Danishness. They either accept this discourse by interpreting their conversion as an act that excludes them from Danish society, or else they challenge the discourse by offering other, more heterogeneous and inclusive definitions of Danishness. The next part of this chapter explores their conversions from a micro-level perspective and goes further into their self-perceptions as converted Danish Muslims and their personal relationships with both other Muslims and their non-Muslim families.

Biographical narratives: "integrated"

Biographical interviews conducted during fieldwork yielded insights into the various individual stories of Danes who have converted to Islam. The following three stories of one female and two male converts, Aisha, Morten and Yousef, have been chosen because they illustrate the variety of people who have converted to Islam and the variations in gender, age, social background, ways of becoming Muslim, and patterns of interacting with Muslims. While a majority of converts are female, an increasing number of men are also converting. The three stories show how both gender and ethnicity conditions ways of relating to Muslims. The stories furthermore express different ways of being religious and of practising Danish and Muslim identities. Whereas the external categorizations of what it means to be a Muslim reflect one stereotype, these personal narratives illustrate the different meanings of Muslim identity to the converts.

Aisha

Aisha, 41, who used to be known by the common Danish name of Mette, unofficially changed her name when she converted to Islam fourteen years ago. She grew up in a small town in the north of Jutland[1] in a family of six siblings. Her father worked at the local railway station, and her mother was a housewife. After graduating from a vocational school, Aisha moved to a major town nearby, where she worked as an assistant in a bookshop. Eventually becoming unemployed, she signed up for various courses for the unemployed, including one on handicrafts for women. There she met an immigrant from Iran, who introduced Aisha to her family. Driven by both curiosity and a sense of adventure, Aisha started to visit this family regularly, which introduced her to Islam (albeit in another form than the Islam she practices today). Aisha converted to Islam when she was 27.

After three years as a Muslim, she was, as she describes it, "integrated, you may say, in that milieu, that community of Muslims." She was also very eager to get married, reasoning that what she needed to complete her religious practice was a Muslim husband.[2] It was not that she lacked suitors, but rather that she deeply wanted to find a man who was genuinely religious. Her choice of marriage partner was thus primarily influenced by her religious sensibilities. One day, when she was drinking coffee in a local cafeteria, she met her future husband, a Palestinian refugee. They were married fourteen days later. At that point, while Aisha had been a Muslim for two years, she was not fully practicing Islam. After her marriage she started to follow Muslim rituals such as the five daily prayers (*salah*), Ramadan, and wearing the veil (*hijab*) and Muslim dress (*jilbab*). She explains that her marriage fulfilled her identity as a Muslim.

Aisha and her husband started to live a traditional married life, with Aisha as a housewife and her husband going to work. Aisha describes her situation as a Muslim convert living in a small town in Jutland as "lonely." As she had heard about the vibrant Muslim milieus in Copenhagen, she persuaded her husband to relocate there. They moved into an apartment in Mjølnerparken, a social housing project in an immigrant neighborhood which has the reputation of being one of the most ghettoized neighborhoods in Denmark. Aisha was happy to live in a neighborhood with so many other Muslims. She gave birth to three boys and took care of the home. She also went to Islamic classes (together with other female Danish converts) at the local mosque, which was otherwise mostly frequented by Arab immigrants.

Aisha and her husband then started making plans to live for a year in his country of origin, Lebanon. This journey was motivated both by her husband's wish to return home and by Aisha's dream of living in a Muslim country, where she could live her religious identity to the full. Yet the stay in Lebanon turned out to be a disappointment: Aisha found the country "uncivilized," and she describes her experience in their new environment as a culture shock. Furthermore, her expectations of life in a Muslim country were not fulfilled. She found that her Palestinian relatives mixed Islam with "culture" and "customs" in ways that appeared rather "un-Islamic" to her; for example, the women wore Western clothes and make-up. Conversely, her in-laws thought that she was a fanatical Muslim. At Aisha's request, she and her husband returned to Denmark after only six months.

Morten

Morten, 22, has been a Muslim for four years. He comes from a religious Christian family and was born and raised on Funen,[3] in a social housing project in which many immigrant families lived. Morten said that he has "always been acquainted with Muslims," with whom he had established friendships from childhood. However, these Muslim friends did not come from particularly religious homes. They did not experience an awakening to Islam until their adolescence, and then it was to an Islam that had nothing in common with that of their parents. Morten and his friends had many discussions over the differences between Islam and Christianity, and Morten's subsequent conversion to Islam was a result of his theological reflections. At the time of his conversion, Morten was eighteen years old and was living in Copenhagen, where he was a student. Despite being accustomed to hanging out in immigrant milieus, Morten found it very difficult to go to mosques as nobody believed he was a Muslim – "because of my blond hair," he said. Consequently, instead of going to the *imam* in person, Morten became a convert through a telephone call to the *imam*, who witnessed Morten pronouncing the *shahada* in that way.

Morten neither signals his piety nor cares much about what is *halal* (allowed) or *haram* (forbidden) according to Islam. He enjoys being with his old (non-Muslim) friends and still participates in parties and nightlife. Nevertheless, he emphasizes that he does not drink alcohol. He also spends a lot of time with his Muslim friends, discussing their respective cultural prejudices. Morten regards himself as a "cultural translator." He has had several Muslim girlfriends, and has proposed to some of them in the Muslim way by negotiating with the girl and her family. But either the family or the girl had rejected his proposal each time because he "comes from a different culture." The same goes for his mother, who is also against the idea of being related to non-Western in-laws and is afraid that Morten will not "father Danish children," as she puts it. Like other Danish parents, she perceives Morten's conversion as a loss in many ways, in terms of both identity and future family relationships.

Yousef

Yousef, 38, was born in a small town in the north of Zealand.[4] Like Morten he comes from a strongly religious Christian family. When he graduated from high school he chose to study theology. He moved to Århus, the main city in Jutland, and while studying there volunteered to do social work with various Christian aid organizations. After finishing his studies he went to Copenhagen, where he continued doing social work. He was a bachelor with only a few friends and spent most of his time working. One evening, when watching TV and channel surfing, he found an Arabic channel that showed recitations from the Koran taking place in Mecca. For Yousef this was an extraordinary experience, and he watched the program for the next two hours: "Something happened, because I was stuck on the program without understanding a word of what was happening – only that it was fascinating." While Yousef had previously had no special knowledge about Islam, now his interest was aroused. After his first difficult attempts to find shops selling Islamic literature, he started to read the Koran and other books about Islamic theology. This experience made him question Christian theology. After some time, he started having recurrent dreams forcing him to make a religious choice. He chose to convert to Islam without ever having been inside a mosque. He went to see a Danish *imam*, to whom he pronounced the *shahada*: "And it was done within five minutes, we signed the papers, and then I was a Muslim, and then I biked home again. And then nothing really happened."

Yousef, now a Muslim, no longer saw any point in working for a Christian organization and quit his job. He told his parents about his conversion only after three months. His mother was particularly shocked. For his first two years as a Muslim, Yousef did not really practise his religion. He had no social relationships with Muslims, did not know where to find Muslim milieus, and did not want to be tied to any particular religious group. His particular problem was that most Muslim milieus were represented by certain ethnic groups: "I'm not an Arab, right?" Today, Yousef considers himself a practising Muslim, though he still does not frequent any particular Muslim community.

"I don't belong there"

The stories of Aisha and Morten show how social relationships with Muslims may be vital to the conversion process. Some become Muslims after marrying a Muslim. But, like Aisha, others convert to Islam first and take on a Muslim name before eventually marrying a Muslim. Converts like Aisha emphasize marriage as a necessary step, a marking of social and religious belonging which completes the conversion. By virtue of her marriage, Aisha was the most intimately related to Muslims of the three informants. The three cases show how gender conditions kinship relations, that is, patrilineal Muslim families accept converted women more easily than converted men.

The experiences of Aisha, Morten and Yousef illustrate that one does not become an immigrant (i.e. cease to be a Dane) merely by converting to Islam. They did not identify with immigrants just because they shared the same religion, nor did any of them become full members of Muslim communities. On the contrary, converts said that they often felt discriminated against by Muslim immigrants for not being "authentic" Muslims. Aisha often said that she felt excluded from the milieus of Muslim immigrants, whom she consistently called "the Arabs." This ethnic categorization expressed her own need to point out cultural differences and to distinguish herself from Muslim immigrants from the Middle East. Given her experiences of being a blond Dane among Muslim immigrants, she had already been exposed to the curious stares of "the Arab" women and had experienced being kept out of the social networks of "the Arabs." Morten's story also illustrates ethnic boundaries; his "culture" hindered him in marrying a Muslim women from a non-Western background.

Neither Aisha nor Morten were keen on becoming "one of them," not least because they thought that Muslim immigrants mixed religion and tradition, thus practising a form of Islam that these converts saw as "wrong." Stories about how converts rebuke Muslim immigrants for not being properly religious are common. Aisha's story shows that she was so critical of the religious practice of people who were born Muslims that her own Muslim in-laws regarded her as a religious fanatic.

In the interviews, converts often said that being a Muslim did not mean they were "Arabs", thereby rejecting any membership in the category "Muslim immigrant." "I don't belong there" was how Yousef described his first unhappy experiences of going to a mosque full of Arab immigrants. Yousef emphasized that he was regarded as a stranger because he was a "white Dane." He further pointed out that one does not change ethnic identity by converting from Christianity to Islam: "Because my entire life is Denmark, I have just chosen another religion."

The three stories illustrate the lack of natural connections or direct relations between belonging to a category such as "Muslim" and the group identification of "Muslims" (i.e. an internal collective definition based on members' reciprocal recognition of the categorization). The kind of community that others assume a convert to be part of is often imaginary. Converts do not necessarily share any sense of community with other Muslims, not even when it comes to sharing religious identity.

The creation of common social spaces

Just as people who convert to Islam cannot take having a social community with Muslims for granted, nor do they necessarily become radically different after their conversions. The stories of Aisha, Morten and Yousef show that converting to Islam has certain consequences, especially in their relationships with their non-Muslim families. All of them have maintained relationships with their families, yet their stories also illustrate that these relationships are neither wins nor losses. The public, politicized discourses that interpret the conversion as a radical process of leaving Danish identity behind affect the families' initial reactions to their children's conversions. Still, relations between parents and converted children continue, as life goes on.

One of the recurrent themes in converts' life stories is their concern with their families' reactions to the conversion. Telling one's family about the conversion is often fairly dramatic. While the conversion to Islam itself is an issue for the family, the real conflict starts when the son or daughter begins to practise the religion at home. This conflict peaks when the son or daughter begins to mark his or her Muslim identity in public, especially in the case of Danish women who start wearing the *hijab* (veil). It is these incidents of staging difference, not the conversion itself, that may result in families choosing to cut ties with the convert for a while. Still, family relationships are seldom permanently severed. The stories of Morten and Youssef illustrate that their families' reactions to their conversions were negative, yet the conversions did not lead to a permanent break. Both had grown up in strongly religious Christian families in which family discussions often revolved around theology and took place in a common space that dealt with being religious. Today, when Yousef's mother tries to see his choice of religion in a positive light, she often exclaims: "Well, if it can't be otherwise, I'm glad he did not join the Jehovah's Witnesses!"

Between parents and children, various positions between rupture and continuity are at issue. Eventually, parents and children usually reach a common recognition that they are the same persons that they have always been, and that their continuing interpersonal conflicts have simply taken another form. Although the parents may still wish that their child would stop being Muslim, this wish is directed at the external level, as an expressed concern for how the Danish environment will react to the conversion (as in "what will the neighbours say — or do?"). Converts and their families both engage in a process of negotiating the conditions for being together in a way that allows them to participate in each other's lives and thereby reach an understanding of each other's situations.

Aisha's mother, who is now in her seventies, often takes the four-hour journey from her home in Jutland to Aisha's home in Copenhagen and stays in her apartment in Mjølnerparken for several days. This journey takes her from the rural part of Denmark to urban Copenhagen — and into the ghettoized neighbourhood of Mjølnerparken, which is inhabited almost exclusively by non-Western immigrants. Aisha and her mother do not talk much about Aisha's religious identity. Yet one day Aisha happily told me that her mother went with her to the local mosque, and that she felt that she had "set the record straight" with her. Her mother thought the mosque a fine place and was relieved to find that Aisha frequented a "decent milieu over there in Copenhagen." During another visit, Aisha's mother suddenly asked her, "Who is *Allah*?" Aisha told her that *Allah* was God, something her mother did not know. Then they started to talk about Jesus, and Aisha explained that Muslims do not believe that Jesus is the Son of God, but rather that he is one of God's prophets. That made sense to her mother. Aisha was amazed at this sudden common understanding between them, achieved by means of a Muslim interpretation of Jesus.

These exchanges between Aisha and her mother reveal that the two managed to create a mutual understanding rooted in Aisha's life in Copenhagen. It implies that for Aisha's Jutlandic mother, the immigrant neighbourhoods of Nørrebro and Mjølnerparken and the local mosque constitute her image of Copenhagen. Her mother's way of experiencing Copenhagen as a site of Muslim culture illustrates how ways of connecting place and culture are multiple and depend on individual experience (cf. Olwig and Hastrup 1997).

The relationships between converts and their families were generally characterized by compromises and the discovery of common social spaces. Often the parents sought to participate actively in their children's Muslim lives, for example, by preparing *halal* food or giving them presents at *eid*, the Muslim feasts. Conversely, having become a Muslim did not prevent the converts from celebrating a Christian holiday like Christmas in the traditional Danish way. Some converts quite openly said that of course they celebrated Christmas "with presents and everything" with their non-Muslim family – some even ate pork on these occasions—and declared that Christmas was a national and cultural, not a religious holiday. Other converts thought that it was *haram* to speak about Christmas or use words or expressions related to it. Although Christmas in these cases was not spoken of, it often appeared that people still participated in the Christmas celebrations with their families in different ways, for example, by sharing in family lunches during the Christmas holidays or by spending Christmas Eve with the family on the condition that they ate *halal* meat. In that way, converts made quiet compromises with their non-Muslim family's wish to celebrate Christmas as a family.

Equally, the converts' own celebrations of the Muslim feasts were strongly marked by their Danish backgrounds. This was my experience when, during *Ramadan* in 2004, I participated in various *iftar*s, "breakfasts" that take place at sunset. The *iftar*s held in Aisha's home included mainly female Danish converts. The dishes that these women produced to break the fast were typically Danish food such as meat and fish pastries, steak, creamed potatoes and various kinds of Christmas goodies like rice pudding with almonds, *pebernødder* (cinnamon cookies) and *æbleskiver* (ball-shaped pancakes). While sitting around the table in the candlelight, the women spoke of coziness (*hygge*, an important Danish concept) and Christmas. This Muslim feast clearly reminded these women of Christmas. In that way, the sentiment that they created around their celebration of the Muslim ritual of *iftar* was related to their past and present celebrations of Christmas.

These examples illustrate how converts' practices of their new religious identities are characterized by continuity with the lives they led leading up to their conversions. Through her religiousness, Aisha cultivates values related to family life, values she grew up with and that she has emphasized throughout her life. For Morten and Yousef, their conversions to Islam appear to be related to their always having defined themselves as strong believers with strongly religious family backgrounds. Their conversions are developments of their already strong religious sensibilities.

In contrast to the public discourses that associate conversion to Islam with brainwashing and broken relationships, these personal stories show that, while conversion represents an identity change in some way, it involves continuity to rather than rupture with former relationships and practices.

Conclusion

This chapter has shown the importance of interpreting conversions to Islam in Denmark from different levels and perspectives that illustrate both public discourses and personal stories. The public, politicized discourses on immigration in Denmark construct a dichotomy between Muslim and Danish identities, which often involves xenophobic attitudes towards Muslims. This perspective inevitably creates an interpretation of Danes who convert to Islam as people who have alienated themselves from Danish identity and society, an interpretation which affects common Danes' general perceptions of converts. Converts are intensely aware of these external categorizations of them as Muslims. They react and position themselves differently to the external, stigmatizing categorizations, both rejecting and submitting to them.

The personal stories of converts illustrate how, in different ways, converts negotiate and unite their identities as "Danish" and "Muslim," thereby belying public stories claiming that they have left their Danishness behind. The stories of Aisha, Morten and Yousef reveal complex images of what the category "Muslim" may contain, and reject the idea that being part of a category necessarily implies being part of a certain community. Instead, by maintaining identities and relationships that existed before their conversions, Aisha, Morten and Yousef show that they have not "broken with" Danishness. Although their families are affected by the public discourses that interpret the conversion as a radical process of leaving Danish identity, relationships between parents and converted children continue. Converts, their close families and friends may all experience living in separate worlds. Still, they all seek to transcend these separations in their common efforts to create coherence by understanding each other. This takes place through the creation of common social spaces that result from being together and participating in each other's lives.

Converts like Aisha, Morten and Yousef have moved both socially and geographically between different milieus with different cultural codes and ways of being together, while maintaining their relationships with their origins and their families of origin. They exemplify what characterizes most human beings: that we enter into various relationships and cultivate different ways of belonging. They thus show that the polarization between Muslim and Danish identities does not last in the quiet integrations of lived lives (Pedersen and Rytter 2006). What the public debate interprets as a "rupture" – a Dane who converts to Islam – may even be interpreted as a quite contrary case of "integration." What is at stake at the personal level is the integration of the identity of the "Danish Muslim." At the social level what is at stake are interactions with different social actors and one's belonging to different worlds. Consequently, converts are figures who illustrate the heterogeneity and complexity of Danish culture. By doing so, they belie the public discourse that denies the existence of cultural diversity in Denmark.

Notes

1. Jutland is the western, continental part of Denmark, and is associated with the countryside.
2. Muslims generally acknowledge that marriage represents a fulfilment of Islam.
3. Funen is the second largest island in Denmark.
4. Zealand is the largest island in Denmark, where the capital, Copenhagen, is located.

References

Allievi, Stefano. 2006. The Shifting Significance of the *Halal/Haram* Frontier: Narratives on the *Hijab* and Other Issues. In *Women Embracing Islam: Gender and Conversion in the West*, ed. K. Van Nieuwkerk, 120-149. Austin: University of Texas Press.
Goul Andersen, Jørgen and Mette Tobiasen. 2002. Forhold mellem religioner og mellem etnisk og religiøs tolerance. In *Danskernes forhold til religionen – en afrapportering as ISSP 98,* ed. C. A. Larsen, 80-100. Aalborg: Uniprint Aalborg Universitet.
Hervik, Peter. 2003. Det danske fjendebillede. In *Islam i bevægelse*, ed. M. Sheikh et al., 181-198. Copenhagen: Akademisk Forlag.

Islamisk udsyn. 1979. Copenhagen: Islamisk Kulturcenter.
Jenkins, Richard.1996. *Social identity*. London: Routledge.
Jensen, Tina Gudrun. 2008. To be "Danish", becoming "Muslim": Contestations of National Identity? *Journal of Ethnic and Migration Studies* 34 (3): 389-409.
Jensen, Tina Gudrun and Kate Østergaard. 2007. *Nye muslimer i Danmark – møder og omvendelser*. Århus: Forlaget Univers.
Olwig, Karen Fog and Kirsten Hastrup. 1997. *Siting Culture: The Shifting Anthropological Object*. London: Routledge.
Pedersen, Marianne Holm and Mikkel Rytter. 2006. *Den stille integration*. Copenhagen: C.A. Reitzel.
Roald, Anne Sofie. 2004. *New Muslims in the European Context: The Experience of Scandinavian Converts*. Leiden: Brill.
Simmel, Georg. 1950. The Stranger. In *The Sociology of Georg Simmel*, ed. K. Wolff, 402-408. New York: Free Press.
Tobiasen, Mette. 2003. Danskernes verden var den samme efter 11.september: terror, islam og global solidaritet. In *Politisk forandring. Værdipolitik og nye skillelinjer ved folketingsvalget 2001*, ed. J. Goul Andersen og Borre, 347-362. Aarhus: Systime Academic.

Chapter Six

Contesting Danish Civility: The Cartoon Crisis as Transitional Drama

Heiko Henkel

In public debates in Denmark about the related themes of immigration and the place of Islam in Danish society, the cartoon affair stands out. More than any other conflict between established Danish society and the emerging Muslim minority, the cartoon crisis (in Denmark usually referred to as *Muhammedkrisen*) galvanized public attention and animated often acrimonious debates about the nature and limits of Danish civility. What was most obviously at stake in these debates was the question of whether *Jyllands-Posten* had the right or even the civic duty to publish the contested cartoons in defense of a particular view of "freedom of expression", or if – and in what way – the sensitivities of the Muslim minority (or a substantial section of it) should be recognized, so that *Jyllands-Posten* should withdraw the cartoons and apologize for their publication. At the same time, however, the contestations over whether the cartoons were simply a "normal" means of political debate or an outrageous act of defamation were also a debate over which ways of life, and the moral sensitivities tied to them, could count as properly Danish and thus qualify those adhering to them as belonging to Danish society proper.

Theorists of democratic citizenship like Taylor, Habermas and Honneth argue that the legitimacy of political power in democratic societies rests on the mutual recognition of state institutions and citizens within the framework of secular society.[1] The protracted and sometimes violent struggles for recognition (Honneth 1996) that have characterized European nation states since their inception have produced the institutional and discursive frameworks within which these struggles continue today. Large-scale immigration, like the waves of immigration that have led to the emergence of a Muslim minority in Denmark, generate an extra challenge in this respect. "Newcomers" often do not easily fit into the forms of civility that were established as legitimate in previous struggles, whether they find it difficult to be the kinds of citizens the majority society expects them to be, or whether they have demands on the state or their fellow citizens that are perceived as unreasonable. In this light, the cartoon crisis appears simply as one episode in an ongoing struggle for recognition in which the terms whereby Muslims residing in Denmark are recognized as legitimate citizens or residents of Danish society are negotiated, as well as the terms on which Muslims may recognize the demands of Danish majority society as legitimate. A closer look at the cartoon crisis illuminates some of the key issues that were, and continue to be, at stake for the various actors in the public contestations over the legitimate place of Muslims (and the Islamic tradition) in Danish society.

In his now classic formulation, the anthropologist Victor Turner (1974) has suggested that much of social interaction takes the form of *social dramas*. According to Turner, social interactions are dramas in the double sense that they form sequences of events that unfold in certain structured patterns over time, and that, rather than simply enacting given structural formations, the actors involved in social dramas perform and dramatize conflicting interests and positions with uncertain and sometimes surprising results. Examining the cartoon crisis can thus help us understand what social actors may accomplish through the critique of Islam on the one hand, and by foregrounding their indignation over the publication of the cartoons on the other. Taking its cues from Honneth and Turner, this chapter argues that the significance of the cartoon crisis can best be understood if we see it as a transitional drama in a struggle for recognition. What is at stake in this struggle are not only the legitimate claims and counterclaims that actors can make on each other in Danish society, but also the forms of identity that can mutually be recognized as "Danish." However, in the drama that unfolded around the publication of the cartoons, it was not only the relationship between Danish majority society and its Muslim minority that became redefined. At least as importantly, the relationship between various "Danish" actors was redefined. For instance, the public criticism of Islam has enabled tacit new alliances between the Danish nationalist right and the left in the wake of the cartoon affair. And finally, it has also helped Danes re-imagine themselves as Europeans in new ways, defining a particular communality with their German and Swedish neighbours (and old rivals) in contrast to practising Muslims near and far. In this performance of Danishness *as* Europeanness, a new emphasis on 'secularity" has come to play a central role. And it is in this dramatic performance of secularity that the Danish drama converges most strikingly with other European dramas currently being played out across the continent.

The Muhammad cartoons: local crisis, global alignments

On 30 September 2005, the Danish broadsheet newspaper *Jyllands-Posten* published the twelve now (in)famous "Muhammad cartoons" it had solicited from members of the Danish national association of cartoonists. In the following weeks and months, the publication of the cartoons became the object of heated condemnations by many Muslim associations and at public rallies and meetings. Numerous demands were made that *Jyllands-Posten* should withdraw the cartoons and apologize to "the Muslims." In response, *Jyllands-Posten*'s editor-in-chief insisted that he "would not dream" of withdrawing the cartoons or apologizing for their publication.[2]

It soon became clear that the publication of the cartoons had severely escalated the simmering conflict between major sections of the Danish public and Denmark's Muslim minority. Increasingly over the past decade, many Muslims, especially religious Muslims and their organizations, had begun to feel that Danish society and the state had failed to recognize fully what they saw as their legitimate demands. This non-recognition was felt in the widespread and often harsh criticism of religious Muslim practices, ranging from public condemnations of the Muslim headscarf as unsuitable for Danish society to the bureaucratic regulations that require Muslims to arrange burials through a pastor of the Danish *Folkekirke,* the Lutheran state church. It is most visible in the intensely negative representation of Muslims in the Danish media (Hervik 2002, Hussein 2000) and the almost ubiquitous display of suspicion towards practising Muslims since the September 11th attacks. The publication of the Muhammad cartoons, and the subsequent official and public support for *Jyllands-Posten*, were broadly perceived by Danish Muslims as a dramatically staged escalation of this non-recognition of Muslim residents of Denmark *as Muslims*. In the following weeks, the Danish media repeatedly reported threats against *Jyllands-Posten* and individual cartoonists that were, in turn, widely discussed and angrily condemned in the media and in everyday conversations. While many in the Muslim community were seriously outraged at the publication of the cartoons, the Danish majority public was seriously outraged at their outrage, a pattern that would continue to define the entire affair.

The cartoons themselves were varied in style and content. While some of the cartoonists interpreted *Jyllands-Posten*'s call to provide images of the prophet Muhammad by presenting more or less aggressive critiques of Islam through the use of heavily stereotyped images of a dangerous and misogynist Oriental, others appear to have sought to present non-confrontational drawings. In a self-reflexive move, one contributor submitted a representation of his own anxiety on the issue, and one of the drawings pokes fun at the newspaper's contest itself, though in a way that was not immediately recognized either by the newspaper or by its readers.[3] The twelve cartoons were presented together with a commentary by the journalist Fleming Rose, who explained that they had been initiated by *Jyllands-Posten* to challenge what he described as the creeping submission of the Danish public to illegitimate Muslim demands. Contrary to these Muslim demands, Rose argued, it was not only the right, but in fact the duty, of the press to disregard and challenge such religious sensitivities when Muslims sought to impose these concerns on society in general.

Already ten days after the cartoons' first publication, the affair had created an echo far beyond Denmark. On 10 October, al-Jazeera's Arabic-language website published an interview with a Denmark-based imam, Raed Hlayhel, in which he discussed the offensive cartoons and aired his anger at their publication. Many other reports and comments on al-Jazeera and on a wide range of news outlets in the Middle East and elsewhere were to follow.[4] The affair quickly developed into an international diplomatic crisis: on 12 October numerous ambassadors of Muslim-majority countries called on Prime Minister Fogh Rasmussen to take legal action against the cartoon's publication. Fogh Rasmussen not only refused to intervene, but refused to meet the ambassadors at all, and insisted that the government had no role in the dispute other than protecting the press's freedom of expression. Over the next weeks and months, the cartoons became the focal point of angry demonstrations in a number of Muslim-majority countries, condemning Denmark and the West. Most of these remained non-violent. However, in a number of incidents in Syria, Lebanon and Libya, for instance, violent clashes erupted with the security forces and dozens of people were killed, Danish embassies and consulates were torched and other buildings associated with Denmark attacked. Although protesters linked the violence to the Danish cartoons, in most of these incidents the organizers and their motives remained unclear.

As the protests against the cartoons spread around the globe and for months became a mainstay on the news the world over, the cartoon crisis also became a major topic in public debates in Europe and North America. While the public (with the exception of religious Muslim communities) almost unanimously dismissed Muslim claims of state intervention against their publication, the assessment of the cartoons was divided. While many supported their publication, and a number of European newspapers republished the cartoons in solidarity with the embattled *Jyllands-Posten*, many others worried that they would further worsen relationships with Muslims both within and outside Europe, which were already under strain from unresolved conflicts in Afghanistan, Iraq and Palestine and the ongoing controversy over the wearing of the Muslim headscarf in Europe.

In Denmark, a string of demonstrations by Muslim organizations condemning the cartoons (with sporadic threats of retaliation against *Jyllands-Posten*) on the one hand, and an outpouring of commentary in the media condemning Muslim protests on the other kept the affair at the centre of public debates throughout much of 2006. The debate became especially heated when in early 2006 it emerged that a number of Danish imams had travelled to the Middle East to seek active support for their protests against the cartoons" publication from the Muslim public, media organizations and governments. In the ensuing debate the imams claimed that they had been forced to shore up support from outside Denmark because the Danish state and the majority public had failed to respond to their legitimate demands to protect Danish Muslims from *Jyllands-Posten*'s defamatory publications. Almost unanimously, public commentary in Denmark denounced the move by the group of imams, seeing it as further proof that their allegiances were not with Danish society but with the Muslim world. The public and the media overwhelmingly supported the view that *Jyllands-Posten* was within its rights to publish the cartoons and that it had good reasons for doing so, and it condemned Muslim protests as an infringement of the right to free speech. A minority of commentators, among them the widely respected former foreign minister Ellemann-Jensen (like Fogh Rasmussen a member of the liberal-conservative Venstre party), criticized the cartoons' publication and the government's defiant stance. A poll from January 2006 shows that of those interviewed 54 per cent thought it was wrong of Fogh Rasmussen not to have met the eleven ambassadors. At the same time, 77 per cent were against Fogh Rasmussen issuing an apology, whereas thirteen per cent were in favour.[5]

In the course of 2006, the feeling of immediate crisis at the cartoons' publication slowly receded and was replaced by a more general discussion of the legitimate place of (religious) Muslims in Danish society. As in other European countries this debate is far from over, and the continuing profusion of news items pertaining to a wide range of problems associated with the presence of Muslims in Denmark (suspected political radicalism, problematic social practices linked to Islam, issues of delinquency linked to Muslim youth) indicates that the "Muslim problem" remains at the centre of the public consciousness in Denmark. Fortunately, the protests over the cartoons had not caused casualties on either side, either in Denmark or elsewhere in Europe, and thus the relationship between the major Muslim organizations in Denmark and the state never broke down entirely.

The dispute at the centre of the crisis, namely whether or not the publication of the cartoons was legitimate or not and whether the state had the duty to protect the Muslim minority from what many Muslims saw as a vicious attack on their religious identity, remained unresolved in the sense that no agreement or compromise was reached between the struggling parties. However, the issue was *de facto* resolved in *Jyllands-Posten*'s favour by the non-intervention of the government and the broad public support for *Jyllands-Posten*. Nevertheless, the process of negotiation and dialogue between Muslim organizations and Danish majority society continues, and has even gained a new sense of urgency and purpose since the crisis. While in many ways not much had changed, things were not quite like they were before either.

Before we turn in more detail to the conflict in Denmark, it is instructive to consider briefly the dynamics of the cartoon affair's international dimensions. Clearly, by travelling to the Middle East and actively soliciting support in their struggle with the Danish state and majority public, the imams had seriously escalated the dispute. Not only did they radically extend the stage on which they could voice their discontent, they also mobilized a transnational alliance that transformed the marginalized Danish Muslim minority into a formidable adversary. The enormous global echo of the affair shows that a "local" conflict over the publication of a number of cartoons in a nationally influential but internationally virtually unknown newspaper in 2005 was "legible" for a global audience This was so not in the sense that this global audience was necessarily able to understand the drawings" content fully (or were even likely to have seen them), nor the local context of the controversy.[6] But across the globe, many people evidently assumed that they understood the main aspects of the conflict well enough, and many felt sufficiently addressed by what seemed to be at stake that they felt compelled to mobilize – and to a considerable extent polarize – public opinion on a perhaps unprecedented scale.

Two factors are often mentioned to explain the enormous resonance of the cartoons with the Muslim public: (1) within Islamic traditions the representation of the prophet Muhammad is generally (although not uniformly) seen as prohibited by Islamic law; and (2) the cartoons constituted (and were meant as) a direct provocation of Muslim sensitivities.

While both are important factors, taken separately they are hardly enough to explain the reaction the cartoons provoked. After all, there is surely an almost infinite number of practices around the world that contradict Islamic legal reasoning, and provocative criticisms of Islam are evidently fairly common. However, the cartoons connected these two aspects in a particularly effective way, by some of them, anyway, not only depicting Muslims in a derogatory fashion, but also doing so in a highly stylized and recognizable manner by commenting on the most venerated figure in the Islamic tradition, the prophet Muhammad. The drawings thus became iconic in that they both represented Western non-recognition of Muslim sensibilities and dramatically performed this non-recognition. Once the Danish cartoons and their story had been taken up by the media in the Middle East and elsewhere, they could be mobilized to unite a usually fragmented Muslim public that was already fluent in the language of Muslim-Western antagonism.

If the Muhammad cartoons therefore presented the Danish imams with an almost perfect opportunity to mobilize a pan-Muslim public, the angry condemnation of the cartoons by religious Muslims also provided a potent rallying point for a broad range of critics of Islam. Not only did many observers in Europe, North America and elsewhere sympathize with the critical commentary the cartoons sought to make, the angry condemnation of the drawings, and especially the often perceived (and sometimes real) threats of violence related to these condemnations, exemplified to these commentators the problem they connected with Islam: its apparent intolerance. To show, in fact, to provoke this "intolerance" was, of course, the explicitly stated purpose of the cartoon's publication in the first place.

The indignation about the cartoons" publication and the criticisms of Muslim "intolerance" quickly created an opposition between "Muslims" and 'secularists" in the globalizing public, an opposition that was reinforced in the ensuing public debates in a process that the anthropologist Gregory Bateson (1958) described as *schismogenesis*. As is characteristic of schismogenetic processes, each side began to define the other in increasingly strong terms as its opposite, leading to a discursive constellation in which "Islam" became juxtaposed to "freedom of expression" and vice versa. The alignment produced by this schismogenetic process thus made plausible a particular dualistic imaginary within which people, despite their wide range of experiences and life-histories, could inscribe themselves into a simple dichotomy. The emergence of this global dichotomy, in its turn, enabled actors in the Danish conflict quickly to feel part of a much larger contest, extending solidarity along a line that divided those who felt offended by the cartoons and those who did not. Despite the apparent ability of the conflict to polarize public opinion on a global scale, however, much of the commentary around the world was actually markedly guarded. This was notably the case with the Anglo-American public, where the anger expressed by many European commentators found little echo.[7] The then British foreign minister, Jack Straw, for instance, known for his otherwise hawkish criticisms of political Islam, attacked the publication of the cartoons. Also notably guarded was the response of *Yeni Safak*, one of Turkey's most influential "Islamist" newspapers, which hedged its own criticism of the cartoons by citing a long list of prominent (non-Muslim) European critics of them.

In Denmark, the cartoons provoked not so much a single Muslim response but a cluster of responses. In spite of this diversity, two poles can be distinguished. For many Danish Muslims, the cartoons provoked an immediate and angry response as the news of their publications filtered through media outlets and the social networks connecting Muslims resident in Denmark. For others, the response was equally prompt and clear, as they defended *Jyllands-Posten*'s right to publish the cartoons in the name of freedom of expression. For many others, however, the publication of the cartoons provoked an often slow and reluctant, sometimes agonizing and contradictory response as they tried to weigh their conflicting impulses and alliances that impacted on their assessment of the stormy public dispute over the cartoons. One thing, however, was shared by virtually all those who lived in Denmark and who identified themselves as Muslims (or were identified as such by others), and which radically distinguished their position from the "international" contestation over the cartoons: as Muslims living in Denmark they were compelled to take – or rather, they had to find and modulate – a position in the hostile public contestation over the cartoons.[8] They had to declare *in which sense* they were Muslim in a public debate in which the very legitimacy of Muslim identity in Denmark was at stake. In other words, they had to show that as Muslims they could conform with a "Danish" way of life.

The terms of this challenge were not entirely transparent, however. Although throughout the cartoon crisis it often appeared as if Danish Muslims were facing the demands of a virtually united Danish majority public to demonstrate their Danishness, these demands contained different, even conflicting impulses. On the one hand, the demand for Muslims to demonstrate their Danishness often entailed a call for their assimilation to a particular ethno-national tradition. On the other hand, the reference to Danishness often referred not so much to a particular (Danish) national tradition, but to Danishness as a national variety of a more universal liberal model of society. Perhaps the most significant aspect of the cartoon affair was that it enabled these conflicting versions of Danishness to converge in their criticisms of Islam. To understand the emergence and significance of this hegemonic configuration better, we need to take a step back for a moment and consider the demand for "tolerance" as a central topic in contemporary public debates.

Two sides of "tolerance"

Across Europe, the intensified push towards globalization that followed the disintegration of the Warsaw Pact in 1989 provoked a renaissance of nationalist sentiments. In Eastern Europe, this renaissance was nourished by aspirations of nationalist movements to state power; in Western Europe, the major focal points of this renaissance were the emergence of new minorities through immigration and the challenges that increasingly pluricultural societies seemed to pose for the social cohesion of established nation states (Appadurai 1996; Beck 2000; Gingrich and Banks 2006). These debates often generate two opposing camps. On the one hand, there are those who emphasize the necessity for nation states (or ethnic groups aspiring to nationhood) to assert the primacy of one distinct "national culture" over other cultural traditions in society and to make this "national culture" the source of national identity, the normative basis of state legislation and of a national code of civility. On the other hand, critics of these neo-nationalist tendencies argue that liberal democracies must take their cultural plurality into account in order to maintain their democratic legitimacy and must not discriminate against and marginalize minority communities, whether these are long established or recently emerged through immigration in the name of defending what are in any case spurious "national values".

The public debate in Denmark about immigration and the legitimate place of "new" cultural traditions in Danish society is in many ways recognizable in these terms. Although the supposed threat to Danish society from immigration had been on the political agenda in Denmark since the 1970s, it had mostly been a fringe issue evoked by the populist right-wing *Fremskridtsparti* (the Progress Party). By the late 1990s, however, immigration had become a central topic in Danish political debates. Under the leadership of Pia Kjærsgård, the Progress Party morphed into the more successful *Dansk Folkeparti* (DF, Danish People's Party), which a sharpened nationalist profile and an agenda claiming to defend the interests of "ordinary" Danish people. Moreover, the then Prime Minister, Anders Fogh Rasmussen from the liberal-conservative *Venstre* party, had fought a successful and unusually aggressive campaign to oust the Social Democrat-led coalition government in 2001, central to which was the accusation that the Social Democratic government had been too lenient in its immigration policies. From 2001 to 2009, Fogh Rasmussen led a coalition government with the smaller *Konservative* party that depended for its majority in parliament on the support of Kjærsgård's *Dansk Folkeparti*.

In many ways, therefore, the conflict over the cartoons neatly fits into a trend in Danish society that Ulf Hedetoft (2003: 1) has described as the replacement of the "humanist" framework that underpinned earlier Danish approaches to immigration by a new "cultural absolutism." While he notes that the assimilationist discourse is nothing new, Hedetoft suggests that today it is accompanied by three elements that give it a new virulence: "its near-total hegemony; the assumed link between 'culture', 'cohesion' and 'social functionality' ... and the way in which this discourse has, on its own terms, started to assimilate and demote pluricultural discourses". As scholars of nationalism have often pointed out, the "cultural absolutism" of ethno-nationalism is not simply the reflection of strongly integrated societies but a product of what Arjun Appadurai has called "ethnic mobilization": the mobilization of nationalist discourses and forms of identity for the purpose of achieving and maintaining political power. Without doubt, Denmark's historical trajectory provides rich resources for the mobilization of such a nationalist discourse. In the second half of the twentieth century, Danish society emerged as a socially, culturally, and indeed ethnically unusually integrated society – if one chooses to look past the immigration of "new Danes" with a wide variety of cultural traditions since the 1960s.

A decisive moment for this process of integration is the year 1660, when King Frederik III, after a virtually lost war with neighbouring Sweden, disempowered the Danish landowning nobility, aligned himself with the emerging urban bourgeoisie and declared absolutism (*enevælde*) the official state form, thus giving the king and his cabinet direct administrative power over all citizens. The emergence of the characteristically strong Danish state over the next three centuries, with its centralized bureaucratic administration and an increasingly well-integrated society, coincided with the progressive loss of territory. As a nineteenth-century saying had it, what Denmark had outwardly lost was to be inwardly gained.

Among the many developments that contributed to the progressive integration of Danish society, three deserve particular mention. First, the privileged place of the Lutheran Protestant church as a state church (today known as *Folkekirke*, literally "The People's Church") has been a cornerstone of Denmark's constitutional order since 1848. Within this institutional framework, it was the Lutheran reform movement led by Nikolai Grundtvig (1783-1872), whose influence is still felt in Denmark today, that defined the central place of the *Folkekirke* in Danish society. Grundtvig turned the fostering of a combined Christian-national sentiment in *all* Danes (including the rural poor) into a national credo in Denmark. Secondly, the wide reach of Denmark's cooperative movement (*andelsforeninger*) contributed to the strong economic integration of Danish society. These cooperatives became crucial actors in Denmark's soaring agro-industry in the second half of the nineteenth and first half of the twentieth century. They were also central in shaping both Denmark's food retail business and the structure of its urban housing supply. Thirdly, while the early decades of the twentieth century had seen its share of divisive political conflict and polarization, the so-called *Kanslergade* agreement of 1933 laid the basis for a rapprochement between all the major social and political segments of Danish society. Politicians representing the working class, the bourgeoisie and the rural classes agreed on a political platform that centred on the creation of a social welfare state that was to benefit all social levels. This agreement pioneered a social model that was to be adopted by most western European states after World War II. On the basis of this social consensus, Danish society emerged as one that was exceptionally integrated politically, economically, socially and not least culturally. As Steffen Jöhnke points out elsewhere in this volume, the welfare state can be seen as an extraordinarily effective integration machine, one not designed in the first place for integrating "foreigners" but to forge successive generations of Danish citizens into proper Danes. The acquisition of a particular canon of civic virtues, of Danishness, is thus simultaneously the likely result of this historical process of integration and the precondition for being recognized as a proper citizen of Danish society.

In Denmark, as in many other European countries, debates concerning immigration have often been entangled with other debates about the plurality of social life. While conservatives tended to criticize both immigration and the emergence of "alternative life-styles" on the basis that public norms and values should be derived from an apparently inherited "national culture," others, who argued that society should reflect the plurality of people's inclinations, championed openness to "alternative" ways of life (like communal living arrangements, the use of 'soft drugs," the recognition of gay civic unions, radical ecological projects, etc.) and tended to champion the toleration of life-styles related to foreign cultural traditions. At least initially, the publication of the Muhammad cartoons and the crisis that followed seemed to mirror this constellation. It is significant that the cartoons were published in *Jyllands-Posten*, a conservative newspaper with a track record of calling for "tougher" immigration policies and worrying about the undermining of "Danish" values by immigrant communities apparently unwilling to "integrate" properly. And it was the government of Anders Fogh Rasmussen that fuelled the crisis by long refusing any kind of conciliatory gesture towards the Danish Muslim minority or the ambassadors who tried to intervene. But as the cartoon crisis unfolded, it quickly became clear that this opposition between an ethno-nationalist right and a multicultural left had lost much of its meaning in Danish political debates and that it hardly helped to explain the lines drawn up in the conflict. In fact the two camps seemed to have merged into one, and "all of a sudden" a new political constellation had emerged: on the one hand, Denmark's Muslim minority, and on the other a broad majority of the Danish public, defined by its criticisms of the Muslim minority. While this Muslim minority was defined by its indignation over the cartoons (on various grounds), the Danish majority public demanded that Danish Muslims put up with the offensive cartoons and sharply criticized them for refusing to do so. In other words, while previously the demand for "tolerance" was primarily directed towards "illiberal" tendencies within Danish (or German, Dutch, etc.) society, now it was directed towards the Muslim minority. Whereas previously the demand for tolerance demarcated a space of possibility, it now described a *conditio sine qua non* to be fulfilled by those who are not seen as being fully qualified to be members of Danish society.

As Wendy Brown (2006) has pointed out, in recent years the concept of "tolerance" has been central to public debates in Euro-American societies. While "tolerance" has also been an important concept in liberal social theory, over the past decade or so it has emerged as central in a broad range of discourses and policies that seek to regulate civic conduct within Euro-American societies, as well as to legitimize political and military interventions outside the territories of these societies. Brown notes that almost all political projects within these societies now claim to be "tolerant," although disagreements over the degrees and modalities of tolerance certainly persist. Drawing on the work of Michel Foucault, Brown suggests that current discourses and practices of "tolerance" can best be understood as examples of "governmentality," that is, the assemblage of concepts, rules and practices that define and modulate the modes of legitimate practice of the inhabitants of liberal societies. Brown argues that, just as in Foucault's classic formulation, the concepts and practices of "tolerance" have become a "conduct of conduct" in the sense that, without providing an overt and rigid set of rules, they regulate the actor's opportunities, as well as what restricts him or her. As Brown and also Saba Mahmood (2006) point out, religious Muslims in particular have become objects of this new concern for "tolerance", as they are widely perceived as posing a particular problem for the regime of tolerance in liberal societies.

How seamlessly "humanist" and "nationalist" criticisms of Islam can go together becomes clearer if we look, as an example, at the comments of the Danish politician Villy Søvndal in 2008.[9] The remarks made in his official blog and a subsequent interview were Søvndal's response to a rally by Danish Muslims voicing their discontent with the renewed publication of some of the cartoons in the Danish press. This, in turn, had happened as a response to the apparent last-minute uncovering of a murder plot against one of the original cartoonists a week earlier. The police operation was widely publicized by the security services and hailed in the press, but it quickly became apparent that, despite lengthy observations, the security services had very little evidence to substantiate their dramatic allegations. Indeed, the case against the accused had to be dropped: one of the accused, who had acquired Danish citizenship, was freed shortly afterwards, while the two others, who had acquired permanent residence, were to be deported without a judicial hearing. At the time of writing, one of them has left Denmark, while the case of the other is still pending.

Søvndal is the leader of Denmark's *Socialistisk Folkeparti* (SF, Socialist People's Party), which, with a "progressive" and explicitly multicultural political platform, gained 12% of the vote in the last elections. At the same time, leading members of the party have been highly critical of Muslim organizations in Denmark, not least their stance in the cartoon crisis. Søvndal's comments are framed as a strong criticism of Hizb ut-Tahrir (HT), a group with branches in many countries known for its provocatively confrontational (if non-militant) critique of liberal society, and its project to establish a new "Kalifat." There is thus nothing surprising in Søvndal's dismay with the group, and Søvndal correctly points out that it represents only a fraction of Muslims in Denmark. What makes Søvndal's comments relevant for this discussion, however, is that his criticism critique of HT becomes the conduit through which he sketches the contours of the conflict surrounding the Muslim presence in Denmark more generally.

From the outset, Søvndal's criticism has been two-pronged, directed both at HT and at all those who do not distance themselves explicitly (enough) from HT. Søvndal singles out a leading member of *Islamisk Trossamfund* ("Islamic Congregation," the largest Muslim association in

Denmark, with a longstanding record of accommodation with the Danish legal system), who had joined members of HT in demonstrating against the renewed publication of the cartoons. Having established a chain of associations between HT, Islamisk Trossamfund (IT) and all those who feel offended by the publication of the cartoons, Søvndal then draws a line between what is proper to Danish society and what extends beyond its limits and thus cannot be part of an inner-Danish political debate or indeed of Danish society proper. Those holding these "fundamentalist" views, Søvndal suggests, should therefore go elsewhere (presumably to the Middle East), where their medieval views would be welcomed. (It should be added, perhaps, that it is not immediately clear which Middle Eastern regime would welcome the political demands voiced by HT.) For Søvndal and critics like him, Muslims associated with "fundamentalist" Islam are thus in a position that is categorically different from that of other political opponents, say, supporters of the Danish People's Party: while the latter can be politically engaged with, the former are beyond the pale of political debate.

Søvndal's comments indicate some of the challenges that practising Muslims especially face in the current debate about Islam in Euro-American society. In the polemical polarization between "we Danes" and "those fundamentalists", there is little place for those who wish to register their dismay with the publications of the cartoons and/or their association with the mainstream of Islamic traditions, and yet also claim to belong to Danish society. This is emphasized in a passage where Søvndal criticizes Birthe Rønn Hornbech, Minister for Integration and Church Affairs, for her public offer to meet with a representative of IT. Undeterred by the fact that IT is the biggest Muslim organization in Denmark and has agenda record of interpreting Islam within the Danish legal framework and of explicitly aiming to be compatible with liberal society, Søvndal suggests that such a meeting would give undue legitimacy to fundamentalist organizations that lack democratic legitimacy but still claim to represent Muslims.

As Minister for Integration and Church Affairs, Hornbech is both responsible for the administrative leadership of the *Folkekirke* and for overseeing other religious traditions in Denmark. By assailing Hornbech for her public offer to meet with a representative of IT, Søvndal presents us with a candid reading of the state of Danish secularism: clearly, in his reading, religious traditions are not to be treated equally in Denmark. While we can assume that Søvndal has no qualms about Hornbech meeting representatives of the Folkekirke (in fact, as minister she is the church's chief representative), in his view the largest Danish Muslim organization is unfit to be met by the minister of religious affairs. Søvndal's position reflects a political configuration in Denmark in which the *Folkekirke* is an accepted part of a broadly hegemonic social consensus, whereas Muslim religious organizations are not.

Some commentators were quick to point out that Søvndal's position converged with the rhetoric of Denmark's other "people's party," the chauvinist *Dansk Folkeparti*, which routinely argues that Muslims are alien to Danish culture and society. Perhaps, it was suggested, Søvndal's comments even constituted an attempt to reach out to its voters. My point here is not to suggest that Søvndal's comments were intended to signal a divergence from SF's traditional support for cultural pluralism in Denmark in favour of joining DF's xenophobic political platform. However, the criticism of Muslim protests over the publication of the Muhammad cartoons allows commentators such as Søvndal to expand their criticism of a particularly provocative "fundamentalist" group to mainstream Muslim organizations in a casual manner, and to establish in the name of Danishness a tacit alliance across the political divisions in Danish society on the grounds of a shared outrage over the un-Danish demands of Muslim political activists. The critique of Islam has become an avenue through which a particular inner-Danish, and indeed inner-European communality and solidarity can be claimed and, at least rhetorically, established.

Conclusion

As with other struggles for recognition, the conflict over the legitimate place of Muslims and their alliance with the Islamic tradition in contemporary Denmark is no one-sided affair. While Danish civil society and the state seek to define the conditions on which Muslims and other new Danes are accepted as fellow citizens (whether with or without formal citizenship), in their turn Muslims residing in Denmark are vying to carve out such spaces in terms acceptable to them. Of course, neither side is itself homogenous but contains groups and individual actors with diverse and often conflicting interests and demands. And, as Honneth (1995) suggests, all actors in struggles for recognition are likely to be transformed in these contestations in often unforeseeable ways.

As citizens or residents, Muslims in Denmark have the same legal, political and social rights (to use the classical typology developed by T. H. Marshall (1964)) as other Danish citizens and residents. Nevertheless, many Muslims in Denmark, especially practising Muslims, have long felt that Danish society does not properly recognize them *as Muslims*, thus denying them a central aspect of their identity. To put it in Habermasian terms, it could be argued that, in the Danish debate over the legitimate role of Islam in society, the Danish majority public fails to separate its own cultural tradition from Denmark's political culture. Whereas the former is rooted in a particular historical experience shared only by this majority society, the latter must be negotiated between all citizens. According to Habermas, this distinction between the cultural tradition of a majority society and a country's political culture is the structural condition for democratic society under pluricultural conditions.[10]

Whether or not this is the case or whether it is the Muslim side that is seeking to universalize its own particular cultural tradition continues to be disputed. Whatever the truth of this, in the current situation Muslims in Denmark too have a wide range of possibilities for pursuing their claims to recognition. One avenue is for Muslims to embrace the mainstream version of "Danishness" and to downplay or abandon links to the Islamic tradition. Another avenue, pursued by many religious Muslims in Denmark, is the ongoing construction of networks and associations that provide the infrastructure for Islamic forms of discourse and practice, as well as making use of the space provided by legal, political and social rights to project Muslim forms of life into Danish society. In the dispute over the cartoons, moreover, religious and non-religious Muslims often had the opportunity to have their views heard in the media, if seldom to the same extent as critics of Islam. Most dramatically, they were able to extend the stage on which the debate over the legitimacy of the cartoons took place. This strategy proved extraordinarily effective, even though it carried both costs and benefits. As the chorus of Muslim protests grew louder, and especially when embassies were torched and people died in clashes with the security forces, when Danish firms became the target of consumer boycotts and when Danes at home and abroad found themselves the targets of anger and potentially of violence, many Danes saw their suspicions of religious Muslims confirmed. At the same time, the dramatic show of solidarity by Muslim public opinion, and not least the spectre of violence, suddenly made the Danish Muslim minority appear as a very serious adversary that could hardly be ignored. After all, as Honneth also points out, in many struggles for recognition majority publics have historically extended recognition to minorities in exchange for social peace.

Danish society (the state as well as civil society) responded to the escalating conflict strategy in a complex way. Muslims became the object of an intense process of "securitization" (Buzan, Wæver, and de Wilde 1998) and often exceedingly polemical criticisms by pundits and politicians. At the same time, both the state and civil society actors put forward a wide range of offers for dialogue that held out the promise of working towards a recognition of Muslim demands. To use again Victor Turner's model of the social drama: after an agonizing period of crisis, during which the very foundations of coexistence between Danish mainstream society and the Muslim minority were brought into question, during 2006 this coexistence found a new (albeit preliminary) equilibrium. In the end, Danish Muslims accepted, albeit grudgingly, the publication of the cartoons; and the Danish public accepted, equally grudgingly, Muslim discontent with them.

But if the Muslim struggle for recognition in Denmark is not one-sided, it is clearly uneven. Muslims in Denmark are a politically marginal minority and therefore have little influence on the enormously powerful institutions that regulate modern societies. Further, the dispute over the legitimate role of the Islamic tradition in Denmark has evolved in such a way that certain Muslim demands, such as the request for the government to censure the publication of the Muhammad cartoons, appear to many Danes to challenge the very foundations of Danish society, and indeed of liberal society more generally. Countering these demands has thus emerged as the passionately held project of a wide range of political actors in Denmark and other Euro-American societies. Moreover, as I have tried to show, the critique of Islam has acquired a positive, solidarity-inducing aspect in which the cohesion of Danish society is experienced and reinforced. There is, in other words, a "speaker's benefit" connected to the critique in the demarcation and enactment of community through a sharp drawing of the limits of solidarity and belonging. As I have noted, something similar holds true for Muslim critics of Denmark across the world, who experience common bonds across other divisions in their condemnation of the cartoons and those who support them. But if – as surely they must to pursue a future life for themselves and their children in Denmark as (practising) Muslim citizens – they maintain ties *both* to the Islamic tradition *and* seek to be recognized as legitimate members of Danish society by the Danish state and majority public, Muslims in Denmark face a painful dilemma.

If, as I have tried to show, the demand for "tolerance" articulates as a shorthand the demand to comply with a particular, historically emerging form of civility, as both proponents and critics of liberal society seem to agree,[11] the question is whether these demands are formulated in terms of "ethnic" citizenship, thus requiring assimilation to a particular cultural tradition, or in terms of republican citizenship, thus opening up the possibility of a process of the incorporation of new cultural traditions into a pluricultural context. Or perhaps, as the Danish case suggests, we should rather ask whether these conflicting notions of citizenship can be sufficiently disentangled so as to offer aspirant members of society the possibility of becoming members of that society without denying their own sense of historical experience and identity.

The question, in other words, is whether Danes and Muslim residents of Denmark will find a formula in which they can recognize each other's demands. What is called for is thus nothing less, but also nothing more, than an update of the *Kanslergade* agreement of 1933 in which the major sections of Danish society worked out a framework within which their mutual demands were recognized for decades to come. In the absence of this, both Danish majority society and Muslim new Danes are likely to face considerable challenges in the future. If Danishness is not expanded to incorporate hyphenated identities such as Muslim-Danes (similar to Muslim-American), it is difficult to see how the antagonism between the Danish majority and the Muslim minority can be overcome, with obvious repercussions for the life chances of Danish Muslims and for social peace and security in Danish society.

Moreover, the enormous pressure on Muslim minorities to conform to narrowly defined versions of secularity is in danger of undermining the very foundations on which Danish society (like other contemporary Euro-American societies) claims to build its moral superiority: a liberal constitution that grants every citizen the same opportunities to pursue his or her life project. In his blog, for instance, Søvndal criticizes the continuing discrimination against Muslims in Denmark. But in his commentary on the second cartoon affair, not even in passing does he engage with the problematic conduct of the Danish state in its handling of the alleged murder plot, which overruled established legal safeguards by referring to the allegedly exceptional danger posed by Muslim militancy. It is difficult not to be reminded here of the figure of *homo sacer*, used by the Italian philosopher Giorgio Agamben (1998), to draw attention to the common recourse of modern states to a "rule of exception" in order to justify the suspension of legal norms in relation to certain groups. Although the claims touted by the security forces, the government and an endless stream of public commentators were never confirmed, the suspects remained in custody, apparently both beyond the rules of due process and even the residual sympathy of the public. The accusation that he was a Muslim terrorist made the released suspect quite literally an outcast in Danish society, the sad centrepiece of a public spectacle in which the authorities demonstrated the extent to which they were prepared to claim a state of emergency that allowed them to circumvent due legal process. As Hannah Arendt (1951) has famously noted, rather than following on from universal human rights, access to civic rights is in fact the precondition for human rights to become meaningful. The disconcerting ease with which the Danish government and large sections of the public are prepared to suspend long-established legal safeguards in dealing with those associated with Muslim militancy can only be explained, it seems to me, against the background of the dramatically staged suspicion that religious Muslims – both within and without – represent the very opposite of Danish civility.

Notes

An earlier version of this paper was originally published in Human Architecture (vol. VIII, issue 4, Fall 2010) under the title "Fundamentally Danish?" This is an updated and revised version.

1. Honneth 1996; see also Taylor 1994; Habermas 1994.
2. Carsten Juste, quoted on Danish TV2's news website of October 9th 2005. (http://web.archive.org/web/20060215191239/http://nyhederne.tv2.dk/article/2986 433/Muslimer_Avis_skal_sige_undskyld.html)
3. Lars Refn's drawing shows a Danish schoolboy named Muhammed in front of a blackboard covered with Arabic script. The boy with his curly black hair wears a football shirt of a club called Fremtiden (the Future) and teasingly sticks his tongue out at us. The note on the blackboard behind him says, in Farsi, "The Journalists of Jyllands-Posten are a bunch of reactionary provocateurs".
4. Al-Jazeera's English-language website provides an easily accessible overview over Middle Eastern perceptions of the controversy, while http://da.wikipedia.org provides a useful chronology over the events from October 2005 to February 2006.
5. Percentages according to a Vilstrup poll cited in the newspaper Politiken, 30 January 2006.
6. To my knowledge, there have as yet been no studies of the perception of the cartoons in the Middle East.
7. "US, British media tread carefully in cartoon furor", Christian Science Monitor, 2 June 2006.
8. For a compelling compilation of responses by Danish Muslims (in Danish), see Fole Kaarsholm (2006).
9. Information, 21 February 2008.
10. Habermas (1998: 105ff.).
11. The most prominent of those I have in mind are Jürgen Habermas, Axel Honneth, Charles Taylor, Sheila Benhabib, Talal Asad and Wendy Brown.

References

Agamben, Giorgio. 1998. *Homo sacer: sovereign power and bare life*. Stanford, Calif.: Stanford University Press.

Appadurai, Arjun. 1996. *Modernity at large: cultural dimensions of globalization*. Minneapolis, Minn.: University of Minnesota Press.

Arendt, Hannah. 1951. *The origins of totalitarianism*. New York: Harcourt.

Bateson, Gregory. 1980. *Naven*. Stanford, Calif.: Stanford University Press.

Beck, Ulrich. 2000. *What is globalization?* Cambridge: Polity Press.

Brown, Wendy. 2006. *Regulating Aversion: Tolerance in the Age of Empire and Identity*. Princeton: Princeton University Press.

Buzan, Barry, Ole Waever, and Jaap De Wilde. 1998. *Security: A New Framework for Analysis*. Boulder, Co.: Lynne Reiner Publishers.

Gingrich, Andre and Marcus Banks. 2006. *Neo-Nationalism in Europe and beyond*. Oxford: Berghahn Books.

Habermas, Jürgen. 1994. Struggles for Recognition in the Democratic Constitutional State. In *Multiculturalism,* ed. C. Taylor, 107-148. Princeton: Princeton University Press.

—. 1998. *The inclusion of the Other*. Cambridge, Mass.: MIT Press.

Hedetoft, Ulf. 2003. 'Cultural transformation': how Denmark faces immigration. *Open Democracy* web journal (http://www.opendemocracy.net/ accessed 30 October, 2003).

Hervik, Peter. 2002. *Mediernes muslimer*. Copenhagen: Nævnet for Etnisk Ligestilling.

Honneth, Axel. 1995. *The struggle for recognition: the moral grammar of social conflicts*. Cambridge: Polity Press.

Hussein, Mustafa. 2000. Islam, Media and Minorities in Denmark. *Current Sociology* 48 (4): 95-116.

Mahmood, Saba. 2006. *Politics of Piety*. Princeton: Princeton University Press.

Marshall, T. H. 1964. *Class, citizenship, and social development*. Garden City, N.Y.: Doubleday and Company, Inc.

Taylor, Charles. 1994. The Politics of Recognition'. In *Multiculturalism,* ed. C. Taylor, 25-74. Princeton: Princeton University Press.

Turner, Victor. 1974. *Dramas, Fields, and Metaphors: Symbolic action in human society*. Ithaca: Cornell University Press

PART II

INCLUSION AND EXCLUSION IN THE WELFARE SOCIETY

Chapter Seven

Day-Care in Denmark: The Key to Social Integration

Helle Bundgaard

This chapter explores central notions of appropriate social behavior in what is arguably the most important institution in Denmark when it comes to social integration, namely day-care, also known as pre-school.[1]

Moral values guiding everyday practices are generally taken for granted. When interacting with ethnic minority children and their parents, however, staff are occasionally forced to make explicit the reasoning behind their actions. A focus on the interaction of ethnic minority children and their parents in day-care centres therefore provides insights into the cultural beliefs and values which structure daily socialization practices in a Danish day-care, and by implication in Danish society.

Using a narrative approach, this chapter presents an experience-near analysis of incidents related to the introduction of an ethnic minority child to a Danish day-care institution. The chapter focuses on dominant conceptions in relation to, first, whether it is appropriate to give children responsibility for looking after other children and, secondly, the extent to which the institution can draw on family relations. The analysis shows that distinct conceptions of the independence and responsibility of children are at play and discusses what consequences this has for the process of *settling in*. It will be seen that misunderstandings and gaps in communication arise because of well-established but unspoken conceptions of the role of parents in a day-care and what children are able to and, not least, allowed to do in relation to other people.[2]

The chapter is based on six months of ethnographic fieldwork carried out in 2002-3 amongst people of different social and cultural backgrounds in an area of Zealand with both social housing and single-family houses (see Bundgaard and Gulløv 2008).[3] The author carried out participant observation in the local area and within the institutional setting. Observations of actions and interactions were used as a point of departure in formal interviews with staff and parents in their homes, as well as in more informal discussions centered on perceptions of day-care at any suitable occasion.

The social institution of day-care

The majority of parents in Denmark work full-time even when their children are very young. This is reflected in the fact that 96 percent of all children between three and five attend day-care (Statistisk Årbog 2007: 162). Day-care institutions are part of a system of non-compulsory, early childhood programs, which include *vuggestuer* (nurseries) for children from six months to the age of three, and *børnehaver* (pre-schools or kindergartens) for children between the ages of three and six or seven, when compulsory school begins. Children younger than six thus spend between five and eleven hours a day in institutions (Winther 1999), where professional staff are responsible for care and for arranging activities in line with educational goals. Young children spend the major part of their day, five days a week, in day-care, where they learn to argue for their wants and interact with other children in socially acceptable ways – crucial skills for citizens in a welfare society. Moreover, they are trained in verbalizing their feelings (*sætte ord på sine følelser*). Children as young as three are expected to explain what they feel about things: "I can see that you are angry, but it makes me sad when you hit me." It is not only children, however, but also their parents who learn or are reminded what is considered appropriate. Parents are encouraged to ask staff for advice regarding matters of upbringing, while for their part staff are obliged to address problems considered potentially harmful to the child.

In Denmark day-care thus plays a crucial role in the organization of family life and in shaping future citizens. This is particularly evident when it comes to low-income families and families with immigrant backgrounds. Despite the fact that the former might be on unemployment benefit or social welfare and therefore not in obvious need of child-care facilities for their children, they will often be offered a place in a day-care institution free of charge to ensure that their children receive social stimulus. This is thought to be crucial if children are to stand a chance breaking their supposedly negative social heritages. When it comes to immigrant families, visiting nurses employed by the municipality often advise parents to sign up their children for day-care so that they can become exposed to Danish social norms and cultural values and the Danish language.[4] It is commonly agreed that immigrant children should attend day-care sooner rather than later, and it is considered preferable if they are enrolled when they are between six and eighteen months old.

Day-care institutions have been part of Danish society since the eighteenth century. The first *asylum* opened as early as 1828, targeting children from the lower classes whose parents were working. The first kindergarten opened in 1871, inspired by the German pedagogue Friedrich Fröbel (see Sigsgaard 1978). In contrast to the earlier asylums, which were characterized by severe discipline (Coninck-Smith 1995: 10-11), kindergartens offered stimulation through play to children from wealthy families (Gulløv, in press). In 1919 the Danish state passed a law granting economic support to day-care institutions (Borchorst 2005: 133-146 in Gulløv in press) and thus became involved in the care of children, an involvement which has increased significantly since then.

Until the 1960s day-care institutions were not widespread, but with the entry of women (including mothers) into the labour market this changed radically. The number of day-care institutions increased markedly, and they have become a decisive element in the organization of the Danish welfare society (Gulløv, in press). The second part of the twentieth century thus saw an increasing professionalization of children's upbringing in Denmark (ibid.).

Towards individual emancipation

Although it is not possible to discuss developments in pedagogy in detail here (see Sigsgaard 1978; Vejleskov 1997), a few words on the subject are necessary. In the middle of the twentieth century, progressive education changed patterns of upbringing at home and in school in the direction of less authoritarian practices (see Hermann 2007 for a detailed analysis of the development of progressive education in Denmark). Strict discipline was thought to result in orthodoxy and passivity, attributes which were not in demand when constructing a welfare society. The values of emancipation and independence continued to play an important role up through the last part of the twentieth century. In the 1990s, this was reflected in the reception of Jesper Juul's book *Dit komptente barn* (*Your competent child*) (Juul 1995), who argued for the importance of acknowledging that generally children will behave in a competent manner if only adults let them.

Since until quite recently the main purpose of activities in day-care was to increase the social awareness of children, the focus was on behaviour rather than a set curriculum. This is gradually changing as neo-liberal policies leave their traces in day-care institutions too (see Gulløv in press for a discussion of recent changes). In the first decade of the new century, a tendency towards increasing state intervention when it comes to determining matters of content in day-care activities can thus be seen. Nevertheless, compared to day-care abroad (see Tobin, Wu and Davidson 1989; Connolly 1998), day-care in Denmark can still be said to be influenced by the post-60s ideology of emancipation and self-determination. To a large extent children are still free to decide how they want to spend the majority of their day. Adults might decide whether children should be indoors or outdoors, but otherwise it is for the children to decide what they want to do. Adults will not introduce activities during what is known as *free play*. *Free play* might involve anything from swinging to cycling, from playing a board game to building a house of mud or Lego, or dressing up or throwing pillows at each other, just to mention a few popular activities.

It is, however, a guarded freedom, a protected existence in which the problems of this world and related responsibilities are classified as belonging to the world of adults. As this chapter shows, this understanding occasionally causes problems, not least for ethnic minority parents, some of whom have different notions of what one can expect from children in relation to their fellow human beings.

Between two worlds

Amina snuggled up to her mother, holding on to her ankle-length coat.[5] It was her third day in the day-care. Her mother, Kirdan, spoke quietly to her daughter, attempting to encourage her into the classroom, but her little body stiffened and she clung on to her mother's legs. When Kirdan gently pressed her daughter, she began to cry in earnest. For the first three years of her life Amina had been at home, but now she had to join a world in which the majority spoke a language she did not understand. From an institutional point of view, Amina would have been better off starting her institutional career earlier in life.

Kirdan chose to sit in the front hall, hoping that her daughter would quieten down. She stroked her hair and spoke soothingly to her. Occasionally the day-care assistant, Anne Mette, entered the front hall, indicating with increasing frustration that they should join the group in the classroom, but Amina refused to move. With a gesture of rejection, Kirdan signalled that the two of them needed peace. But Anne Mette soon returned to say that Kirdan had to make a decision: either she must bid farewell and leave Amina there or take her home. Kirdan responded by saying, "I do not understand." To Kirdan's relief, Amina's cousin, Fakhri, passed by while Anne Mette was speaking. Kirdan got hold of him and asked him to look after Amina during her day in the day-care. Fakhri, who was two years older than Amina, took her hand and guided her into the classroom. Amina briefly turned to look at her mother but accepted the situation. Shortly afterwards, Kirdan left the institution.

Settling in as praxis

In a Danish day-care institution, *settling in* is a central concept. First-time parents of a child starting in day-care will only have a vague idea of what the concept entails, whereas parents who have to help their third child *settle in* will be very familiar with what is required. The process of *settling in* is influenced by the institutional framework, including the number of staff. However, the degree of success is mainly understood to be related to the parents' ability to *settle in* their child and their willingness to assume the responsibility for doing so. Staff will generally expect that one parent spends some days in the institution together with the child and then gradually, as the child grows more comfortable (*er blevet trygt*) with its surroundings, to let her cope (*stå på egne ben*, literally, "stand on her own legs"). This is no easy task, as any parent who has experienced the process will know. One has to strike a balance between on the one hand being present and ready to help one's child, and on the other hand keeping a distance and not interfering without reason, in order to encourage the child be part of the social life of the institution. *Settling in* a child gives the parents an opportunity to acquire an impression of everyday life in the institution as well as of the staff. At the same time, the staff observe parents in order to decode "signs of care" (Thorne 2001: 368ff.), or in other words their competence as parents. Have they "cut the umbilical cord" (*klippet navlestrengen*)? Are they capable of "saying no" (*sige fra*)? Do they take upon themselves their responsibilities in an appropriate manner? These are the kinds of evaluations to which parents are subjected and which, among other things, indicate that institutions are guided by a dominant set of norms of behaviour (Bundgaard 2004).

There is a conception that a successful institutional stay depends upon close collaboration between the parents and the staff of the institution. In principle, parents have the main responsibility for the well-being of their children, although the staff have the responsibility for care while the child is attending day-care. Three weeks before Amina started day-care, her father spoke with the day-care teacher responsible for the group of children she was going to join. However, the gist of their conversation was never relayed to the assistant who took over during the summer vacation, nor, it seems, to Amina's mother. Kirdan did not give the impression of being familiar with the expectations of the staff and seemed at a loss and uncertain of her role.[6] As mentioned earlier, Kirdan stayed in the front hall with Amina and thus did not strike an appropriate balance between closeness and distance. This was noticed by staff, who felt that she did not perform well when it came to *settling* Amina *in*. For weeks, Kirdan sat with her crying daughter in the front hall. Some members of staff felt that Kirdan was not taking on her proper parental responsibility. Staying in the front hall was not considered a fitting alternative to guiding Amina into the classroom.

Staff never explicitly stated what they expected of Kirdan. In this respect day-care resembles other social institutions. Behavioural norms are not made explicit or explained, but nevertheless they are inherent in the institution as hidden statements to its users concerning who has what rights and how one behaves responsibly in accordance with the purpose of the institution (cf. Barth 1994: 91-2). As I have shown elsewhere (Bundgaard and Gulløv 2008: 22-5), minority parents and children, who are not familiar with the social codes, may break them and therefore be corrected or commented upon without knowing that they are not following these implicit expectations. They are not able to protest against this treatment in a way that will be acknowledged, and consequently they are prevented from influencing the social norms of interaction. The fact that expectations are implicit therefore enforces the unequal power relations between majority and minority.

Who has the responsibility?

The young assistant, Anne Mette, who had the main responsibility for *settling in* Amina due to the summer vacation, felt uncertain about how to handle a situation which she experienced as extremely difficult due to the language barrier. She was, moreover, aware of Kirdan's personal insecurity, but did not know how to deal with it. The situation was not taken up during the weekly staff meetings, and therefore my impression of how staff responded comes from more spontaneous comments. A few staff members expressed increasing frustration, made evident in the beginning in ironic or snide remarks, but later developing into direct criticism of the mother's and to some extent also the daughter's inability to communicate in Danish. One day-care teacher remarked that she simply could not understand how the mother could be so irresponsible as to not learn Danish so that she might understand the world in which her children would be growing up. An assistant also expressed incomprehension at

Amina's lack of Danish, knowing that her elder brother was fluent; and yet another member of staff from a neighbouring class described Amina as "completely blank." She found this incomprehensible when comparing Amina with a boy of similar age and background in her own class, who understood and spoke a little Danish. The staff member apparently forgot that this boy had started day-care when he was one-and-a-half years old.

Despite the great emphasis in the institution on the importance of communication between staff and parents, staff did not request an interpreter. Apparently, the assistant in charge of Amina's class associated the use of an interpreter with official meetings between parents and staff and therefore did not consider the possibility or need to hire an interpreter. Other staff members in the institution who had long experience of working with minority parents and therefore might have helped the process did not intervene, probably because they were generally overworked and had more than enough to do just dealing with their own classes. Furthermore, they were hesitant to interfere in the work of classes that were the responsibility of other teachers.

It was not only Kirdan's lack of competence in Danish which attracted the critical attention of the staff, but also her behaviour more generally. This might have been another reason why an interpreter was not thought to be the solution to the problem of settling in Amina. When she was asked about Kirdan's problems in *settling in* Amina a few months after she had started day-care, one member of staff replied:

> She [Kirdan] was not there, was she? But she clearly thought that not only she but also Amina's cousin had responsibility for Amina. It's a heavy burden for Fakhri and so unlike our way of thinking.

This last remark indicates that the social interaction in the front hall not only represented an encounter between single human beings but, as we shall see, a meeting between two stereotyped groups. The remark also suggests how categories are always ready to be activated in response to behaviour that is not considered normal (McDermott 1993).

It was the explicit aim of staff that all children should have a pleasant start in day-care. It is therefore not surprising that the assistant in charge of Amina experienced great frustration and powerlessness when she did not succeed in her attempt to reach the child. A sympathetic colleague in charge of the class next to Amina's explained that the deadlocked situation was due to Kirdan being a "bilingual foreigner".[7] To this more critical member of staff, Amina's *settling in* exemplified how certain minority parents relegate their parental responsibilities to the staff when their children are enrolled in an institution. This might lead to the conclusion that two distinct cultural models concerning childcare were at work.[8] However, it is not that simple, as will become evident in the following.

A relationship is strengthened

As already mentioned, Kirdan's response to the problem of *settling in* Amina was to ask Fakhri to take care of the girl. This solved the problem to the extent that Amina stopped crying and agreed to leave her mother. She followed Fakhri wherever he chose to go, first to the playground, where she sat on a bicycle and watched her cousin's ball game with a male employee, and later in the classroom, where Fakhri showed her how she had to find her lunch box herself in the fridge. Then they had lunch together. After lunch, Fakhri returned to the playground, while Amina washed her hands in the bathroom. Entering the classroom, she realized he had gone and immediately started calling him. Anne Mette felt sorry for her and helped her find Fakhri in the playground. Fakhri, however, was on his way to the bathroom and Amina was exceptionally allowed to follow him.[9] While he was using the bathroom, he supervised her examination of the water taps. They spoke in Arabic, only interrupted when Fakhri declared in Danish that he was done. Later, he showed her where her mug was kept and how she should turn on the taps to fill it. This was followed by instructions about where outdoor toys, the sand pit and the swings were located. When Amina was picked up after lunch, Fakhri had guided her through the practical aspects of everyday life in the institution and had thus fully fulfilled Kirdan's expectations of him as an elder cousin.

It was quite clear that Amina was content the first day as long as she was allowed to follow Fakhri. Her role as "follower" made her familiar with the routines of everyday life. For his part, Fakhri did not seem bothered by the task, which he carried out without any protest. Nevertheless Fakhri's role was met with scepticism from the members of staff. During the first days, several of them pointed out that, "after all it was not his responsibility". Despite these objections, there were occasions at the beginning of Amina's stay in the day-care when the staff asked Fakhri to carry out tasks related to Amina, even if he did not at first want to. For example, one day-care teacher unsuccessfully attempted to take Amina to the bathroom, since she was jumping up and down with crossed legs and a tense expression. Amina, however, refused to follow her, and the teacher then asked Fakhri to take her. But he was busy and did not want to take his cousin. After a while, however, he agreed and they went together.

The teachers' scepticism in relation to Fakhri's assumption of responsibility for Amina was caused by their concern for whether Fakhri would be able to "say no" (*sige fra*) if he felt this was too heavy a burden. At a point in time when the book *Your competent child (Dit kompetente barn)*, mentioned above, still was highly influential, it is noteworthy that the staff did not trust Fakhri to be able to handle his task in a way which would be acceptable to both his cousin and himself. How does the institutional aim (stated explicitly in the institutional management plan) that children must be supported in developing responsibility relate to the idea that they must be able to "say no" (*sige fra*)?

To be able to "say no"

Amina had been in the day-care for a week and continued to follow Fakhri. Sometimes they conversed, but generally she simply followed him either to do what he was doing or to watch him at a close distance. One afternoon they were joined by four-year-old Mitra. He was from another class, but they both knew him well. They shared the same mother tongue, and he lived in the same area of town. Shortly after he had joined them, Fakhri moved slightly away, soon leaving them on their own. In other words, rather than "saying no," he had passed his task to another child for a while. Mitra walked while he quietly spoke to Amina in Arabic. She gave the impression of listening but did not reply. Ibrahim joined them and the boys entered a shed, while Amina sat on a bicycle Mitra had pointed out to her. She did not at any point stop watching Mitra, and when he returned they continued their quiet walk in the playground, punctuated by Mitra's occasional comments, and interrupted by breaks in which they quietly watched other children, adults or things. Mitra's best friend in the day-care, Umar, had his third birthday that day, and his father brought a big cake for the children in Umar's class. On his way through the playground he saw Amina with Mitra and stopped to have a little chat, stroked her chin and then proceeded to hand over the cake.

Mitra and Amina were sitting on a bench watching the passers-by, with Amina sobbing now and then. "Amina is crying," Mitra said quietly, maybe to himself, maybe to me. He found a ball and threw it to her; she hesitantly picked it up to throw it back to him, but it never really developed into a game, as Amina let many balls go by. They then clambered on to a fence and sat on it without saying anything. Mathias, who was five years old, placed himself next to Mitra, and the two boys began an intense discussion. It was quite clear that the conversation engaged Mitra much more than the game with Amina had done. She got down off the fence and placed herself with her back to the boys. When Mathias left, Mitra joined Amina and they went into the institution together. Shortly afterwards Mitra came out again alone, having handed over his task to an adult.

These accounts indicate that the boys handled their responsibility for Amina in a way which also allowed them to play on their own. When Mitra appeared, Fakhri saw an opportunity to have a break: without rejecting his responsibility, he simply shared the task with someone else. Mitra, who had never been instructed to take care of Amina, did not leave Amina at any time, but handed her over to an adult when he did not want to have her around anymore.

Responsibility and degrees of relatedness

Amina had been in the day-care for two weeks. The children were in the playground. One of the older girls, Nana, crossed the lawn, closely followed by Amina. Fakhri appeared, calling "Amina, Amina." They stopped and looked at him. A short conversation followed in Danish.

> Fakhri (to Amina): What a nice necklace you are wearing.
> Nana: It's a bracelet, not a necklace.
> Fakhri: I don't care.
> The girls sat on a blanket and were joined by Signe and Sarah.
> Signe (to Nana): Are you her friend?
> Nana: No, I am not her friend. I take care of her.

One of the members of staff from Nana's class had asked her to take care of Amina, a task she had proudly accepted. The task marked her position as one of the older children in the day-care. She accepted her role with great empathy for the little girl she had been asked to take care of. For her part, Amina clearly understood that it was Nana who was supposed to take care of her, and she followed Nana wherever she went.

Nana and Fakhri were about the same age, and they were both in the same class as Amina. What then caused several staff members to conceive it as problematic that one of the two, Fakhri, was given responsibility for Amina, while they themselves asked the other, Nana, to carry out the same task? The main difference between Nana and Fakhri was gender. Gender might therefore be one possible explanation, but this is not borne out by the staff's emphasis on gender equality in the day-care centre. Staff was especially careful not to give minority girls roles that were considered traditionally female. For example, it was common to perceive minority girls' wish to help lay the table as an indication of their familiarity with this kind of task in their homes, while nobody took any notice of the boys' eager participation in the same activity. From a gender perspective, one would therefore expect the staff to prefer Fakhri as the child minder. To understand why the staff regarded Nana as more suitable to take care of Amina, I suggest that we turn our attention towards the relationships between the children themselves. Whereas Nana's relationship to Amina was purely one of friendship, based on their attending the same institution, Fakhri and Amina's relationship was grounded in kinship. For this reason, the staff conceived of Nana's role in minding Amina as voluntary, as she could say no at any time if she did not wish to continue doing so. When it came to Fakhri, however, staff thought that, as Amina's cousin, he would find it difficult to say no. Since it was Amina's mother who had asked him to look after Amina, it would not have been possible for him to stop carrying out the task without disclaiming the responsibility he had been given by an adult relative. Asking a child to be responsible for a younger relative would not have been acceptable to the staff. This is borne out by the fact that it is very common in day-care institutions to put siblings in different classes so that the elder sibling will not be laden with the responsibility for looking after the younger sibling, a responsibility that is considered "too heavy a burden for a child."

However, it was not only the family relationship that was considered problematic. During fieldwork, staff mentioned several times that, when minority children start day-care, their parents often expect that older children who have the same mother tongue will look after the child. What staff found problematic was not so much the family relationship as the strong bonds of social affinity resulting from common language, neighbourhood, area of origin, etc. While Amina's social bond with Nana was relatively weak, her bond with Fakhri was strong. In the institutional context, this meant that it was not considered problematic to ask Nana to take care of Amina because she, unlike Fakhri, was understood to be able to "say no." Fakhri, on the other hand, who knew Amina from home, was tied to her in a way which made it too difficult for him to say no.

Interpretations of appropriate responsibility in relation to children

For Amina, Fakhri was a support during the first difficult period in the institution. Fakhri drew on his experience when mediating between Amina and the staff, as well as between the world she knew at home and this institutional context, which was completely foreign to her. Fakhri's central role in her adjustment to the day-care centre meant that it was difficult for

Amina to get through a day if he was not present. She cried a lot and would not leave the adults even for a minute. Thus the relationship between the two children was not equal, as Fakhri did not depend upon Amina's presence for his well-being, as she did on his.

The two children developed a closer relationship during Amina's period of *settling in*. This closeness consisted of more than mere language dependency. During difficult periods, when she was missing her mother and felt most miserable, only Fakhri was allowed to touch her, and she refused the adults' attempts to cuddle her. Their relationship thus also contained a bodily dimension. They were emotionally connected to each other in a way which meant that the pain of one of them affected the other. When Amina cried one day in a heart-rending fashion because her mother was leaving her, Fakhri was so strongly affected by the situation that, quite uncharacteristically for him, he was not able to do anything at all but stand there and watch them, shaken and motionless. Fakhri, however, was not the only one affected by Amina's sorrow. While Fakhri was incapable of acting, two-year-old Kabir attempted to comfort Amina by showing her the place to put her clothes. Several other small children watched silently and unsure while rocking from one foot to another.

This ethnographic example shows that what staff regarded as a "heavy" and inappropriate responsibility for a child can, from the children's perspective, be described as a relationship of great personal commitment, emotional engagement and strong connectedness. If Fakhri experienced difficulties handling his relationship with Amina, this was because of the close emotional relationship that it entailed, which made it difficult for him to handle Amina's distress when her mother left. If Fakhri occasionally experienced his responsibility to Amina as "heavy" in the staff's sense, he was, as shown, able to hand over this responsibility to others, just as other children tried to help when asked or when they thought the situation called for this. In an institutional environment which aims at developing the responsibility of children and their ability to enter binding social relations (Law on Social Services, § 8, part 4), it is noteworthy that such displays of responsibility for another human being were not praised by the staff, but only considered unfortunate incidents connected with a problematic process of settling in.

The front hall: a neutral place

Amina's mother Kirdan came to Denmark to marry when she was eighteen years old. Eleven years after her arrival in Denmark, her life was quite full, with four children already, one on the way and a sick husband. When I spoke to her she had not yet given up hope of learning Danish, and she thought she would begin learning the language when her fifth child entered day-care. Kirdan's personality was restrained. That made it so much more difficult to tackle Amina's negative response to day-care. She explained later in an interview with an interpreter that she could not face sitting in the classroom with a screaming child, being watched by others and incapable of understanding anything when people spoke to her. For this reason she preferred the front hall, hoping that she might get some help while there. To a certain extent the front hall represented a neutral room between the different worlds of the Danish institution and her private home, a place where one could be left in relative peace. Kirdan's encounter with the staff in the day-care was influenced by body language and style of dress and only confirmed mutual stereotypes represented by Kidan's headscarf and *jelbab* on the one hand, and Anne Mette's bare stomach, small top and tight jeans on the other. Neither Kirdan nor Anne Mette could go beyond this initial experience, and thus they were unable to do or say anything which might have changed things.

Anne Mette could not understand why the mother would choose to say goodbye to her daughter in the front hall. Why did she not do what would be "best" for her child, namely enter the classroom with her and stay there until the child was relatively at ease? Kirdan's choice showed her insecurity in relation to the institutional expectations of behaviour, but she also had a vague impression that the classroom was the domain of the head teacher and therefore would have been marked by inequality. Keeping this in mind, Kirdan's choice of the front hall as a place for negotiations with her daughter indicates a certain understanding of institutional ways: here she could to some extent escape the area under the authority of the teacher.

Untimely interference: guarding the nuclear family and the peace of private life

Three weeks after Amina began day-care, there were still long sequences in the front hall during which Kirdan unsuccessfully attempted to make her daughter accept that she had to leave. The situation seemed completely at a standstill. The staff were increasingly frustrated by Kirdan continuing to linger ineffectually in the front hall. However, nobody took any action. When occasionally staff attempted to explain to Kirdan that she had to take a decision, it was in a language she did not understand. As other Arabic-speaking parents in the local area, who had children in the same institution, noticed what was going on, rumours began to circulate about racism as an explanation for what was seen as the staff's lack of assistance to Kirdan and Amina.

One morning, having watched this painful interplay for several weeks, I spontaneously asked Fakhri's father to explain to Kirdan what the staff wanted her to do. The two spoke quietly together, and Kirdan attempted gently to push Amina into the classroom, but the child refused to let go of her mother. Fakhri's father decided to carry Amina swiftly into the classroom, closely followed by Kirdan, who, however, hesitated in the doorway. A member of staff took hold of her arm and gently guided her into the classroom, where she evidently felt ill at ease, and sat her in an armchair with her daughter in her lap. Half an hour later she left with only a mild protest from Amina, who accepted that her mother had to leave.

Three days later, when a staff member became irritated at Amina and her mother again just sitting in the front hall, I mentioned that Fakhri's father had tried to help. "Yes," she answered, "however, we prefer Mom to do it. Besides he is not part of the family." Slightly confused, I remarked that Amina and Fakhri are cousins. This, however, was considered irrelevant. Family referred to the nuclear family only. Respect for the integrity of individuals meant that staff would not turn to the extended family for assistance.

This exchange illustrates the principle that problems must be taken care of by those directly involved, that is, parents and staff, and if this is not possible, then by "neutral" professionals such as psychologists or consultants. This logic respects the integrity of individuals but means that no one else can be involved, as this would mean mixing lives which otherwise might not intersect.

The fact that staff respected this logic led to difficulties in relation to concrete problem-solving. Despite the fact that the situation with Amina and her mother was not making any progress, it did not occur to staff to ask other Arabic-speaking parents present in the institution for help. The conception of the staff can be seen as indicating that they were guarding Kirdan's integrity. But what does the concept entail in this context? In this situation, guarding her integrity meant cutting off relations that might have helped Kirdan to act and thus make a positive difference for her child in a difficult situation. When Kirdan asked Fakhri to help her daughter, she was met with critical looks and comments that signalled that her action was wrong. It was, however, difficult for her to know how best to deal with the situation, as nobody could tell her what to do in a language she could understand.

If we conceive a human being as a closed entity, or in the words of Michael Jackson "some skin-encapsulated, seamless monad possessed of conceptual unity and continuity" (1998:6), Kirdan's inaction cannot be understood. However, if we perceive people and their actions as something that come to be in relation with others, then the many occasions of waiting in the front hall are understandable. In an unfamiliar environment, where her turning to her extended family relative was criticized, Kirdan withdrew. There was no room for her extended family network in a cultural context in which the only acceptable actors are members of the nuclear family, or more precisely the parents of the child.

Conclusion

Amina's experience was in some ways exceptional. The majority of minority children *settled in* much more quickly than she did – and even she was eventually integrated into the social life of the institution. Can racism, as some of the other Arabic-speaking parents suggested, explain why *settling in* was so complicated in her case? This explanation was explored, and although one member of staff was indeed very critical of Kirdan and her choices in life, the notion of racism does not help us understand what generally took place between the individuals involved. When staff members did not act, it was partly due to the language barrier and partly because they, like Kirdan, did not know what to do.

Merleau-Ponty writes that we understand others through the "blind recognition" of reciprocal gestures, common metaphors, parallel images, and shared intentions (quoted in Jackson 1998: 12), rather than through cognition and intellectual interpretation. If we accept this, it follows that we decode each other's body language and statements without further reflection. Just like Kirdan, members of staff were not sure how to tackle the problem, and Amina's *settling in* was therefore affected by insecurity. They each tried to interpret the mime and gestures of the other for want of a common language. In such a situation, for example, Kirdan´s gesture of rejection to indicate her need for peace to talk with her daughter might be interpreted as a more general rejection of the involvement of the staff.

Due to the lack of verbal communication through a common language, body language and other non-verbal signs such as clothing came to play a central role. The different forms of clothing worn by Kirdan and the staff respectively might have had an alienating effect. Thus, they may have acted as disturbing elements that made it difficult to see an individual and ways of action rooted in a personal history rather than a stereotypical cultural category. This unnecessarily complicated the interaction reducing the likelihood of either party taking any action.

The idea of the integrity of the single individual or nuclear family means that staff in day-care institutions generally prefers to solve problems with the people directly involved. Alternatively, professional, so-called "neutral" assistance might be called on, but in a period marked by continual financial cuts this is not always realistic. The fear of creating relations of dependence among people who might prefer not to interact means that members of an extended family network or other parents who have children in the institution and speak the same language will not be called upon to help find a solution. This professionalism hinders unwanted interference but simultaneously also cuts off relations which in some situations might prove crucial in reaching a meaningful understanding between staff, parents and children.

As this chapter illustrates, it is culturally unacceptable in Denmark to defer responsibility for playmates to other children. A "competent child" is a child who has a strong sense of what she wants, an ability to communicate what she wants and who knows how she can go about getting what she wants in an acceptable manner. Responsibility for other human beings must not stand in the way. To understand this cultural phenomenon, it is necessary to recall the historical context, specifically developments in pedagogy and the post-1960s ideology that stresses emancipation and self-determination as fundamental to the process of individualization. Seen in this light, it is evident that what in the encounter between staff and ethnic minority parents appear to be fundamental Danish values are in fact a relatively recent product of the Danish welfare state and its emancipatory project of individualization.

Notes

1. Public schools are the only other social institution which can claim a similar key role.
2. The chapter has been published in Danish in a different version (Bundgaard 2002).
3. The research project was carried out by the anthropologist Eva Gulløv and the author and was funded by the research council known at the time as Det Humanistiske Forskningsråd.
4. In Denmark, mothers with new-born babies receive a number of visits from a nurse, who gives advice on issues of care.
5. All names are pseudonyms.
6. In the two institutions attended during fieldwork, only one leaflet was translated into other languages. This leaflet informed readers that it is illegal to beat children according to Danish law and that it can cause psychological damage. There was hardly any information – and then only in Danish – on the purpose of an

institutional stay, apart from care activities, or for that matter any practical information on opening hours, holidays, lunch boxes or settling in.
7. In Denmark, "bilingual" is an official term used for people whose parents do not have Danish as their mother tongue.
8. See Bundgaard (2006) for a critique of the inherent concept of culture.
9. The bathroom was placed right next to the classroom. The children did not close the door separating the bathroom from the classroom, giving me an opportunity to follow their interaction at a distance.

References

Barth, Frederik. 1994. *Manifestasjon og prosess*. Oslo: Det Blå Bibliotek.
Bundgaard, Helle. 2002. Hvem har ansvaret? En immigrantfamilies møde med den danske institutionsverden. *Tidsskriftet Antropologi* 46: 121 134.
—. 2004. Normalitet. Positioner og Kategoriserings-processer i det institutionelle rum. In *Viden om verden.En grundbog i antropologisk analyse*, ed K. Hastrup, 95-116. Copenhagen: Hans Reitzel.
—. 2008. *Forskel og fællesskab. Minoritetsbørn i daginstitution*. Copenhagen: Hans Reitzels Forlag.
—. 2006. Et antropologisk blik på kultur. In *Tosprogede børn i det danske samfund*, ed M. Karrebæk. Copenhagen: Hans Reitzels Forlag.
Bundgaard, Helle and Eva Gulløv. 2003. Sprog-lighed og ulighed. *Magasinet Humaniora* 2: 18-21.
Connolly, Paul. 1998. *Racism, Gender Identities and Young children. Social relations in a Multi-Ethnic, Inner-City Primary School*. London: Routledge.
De Coninck-Smith, Ning. 1995. Byggeri for børn. Daginstitutionsbyggeri før, under og efter 2. verdenskrig. [Buildings for Children. Daycare buildings before, during and after World War II]. *Architectura* 17: 7 30.
Gulløv, Eva. In press. Kindergartens in Denmark – reflections on continuity and change. In *The Modern Child and the Flexible Labour Market: Child Care Policies and practices at a Crossroads?*, ed. J. Qvortrup and A. T. Kjørholt. Basingstoke: Palgrave.
Hermann, Stefan. 2007. *Magt og oplysning: Folkeskolen 1950-2006*. Copenhagen: Unge pædagoger.
Jackson, Michael. 1998. M*inima Ethnographica. Intersubjectivity and the Anthropological Project*. Chicago: The University of Chicago Press.
Juul, Jesper. 1995. *Dit kompetente barn: På vej mod et nyt værdigrundlag for familien*. Copenhagen: Schønberg.
Law on social services § 8, part 4.

(http://www.social.dk/tvaergaaende_indgange/lovgining/reglerogafgor elser/allegaeldende/serviceydelser/index.aspx)

McDermott, Ray. 1993. The acquisition of a child by a learning disability. In *Understanding Practice*, ed. S. Chaiklin and J. Lave. Cambridge: Cambridge University Press.

Sigsgaard, Jens. 1978. *Folkebørnehaver og social pædagogik. Træk af asylets og børnehavens historie.* [Folk kindergarten and social education. Outline of the history of the asylum and the kindergarten]. Copenhagen: Forlaget Børn og Unge.

Statistisk Årbog [Statistical Yearbook]. 2007. Copenhagen: Statistics Denmark.

Thorne, Barrie. 2001. Pick-Up Time at Oakdale Elementary School: Work and Family from the Vantage Points of Children. In *Working Families. The Transformation of the American Home*, ed. R. Hertz and N. Marshall. Berkeley: University of California Press.

Tobin, Joseph. J., David Y. H. Wu and Dana H. Davidson. 1989. *Preschool in Three Cultures*. New Haven: Yale University Press.

Vejleskov, Hans. 1997. Den danske børnehave. Studier om myter, meninger og muligheder. *Skrifter fra center for Småbørnsforskning* 8. Vejle: Krogs Forlag.

Winther, Ida. 1999. *Småbørnsliv i Danmark – anno 2000* [The Life of Young Children in Denmark – anno 2000]. Copenhagen: Danmarks Pædagogiske Institut.

CHAPTER EIGHT

PSYCHIATRIC PATIENTS WITH A NON-DANISH ETHNIC BACKGROUND: CATEGORIZATION IN A DANISH WELFARE INSTITUTION

KATRINE SCHEPELERN JOHANSEN

The fact that, in many European countries, immigrants and refugees have an increased psychiatric morbidity compared to the general population has been extensively documented (e.g. Jarvis 1998; Cantor-Graae et al. 2003, Cantor-Graae and Selten 2005). This is also the case in Denmark, where patients with a non-Danish ethnic background make up a comparatively larger part of the patient population in Danish psychiatric wards than would be expected from their proportion of the total population (Cantor-Graae et al. 2003). The Danish welfare state offers free psychiatric treatment to patients who are citizens of Denmark, but patients with a non-Danish ethnic background challenge this approach. Being not Danish sometimes causes staff to categorize these patients as not being proper patients and therefore not being subjects of the Danish psychiatric treatment system.

Danish psychiatric wards are thus one important institution where the encounter between immigrants and refugees and the Danish welfare state takes place. This particular encounter is the subject of this chapter. More specifically, I discuss how psychiatric patients with a non-Danish ethnic background are categorized: are they categorized as patients in need of treatment or rather people who do not belong in the wards? The analysis shows that processes of categorization are influenced by both the specific institutional context of psychiatry and more general processes and discussions that take place in Danish society. To understand how immigrants and refugees are received and treated in the institutions of the Danish welfare state, this analysis shows that we must pay attention to both levels: the specific institutional level, and the general societal level.

The analysis of the psychiatric wards shows that the categorization of some patients as having a non-Danish ethnic background is not the only kind of categorization that takes place. Other kinds of categories are also at work, such as diagnosis, and the categorization of some patients according to ethnicity thus takes place in competition with other categories within the psychiatric system. The category "patients with a non-Danish ethnic background" is in practice a rather vague, ad-hoc category that is primarily used for patients whom the psychiatric staff consider difficult to treat. Immigrants and refugees who are easily treated within the psychiatric system are typically not categorized as having a non-Danish ethnic background. However, other patients are also difficult to treat and thus risk being categorized as someone the psychiatric wards are not obliged to treat. For example, patients with a dual diagnosis (co-occurring drug use and psychiatric disease) are often categorized primarily as drug users and therefore not eligible for psychiatric treatment. The ethnic categorization is thus part of a more general practice in the psychiatric wards – that of categorizing some patients as the right type of patients and other patients as wrong and hence as people who do not belong in the wards.

Before presenting my study and analysis, I offer a brief description of the Danish psychiatric system.

Immigrants and refugees in the Danish psychiatric system

In Denmark, the psychiatric system is part of the general health-care system. This system is publicly funded through taxes and gives everybody equal access to the treatment facilities. The psychiatric treatment system in Denmark consists of hospital wards that take care of patients in need of intensive treatment, often in the short term, and outpatient clinics for patients in need of long-term but often less intensive care.

Danish psychiatry is dominated by a biological approach to psychiatric disorders, and the dominant treatment offered is medicine: primarily anti-psychotic medicine, anti-depressive medicine, mood-stabilizing medicine and tranquilizers. Most wards also have a psychologist, who offers different kinds of psychotherapy, but only to a minority of the patients. Social workers are also employed to help patients out with the many programmes that the welfare state provides for the individual citizen. The social worker is thus often engaged in helping out with welfare benefits, living facilities, settling debts, organizing different services for the period after the stay in hospital, etc.

On the wards the most important treatment staff are the psychiatrist, the nurses and the nursing assistants. Most wards have room for approximately twelve to twenty patients. Wards are built to be comfortable facilities with common rooms, dining rooms and individual rooms for the patients.

The Danish psychiatric system, like most of the other welfare-state institutions in the country, was originally created to serve a mono-cultural and mono-ethnic population. Treatment is thus free of charge and in principle depends only on the patient's diagnosis, not on his or her social or cultural characteristics. As with other welfare institutions, psychiatry categorizes people as belonging or not belonging to the target groups for their specific programmes, categorizations that often provide the basis for the interventions of the programme. There is no tradition in Danish psychiatry of working systematically or professionally with the ethnic or cultural background of minority patients, as is the case in, for example, US psychiatry.

During the last ten years, increased attention has been paid to patients with a non-Danish ethnic background in the Danish psychiatric system. This is partly due to the growing number of these patients, and partly to the general attention that immigrants and refugees have received in Danish society. Discussions have been conducted regarding how these patients are to be treated, whether they suffer from different psychiatric diseases than ethnic Danish patients, and whether their foreign cultures and religions create special problems for the psychiatric wards. This growing attention has, however, not led to systematic changes or adaptations of the treatment. Patients with a non-Danish ethnic background continue to be treated within the existing psychiatric system and are given the same treatment as Danish patients. The only change is the use of interpreters when a patient speaks no Danish or English at all. The only exception to this rule are traumatized refugees, for whom specific outpatient clinics have been created.

The study

As there are no official guidelines in the Danish psychiatric system for treating patients with a non-Danish ethnic background, I examined how psychiatric staff work with this group of patients in practice (Johansen 2006). Among other things, I recorded how psychiatric staff talked about this group of patients and how they categorized them. I also researched the more general psychiatric treatment practices so as to compare the treatment of non-Danish ethnic patients with Danish patients.

The data were collected during thirteen months of fieldwork in five different psychiatric wards in the Greater Copenhagen area. Some of the wards were forensic psychiatric wards, while others were ordinary psychiatric wards. In Denmark, forensic psychiatry is an integrated part of the ordinary psychiatric treatment system and to a large extent resembles it. Also, the ordinary psychiatric wards often admit several forensic psychiatric patients. Therefore in this chapter the different wards will be treated as representatives of the general psychiatric system in Denmark, and no special attention will be paid to the forensic aspects of some of the wards.

The methods used in the fieldwork were participant observation in the hospital, for example, in the patients' living rooms, the staff's offices and the gardens of the different wards. I participated in conferences, meetings and conversations between staff and patients and among staff. I also interviewed a number of members of staff and patients.

The majority of patients who in one way or the other became part of this study had a diagnosis of schizophrenia. Schizophrenia is one of the most severe mental illnesses. The best known symptoms are hearing voices or having other hallucinations, feeling that one is being persecuted and megalomania. But many patients also have what are called "negative symptoms", which include autism, difficulties in establishing and maintaining social relations, feelings of ambivalence, etc.

The Analytical Approach

As mentioned in the introduction to this chapter, my empirical object is the categorization of some psychiatric patients as patients with a non-Danish ethnic background: why are some patients categorized as "ethnic", and why are other patients, despite also having a non-Danish ethnic background, not categorized as such? In analysing this phenomenon I have found it useful to maintain a double analytic approach. This double approach developed during the analytic work to mirror the two levels, or influences, in the categorization that takes place in the psychiatric wards: the specific institutional level, and the general social level.

In analysing the categorization linked to the specific institution, and to psychiatry, I use the concept of "social technology" as developed by the anthropologists Steffen Jöhncke, Mette Nordahl Svendsen and Susan Whyte (2004; see also Spector and Kitsuse 2001). They argue that social problems are defined by the available solutions. Put very simply, if a treatment institution is offering treatment for alcohol problems, all the clients' problems will be defined as being caused by alcohol and therefore as being amenable to treatment for excessive drinking. Defining the problems therefore also means defining the target group for the institution, that is, the group with this kind of problem. In the context of the psychiatric wards, this approach shows how the treatments offered by the wards categorize some people with psychiatric problems as proper patients and other people with psychiatric problems as not proper patients, as their problems are not objects of the social technology on offer. The social technology approach will be presented more thoroughly below.

The general social level in the categorization process can be explored with reference to the literature concerning the relationship between minorities and majorities in modern states (Kragh 2007; Hvenegård-Lassen 1996). This approach is built on the theoretical conception that a majority in a society is the group of people that defines the norms for that society. Minorities are groups that in one way or the other are not associated with these norms, either because they choose not to be or because they are excluded by the majority. These minorities may in principle have many different origins and may be political, sexual, linguistic, and so on. However, many will be grounded in ethnicity and hence be ethnic minorities. Before I elaborate further on this approach, I will briefly discuss why I have chosen to focus on categorization rather than on the issues of ethnicity and ethnic identity.

In trying to understand what this categorization is all about, one might think it would be useful to describe the shared cultural values of these patients with a non-Danish ethnic background and thus conceptualize them as an ethnic group. However, this is problematic as the category "patient with a non-Danish ethnic background" is primarily one invented and used by the psychiatric staff and not by those placed in the category themselves. The latter group shares no common cultural values and has no common identity. The categorization is not meaningful for the people placed within the category. In other words, here we are dealing with an ethnic categorization for which there is no corresponding ethnic group (Jenkins 1997: 54). The distinction between ethnic group and ethnic category draws on Barth's distinction between the internal and external identifications of a group (2001: 252). An ethnic category is externally defined by the surrounding community, whereas an ethnic group is an internally defined group with subjective feelings of belonging.

When I interviewed some of the patients who staff stated belonged to the category of patients with a non-Danish ethnic background, they did not focus on their ethnic background themselves. When I asked them about their ethnic identities, they told me how many years they had been living in Denmark, how they had worked and paid taxes as good citizens and how their children had attended the Danish public school system (*folkeskole*). Others, who had not lived in Denmark for many years, spoke of the ways Denmark and their country of origin were alike, how the education that they had received before coming to Denmark was very similar to a Danish education and how they felt at home in Denmark. They thus seemed to be eager to situate themselves in Danish society. Perhaps they were aware of the categorization in use at the wards and also that it was not beneficial to be categorized as such, and therefore tried to escape this category by telling an alternative story of being part of Danish society.

What is at stake when some patients are categorized as patients with a non-Danish ethnic background thus does not seem to be about the ethnic identity and common cultural values of these patients. We rather need to look in the other direction, to the psychiatric system itself and the psychiatric staff, and analyse why they categorize certain patients as not having a Danish ethnic background. This brings us back to the concept of categorization and the two approaches mentioned above.

Studies of majorities and minorities

In the social sciences, studies of majorities and minorities often use an approach in which these definitions are seen as the results of social and historical processes, rather than as naturally given (Kragh 2007). Of interest are the questions why a certain group is perceived as a minority, how this group is constituted, who is perceived as being part of it, and what the consequences of minority status are for the people who are part of the group.

Often previous research uses a definition of these groups based on power relations rather than on numbers: a majority is the group of people who have the power to make the categorizations and carry through the political consequences of them (Hvenegaard-Lassen 1996). An example of this is the white population under apartheid in South Africa. Though a numerical minority, they had the power to control society and define other groups of people within it as second-class citizens.

The majority is also characterized by being the group that can define what is normal and what is abnormal (Kragh 2007). The abnormal is often perceived as something that should be controlled. According to Hvenegaard-Lassen, the reason for categorizing a group of people as a minority is the possibility it provides of justifying placing restrictions on the symbolic and material resources available to this group (1996). As the minority is not associated with the norms of or form part of normal society, they do not have any right to make the same demands for societal resources as the majority. Even in situations where a minority identity provides access to specific rights or resources, it is still the majority that establishes the framework, makes the rules within which this access is allowed and defines which extra resources the minority should have access to.

In this perspective, psychiatric patients will make up a minority, as they are subjected to the majority's – here the staff's – categorizations and the social and political consequences of these categorizations. The limited resources are, in this setting, the patients' freedom and self-determination. Patients who are categorized having a non-Danish ethnic background are, as I will show below, also given limited access to psychiatric treatment.

Categorization as a consequence of social technology

Another approach to categorization has been developed by the anthropologists Jöhncke, Svendsen and Whyte (2004), who describe categorization as being an example of "social technologies". A social technology is an act of intervention in other peoples' lives; the "social" highlights the fact that this intervention takes place in social relations. Their idea is that social problems are defined by their imagined solutions (Jöhncke et al. 2004: 385). Instead of finding the best possible solution to a given problem, the process is often the opposite. Within a given social context there are a range of possible solutions available, and any given problem to be dealt with in this social context should fit one of the available solutions.

In the process of defining the problems, the target group for the solutions is also defined, as are those who are *not* part of the target group: "This means that social technologies create certain target groups, certain categories of individuals or groups that are characterized by possessing the problem that the solution can surround and handle" (Jöhncke et al. 2004: 392; my translation). This means that there will also be people categorized as not belonging to the target group (ibid.: 393).

According to this approach, categorization is part of any social technology. This means that, when working with the treatment of specific groups of people, certain people are categorized as those who belong to this treatment institution or are in need of the treatment it offers, while others are defined as not being part of this target group and therefore as not belonging in this treatment setting.

This perspective on categorization is different from the one presented above, where the focus was on access to resources. The disadvantage with the social technology approach is that it makes the categorization process unique, as it is linked to the specific institution, instead of placing it within a broader social process, which is the strength of the minority perspective. Therefore, I suggest that this double analytical approach, which combines general categorization processes with specific processes that are part of a specific institutional practice and its social technology.

Categorization in Danish psychiatric wards

The categorization of some patients as patients with a non-Danish ethnic background takes place in a psychiatric setting that is full of categories and categorization, including the formal process of diagnosis, whether or not the patient is using drugs, their gender, their forensic status, etc. The category "patients with a non-Danish ethnic background" is not a definitive category – not every non-Danish patient is categorized as such. It is rather a categorization that staff sometimes use to explain problems in their relationships with certain patients. I will return to this category below. First I will introduce some of the other categories that exist in the psychiatric field.

The most important categorization is that between patients and staff, but within these two dominant categories a range of other categorizations takes place. Among the staff, these categorizations distinguish different professions. Thus staff are categorized as nursing staff, doctors and others (psychologists, occupational therapists, physiotherapists, social workers). Another distinction is that between the nursing staff and all the other professions, a matter of who has the closest contact with the patients and who needs to confront patients physically if they become too upset or aggressive (see also Barrett 1996). There is also a distinction between male and female staff that is activated in situations where a patient is aggressive or is threatening to be, as male staff are perceived to have more physical strength if a patient needs to be strapped down.

As for the patients themselves, they divide staff into nice staff members and not-so-nice staff members. This distinction reflects whether the individual staff member likes to spend time with the patients or rather prefers to stay in the staff office. Patients are also aware of the different professions and their various competences – they know that the doctor has the final say in relation to medicine and being discharged, that the social worker can help in relation to money, and so on. The gender of the staff is also important for patients in some situations. They seem to be aware that when many men suddenly appear in the ward, this means that a physical confrontation is about to take place. Psychiatric work experience is also important for the patients. I experienced being categorized as "inexperienced staff" by patients several times, which meant that they asked me to do favours for them that they knew more experienced staff would not do. I think this is an experience I share with many students and new staff members.

Patients are categorized by staff according to diagnoses: there are the schizophrenics,[1] the depressives and those with personality disorders. On the wards where I did my fieldwork, staff members preferred the patients with schizophrenia. These patients were considered to be the true psychiatric patients that really needed to be in the hospital. Staff were in no doubt what was the matter with these patients, whom they were able to help with treatment and care, at least as long as they were in the hospital.

Another distinction in the patient group concerns whether or not the patient was using drugs. This is a rather common occurrence, as approximately half of all patients hospitalized with psychoses also have a drug use disorder (Vendsborg 2003). However, this distinction is not an absolute one. If staff members regard drug use as the patient's own attempt to treat his psychiatric disorder (self-medication), the patient is not considered an abuser. Instead, the drug use is seen as a symptom of psychiatric disorder instead of as a problem in its own right. However, for some patients drug use is not seen as self-medication, and these patients are categorized as abusers. This is not a positive category, as in the Danish psychiatric system drug users are seen as taking time and beds away from the "real" patients. This in turn means that drug users are discharged from the psychiatric wards as quickly as possible. Finally the staff categorize some patients as ones with a non-Danish ethnic background, a categorization I return to below.

There is a strong normative element in the two different approaches to categorization presented above. Some patients are categorized as being right, some as being wrong and therefore as not belonging on the ward. It might seem a bit paradoxical to talk about "being right" in relation to psychiatric patients, who by definition are abnormal and therefore "wrong." But there is no doubt that some psychiatric patients are considered more right than others. On the wards where I did my fieldwork, the patients with schizophrenia made up just such a category of right patients. In relation to the above list of different kinds of patients, there were several examples of patients who were not considered right. One example was patients who used drugs in a way that was not considered self-medication. As we shall see below, patients with a non-Danish ethnic background were another example.

The place of patients with schizophrenia as an ideal target group fits nicely with the social technology model. In this case, the social technology is the treatment that the psychiatric wards offer their patients. And in this technology there is a target group: those who can be helped by the technology. The primary treatment in the wards is medical treatment with anti-psychotic medication and tranquilizers and a structured environment, meaning clear rules for behaviour, a planned day and limited stimuli from the outside world. These types of treatment are thought to have a good effect on people with schizophrenia, but they are less suitable in treating, for example, cannabis abuse. Patients with such problems therefore present a challenge to the social technology of the wards.

Patients with a non-Danish ethnic background

Another group of patients who challenge the social technology and the ideal category of the schizophrenic patient are those categorized as patients with a non-Danish ethnic background. These patients often have one or more of the following characteristics: they have a different physical appearance (skin or hair colour, different clothes), they have a strong accent or do not speak Danish at all, or they have some obviously different cultural habits, such as praying five times a day, as some Muslim patients do.

It is by no means certain, however, that a patient will be categorized as having a non-Danish ethnic background, even if he or she has some of these characteristics. In practice, the category is rather vague. Some staff members refuse to make a distinction between Danish and non-Danish patients at all and say that the important issue in a psychiatric ward is that one is a patient in need of treatment. The general tendency, however, is for staff to consider patients, who are categorized as having a non-Danish ethnic background, to be difficult. Patients from another country or culture whom staff consider easy to work with are seldom referred to as ethnic or non-Danish: they are just patients.

From the perspective of social technology, however, the category non-Danish ethnic background is yet another category that does not fit the technology of the psychiatric ward. Describing a patient as having a non-Danish ethnic background means describing a patient as having some characteristics that can make treatment and care difficult. Some staff members describe how they must spend extra time with these patients because they need more explanations or because working with an interpreter takes more time. Some members of staff explain that they try to make the treatment fit the patient, for example, by involving the family more in the treatment – something that also takes up more time and makes the treatment more complicated, as more people are involved. However, there are reservations about many of these attempts to make the treatment different, as staff are not sure they will succeed in making the treatment suit the non-Danish ethnic background. Invoking such backgrounds, while representing an attempt to adapt the treatment, is also an excuse for not being able to do it properly (see also van Dijk 1998). Often staff could not point to specific problems or areas of conflict. Categorizing a patient as non-Danish was often based on a diffuse feeling of not being able to establish a proper relationship with the patient. Staff often explained that the non-Danish ethnic background of a patient gave them a feeling of literally not being able to reach the mental illness in the patient because the foreign culture stood in the way (Johansen 2008; Littlewood and Dein 2000). The staff's experience of this patient group as particularly difficult or different is further strengthened by the various courses offered in hospitals that focus on "the ethnic patient" or "the Muslim patient", not to mention research projects such as my own that placed a special emphasis on this particular group of patients.

For some staff members, categorizing some aspects of patients' behaviour or problems as cultural or ethnic is a way of saying that this is beyond the limits of what they can or want to deal with professionally. As one staff member said in an interview: "We are psychiatric staff, not ethnic consultants. If they are having problems with their culture, they will have to go somewhere else with those problems."

Language

Patients who do not speak Danish will almost invariably be categorized as having a non-Danish ethnic background. The daily contact between patients and staff, which staff consider very important and which is a central part of the non-medical treatment, is very limited in relation to these patients and takes place only in a few formally arranged conversations when an interpreter has been called. In these conversations it is often only the doctor who talks with the patient, and the topics raised often centre on issues such as medicine, its effects and side effects. The fact that conversations are few and very formal fundamentally limits how well staff and patient can get to know each other. Patients who speak Danish will have at least one daily conversation with a staff member. This conversation may be relatively brief and only focus on how the patient is doing that day, but for other patients it can develop into a real therapeutic relationship, where problems and solutions are discussed. Such a conversation will only rarely take place with a patient who does not speak Danish.

The wards use interpreters when it is not possible to communicate with a patient in either Danish or English. In practice this means that no interpreter is used when a patient comes from the other Nordic countries or from most Western European countries. The frequency with which psychiatric staff use interpreters varies. Some patients have an interpreted conversation every week, others – especially long-term patients – will only have an interpreted conversation every other month.

When I interviewed staff on their practices with regard to interpreters, many explained their very limited use with reference to money and resources. It was expensive to use interpreters, as well as difficult to arrange, as the relevant people (doctor, staff, patient, and interpreter) all had to be present at the same time. Interestingly, the issue of cost was never raised officially in relation to interpreters. But the issue of resources is never far away in a modern health-care setting, and staff themselves invoked it in relation to the issue of interpreters. If we return to the discussion of why some groups are categorized as minorities, one of the suggestions was that it is about access to resources – symbolic and material. The issue of interpreters and language is the only one where resources are explicitly mentioned by staff in relation to ethnicity. Categorizing some patients as having a non-Danish ethnic background is thus also a legitimization of why the staff do not talk very much with these patients.

Above I described how the category "patient with a non-Danish ethnic background" connoted a difficult patient, as opposed to a patient with schizophrenia for whom there was a ready treatment. In a way, in not speaking Danish, a patient merely reinforces his or her categorization as a difficult patient. The question of interpreters is also very much a question of the practical arrangements of the wards. The social technology of the wards thus does not seem to consider the use of interpreters as logical or appropriate.

This part of the analysis has focused primarily on categorization from the perspective of social technology. As such has been explicitly linked to the psychiatric wards. Next I will turn to an analysis of the influence of the surrounding society.

The Muslim patient

Among the staff I have worked with, there is general agreement that patients with non-Danish ethnic backgrounds are typically from the Middle East or are Muslim patients, the two characteristics often overlapping. This close connection means that many patients whom staff consider to have a non-Danish ethnic background are also automatically perceived to be Muslims. I have encountered one patient from Montenegro and another from Armenia – both Christians – whom staff talked about as Muslims.

In the staff's perception Islam is fundamentally different from Danish culture, and Muslim patients are therefore considered to have great difficulties in adapting to the environment and culture of the wards. Staff perceive Muslims to be very religious, very patriarchal, very family-oriented, very traditional or old-fashioned and very much influenced by their culture and religion. Their religion is viewed as standing in the way of these patients' adjusting to the rules and culture of the psychiatric wards and hence to the requirements of their own treatment and possible cure. Staff will sometimes voice a need to re-educate these patients into Danish culture and the Danish way of life, which staff see as characterized by notions of equality, democracy and rationality. The culture of the wards is thus seen as being identical with Danish culture in the wider society.

This focus on Islam and Muslims is not unique to the wards in which I did my fieldwork, but is found in the Danish health-care system more generally, as well as in the wider welfare state in the country. One can find courses in "Muslim culture" and "Muslim perceptions of health and disease" in many hospitals, and the words "Islam" and "Muslim" have become part of the ordinary vocabulary of Danish psychiatric wards. When management at the different hospitals writes about ethnic minorities in policy papers, they are often simply referring to Muslims.

I have not managed to trace systematically the emergence of the category "Muslim patient" in the Danish health-care system, but there is no doubt that it is linked to the general, public debate on foreigners in Danish society over the last approximately ten years, in which immigrants and Muslims have become synonyms, and in which immigrants have come to be considered a central problem, even a threat, to Danish society. In many situations in Denmark today, Muslims are considered fundamentally different from the native Danish population (Hervik 2004; Simonsen 2004). We thus find the same idea in the wider society that I found at the psychiatric wards: that the culture of Muslims is inconsistent with Danish culture, and that Muslims need to adapt to this Danish culture to be part of Danish society – in other words, they should stop being Muslims.

Muslims have thus become a minority that is considered fundamentally different from the majority in Danish society, both in the psychiatric system and in the wider society. As they are not perceived as sharing the cultural values that are part of the different institutions in Denmark, they cannot expect to be given the same, good treatment as proper Danes. When, from the point of view of the psychiatric staff, these patients do not share social and cultural values, they also do not have the same right of access to the resources of the society, in this case to treatment in psychiatric wards.

As mentioned above, established professional guidelines on how to work with the cultural background of patients with a non-Danish ethnic background do not yet exist in Denmark. In practice a focus does seem to be emerging on the Muslim patient as a typical representative of such patients.

A comparison with the United States[2]

This situation is different from that in USA, where several different approaches exist regarding how to accommodate the psychiatric treatment system to an increasingly ethnically diversified population. One approach is to use an ethnic consultant to translate linguistically and culturally between the treatment system and the ethnic patient (Budman et al. 1992). Another involves the clinician him- or herself being or becoming aware of a range of cultural differences in the clinical encounter (Johnson and Kleinman 1984). Yet a third approach is to develop psychiatric services that aim to treat people with a specific minority background. The anthropologist Vilma Santiago-Irizarry describes the establishment of a psychiatric clinic in New York for Latino patients. In this clinic, the majority of staff themselves have a Latino background, the dominant language spoken is Spanish, and the clinic's interior and decorations have been designed to make Latino-patients fell more at home (Santiago-Irizarry 2001). However, Santiago-Irizarry also points out some problems with this approach, among others that the representation of Latino culture is rather stereotypical and that the culture itself becomes pathological: as patients have to be both mentally ill and Latino to be admitted to the clinic, a structural similarity appears to be constructed within the clinic between the mental illness and the culture, thus turning both into objects of treatment.

The most systematically and professionally well-grounded work on how to treat psychiatric patients with an ethnic minority background is probably the cultural formulation of the DSM-IV. The DSM is the Diagnostic and Statistical Manual of the American Psychiatric Association (APA 1995). When the fourth edition was published in 1994, it included an appendix on the cultural formulation, a question guide aimed at disclosing culturally specific issues in relation to the psychiatric patient.

The cultural formulation was developed by a group of anthropologists and psychiatrists in cooperation. The group was established to make suggestions to the editorial board of the DSM on how to make the manual more usable both in the USA, where the population is becoming increasingly multi-ethnic, and abroad, where the DSM has increased in popularity. Many of the suggestions were rejected, and many participants in the group were very disappointed with the role that culture was given in this fourth edition (see Kirmayer 1998; Mezzich et al. 1999; Lewis-Fernández 1996). But one of the few suggestions to be incorporated was the cultural formulation, which is made up of five specific points that the clinician should collect information about as part of the diagnostic process. These are: 1) the cultural identity of the individual; 2) cultural explanations of the individual's illness, 3) cultural factors related to the psychosocial environment and levels of functioning; 4) cultural elements of the relationship between the individual and the clinician; and 5) an overall cultural assessment for diagnosis and care. For each point, the working group developed a range of interview questions. They also recommended that, in filling out the cultural formulation, the clinician should use the patient's own narrative to prevent the use of cultural stereotypes (Lewis-Fernández 1996).

In clinical practice, however, the cultural formulation has not been much used. One of the problems is that it takes a long time to go through and produces very long descriptions (se for example Flemming 1996), and as such it is not very popular in the busy days of ordinary psychiatry. Also, American psychiatry is becoming increasingly dominated by a biological paradigm that leaves little room for social and cultural aspects, much as in Denmark (Kleinman 1988, Luhrmann 2000).

In comparing these approaches with the Danish material, it is interesting that there are different, established ways of working with culture within psychiatry in USA; clinicians are thus not necessarily left to themselves or to the media debate when encountering patients with an ethnic minority background. Part of the explanation for this is probably the long history of the USA as a multicultural society because of the immigration history of the country and the existence of native peoples (Proulx 2007; Kymlicka 1995). The multi-cultural discourse in the USA has established a range of different categories concerning ethnicity and culture which it is possible to draw on in medical and psychiatric practice. Additionally, not least because of the various civil rights movements, the USA has developed a social practice in which it has become legitimate to categorize people with reference to, among other things, ethnicity and gender to guarantee fair treatment. The recognition of differences with the aim of ensuring fairness is thus a well-known phenomenon in the USA, which in some institutional settings has developed into affirmative action (Skrentny 2002).

But, as the above presentation has also shown, psychiatry in the USA has not yet found an unproblematic way of handling patients with ethnic minority backgrounds. Nevertheless, the experiences of the USA have an important part to play in inspiring discussions within Danish psychiatry on how best to treat patients with non-Danish ethnic backgrounds.

Conclusion

The categorization of some patients as "patients with a non-Danish ethnic background" is a complicated process that brings together categorizations from Danish society generally and categorizations that are unique to the psychiatric system. From the perspective of the social technology of the psychiatric system, "patients with a non-Danish ethnic background" form a category of patients who challenge the social technology of the wards. They are patients who cannot access the treatment to the same extent as other categories of patients. At the same time, the categorizations of the psychiatric wards also draws on some more general processes in Danish society. Here Muslims in particular are considered as having difficulties in fitting in, and therefore patients with a non-Danish ethnic background are often considered to be Muslims. An analytical conceptualization of these parallel processes should mirror this duality to draw attention to both. In my analysis I have chosen to use two approaches to categorization, one from the literature on minorities, and one from the literature on social technology.

This chapter therefore concludes that the categorization of some patients as patients with a non-Danish ethnic background takes place because they are perceived as more difficult to treat than others, and ethnicity becomes a possible explanation of this difficulty. In comparison with the material from the USA, it is apparent that being categorized as different in the Danish context does not release any special rights, but on the contrary establishes a demand on the patients that they adapt to the existing system.

Notes

1. In medical journals, it has become common practice not to use the word "schizophrenics," but rather to write "people with a diagnosis of schizophrenia".

My use of the word mirrors the terminology of the psychiatric staff, who commonly used it to describe these patients.
2. The argument in this section was originally developed in the article "Islam in Danish psychiatry" ["Islam i dansk psykiatri"], Johansen and Johansen 2008.

References

APA. 1995. *Diagnostic and Statistical Manual of Mental Disorder: DSM IV*. Washington: American Psychiatric Association.

Barrett, Robert J. 1996. *The Psychiatric Team and the Social Definition of Schizophrenia*. Cambridge: Cambridge University Press.

Barth, Frederick. 2001[1969]. Introduction. Ethnic Groups and Boundaries. In *Socialantropologiske grunntekster*, ed. Thomas Hylland Eriksen, 251-280. Oslo: Gyldendal Norsk Forlag AS.

Budman, Cathy L., Juliene G. Lipson and Afaf I. Meleis. 1992. The Cultural Consultant in Mental Health Care: The Case of the Arab Adolescent. *American Journal of Orthopsychiatry*, 62 (3): 359-370.

Cantor-Graae, Elizabeth, Carsten B. Pedersen, Thomas F. McNeil and Preben Bo Mortensen. 2003. Migration as a Risk Factor for Schizophrenia: a Danish Population-Base Cohort Study. *British Journal of Psychiatry* 182: 117-122.

Cantor-Graae, Elizabeth and Jean-Paul Selten. 2005. Schizophrenia and Migration: A Meta-Analysis and Review. *American Journal of Psychiatry* 162 (1): 12-24.

Flemming, Candace M. 1996 Cultural Formulation of Psychiatric Diagnosis. Case No. 01. An American Indian Woman Suffering from Depression, Alcoholism, and Childhood Trauma. *Culture, Medicine, and Psychiatry* vol. 20 (2): 145-154.

Hervik, Peter. 2004. Anthropological Perspectives on the New Racism in Europe. *Ethnos* 69 (2): 149-55.

Hvenegård-Lassen, Kirsten. 1996. *Grænseland. Minoriteter, rettigheder og den nationale idé*. København: Det Danske Center for Menneskerettigheder.

Jarvis, Eric. 1998. Schizophrenia in British Immigrants: Recent Findings, Issues and Implications. *Transcultural Psychiatry* 35 (1): 39-74.

Jenkins, Richard. 1997. *Rethinking Ethnicity. Arguments and Explorations*. London: Sage Publications.

Jöhncke, Steffen, Mette Nordahl Svendsen and Susan Reynolds Whyte. 2004. Løsningsmodeller. Sociale teknologier som antropologisk arbejdsfelt. In *Viden om verden*, ed. Kirsten Hastrup, 385-407. København: Hans Reitzels Forlag.

Johansen, Katrine Schepelern. 2006. *Kultur og Psykiatri. En antropologi om transkulturel psykiatri på danske hospitaler.* Copenhagen: Institut for Antropologi, ph.d.-rækken nr. 37.

—. 2008. Der er to i et møde – perspektiver på kulturmødet fra psykiatrien. *Tidsskriftet antropologi,* 57: 27-45.

Johansen, Katrine Schepelern and Birgitte Schepelern Johansen. 2008. Islam i dansk psykiatri. *Tidsskrift for Islamforskning* 1: 30-43.

Johnson, Thomas M. and Arthur Kleinman. 1984. Cultural Concerns in Consultation Psychiatry. In *Manual of Psychiatric Consultation and Emergency Care,* ed. F.G. Guggenheim, 275-284. New York: Jason Aronson.

Kirmayer, Lawrence J. 1998. The Fate of Culture in DSM-IV. Editorial. *Transcultural Psychiatry* 35 (3): 339-342.

Kleinman, Arthur. 1988. *Rethinking Psychiatry. From Cultural Category to Personal Experience.* New York: Free Press.

Kragh, Helen. 2007. *Mangfoldighed, magt og minoriteter: Introduktion til minoritetsforskningens teorier.* Frederiksberg: Samfundslitteratur.

Kymlicka, Will. 1995. *The Rights of Minority Cultures,* Oxford: Oxford University Press.

Littlewood, Roland and Simon Dein. 2000. Introduction. In *Cultural Psychiatry and Medical Anthropology. An Introduction and Reader,* ed. Roland Littlewood and Simon Dein, 1-34. London, The Athlone Press.

Lewis-Fernández, Roberto. 1996. Cultural Formulation of Psychiatric Diagnosis: Introduction. *Culture, Medicine and Psychiatry,* 20 (2): 133-144.

Luhrmann, Tania M. 2000. *Of Two Minds. The Growing Disorder in American Psychiatry.* New York: Alfred A. Knopf.

Mezzich, Juan E., Arthur Kleinman, Horatio Fabregga and Dolores L. Parron. 1996. *Culture and Psychiatric Diagnosis. A DSM-IV Perspective.* Washington: American Psychiatric Press, Inc.

Proulx, Pierre-Luc Dostie 2007. American Citizenship and Minority Rights. *Critique: A worldwide journal on politics,* Spring 2007: 43-63.

Santiago-Irizarry, Vilma. 2001. *Medicalizing Medicalizing Ethnicity. The Construction of Latino Identity in a Psychiatric Setting.* Ithaca: Cornell University Press.

Simonsen, Jørgen Bæk. 2004. *Islam med danske øjne. Danskeres syn på islam gennem 1000 år.* København: Akademisk Forlag.

Skrentny, John D. 2002. *The Minority Rights Revolution.* Harvard: Harvard University Press.

Spector, Malcom and John I. Kitsuse. 2001. *Constructing Social Problems*. New Brunswick, Transaction Publishers.
van Dijk, Rob. 1998. Culture as Excuse: The Failures of Health Care to Migrants in The Netherlands. In *The Art of Medical Anthropology. Readings*, ed. Sjaak van der Geest and Adri Rienks, 243-250. Amsterdam: Het Spinhuis Publichers.
Vendsborg, Per B. 2003. Indsatsen for mennesker med dobbeltdiagnose. In *Cocktail med udfordringer. En antologi om mennesker med sindslidelse og misbrug*, ed. Kristian W. Andersen and Dorthe Perit, 19-35. København: Socialt Udviklingscenter SUS.

Chapter Nine

Suffering for Benefits? Integration and Social Exchange between Iraqi Refugees and Danish Welfare Institutions

Sofie Danneskiold-Samsoe

The issues of the influx of refugees and immigrants and their integration into Danish society have been given a great deal of attention in the public health sector, and the Danish authorities have formed a system for the medical and psychological treatment of traumatized refugees. An institutional framework has been set up to organize and perform the work of rehabilitation, now based on a considerable knowledge of and experience with diagnosis and treatment. In the past 28 years, 13 specialized centers for the treatment of torture victims and traumatized refugees have been established throughout the country (traume.dk). The Rehabilitation Centre for Torture Victims (RCT) was the first of these centres to be established, in 1982. It was also the first centre in the world for the rehabilitation of survivors of torture founded by medical doctors engaged in Amnesty International's medical group. The aim was to improve the treatment of victims of torture who had sought asylum in Denmark from the military regime in Greece and from South American countries during the 1970's by specializing and doing research in the field of rehabilitation (RCT 2003). Since then, the centre has supported the establishment of other rehabilitation centres throughout the world and urged the UN to draw up the "Convention Against Torture and Other Cruel, Inhuman or Degrading Treatment or Punishment" in order to eliminate torture and the suffering torture induces.

Today, one of the main groups among the clients of the RCT is refugees from Iraq – in some rehabilitation centres, up to half of the clients come from Iraq. They participate widely in rehabilitation programs for traumatized refugees and victims of torture and other forms of organized violence, and in this respect they are also the major targets of integration efforts by rehabilitation centres and the welfare system. In this chapter, I examine the role of welfare institutions in the incorporation of Iraqi refugees into Danish society. I argue that suffering has become a focal point in Iraqi refugees' interaction with Danish welfare institutions and demonstrate how divergent ideas among Iraqi refugees and Danish welfare professionals on suffering, politics and position in a globalized world inform this interaction. While different notions of suffering bring about misunderstandings and are disputed, the social exchange of suffering – however diverse the value of suffering may be – is also the motor behind the social interaction that takes place between Danish society and the Iraqi newcomers. Thus, suffering is a ticket to the granting of refugee status, to pensions, aid and appliances, as well as the special assistance that the supposedly traumatized refugees receive. To put it simply, welfare institutions provide residence, services and economic benefits, while refugees contribute with the social currency of suffering.

Let me introduce the problem with an example from the field. In the spring of 2004, the Danish-Iraqi Friendship Organization held a party in the gym of an inner-city school in Copenhagen. The gym was crowded with dressed-up men and women playing music, making speeches, reciting poetry and playing bingo. The adults were seated at the tables, while a group of 6- or 7-year-old sisters and cousins were playing their own game. One of the girls was sitting cross-legged above the others on a table with a pile of bingo cards in her hands. She ordered the other girls to stand *bil-kø* (an expression combining the Arabic preposition for "in" with the Danish word for "queue"), and the girls lined up in front of her. They were supposed to be clients at the local welfare office. The girl in front approached the social worker and presented her case: "I am ill and have a headache. I want to be excused from school!" Her claim was approved, and she was asked to write her name by being handed a pen and a bingo card to write on. "Should I write my name in Danish or Arabic?" she asked. "Both!" was the answer. The next girl in line claimed to be ill and to have a pain in her throat. She also wanted to have a day off to go to the doctor. And so the game continued, with varying sore body parts and permissions being granted or rejected by the "caseworker".

Here the girls were presenting an episode in which illness justifies exemption from demands and activities imposed on the refugees by the local social security office. Suffering becomes a resource by which they can act on an inscrutable caseworker, and they try to surpass each other in the illnesses they depict. In doing so they imitate the actions of their parents and the world in which they live, and as such their play not only illustrates a life marked by illness and suffering from persecution and oppression in Iraq, but also negotiations on suffering between Iraqi refugees and Danish welfare institutions. In other words, the girl's play is a representation of a social exchange that takes place with suffering as its core currency.

Social exchange

It has long been recognized within anthropology that certain obligations and moral conventions are attached to social exchange. Marcel Mauss was the first to explore reciprocity through an analysis and comparison of gift exchange within different societies in his pioneering essay *The Gift* (Mauss 2001 [1923]). He noted the triple obligation to give, receive and return a gift, this being a general moral obligation in all societies, despite the cultural varieties of reciprocal practices. Through compliance with these obligations of gift-giving, social relations are formed and affirmed. Conversely, not complying with these obligations, that is, not receiving or returning a gift, will disturb social coherence. The point is not just that the gift is a transfer of value from one person to another, but that in the act of giving a gift the gift-giver conveys a part of her- or himself, thereby forming a social bond with the receiving party. The person receiving a gift can never forget the gift-giver, since returning a gift will never clear the debt.

In his attempt to formulate a theory of exchange, Mauss has been followed by a number of anthropologists and other social scientists. The French anthropologist, Pierre Bourdieu, includes immaterial values, like services, and symbolic values, like honour, in social exchange (Bourdieu 1990). Within the period of time within which a gift is given (or a service provided) and reciprocated, the gift-giver is morally superior, thus winning esteem or prestige. Though the gift is apparently given selflessly and without any demand for a return, the price is an unspoken debt of gratitude.

Social rank and prestige thus become crucial for social exchange. On the one hand, social stratifications prescribe who is expected to give and return, the value of the gift, and the length of time between gift and return. On the other hand, the exchange in itself produces – and sometimes challenges – social stratifications like rank and prestige. This applies to social differences like gender, generation and ethnicity. It makes up a complex account of unspoken debits, an implicit moral making-up in which debtors are tied up by mutual liabilities. This is also the case when someone tries to override or evade a debt – the occasion on which implicit expectations of return become manifest.

This study of the social exchange of suffering and benefits is concerned with the tension between the integrating effect of exchange on the one hand – that is, the creation of social ties – and on the other hand the conflicts that arise as a consequence of disparate ways of understanding and valuing suffering. From this perspective, the heart of the matter is not who is the victim of integration – Iraqi refugees or Danish welfare state – but rather the social processes by which victims are produced. Thus, I do not intend to evaluate the integrating effect of the rehabilitation of torture victims as such. Instead I examine how the social exchange of suffering, as well as negotiations of the value of suffering, simultaneously creates binding social relations and reinforces victimization.

From the perspective of the welfare state, this reciprocal relationship leaves the sufferer as a debtor if they continue to suffer despite a massive effort to rehabilitate them, and therefore they do not contribute to society with valuables or by creating value that corresponds to the benefits they have received.[1] From the perspective of Iraqi refugees, continuous suffering confirms their position as creditors, since from their perspective, treatment and simple compensation do not correspond to the immense injustices they are the victims of and are suffering from. Suffering as a loss of what is of value in life plays a significant part in Iraqi social life. Everybody has a story of loss, most visibly the loss of health and of being able-bodied, as many were made invalids by warfare and torture. But loss of property, jobs, education and youth are also important. As such it is not only the loss of value that is of concern, but also the loss of any ability to produce value. This ability to generate value is the great pleasure and pride of these Iraqi refugees: to have children and to establish some kind of business, often in the form of a shop or service. They struggle to win some recognition for their gains and valuables, yet it is losses more than gains that seem to attain recognition.

A quest for recognition

As members of Shia Muslim opposition parties, one of the Iraqi communist parties or Kurdish opposition groups, four million Iraqis fled the country in the thirty years of Baathist rule (Jensen 2003: 49). Today 29,000 of these refugees and their families live in Denmark, where they constitute the largest group of refugees (Statistics Denmark 2010). The vast majority arrived in the 1990s, mostly in response to one or more of political events in Iraq, including the first political cleansing in 1979; the war against Iran 1980-88; the genocide al-Anfal on Iraqi Kurds in 1988; the attack on Kuwait and the subsequent defeat of Iraq and public revolt, al-Intifada, in 1991; and the international sanctions against Iraq in the 1990s, which caused poverty and a lack of medicine and food for large swathes of the Iraqi population. Every Iraqi I met during fieldwork recounted massive suffering as a result of these political events. Everyone had lost a relative or friend and had themselves been the victims of violent assaults, like forced conscription into war, imprisonment, torture, house searches, poison gas attacks, escape, loss of job, house and property – and many other things.

All these are common experiences of suffering, which are retold and re-enacted at political meetings and religious rituals and communicated through various forms of art, especially poetry. Every year the greatest martyr in Shia Islam, Hussain, the third imam and grandchild of the prophet Muhammad, is commemorated and his martyrdom celebrated in the ten days of mourning or *ashura* in the month of *Muharram*. Imam Hussain was brutally killed at Kerbala (in present-day Iraq) in AD 680 by the absolute ruler of the Arab world at that time, the caliph Yazid. Through passion plays, recitations of poems and collective flagellation (symbolically by slapping the right hand on left chest or forehead), the suffering of Imam Hussain is portrayed. This suffering is understood as resonating with the following 1,400 years of repression of Shia Muslims, and most recently the dictatorship of Saddam Hussein.

The period of my fieldwork[2] was characterized by hopes for the future and concern about whether relatives that had long since disappeared would be found and set free. For many, though, the invasion ended up causing sorrow when relatives and friends did not turn up or were found in mass graves or on lists of executed prisoners or, as happened for some, relatives died as a consequence of the military invasion. Lost relatives were commemorated in *fatiha* where friends and relatives gather in a common mourning ritual. A collective *fatiha* was organised for all missing martyrs (that is, those who had lost their lives as a consequence of oppression). At these gatherings suffering is presented through strong emotional expressions in sympathy with the sufferers.

My Iraqi informants tried to explain the suffering and to make it clear to me by showing video clips of torture and war, reciting poems about oppression and loss, and pulling out diaries hidden in closets. Photos from prisons, partisan and military camps, refugee identification papers, scars and other marks of violent attacks left on the body were shown to me. In other words, artefacts of suffering were put forward as proof and a call for recognition and sympathy.

My informants provided me with information and evidence as a researcher who would eventually write about their suffering. Yet, I was not the only recipient of this information. In many ways, Iraqis tried to inform the Danish authorities and the Danish public in general about the political situation in Iraq, and how they and fellow Iraqis back in Iraq were still victims of oppression. Iraqis told me how they had informed the Danish authorities for years about the existence of Iraqi spies working from Denmark and reporting to the Iraqi authorities (at the time of Baath party rule) about other Iraqis living as refugees in Denmark, and how they were harassed by the Iraqi authorities with anonymous telephone calls and enquiries to relatives in Iraq. For this reason, almost every Iraqi person I met had unlisted telephone numbers, and many changed telephone numbers frequently in order to prevent Baathist authorities tracking them down (before March 2003). Yet my informants told me that the tips they gave to the Danish authorities were ignored, and they regretted the lack of action against what they experienced as a threat to the security of themselves and their families. They experienced this lack of understanding as contributing to their continuous suffering. They explained the Danish indifference as being caused by what they perceived as Danish ignorance of the consequences of unequal power relations and political dominance.

Likewise Iraqi associations invite Danish people to political debates about Iraq, film showings and poetry readings. However, usually only a small number of Danes show up at these gatherings. Health professionals are the main audience for the sufferings of Iraqi refugees, since they recognize suffering as a health problem for which solutions are to be found within health technologies, rather than regarding suffering as a social condition to be understood and dealt with from a political and social perspective. Hence, it is mostly through rehabilitation and medical treatment that the suffering of Iraqi refugees receives a response from and recognition in Danish society. This chapter argues that this predominantly medical perspective on Iraqi suffering must be considered in relation to the practice of integration as a social solution model.

Integration as social solution model

In Denmark, integration has become an organized and politically motivated activity for the management of the social integration of immigrants, or what can be termed a social solution model (Jöhncke et al. 2004). These activities are attached to certain institutions, including a set of professionals who aim at solving the social problems of a specific target group. Recent anthropological studies show that social solution models not only apply to solving social problems, in the very attempt to do so they define the problems according to specific assumptions (ibid.). The point is that the solution predefines the social problem as well as the target group (for a more advanced discussion of the social implications of the social categorization implied in the definition of target group, see Johansen this volume). In the case of integration the target group is immigrants, the problem is the lack of their social integration into Danish society, and the solution is a number of institutional activities directed to them.

According to the current Integration Act, any newly arrived immigrants must sign a "Declaration of active participation in Danish society" as well as an "Integration contract"[3] with the local authorities within a month of arrival. According to the Ministry for Integration, the purpose of the declaration is to:

> render the values of Danish society visible for the individual foreigner and to make the foreigner aware about what Danish society expects and that one has to make an effort to be integrated as a participating and contributing fellow citizen on equal terms with other citizens.[4]

The integration contract sets out the specific content of a compulsory "Introduction programme," lasting up to three years on a full-time basis, in which local authorities organize activities for newcomers, including Danish language courses, counselling, and occupational training. According to the Ministry of Integration, the purpose of this program is to integrate newly arrived foreigners as appropriately and as quickly as possible into Danish society by assisting them in acquiring linguistic, cultural and professional qualifications and to make them independent of social benefits. All newly arrived immigrants have to comply with this objective, though special cases of foreigners with physical or psychological handicaps, experiences of torture or intense traumatization may be exempted.

The social solution model is based on practical interventions, yet it implies a moral imperative, that is, an idea of "the good society" or "the good citizen" and thus the morally correct or proper ways to address a certain problem. In the case of integration, the good immigrant makes an active and deliberate effort to acquire the Danish language, to learn about and assimilate into Danish culture, and to strive to be self-supportive through participation in the labour market. In order to achieve these objectives a number of social remedies are set up, like Danish language courses, social counselling, etc. These are what Jöhncke et al. term social technologies, that is, the processes through which social solution models are practised (Jöhncke 2004: 388-90). They are *social* because they aim to (trans)form social relations, and they are *technologies* because they function as tools in a practical as well as a metaphorical sense, including educational and therapeutic methodologies and activities.

Some refugees cannot comply with the demands of conventional social technologies for integration as they find it difficult to participate in the integration programme, let alone conform to the ideal of participation in Danish society as set out in the integration contract. It is hard for them to concentrate and learn in school and to hold a job due to physical handicaps and chronic pain from violent assaults. As an effect of violent assaults, many people lose the ability to concentrate and remember, or to learn altogether. As already mentioned, foreigners can be exempted in some cases if there is valid documentation for traumatization or sequelae from torture. In this case, treatment is often brought in as a remedy in order to document and rectify the requirements of the authorities. Therefore the local authorities often refer refugees to specialized rehabilitation centres.

Thus, in the Danish welfare state the suffering of refugees becomes an obstacle preventing them from participating in integration. As a social technology, rehabilitation represents a practical attempt to solve social problems of suffering derived from trauma and torture, implying a set of techniques as well as moral perspectives on the social problem at issue. Specially organized treatment and rehabilitation courses become social technologies set up in order to eliminate or alleviate the suffering that impedes refugees in participating in integration.

In the effort at rehabilitation, additional and specialized social technologies are applied. One notable example is the diagnosis of Post-Traumatic Stress Disorder (PTSD), a psychiatric diagnosis developed in the USA on the basis of the traumas of American veterans of the Vietnam War. The diagnosis has since spread to other parts of the world and been applied to other contexts, including the rehabilitation of traumatized refugees. At the same time, the diagnosis has obtained status as a valid proof of traumatization, which is of vast importance for the legal status of many refugees and their attainment of social benefits. As such, PTSD is not only a health technology, defining and solving health problems, it is also a social technology, solving social problems. As a result, it has social effects itself.

The solution of the welfare state to the suffering of refugees is based on the assumption that suffering from torture and other forms of organized violence takes the form of trauma (including PTSD). These traumas are difficult to treat, requiring a vast number of treatment sessions and a relationship of trust between the therapist and the client to make traumatic memory accessible and to allow the client to speak about painful experiences. A long process of treatment thus becomes the welfare state's solution to the social problem of suffering.

In Denmark, the rehabilitation of torture victims is now a generally recognized and specialized field among health professionals (assisted by a research department and documentation centre at RCT). Medical doctors and nurses are supplemented by psychologists and social counsellors and other professionals, so that rehabilitation has turned into an interdisciplinary working field, focusing less on recovery and more on coping. In addition, a considerable part of the professional's work is directed at assisting clients in their negotiations with the authorities in their struggles to obtain benefits and to meet the demand for integration. The professionals I met in fieldwork regarded themselves as mediators between their clients and the welfare state: having privileged knowledge of the suffering from torture and trauma, and knowing their clients well, they are able to explain particular difficulties and handicaps impeding participation in integration programs, and they were thus able to assist their clients with the required documentation of trauma and knowledge about the practice of welfare institutions.

This assistance was particularly appreciated by my Iraqi informants. Generally, they praised the welfare system and the specialized treatment they received. However, the idea that suffering can be treated or at least "left behind" provoked some of my informants. As Mariyam, a woman who spent her youth waiting for her husband to get out of Abu Ghraib prison in Baghdad in which he was kept for eleven and a half years, phrased it as follows:

> People say "forget it, leave it behind you". It is difficult because we are tied to our country and our history, and our families are still suffering there. We see it constantly: we find our family as bones, as bones in black plastic bags. This is not a simple case. Invasion after invasion. All we know is oppression. We shall never forget. Every day we sit and watch television [showing pictures from war In Iraq] and our children watch it....

Mariyam gives an example:

> When we came here [to Denmark], we lived in Jutland. There was a caseworker, and everybody thought she was racist. Anyhow, she sketched a car driving up a hill. She explained that the more load that is thrown overboard, the easier the car will drive up the hill. We went mad, we didn't understand. It didn't make sense. We are tied to our land and to our family there. We told her [the caseworker] to leave the subject alone.

Mariyam, who told me this anecdote, referred to a general demand on the part of the Danish authorities that refugees leave their suffering behind, as articulated metaphorically by the caseworker. The caseworker depicts integration as a hill to be climbed: the more you leave the past behind, the better you will integrate. According to this image integration is an individual effort, and the job of the caseworker is to motivate and assist the newcomer in it. This confirms the idea of integration as an institutional set-up organized in order to assist the newcomer, or in other words a social solution model.

Perhaps professional approaches to suffering do not conform with how Iraqi patients value their suffering and how they think it should be addressed, yet the very concern for their suffering is valued, and Iraqi refugees often compared the care they received in rehabilitation and from the state in Denmark in general with the humiliation and violence they were subjected to in Iraq. For some of them, the care they receive in health-care institutions is a crucial part of coping, even when the therapy is not progressive.

My Iraqi informants nonetheless appreciated these attempts, partly because treatment and compensation imply some recognition of suffering, and partly because it makes it possible for those who cannot work to survive economically. Moreover, it implies being included in a society based on the principles of equal rights and caring for the needy – principles that they did not find in Iraq and which they hoped to find in Europe. At times they would be overcome by gratitude to the receiving country and the welcoming therapists who tried to alleviate their suffering.

Generally, my Iraqi informants praised the Danish welfare system, some even describing the idea of a welfare system through which wealth is redistributed and the underprivileged are cared for as the kind of society they had envisaged in their struggle for a different Iraq. The Iraqi imam, al-Talkani, told me how he portrayed the Danish welfare system when Iraqi people came to listen to him on his visit to Iraq in the summer of 2003. He told them that he had been welcomed in Denmark with a warm heart and a yellow public health insurance card. "Denmark offers free health services," he said, "even though the country is not rich in natural resources like Iraq, a rich country in this sense, yet Iraq does not provide the same services to its people." He said this was proof of the cruelty of Saddam and how he spent all the wealth of Iraq on himself and on the most gruesome wars in the world.

With respect to the efforts of the Danish welfare state to eliminate suffering, the system of securing health and welfare for all citizens represents an ideal for many Iraqi refugees who have been deprived of their health and property. Alternatively, some Iraqis suggest that the idea of the welfare state is initially a vision deriving from socialism or Islam, from the idea of redistribution in communism, or from the obligation in Islam to give alms (*zakat*) and to do charity (*sadaqah*). In fact, the Danish word *skat* (tax) derives from the Arabic *zakat*,[5] as my Iraqi informants often reminded me.

Integration as social process

Despite appreciation of the welfare system in general and the care provided by rehabilitation programmes in particular, the suffering seems to continue. Recent medical surveys have shown that victims of torture do not experience positive effects on their health, even after extensive and specialized rehabilitation treatment (Carlson 2006; Olsen 2006). Yet, the same surveys show that those undergoing prolonged periods of treatment do appreciate the treatment to a great extent. My ethnographic study of suffering among Iraqi refugees (who constitute half the clients in the surveys mentioned) confirms the paradox, in the sense that my Iraqi informants describe themselves as suffering even after many years of treatment, but at the same time they value the treatment as a token of care and acknowledgement of their suffering.

I explain this paradox through the discrepancy of the value of suffering between the therapists and their Iraqi clients. My Iraqi informants do not think the treatment can make up for the magnitude of their suffering, and they think their suffering is being reduced when a day off can be exchanged for a headache, as the young girls showed in their play caricature of the relationship between the client and the caseworker. When suffering enters into a transaction as a form of currency in which it is measured and exchanged for a minor social benefit, its nature and magnitude is not sufficiently recognized. My Iraqi informants were therefore ambivalent towards assistance and social benefits. Because social benefits are regarded as a social gift, Iraqi beneficiaries are profoundly grateful and believe they are the objects of great generosity, which few of them ever will be able to repay. At the same time they do not think the assistance they receive really makes up for the suffering and malice they have been the victims of.

Few clients at rehabilitation centres are thus able to engage in integration in the form of organized and politically motivated activities, even after years of treatment, and many are permanently exempted from such demands by being granted a disability pension. From a Maussian perspective, however, one might argue that this social exchange of suffering, care and benefits is what social integration is all about, since social exchange creates social ties. The treatment of suffering implies a degree of concern and care that Iraqi patients appreciate as forms of response to their suffering, or which they search for when they do not seem to find it. Caring in this sense creates social ties in the world of suffering. Hence, the girls playing at being welfare officers are busy with social integration and are practising how to negotiate with welfare institutions. Yet, the currencies are not only headaches and other minor illnesses in a relatively simple exchange of social benefits: the girls are imitating a social practice of exchange in which there is much more at stake. In opposition to this simple form of exchange and uncomplicated responses to suffering are discussions about how to give an adequate response to suffering of a more profound kind.

One commentary in this heated debate is a caricature of a wounded soldier in the invasion of March 2003. In the days of the American-led coalition's invasion of Iraq, I found a cartoon hanging on the front door of one of my informant's, Jamil's, apartment block. An Iraqi man is lying wounded in a hospital bed, bandaged from head to foot, while an American soldier approaches him with a burger and a Coca-Cola. The symbolism is clear: the wounded Iraqi is an image of the Iraqi people suffering from decades of wars and oppression, unable to move and act, waiting for relief. Relief is coming in the form of burgers and Coca-Colas, the icons of American consumerism. The joke comes from the contrast between the immensity of the suffering and disability and the poor and ludicrous gifts of fast food.

I suggest that the cartoon is not only a political commentary on the current invasion, but also a statement on the reciprocity of suffering. The disproportion between genuine suffering and half-hearted responses to alleviate this is all too evident. As the cartoon indicates, Iraqi suffering is of such a magnitude that no liberating force will ever be able to make up for it fully, and any attempt to do so will simply devalue it. Despite some approval of the invasion, none of my informants believed that the USA intervened for the sake of the Iraqi people. For them, the true motive was to be found in Iraq's oil reserves, and the claim to be bringing freedom and democracy to the country was just a screen for the real policy of controlling and exploiting Iraq's natural riches. The cost of freedom was thus access and control of oil resources. In political debates over the invasion, Iraqi refugees only reluctantly accepted a balanced reciprocal exchange of oil for liberation with the liberators, and they insisted that liberation from a cruel dictatorship should not be quantified or balanced.

The situation played out by the girls playing at being welfare officers stands in stark contrast to this experience: their illnesses are quantifiable, and they present them for the municipal caseworker to respond to with measured benefits. The relationship between the girls and the caseworker is based on a reciprocal exchange that is balanced and terminated by the return.

These examples of reciprocity are parodies of social life based on children's imitations and a satirical cartoon. In the case of the children's play, suffering is apparently easily assessed and reciprocated, while according to the cartoon suffering is of a much more profound nature, making any possible return much more contested. As parodies, they are cultural reflections on the value and reciprocity of suffering. As such, they push the point to an extreme while illustrating different forms of social exchange according to the assessed value of the suffering. Together the two cases illustrate the two extremes of a hierarchy of suffering.

The American anthropologist David Graeber suggests we think about reciprocity as relatively either "open" or "closed." In an open reciprocal relationship of mutual commitment, no one keeps accounts, whereas a closed social relationship is based on the understanding that the relationship will eventually be closed by a balancing of accounts, whether or not this actually happens at some point (Graeber 2001: 220). By applying the terms "open" and "closed," reciprocity becomes a matter of degree rather than of kind, which I believe accommodates an understanding of reciprocal relationships as negotiable. How open or closed such relationships are is not definite, and the understanding of them might also change over time. Categorizing reciprocity as an academic exercise without including how others interpret, categorize and negotiate reciprocity as more or less open or closed will not allow one to understand the matter fully.

Where one's suffering is to be placed in the hierarchy of suffering therefore depends on how the suffering is recognized and how this recognition is negotiated. The examples demonstrate that illnesses at the lower end of the ranking system such as headaches and back pains can easily be measured and responded to with treatment and compensation. Here, a social exchange of suffering takes place through principles of closed reciprocity. At the other end of the system, suffering caused by political persecution and torture has no equivalent response, and any attempt to provide one will be regarded as demeaning. Only unselfish concern and care will provide some easing of the suffering, not in the form of its elimination, but rather as confirmation of its validity. Iraqi sufferers regard the relationship between caregiver and sufferer as an open reciprocal relationship with no expectation of return. Anything else would be an offence to a genuine sufferer.

The idea that extensive suffering can be compensated sometimes creates frustration among Iraqi beneficiaries of social and health services. Compared with the moral status of their suffering, they believe it is being reduced to mundane disabilities and thus is not really recognized for what it is by the welfare institutions that are meant to help and provide care for them. For instance, Jamil told me with exasperation how his doctor suggested that he eat cornflakes as a treatment for indigestion and stomach pains. He told me the story after a prolonged account of his imprisonment and torture as a young communist in Iraq, how he escaped by hiding in Bagdad, how he was caught and forced to serve in the army in Iraqi Kurdistan, and his time as a soldier in the first Gulf War, which ended with his capture and four years of imprisonment in a Saudi Arabian military camp. "Cornflakes!" he snorted; "How would that help? I don't even like cornflakes, nor milk for that matter.... Well, maybe I could eat cornflakes with beer!"

Jamil laughed at his ironic suggestion that he should eat the cornflakes with beer as a solution, not only because beer and cornflakes do not go well together, but also because his response to suffering and the doctor's understanding of it were incompatible. The doctor suggested addressing his illness by simply changing his diet and thus presented it as a shallow problem that could be rectified by a simple act of eating cornflakes. Jamil was offended by the suggestion. To his mind, the act of eating cornflakes did not correspond to the genuine and complex nature of his suffering.

In fact Jamil often resorts to drinking beer as a way to endure his suffering, he told me. He also goes out on Friday and Saturday evenings to meet friends and talks and drinks with them. On these occasions, he will engage in heated political discussions and reminisce about the Iraq of his childhood and youth, while beer and vodka ease his words and his nostalgia. I often met him on occasions like this, always in a good mood and very talkative. It seemed that he was helped by engaging in these social activities, where his suffering was recognized and affirmed.

Coping strategies like these are exactly what professionals in rehabilitation are working towards (though they do not prescribe the excessive drinking). The word "rehabilitation" suggests becoming capable or competent again after the ability to function fully has been damaged. In counselling for coping, rehabilitation implies the modest and pragmatic aims of acceptance of the limitations of a cure and the taking of small steps to improve everyday tasks like economizing one's strength and energy and avoiding situations that trigger pain. The assessment of one's level of functioning and the focus on coping in counselling thus refer to the same idea of rehabilitation. The idea is that, when the causes of suffering cannot be treated and when there is no cure, the next best thing is to help the patient find ways to cope. Counselling is an activity in rehabilitation in which a professional will try to investigate possible coping strategies for the individual patient, like going for a walk, reading or other activities, depending on the individual, as long as they are not self-destructive or harmful to others. However, this does not correspond to Iraqis' own ideas of suffering and therapy.

Fatima is another Iraqi refugee searching for recognition of her suffering. I visited her, her husband Sadik and their four children once a week for about a year and joined her on her frequent visits to the doctor. Fatima would go to the doctor, leaning on the doctor's desk, while putting her hand to her forehead in pain, telling the doctor how she suffers from headaches, backache, weariness, pain in the eyes, a heart disorder, high blood pressure, irregular menstruation, unwanted pregnancies and depression. To me she described her life as miserable and desperate. She told me of her father who was killed when a bomb hit her family's house, about living in (relative) poverty and not seeing any way out, about living with a husband who had been handicapped and traumatized by war and imprisonment in Iraq and Saudi Arabia, and at the same time about being responsible for maintaining a home and raising four children.

One day Fatima took a plastic bag full of medicines and poured the contents out on to the floor. She had a strong headache that day and she was not sure what medicine to take against it, so she asked me for advice. I noticed that many of the packets of medicine had never been opened. Every time Fatima goes to the doctor, she explained, she is given another medicine but does not understand what for. "Does it help you?" I asked. Fatima said she did not really know, and she finished off the subject by lying on the floor stretched out and exclaiming, "I'm going to die soon!"

She was saying this with a wry smile on her face, half serious, half joking, as she was contemplating the melodrama of her lying among the scattered glasses and packets of medicine, at the same time seeing no way out of the deadlock of her hopeless situation and genuinely feeling miserable, underlined by her lying down as if dead. Not even medicine would ease her suffering, its efficacious effects being itself evidence of her suffering. The point was not to elaborate on her exclamation because that would narrow the suffering. The effect was one of being inscrutable, emphasized by the drama of her lying down, as if she were in fact already dead. In her exclamation on her seemingly imminent death, she summarizes her experience of a complexity of suffering, symbolized by the total collection of medicine spread out randomly on the floor. Just as the total collection of medicine symbolizes a complex of suffering, Fatima's frequent visits to the doctor becomes a ritual confirming her experience of being the victim of a "generalized malaise" (Desjarlais and Kleinman 1995) which is not easily divided into particulars. Considered separately, every visit to the doctor can be seen as a request for the treatment of an isolated symptom. But taken together, the many consultations outline another picture. A complex of suffering is not easily defined and thus not easily treated. Any attempt to treat a single symptom will be inadequate, and consequently Fatima omitted to take most of the prescribed medicines.

The purpose of rehabilitation is to alleviate or (at best) eliminate suffering and to make sufferers capable citizens. This aim is approached by defining (or in this case diagnosing) suffering in order to make it manageable, that is, to divide it into units that specialists can handle. This approach to suffering frames how suffering is represented and valorized in social exchange. The response to suffering is set within this framework of rehabilitation and compensation. However, Fatima does not find space within this framework to express her suffering thoroughly, and Jamil complains how the response to his suffering from war and torture is advice on a change of diet.

These examples, of course, push the point to an extreme. The point is that the suffering of Fatima and Jamil is not alleviated in any substantial way. Their martyrdom cannot be boiled down to a list of symptoms and diagnoses. Nevertheless, my Iraqi informants did appreciate the responses of the welfare state to their suffering due to the recognition and care that is implied in rehabilitation and compensation. They had the experience of being included in a caring society in which everyone has access to welfare benefits. They valued the rejection of dominance and praised the efforts to eliminate their suffering through the provision of free and general health services and the generosity of politicians in distributing wealth to the needy. On the other hand, they were sceptical of what they regarded as the political ignorance of Danish institutions.

This ambivalent view of the politics of the Danish bureaucracy reflects the ambiguity of politics in general. As Jamil said, politics are not "pure," but you must somehow analyze human action as political action and engage in that action to understand the world you are living in and ultimately to survive.

The politics of welfare and reciprocity

At a public meeting two weeks after the conquest of Baghdad, the Worker's Communist Parties of Iraq and Iran held a meeting at a community centre in Copenhagen on the issue of the future of Iraq. The last speaker was Abdulatef al-Mashadani from the Communist Party. He criticized the recent invasion of Iraq and urged the UN to support the Iraqi people in its peace-keeping operations and the reconstruction of the country. Now the Iraqi people were victims not only of a "horror dictator" but also of the American "military machine," and he saw the UN as the only guarantor of Iraqi autonomy. "Comrades and friends," he concluded, "freedom can only be accomplished through will and effort. It can never be turned over and obtained as a gift." For Abdulatef, the invasion purported to be a generous gift, a humanitarian response to Iraqi suffering devoid of ulterior motives, while in fact its real intention was to obtain control over vast oil reserves. Instead of an open reciprocal relationship in which the return is indeterminate, the coalition forces were assuming the existence of a closed reciprocal relationship where giving and taking were assumed to correspond immediately.

This analysis suggests that the discussion is not only a commentary on the political situation in Iraq, but also a general valuation of Iraqi suffering in relation to the socio-political order of the world in which the refugees live. However, suffering on this scale is hard to reciprocate, even by launching a large-scale invasion. On the other hand, rehabilitation and other social benefits are offered as responses to Iraqi suffering and as a model for social integration.

The discourse on reciprocity in the welfare state is mirrored by Danish national politics, in which the degree of how open or closed the reciprocal relationship is supposed to be is debated, especially concerning that between immigrants and welfare institutions. At the opening of the Danish parliament on 7 October 2003, Prime Minister Anders Fogh Rasmussen stated:

> The founding principle of our society is that everyone makes an effort and that special efforts are recognized. Consequently, the individual must sense the consequences when he does not fulfil his obligations. The individual must apply the principle of "something for something". [...] For many years immigration policy was characterized by a laxity and lack of consistency. We must make demands and demonstrate consistency in immigration policy. The individual immigrant has a great responsibility to be integrated. They must learn Danish. And they must accept the fundamental values of our society.[6]

The Prime Minister was arguing for a balanced, reciprocal relationship of "something for something" between welfare institutions and citizens. This was supposedly meant to stand in opposition to a dominant reciprocal principle based on generosity, or in Graeber's terms closed and open reciprocity respectively. In announcing the relationship of reciprocity as an object of political debate, this quotation indicates that principles of reciprocity are negotiable. However, it is more of a political signal than a reference to actual reciprocal negotiations. Nonetheless the passage reflects the political climate in which my fieldwork took place. It also summarizes the two major subjects in Danish political debates at the time: the future of the welfare state, and the integration of immigrants, two subjects which are increasingly being associated in current political discourse.

Recently the sociologist Mehmet Necef of the University of Southern Denmark has applied Mauss's notion of reciprocity to an analysis of the relationship between immigrants and the welfare state (Necef 2004), which he suggests should be based on a reciprocal principle of mutual obligations to give and return. He claims that the Danish welfare state has previously been run according to a principle of charity or of "something for nothing" (*noget for ingenting*); now it has to change to a principle of reciprocity or "something for something" (*noget for noget*). In other words, social benefits and services must be reciprocated. According to Necef, this obligation to repay social gifts has to be reinforced and communicated more clearly to immigrants, as they seem not to have recognized that the relationship is reciprocal (Necef 2004: 4).

Exactly how immigrants are to return benefits and by what means is often left unclear in general statements on reciprocity, though the Prime Minister indicated accepting "the fundamental values of our society" as a possible return (though he declined to state what these values are).

Conclusion

In this chapter, I have endeavoured to demonstrate processes of social reciprocity between Iraqi torture victims in Denmark and the welfare institutions that seek to help them. I have shown that, by insisting on the high value of suffering, Iraqi refugees confirm the image of immigrants as those in need of special assistance in becoming integrated. To a great extent they do accept the social solution model of the welfare state, including rehabilitation and compensation as specific welfare technologies. This implies that the integration of Iraqis into Danish society has primarily been taken place in specialized institutions, structuring daily life and framing social encounters with Danish society and Danish fellow citizens. It also implies that suffering has been turned into a core currency in negotiations between welfare institutions and Iraqi clients in the attempt to reciprocate the gift of care and compensation. Paradoxically, the rhetoric of suffering has become a way of consolidating difference by creating barriers that harden or inscribe and rationalize two incommensurate domains of moral humanity.

Notes

1. This position is valid from a socio-political perspective, as well as from the "hardliner's" perspective. In the first case, refugees become victims locked in their position as sufferers, where they could not return the assistance they obtain even if they wanted to. In the second perspective, refugees are suspected of not wanting or not having any incentive to return the benefits and assistance they have received.
2. I did fieldwork for one year from November 2002 to October 2003.
3. An English version of the contract can be accessed at this website: http://www.nyidanmark.dk/da-dk/Blanketter/SearchForms.htm?SearchType=forms&Keywords=aktivt%20medborgerskab&PerformSearch=True (Ministry of Refugee, Immigration and Integration Affairs 2010).
4. Translation from Danish by the author. Original text at http://www.nyidanmark.dk/da-dk/Integration/integration_af_nyankomne/introduktionsprogrammet/integrationskontrakt_og_erklaering.htm (Ministry of Refugee, Immigration and Integration Affairs 2010).
5. Some Islamic scholars argue that Islam constitutes the first social theory for the welfare state (Vroldby 1988).
6. Translation from Danish by the author. Original speech at http://www.statsministeriet.dk/_p_7446.html (Rasmussen 2003).

References

Bourdieu, Pierre. 1990. *The logic of practice*. Cambridge: Polity Press.
Carlson, Jessica. 2006. *Mental health and health-related quality of life in tortured refugees*. Ph.D. Thesis, Copenhagen: Rehabilitation and Research Centre for Torture Victims.
Desjarlais, Robert, and Arthur Kleinman. 1995. Violence, Culture, and the Politics of Trauma. In *Writing at the Margin: Discourse between Anthropology and Medicine*, ed. A. Kleinman, 173-189. Berkeley: University of California Press.
Graeber, David. 2001. *Toward an Anthropological Theory of Value: The False Coin of Our Own Dreams*. New York: Palgrave.

Jensen, Michael Irving. 2003. *Irak fra diktatur til demokrati?* Copenhagen: Lindhardt and Ringhof.
Jöhncke, Steffen; Mette Nordahl Svendsen and Susan Reynolds Whyte. 2004. Løsningsmodeller: Sociale teknologier som antropologisk arbejdsfelt. In *Viden om verden*, ed. Kirsten Hastrup, 385-407. Copenhagen: Hans Reitzels Forlag.
Mauss, Marcel. 2001 [1923]. *The Gift: The Form and Reason for Exchange in Archaic Societies*. London: Routledge.
Ministry of Refugee, Immigration and Integration Affairs. (http://www.nyidanmark.dk/da.dk/Blanketter/SearchForms.htm?Searc Type=forms&Keywords=aktivt%20medborgerskab&PerformSearch= rue, accessed June 1, 2010).
Ministry of Refugee, Immigration and Integration Affairs. (http://www.nyidanmark.dk/da.dk/Integration/integration_af_nyanko ne/introduktionsprogrammet/integrationskontrakt_og_erklaering.htm, accessed June 1, 2010).
Necef, Mehmet. 2004. Lønnen fra FN. *Information om Indvandrere* 8 (1): 1-4
Olsen, Dorte Reff. 2006. *Prevalent pain in refugees previously exposed to torture*. Ph.D. Thesis, Faculty of Health Sciences, Aarhus University.
Rasmussen, Anders Fogh. Opening speech at the Danish parliament, October 7, 2003. (http://www.statsministeriet.dk/_p_7446.html, accessed June 29, 2010).
Rehabilitation and Research Centre for Torture Victims (Copenhagen). Rehabilitation and Research Centre for Torture Victims. 2003. *RCTs 20 års jubilæumssymposium*, 2002–30 October. University Hospital, Copenhagen: RCT Working Papers 1/2003: 20-22.
Statistics Denmark - statbank.dk, select from table FOLK 1 2010M04 (accessed June 1, 2010).
traume.dk, www.traume.dk accessed November 3, 2010.
Vroldby, Jens Due. 1988. *Den første velfærdsstat*. Frederiksberg: Alif.

Chapter Ten

Caught in the Grid of Difference and Gratitude: HIV Positive Africans Facing the Challenges of Danish Sociality

Hanne Overgaard Mogensen

Introduction

It was one of those cold days in January when the streets of Copenhagen were covered in a grey mush of salt and snow. The wind was freezing cold, and the daylight barely made its appearance before again turning into a grey twilight and then darkness. In an attempt to establish a rapport through a recognition of our common connection to Uganda, the very first thing I said was: "One of those days that makes you wonder why you are living in Denmark rather than Uganda, isn't it?"

"No," Harriet said, who was waiting for me at the centre for HIV counselling, where we had agreed to meet. "I never wonder that. I like Denmark much more than Uganda. I like Danish people. Even the weather doesn't bother me."

It was my first encounter with Harriet, and it was the very beginning of a research project that took place in 2006, exploring the life of HIV-positive Africans living in Denmark and receiving antiretroviral treatment. It was well known, and of great concern to organizations counselling people living with HIV/AIDS, that it was as difficult as ever to be HIV positive and African in Denmark, in spite of the fact that free antiretroviral treatment had by then been available and effectively prolonging people's lives for close to a decade. While I took off my coat Harriet went on praising Denmark and Danes, and before I had made it to the chair next to her, she had given me the impression that she would not be able to help me understand the challenges of HIV-positive Africans in Denmark. She seemed to love living in Denmark.

I soon realized though, that, through her account of her journey from Uganda to Denmark, her attempts to distance herself from other Africans in Denmark and her insistence that she was Danish, she took me right to the core of what it means to be an HIV-positive African in Denmark, and thus be un-integrated in more than one way. For Africans on antiretroviral treatment, everyday life is an ongoing struggle to become (re)integrated into the life of the living, as well as into Danish society. It is a struggle during which many experience an exclusion from African networks and yet never really become part of social life in Denmark.

Being HIV positive at times makes it necessary for Africans to redefine themselves and their ethnic belonging. This can therefore provide us with insights into what happens when people actively try to obtain a Danish identity. When we follow the dilemmas, paradoxes and obstacles they encounter on their way, implicit assumptions in Danish debates on integration and on what it means to be Danish will be challenged. From their attempts to become Danish – or simply to establish a social life in Denmark – we catch sight of what characterizes sociality in Denmark.

Integrating HIV-positive Africans into the Danish welfare state

Classical anthropological and sociological debates were often concerned with questions of integration. Émile Durkheim, for instance, pointed out that together individuals create something, a society, which is larger than the sum of the individuals who make it up (Durkheim 1996 [1895]). Georg Simmel was interested in those apparently contradictory processes which together make society an integrated whole. We become integrated as a group, he writes, through a constant oscillation between closeness and distance, intimacy and strangeness, imitation and differentiation. Strangers and difference are fundamental principles in any social interaction (Simmel 1950, 1971). Unlike the present debate on integration in Denmark, which focuses on how divergent individuals and groups can be integrated into a predefined entity, the starting point of these early social scientists was that cohesion arises through differences and internal conflicts. They were not concerned about "whether" integration took place, but "how" it took place, that is, the nature of society's cohesion. From their point of view, the question is therefore not how to integrate HIV-positive Africans into Danish society, but the ways in which they are already integrated through "apparently contradictory processes" and what this teaches us about sociality in Denmark.

The eight women[1] whom I followed for about ten months in my study all came from countries in southern and eastern Africa (Uganda, Kenya, Malawi, Zambia). I visited them between one and five times. Some of these visits were limited to the interview, while others lasted most of the day while we cooked and had a meal together or went for a walk and did some shopping together. However, none of the women wished to invite me to take part in any other social activities in their lives, since, as I shall discuss later, I was a potential threat to their attempts to keep their status as HIV-positive secret. In my interactions with the women, I drew extensively on my fifteen years of fieldwork experience in various African countries, and their past lives in their home countries played a central role in our conversations. Harriet's story is prominent in the presentation of my argument. I will draw on the other women in the study in my analysis of Harriet's experience, but I have chosen to follow in detail the development of one person's story over time. This allows me to show how the apparently contradictory processes discussed by Simmel (1950) come to play a part in a person's life. Harriet was chosen because she was one of those with whom I had the most contact, and because her story and our sense of shared experience acquired a particular depth, thanks to my many years of research on women and HIV/AIDS in Uganda.

According to the national statistics office (Statistics Denmark 2006), all African groups in Denmark (except for Somalis[2]) are counted in the hundreds. Kenyans and Ugandans comprise the biggest groups with respectively 774 and 662 persons in 2006 (plus 144 and 201 descendants from these two nationalities). We are thus dealing with relatively small numbers of people, originating primarily from countries in which Danish development organizations have worked extensively. Some of the Ugandans in Denmark came as refugees during the years of political instability and civil war in the 1970s and 1980s, but many arrived later as the spouses of Danish development workers who have returned to Denmark.[3] Five of the eight women interviewed for the study came to Denmark as the spouse of a Danish man who had worked in their home country. They were all divorced at the time of the study, and they all felt that their husbands had abandoned them after their HIV status had been revealed.

Large public campaigns informing people about HIV/AIDS and encouraging condom use were initiated in Denmark in the late 1980s but eased off in the early 1990s and were replaced by campaigns directed at specific target groups (in particular men who have sex with men and people with non-Danish ethnic backgrounds, especially African communities). AIDS incidence and mortality have been reduced by more than 80% thanks to medical treatment that started improving dramatically in the mid-nineties and which has been provided free to anybody with a Danish residence permit throughout the epidemic. The absence of spread in the heterosexual population of Danish origin, the reduction in morbidity and mortality, and the considerable improvements in the quality of life of people who are infected are all noteworthy and very positive outcomes of the measures taken against HIV/AIDS. But concerns remain that neither the large-scale public campaigns nor the more targeted campaigns, nor the treatment itself, have made any difference with regard to the number of new cases, a figure that has remained stable throughout the years (Cowan and Smith 2006). Since the early nineties, two to three hundred new cases of HIV have been diagnosed every year in Denmark. However, the proportion of people of African origin among the new cases has been steadily increasing (ibid.). About one third of new cases are now found among immigrants and refugees from sub-Saharan Africa, Ugandans being by far the largest group. Due to steady improvements in the treatment, being HIV positive is now by and large considered a chronic condition rather than a deadly disease. This, however, does not mean that a life on antiretroviral treatment is uncomplicated. The treatment may cause a number of more or less serious side effects; it submits one's life to various kinds of regulations and to numerous controls and visits to the hospital. As we shall see below, re-integration into a life among the living is in no way straightforward or uncomplicated, and even less so for people of African origin living in Denmark.

As mentioned above, the ongoing debate on integration in Denmark takes its starting point in the idea that it is a challenge to incorporate what is "different" into an already existing and relatively harmonious entity (Danish society and culture). Gullestad (1991) has pointed out that there is a specifically Scandinavian understanding of "sameness" as a precondition for "equality," which is not as entrenched in the US, for example, where difference is not necessarily seen as an obstacle to equality. Steffen Jöhncke shows that a strong belief that the encompassing welfare state provides a benevolent society for everybody plays an important role in Danes' self-perception (Jöhncke, this volume), and that this idea about the welfare state also takes it starting point in the notion of sameness as a precondition for equality. What characterizes the Scandinavian welfare state model is that it is built on a universalistic principle, according to which all residents receive services to which they are entitled (e.g. retirement pension, education) and can receive other services according to their needs (e.g. health care, disability pension). Financing takes place through general taxation and not through insurance schemes, as in many other welfare states (Jöhncke, this volume). The idea is that everybody contributes and everybody benefits, and that the number of people benefitting more than contributing should remain low. Special provision for and consideration of different groups should be minimized. This is usually done with reference to the principle of "equal treatment," which interestingly is interpreted in general as "the same treatment for all" regardless of manifest differences between people (Jöhncke 1996: 168). One of the consequences of this, for instance, is that service provisions for people living with HIV/AIDS are not directed at the particular group of people (proportionally more and more Africans) who use it (ibid.).

Payment of taxes is proof of social participation and is regarded as a concrete contribution to the community and to the way society works: it is not just a contribution to an anonymous bureaucracy (Jöhncke, this volume). The implicit cultural assumption here is that the system works as long as most residents provide for themselves by working and only make use of the services when necessary. In other words, the welfare system is integrative in the sense that it creates a shared feeling of everybody contributing to a system which everybody benefits from – as long as there are not too many who benefit more than they contribute (Jöhncke, this volume). The people on whom the present chapter is based cannot live up to these ideals. They are painfully aware that, in the eyes of others, they benefit far more than they contribute. They are grateful for this, but they also struggle with overwhelming experiences of loneliness. By listening to Harriet's story and following the concerns and dilemmas that she and other HIV-positive African women in Denmark encounter, we will catch sight of the ways in which the ideas described above about integration, sameness and the welfare system shape the kinds of sociality that characterize Danish society.

From Uganda to Denmark

Antiretroviral treatment has finally reached Africa, and in Uganda it is now available for free or almost for free. Thousands of Ugandans lying on their deathbeds have in the past few years been brought back to life. With the medicine come new ways of living openly with the disease – and new possibilities of hiding it. A box of tablets is easier to hide than rashes on the skin and a wasting body, but you now also see people advertising themselves in the personal columns of the newspapers as "HIV positive and on antiretroviral treatment, searching for a partner in the same situation to start a life and a family with." Life on antiretroviral treatment should not be idealized, but the treatment is changing lives at a dramatic rate in Uganda and other African countries. After years of working with AIDS in Africa, it was therefore puzzling to me to be confronted with the fact that in many ways this is not the case for Africans in Denmark. They still feel increasingly stigmatized, and disclosure remains as – if not more – difficult now as in the 1990s. AIDS counsellors in Denmark therefore approached me, hoping that, with my experience of Africa, I could help them understand why this was so. This resulted in the small study carried out in 2006. For about a year I followed eight HIV-positive women living in and around Copenhagen, as well as the work of a Training, Information and Counselling Centre (TICC) financed by the National Board of Health and providing information and counselling to African communities in Denmark.

"My counsellor tells me that you have been to Uganda," Harriet says. "Yes I spent a year in a village in the East and I still go to Uganda regularly," I explained. "That is where I am from!", she exclaimed, and we soon found out that I had stayed with the ethnic group to which her father belonged, and therefore also she herself. In the meantime, however, she had also explained that she had never known her father, nor even seen a picture of him. "They say he got a passport and lives in England now. I am actually not even sure he is my father. But I went to boarding school in the East, so I know that part of the country very well." Harriet's mother was from the North, where Harriet also grew up, but we had managed to find points of commonality in both Denmark and Uganda, established her as a "Dane" and me as a "Ugandan," and then we went on to the story about her journey to Denmark and her life as an African in Denmark:

> "I am not trying to say that I don't like being black, but the African community is no good to me. They don't have a life. Each time you go to one of those African basement shops, you know, then you always see the same people there. They just sit all day and talk to each other in the shop. It is the same thing in the hairdressing salons where African women go to have their hair plaited. The women just sit and plait and gossip all day, and then social services turn up and remove their children."

"Maybe," I suggested, after her initially telling me how awful other Africans were, "it has something to do with the way foreigners are treated in this country and that Danish people are not so open towards them." "No, absolutely not," she said:

... that is the way they have chosen to live, and it does not have anything to do with Danish people. Danish people are nice and kind. All my friends are Danish, and I live like Danes. Denmark has done so much for me. But Africans, they just live that kind of life, you know. They are busy impressing each other, dressing smartly, walking up and down the street looking smart: 'Here I am. See my expensive clothes.' They expect that when you are completely well-dressed people look up to you. But Danish people are not like that. You cannot impress them that way. [...] In Denmark you can be so rich and famous, and still people do not notice you when you walk on the street. It is not by spending a lot of money [and] looking fancy that you make Danish people accept you. It was my husband who taught me that. He almost divorced me because I was also like that in the beginning. 'Whether you wear a jogging suit or a cashmere coat, you are the same,' he said. But other Africans haven't understood this.

Harriet came to Denmark in the late 1980s, when she was in her early twenties. She had married a Danish man working for a development organization in Uganda. Harriet told me the following about her life in Uganda and her journey to Denmark:

My mother was alone with nine children, and most of us had different fathers. We lived in a town in northern Uganda, where she made a living from brewing millet beer and alcohol from cassava. Then, of course, she became an alcoholic herself, and now and then a man passed by her place, drank her alcohol, and made her pregnant. When we asked who our fathers were she beat us, and she did not give us a good life, so when I got big enough I tried to spend as much time as possible with other relatives. It was during the wars in the 1970s and 1980s. If you knew how many people I have seen getting killed. [...] And you know the way Danish mothers put their children's drawings on the wall, even when they are not particularly good? My mother, when I showed her what I had done in school, she just said: 'Remove that piece of paper. I cannot afford to continue paying school fees anyway.' That is why I started dating men who were older than me. [...] I managed to find somebody who was willing to pay school fees. He did so for three years, but then he found somebody else. So I went to Kampala and started knocking on doors in big houses to hear if anybody would employ me. In one of the houses lived the man who later married me. He said I could work for him, but then he started loving me and brought me to Denmark. The moment I got out of the plane I sensed that this was the place where I wanted to live and die. Since then I have only been back to Uganda once.

Lotte Meinert (2005) has shown that, in Uganda, physical movement is also considered a change in one's social position, and a crucial part of the process towards adulthood. Some young Ugandans just move to their own hut on their father's land, but others move further, for example, to boarding schools in other parts of the country and maybe later to town to find work. The ultimate movement, the one everybody dreams about, is the trip to Europe. It is expected that if one succeeds in this it will improve not only one's own but also one's family's life, and the expectations for those who manage to reach Europe are extremely high (ibid.: 283).

Harriet was partly successful in moving away from her alcoholic mother thanks to accommodating relatives. With the help of an older lover, she made it to a boarding school in a different part of the county. When he let her down, she moved on to the capital and reached the ultimate goal: Europe. It was a huge step for her, both physically and socially.

> But after a couple of years in Denmark my husband said to me: 'You hear so much about this disease, AIDS, that so many Africans have. I would like us to be tested.' That is how I found out that I was HIV positive and he was negative. Afterwards I could feel that he no longer liked being with me. So we got divorced.

Exclusion from African networks

Having lost her husband and his Danish network, Harriet first tried to continue her movements towards a better life through other Africans in Denmark, but as we shall see, it eventually became impossible for her to be part of the African community. Harriet continued her story as follows:

> It was a little lonely for me in the town where we lived before I got divorced, because there were not many other Africans living there besides me. That is why I moved to Aalborg [the biggest town in northern Denmark] and thought that now I would be happy among Africans there. But that is not how it worked out. The medicine they gave us in the beginning had a lot of side effects, and at one stage I lost a lot of my hair. I went to a hairdressing salon in Aalborg to have the rest plaited, but when they saw my head they said: 'Why do you have so little hair?' 'Because of the HIV medicine I get,' I told them, 'but don't worry, just plait what is left and then I will wear a cap so that nobody will notice it is thin on the top of the head.' But once I had said it, they refused to touch me. That is how it has been each time I mention my disease to Africans. They simply turn their back on me. Once I had lunch in a park with six other African women. One of them asked why I had become so thin. So I told them the truth. First they were just quiet for long, but then one of them said, that it was stupid of me to say such things if I wanted to be with other Africans. So now I have stopped saying it.

Harriet's description of life and relationships with other Africans is long and complicated. She informs and warns African friends and lovers that she is HIV positive, but also she always wears sunglasses, even in rainy weather, and avoids going to bars and discos where Africans usually go. She sends her boyfriend – when she has one – to the African shops when she needs things from there because she wants to avoid being confronted by other Africans. She does not tell her stories chronologically, and it is possible that what she is describing is a question of increased isolation and withdrawal over the years, but it is also possible that she moves back and forth between participation in African communities and withdrawal from them.

Everybody I spoke to talked about this ambivalence towards other Africans. They say that they often see other Africans when they turn up for appointments at the hospital, but if you happen to meet any of these same people outside the hospitals, they will refuse to admit they were ever there. If you mention that you have seen the other person at the hospital, you have at the same time disclosed your HIV status and made yourself a potential victim of gossip. The medicine makes it possible to avoid those symptoms that used to be characteristic of AIDS patients (cough, rashes, loss of weight, etc.), but others have replaced them. Some people on antiretroviral treatment have problems with fat distribution, with especially the torso becoming heavy and the legs thin, weak, and at times painful. This is now being recognized as a sign that one is on antiretroviral treatment. Taking tablets morning and night is in itself revealing, even though the number of tablets one has to take has been reduced considerably in the past few years. Having visitors in your home can be problematic. Somebody may open the cupboard where you keep the medicine and see it. Antiretroviral medicine has given people new ways of hiding their disease, but also established new signs that reveal it. There is thus a continued need to control who has access to what kinds of information about one's life.

"After some time it got too complicated to live in Ålborg, where everybody knew I was HIV positive, so I decided to change my name and move to Copenhagen," Harriet continued:

> There were far more Africans in Copenhagen, so I thought I could start a new life there, but then somebody from Aalborg visited somebody in Copenhagen and recognized me. I have had so many problems with those other Africans. As you can see, my life has never been easy. Uganda did not bring me anything good. Then I came to Denmark and thought that finally I was going to be happy, but then this HIV was crammed into my already far too heavy rucksack. After the divorce and the move away from

the Africans in Aalborg my life was ruined, and I was so depressed that I just walked around in the streets and cried behind my sunglasses. At some stage I was so far out, that this was also how I made money. You know. Walking in the streets to make money. When you have a permanent problem that you cannot get rid of, then it really hurts when people use it against you. If people tell you that you are stupid, then you can try to be less stupid. But when it is something that you cannot do anything about, like your HIV status, then it is really painful to have it thrown at you all the time. That is why I feel much better when I am with Danish people. They don't insult me with my disease, and they do not expect me to hide it all the time.

What Harriet describes is very close to the situation depicted by Jens Seeberg (1996), who did fieldwork among HIV-positive Africans in Denmark in the early 1990s. In spite of the progress in treatment that has taken place since then, the fear of discrimination is still an overarching factor in the lives of HIV-positive Africans. "Africans are no good for me," Harriet repeatedly said; "Now I only have Danish friends. "Openness about one's HIV status is a serious obstacle to participation in African networks in Denmark, and Harriet's constant emphasis of her decision to distance herself from other Africans seemed to be an attempt to convince herself that she did not need them, even though she clearly also missed being with them. She was trying to rework the pain caused by their rejection through these kinds of narration. Our experience of the world gives shape to the stories we tell about our life. But the opposite is also true: through our stories we can shape our memories of what happened and our imaginings about where we would like to go from now (Bruner 1986). Harriet's stories about her lack of interest in other Africans must be seen in the light of the fact that their rejection of her had created a need for her to redefine herself as somebody who did not need to be with other Africans.

But why is it so difficult for these networks to include people with HIV? "Because they are so small," explained Peace Kabushenga, the founder of TICC. "News spreads fast, and they are all socially very dependent on each other. In addition, they are extremely careful about not confirming the image, which the surrounding society has of them as a group of people with HIV/AIDS." Seeberg has conducted a systematic reading of the way newspapers portray AIDS and Africa and shows how stereotypic images of African culture and sexuality have influenced news coverage, as well as research about AIDS in Africa, since the beginning of the epidemic (1996: 226-230). This has also been discussed in many international publications (e.g. Schoept 1991; Packard and Epstein 1991; Gausset 2001), and Seeberg (1996) has contributed further with a detailed analysis of how Africans in Denmark respond to these stereotypic categorizations of Africans as carriers of AIDS, and how each person who is infected therefore constantly tries to control information about his or her HIV status. Still many, like Harriet, have felt a need to share their experience with others, and it is their fear of exclusion which has kept them from being open about their HIV status. We must therefore extend our analysis to the network's desire to control information.

Georg Simmel suggests that in any social situation there is a need for discretion and respect for the sphere around individuals and groups, which delimits what is revealed and what is concealed. All social relationships, he says, are based on people knowing something about one another, but relationships also presuppose a certain ignorance and a measure of mutual concealment (1950: 308-9). Lying is but one of a number of possible means to restrict one person's knowledge of another, the most common of which are secrecy and concealment (1950: 316). Discretion thus consists not only in respecting secrets, but also in steering clear of the knowledge of all that the other does not explicitly reveal to us. For the sake of the interaction, we agree that "what is not concealed may be known" and "what is not revealed must not be known" (ibid.: 321). African networks struggle as a group against the surrounding society's categorization of them, and one of their means in this fight is precisely discretion. They tone down the presence of HIV in African communities and exclude those who, through their openness, nourish the negative stereotypes that surround them. Harriet did not respect the group's need for discretion because as an individual she needed to share her situation with other people. She transgressed the limits of what could and could not be said, was too outspoken, and had to suffer the consequences. Others did not come as close to exclusion as Harriet. They respected the group's need for discretion, but decided to withdraw anyway since they did not feel comfortable in social settings where there was no room for the condition that took up the most space in their lives: the fact that they were HIV positive.

Harriet lost her ethnic community and attempted instead to redefine herself as Danish rather than African.

Redefining belonging

Harriet's attempt to take a Danish identity upon herself was hardly noticed by the Danes around her and did not result in any sense of belonging. Instead it left her feeling lonelier than ever:

"I often need to talk to somebody about my HIV. It hurts to always have to be careful about saying what you think and feel. But Danish people have never abused me when I have been honest to them, so they are the ones I talk to about it. And I try to talk Danish. It makes people so happy when they hear that I try and that I do many of the same things that they do."

"Like what?" I asked. "Like going to 'Bakken' [an amusement park in the outskirts of Copenhagen]":

I am the only black person going to 'Bakken.' I also ride the bicycle around Copenhagen, but you do not see any other black people riding the bike. When I visit African people, I bring roasted pork and meatballs prepared the way Danish people make them, and I drink coffee made like Danish people make it. I also like the rice pudding and cherry sauce you eat for Christmas and dancing around the Christmas tree, because I know that now I have to live like Danish people if I want to have a life. Other Africans do not understand that. If just everybody did like me, then Danish people would be happy, and then life here would be much easier for us Africans.

Marianne Holm Pedersen (2005) has described what she calls "quiet integration" at the Danish kindergarten where she conducted fieldwork. By this she means all those things Muslim mothers do, like buying carnival costumes and Christmas trees for their children, so that they can participate in Danish traditions. But like Harriet's meatballs, cherry sauce and bike rides, these efforts were rarely noticed by others. The surrounding society notices the ways in which foreigners are different, but does not pay any attention to their attempts to do as the majority does. During follow-up visits at Harriet's place, it became clear to me that her efforts had indeed had limited results. "I feel so lonely," she explained on the phone, when she called to apologize that it had taken her so long to get back to me:

I am no longer used to being with other people. After our last meeting, I got all scared about meeting you again. Do not misunderstand me. It is just that I am not used to people being interested in talking to me, so I got all confused.

Later we sat on her huge soft couch, drinking tea and eating Danish pastries, and talked about the side effects of the medicine, the civil war in Uganda and her nice apartment. She then told me that she would like to move. The apartment is in a part of town where nobody is unemployed, and she always wonders what they think about her, the black woman who is always at home. She fears talking to them, because then maybe they will find out that she receives a disability pension, and they will think she is one of those people exploiting the system:

> That is also why I don't like looking too stylish. If I leave my apartment with make up and cashmere, maybe they will wonder why somebody like me, who does not work, can afford things like that. When I leave my place during the day, I always wear sunglasses so that other Africans do not recognize me if I am not in the mood to talk to them. But also because – I know it is stupid – but it is as if I can hide myself that way. I don't think you can imagine what it is like to always feel that everybody in the bus can see that you are different. I know that all they can see is that I am black, but it feels as if they can also see that I am HIV positive, on antiretroviral treatment and that I don't work. Actually, I mostly go out at night. Or I don't go out at all, except when I have an appointment at the hospital or with my counsellor.

It should be clear from the above that the challenges with which Harriet is faced cannot be reduced to racism. She is aware that people notice the black colour of her skin and that this may reinforce her position as a stranger, but what really worries her are the other ways in which she differs. She fears that her HIV and her inability to contribute to society are potentially even more damaging to her social life.

The Danes who listen to Harriet, and who do not abuse her when she talks about her disease, are the AIDS counsellors, a therapist she saw for a while, doctors at the hospital – and the anthropologist. Harriet speaks about everybody working within the health care system with warmth and gratitude, but there are not really any other Danes in her life. Those who are there are close, yet profoundly distant. They are professional listeners and caregivers, and they play an immense role in her life, which is structured around her appointments with them. But they do not pass by to hold her hand when she feels lonely and scared. They do not know what it means to miss plantains and enjoy the company of other Africans while having your hair plaited. They do not know either what it was like to grow up with civil war and hunger and only have one's mother's worn dresses to cover oneself with during the cool nights. They have no idea what a big effort it has been for her to come as far as she has, to fight for her continued schooling, to learn English, to be able to socialize with foreigners, and to make it all the way to Denmark.

Danes are close by in the sense that the welfare system is solicitous and considerate – and yet they are distant and uninterested in the person behind the patient. However, it is difficult to complain about this when one receives so much, when you are alive thanks to the solicitous system. "Denmark has done so much for me," was one of the first things Harriet said to me, and she repeated it again and again in the months that followed, often with tears running down her cheeks:

> You have to understand that it is not the photos from Uganda which you showed me that make me cry. It is not that I miss Uganda. I don't. Uganda has done no good for me. Not like Denmark. It is just that my conversations with you remind me how rare it is that somebody comes to me and says that they are interested in what I come from.

Danes' love of the Danish way of life is not something that is ignored by "foreigners." On the contrary, I heard of countless attempts to live up to and do things that were thought to be particularly Danish. For Harriet this included eating roast pork and riding a bicycle. But these efforts do not necessarily result in any new membership of networks or the establishment of new friendships with Danes. Georg Simmel provides useful insights for understanding this. He suggests that collectivity is achieved, in several respects, only through negation (1950: 396). As the size of the group increases, the common features that fuse its members into a social unit become fewer, and obligatory rules of every sort must be simpler and less voluminous (ibid.: 397). Qualitatively speaking, the larger the group is, the more prohibitive and restrictive the kinds of conduct it must usually demand of its participants in order to maintain itself (ibid.: 397-8). "You *must not* exploit the system, refuse to work, or continue to wear cashmere when you become unemployed," has a stronger effect on the sense of collectivity than "you *have to* eat roast pork, ride bicycles and visit 'Bakken.'" In Denmark, increasing attention is being paid to collective identity, sameness and Danishness. Many foreigners in turn try to conform to these standards in order to become part of the "Danish community" (cf. Pedersen 2005). But as Simmel reminds us, it may be the foreigners' negation of sameness (rather than their attempt to obtain sameness) which the Danes use to reinforce their sense of Danishness. The foreigners are therefore kept in their position as strangers, no matter what efforts they make to live like Danes.

Closeness and distance

Simmel suggests that the whole history of society is reflected in the conflicts between socialistic adaption to society and individual departure from its demands (Simmel 1971: 294). More generally speaking, social relationships are always based on attempts to combine the interest in duration, unity and similarity with change, specialization and peculiarity (ibid.: 295). The stranger, he says, is a social form characterized by a particular way of organizing the unity of closeness and distance, similarity and differentiation. A stranger is a person who is fixed within a social group, but whose position within the group is determined by the fact that he has not always belonged to it. By "stranger," Simmel does not mean the one who comes today and goes tomorrow, but rather the person who comes today and stays tomorrow. Simmel's "stranger" confronts the group from within, that is, a negation is necessary for the sense of collectivity and cohesion (Simmel 1950: 402-8).

Following Simmel's line of thought, "African" and "Danish" can no longer be seen as two sharply demarcated identities. Harriet is not simply African or Danish, but she remains a "stranger." She is constantly trying to imitate and differentiate herself in relation to both of these categorical identities. She rides her bicycle in Copenhagen and has her hair plaited in African hairdressing saloons. She brings meatballs and rice pudding to African gatherings and prepares Ugandan food for the Danish anthropologist. At times discretion is required in order for her and others to be able to remain African without differentiating themselves too much from Danes. Through discretion, the striving for the general and the specific, for imitation and differentiation, are united in one and the same action.

Harriet may be neither African nor Danish, but as already mentioned she continues to be perceived of as a "stranger" in Denmark. According to Simmel, a social group will always have members defined as strangers in one way or the other: people from whom to differentiate oneself, in order to obtain a sense of unity and continuity, and to imitate, in order to obtain a sense of dissimilarity and change. Before foreigners started coming to Denmark in large numbers, there were other groups of people who were perceived as "strangers." As Olwig and Paerregaard point out in their introduction to this volume, Denmark was never the culturally homogenous society that Danes now like to claim it used to be. Social and economic differences as well as regional variations characterized Denmark well into the twentieth century. The homogeneity that many Danes experienced in the mid-twentieth century was not due to a Danish heritage of shared cultural traditions and social norms. Rather it was due to several important social and economic developments that took place from the late eighteenth to the mid-twentieth centuries: the emergence of a democratic nation state; territorial losses resulting in the devolution of the multi-cultural Danish empire; modernization of the agricultural sector, followed by rapid urbanization and diminishing regional differences; and finally the introduction of a national welfare system extending services to society at large and not only to those in need (Olwig and Paerregaard, this volume).

But even in this apparently homogenous welfare state of the mid and late twentieth century, one may talk about different kinds of "strangers," that is, people from within the group confronting the group. There were, for example, always people who benefitted more than they contributed and therefore in a sense were "unintegrated" and a challenge to the perceived unity and homogeneity of the welfare state. This group included people who were unemployed, received disability pensions, or had other special needs. It was not until the 1990s that there were concerns about another kind of "stranger": immigrants and refugees and what were perceived as irreconcilable cultural differences between ethnic Danes and foreigners bringing new kinds of challenges to the welfare state (Olwig and Paerregaard, this volume). Refugees and immigrants are now among the ones who confront the group from a position within the group, but in Simmel's terms they are therefore also a prerequisite for the continued integration of the group, that is, for people's ongoing attempts to combine continuity with change, similarity with differentiation, in an increasingly globalized world.

Simmel's insights concerning the unity of closeness and distance in all social interaction may help us in understanding the difficulties of newcomers, who have to learn the ways in which closeness and distance are played out in social relationships in a particular part of the world. As already mentioned, other Africans are in many ways those who are the closest to the HIV-positive women interviewed, but at the same time they are the ones with whom one cannot share intimate information about one's life if one is HIV positive. Discretion is at times necessary to maintain a relationship, but it also entails a distance that can be painful for those who become the victims of this discretion. The balance between closeness and distance is very different in these women's encounters with health personnel and professional listeners. They are in many ways strangers and distant, but as Simmel says, strangers are not woven into one's close social relations, and are therefore often met with a surprising openness (cf. Simmel 1950: 404). This is also the reason why an anthropologist doing fieldwork may obtain relatively easy access to very personal and intimate details about people's lives. It is noteworthy that these professional caregivers often experience frustrations and feelings of insufficiency in relation to HIV-positive patients with a non-Danish ethnic background, while the patients themselves are happy and grateful for the treatment and support they receive from them (Seeberg 1996: 165-95; Mogensen 2007). The patients appreciate the particular constellation of closeness and distance involved in these relationships: they can be open without fearing the consequences, but they also attach a lot of expectations to the people with whom they share the intimate details of their lives. Health workers do not feel capable of living up to these expectations without challenging their need for professional distance. As a consequence, the women interviewed would always praise the professional caregivers in general terms, but they would often feel frustrated after an actual meeting with them. Their expectations were not quite fulfilled: there was not enough time, they did not get to say all they wanted, their problem was not solved, and so on.

The healthcare system, and to some extent also social services, are thus seen as caring but also at times indifferent. The care takes place in short intensive periods, but nobody from the hospital or the AIDS organization turns up at your home and just sits there to make you feel less lonely, the way Africans do for each other when somebody has a problem. Other Danish people do not do that either. As one of the women said: "There are many things which it is much easier to discuss with Danish people, but if you are sick or in sorrow, then they send flowers instead of turning up to be with you." Another woman told me about the attempt of an AIDS counsellor to create a support network for HIV-positive African women in which they were supposed to share their experiences and thoughts about the disease. She said she had joined the group for some time, but they never talked about being HIV positive when they met. She was not even sure that everybody knew that this was what they were supposed to do. "But it was good anyway," she said; "I just sat there and felt a little less lonely."

The women interviewed usually opened up to me very quickly and told me things they would never share with other people, except maybe some of the professional caregivers who also had time to listen to them. But that also meant that I was never allowed to participate in any other social events in their lives, since people were likely to be present at such events who were not supposed to know anything about their disease and who would be wondering who I was, even if we did not say anything directly. I was often told by the women that "it feels as if you are a nurse or a doctor," which meant that they trusted me but also expected me to disappear again. I tried to define myself as somebody who opened herself up to them more than a health worker would. I let Harriet know about my knowledge of Uganda. I showed her photos from my stays there and told her about my Ugandan family who had adopted me during my fieldwork. She acknowledged these efforts and gave me examples of her Danishness and the pain of her loneliness in return. The result was a particular form of closeness and distance, strangeness and commonality, a whole new constellation that confused her and scared her, even though she craved new kinds of relationships. And she was right in being scared. Even though I became increasingly involved in her situation and tried to help her with the challenges she was facing at that time, I did not invite her into the personal sphere of my life. I was indeed, like the nurses and doctors, a professional listener.

As shown in these examples the women are faced with many problems due to their inability to define the terms on which closeness and distance are played out in the relationships they become part of in Denmark. In the following, I will use the challenges they are faced with as a starting point for a discussion of what characterizes sociality in Denmark.

Kinds of sociality in Denmark

Establishing relationships with people in Denmark is never easy for foreigners, whether HIV positive or not, and I will now look more closely at some of the reasons for this. Sally Anderson has studied various aspects of civil society in Denmark (see e.g. Anderson's chapter, this volume) and has also reflected on the particular constellation of closeness and distance inherent in social relations in the country (Anderson 2006). In Denmark, as elsewhere, there is a whole range of different social relations: from close family to more remote relatives, neighbours, friends, acquaintances, colleagues, public institutionalized relationships, etc. However, it is possible, Anderson says, to identify certain characteristics of the ways in which these relationships and social networks are formed and maintained which are particular to Denmark (2006: 21).

One of these characteristics is the tendency to emphasize enduring social networks and to put a lot of effort into maintaining these. Vered Amit (2002: 22-3) writes that personal social networks that arise through particular individuals' efforts, experiences and history are often ephemeral and highly sensitive to the vagaries and life-cycles of interpersonal relationships, as opposed to more enduring social groups sustained by a core of individuals capable of and willing to operate in certain roles (e.g. a family). While this is no doubt also the case in Denmark, Anderson points out that, compared to other parts of the world, a lot of effort is put into controlling and maintaining personal social networks over time, for example, keeping in contact with friends one has known since kindergarten, celebrating New Year's Eve with the same group of people each year, avoiding changing schools too often so that one's child is given the possibility to establish long-term relationships which ideally last into adulthood, and so on. (Anderson 2006).

This emphasis on long-term relationships may be due to the relatively low mobility of the Danish population and the small size of Denmark. But such relationships are also underpinned by many institutions of the welfare state. An example is the Danish school, in which children are divided into "classes" of 15-28 children according to age, who ideally are taught all subjects together during the first nine years of their schooling. Ideally, two teachers (the Danish teacher and the mathematics teacher) also remain attached to the "class" throughout these nine years, while teachers of other disciplines join the team for shorter periods. An effort is made to avoid major changes to the constellation of the group (Anderson 2000: 50-52). In reality such changes do, of course, take place now and then, but continuity is thought to create a safe environment and the best atmosphere for learning (ibid.: 48). The "class" is expected to be the most important point of reference for the children's social life, and an important part of the teacher's work is therefore to assist the children in becoming a well-functioning social unit: to be tolerant, loyal, socially responsible, good friends, be able to solve conflicts, etc. (ibid.: 51). This is taught through implicit rules and physical and bodily practices (ibid.: 244).

Gulløv shows that Anderson's observations about "classes" in school also holds true of pre-school institutions, which are attended by the vast majority of Danish children (96%). Children are taught early on how to get on with each other, how to take part in pre-defined communities and how to develop relationships with people they did not know in advance and did not choose themselves. They are, however, not to the same extent taught how to create communities themselves, and they rarely see the rules of their community be challenged by people who are different or act differently. They are taught how to be tolerant and inclusive of others, but not how to manage deviation and difference or how actively to create relationships outside a pre-defined group (2009). Together, Anderson and Gulløv show that day-care institutions and schools play a central role in creating this emphasis on long-term relationships and the focus on sameness.

Another characteristic of Danish sociality is the fact that most people are part of a broad range of more "contextual relationships" in the civil sphere, in other words, relationships with people encountered in a certain place or in relation to a particular activity. These could be relations with parents who have children in the same kindergarten, or with a group of people who have participated in the same evening class, and so on. These relationships take place in the public sphere but do not become institutionalized, nor do they develop into relationships in the private sphere. Anderson states that there is "the will to create a (non-institutionalized) sense of community in the public sphere," but that this results in "arm's-length relationships," that is, relationships that may last for years, but which never become close personal ones (2006: 22, 25). If over time these relationships do become part of the personal sphere of the members of the group, it happens in a very controlled manner, whereby only those whom everybody agrees can be defined as "legitimately" belonging to the group (as being like us) are incorporated, while others are rejected (ibid.: 23).

Many of my informants expressed confusion and sadness about the difficulty of converting both arm's-length and professional relationships into more personal relationships (e.g. relationships with parents in their children's school, with colleagues, with other participants in evening classes, with doctors, counsellors, etc.). Thanks to antiretroviral treatment, it may have become easier for them to negotiate the role of their HIV status in social relations. However, it continues to be complicated for them to negotiate their African identity, and even when they lose their ethnic community, it remains difficult for them to establish other social relationships. Their loneliness must be seen in the context of the lack of opportunities they have to set the terms for negotiating closeness and distance, and hence to play around with the repertoire of possible relationships (cf. Anderson, this volume). In that sense they are not at all alone. They are "well-integrated" into a much broader group of people in Denmark, who, due to their dependency on the services of the welfare state, are "different" and feel un-integrated into the society as a whole (cf. Jöhncke, this volume). They benefit more than they contribute and they are, therefore, in a sense, not part of the community of equals who contribute more than they benefit (Jöhncke, this volume).

As Anderson writes, in all societies there is a certain "twist" to the balance of closeness and distance in social relations and to the repertoire of possibilities that some people – though not everybody – can play around with (Anderson 2006: 22). In Denmark that "twist" is characterized by an emphasis on long-term relationships and enduring personal networks, by the high prevalence of non-institutionalized communities in the public sphere (arm's-length relationships), by ideas about sameness, and for some, close but professional relationships with caregivers employed by the state.

Conclusion

By following the development of Harriet's story over time, we have been able to catch sight of how apparently contradictory processes work together in social life, such as the confirmation and negation of collectivity, imitation and differentiation, closeness and distance. The challenges faced by newcomers in Denmark include not only becoming proficient at speaking Danish, riding bicycles and eating rice pudding and roasted pork, but also learning how to manage the particular constellation of imitation and differentiation, closeness and distance, that characterizes social relations in this part of the world.

The problems of the women in the present study are usually presented in ethnic terms, but the challenges with which they are faced are parallel to those faced by others, who challenge implicit cultural assumptions about the welfare state and Danish people's perceptions of themselves and their society. The loneliness of HIV-positive African women is a reminder of the challenges that newcomers must negotiate in Danish society. But it is also a reminder of far more general problems of exclusion and loneliness within the encompassing welfare state.

Finally, their problems are emblematic of the challenges that people in Denmark are facing in a globalized world. In Denmark, a person gradually becomes absorbed into networks and communities through welfare institutions such as childcare institutions. These institutions underpin an emphasis on long-term relationships, and this is combined with a non-institutionalized will to community and "arm's-length relationships." Difference is downplayed in both instances, and people are not taught how to manage deviations and differences. For foreigners trying to make a life in Denmark, the challenges lie in the absence of long-term relationships and the lack of experience with professional caregivers and "arm's-length relationships." For Danes, the challenges lie in their inability to handle differences that they are likely to face with increasing frequency in a globalizing world. They may also experience increasing difficulties in maintaining long-term relationships as mobility increases. Lastly, there are challenges to be faced by the welfare state as such. In its present form, it is based on the principles of homogeneity and sameness. These, however, may be an obstacle to its survival in the long run.

Notes

1. Only women volunteered to participate in the study.
2. The biggest group of Africans in Denmark is the Somalis, who came to the country as refugees in the 1980s and 1990s. They are counted in thousands (about 10,000 of Somali nationality and 6,000 descendents of Danish nationality). No Somalis participated in the study, and according to my informants they are "different from the rest of us," "stick to themselves," have few cases of HIV, and

are not part of what is otherwise referred to as "African networks" cutting across other African nationalities.
3. Two thirds of Ugandans in Denmark are women, and the same trend is seen among other nationalities from eastern and southern Africa. In Copenhagen, only about 50% of Ugandans are women, but in other parts of the country almost 90% are women. A plausible explanation for this is that couples and families settle in urban areas, where the African community is bigger. Outside the cities we mostly find women married to Danish men.

References

Amit, Vered. 2002. Part I. An Anthropology without Community. In *The Trouble with Community. Anthropological Reflections on Movement, Identity and Collectivity*, ed. V. Amit and N. Rapport, 13-65. London: Pluto Press.

Anderson, Sally. 2000. *I en klasse for sig*. København: Gyldendal uddannelse.

—. 2006. At ville noget, at gøre noget, at gå til noget sammen – en velplejet performativ genre. In *Begrebet Immateriel Kulturarv, 20-26*. København: Kulturministeriets Forskningsudvalg.

Bruner, Edward M. 1986. Ethnography as Narrative. In *The Anthropology of Experience*, ed. V. Turner and E. M. Bruner, 139-155. Urbana: University of Illinois Press.

Cowan, Susan A. and Else Smith. 2006. Forekomsten af hiv/aids i Danmark i perioden 1990-2005. *Ugeskrift for Læger* 168 (23): 2247 2252.

Durkheim, Émile. 1996 [1895]. What is a Social Fact. In *Anthropological Theory. An Introductory History,* ed. R. J. McGee and R. L. Warms, 85-92. London: Mayfield Publishing Company.

Gausset, Quentin. 2001. AIDS and cultural practices in Africa: the case of the Tonga (Zambia). *Social Science and Medicine* 52: 509-518.

Gullestad, Marianne. 1991. The Scandinavian Version of Egalitarian Individualism. *Ethnologia Scandinavica* 21:3-18.

Gulløv, Eva. 2009. Om institutionalisering af børneopdragelse. In *Individ, institution og samfund,* ed. C. Aabro and S. G. Olesen, 261-280. Værløse: Forlaget Billesø and Baltzer.

Jöhncke, Steffen. 1996. Culture in the Clinic: Danish Service Providers' View of Immigrants with HIV. In *Crossing Borders: Migration, Ethnicity and AIDS,* ed. M. Haour-Knipe and R. Rector, 168-177. London: Taylor and Francis.

Meinert, Lotte. 2005. På vej mod voksenlivet. Modernitet og mobilitet blandt unge ugandere. In *Lokale liv, fjerne forbindelser. Studier af børn, unge og migration,* ed. L. Gilliam, K. F. Olwig and K. Valentin, 283-300. Copenhagen: Hans Reitzels Forlag.

Mogensen, Hanne Overgaard. 2007. Den dobbelte ensomhed og det omsorgsfulde system: Hiv positive afrikaneres møde med fællesskaber i Danmark. *Tidsskrift for Forskning i Sygdom og Samfund* 7: 87-103.

Packard, Randall M. and Paul Epstein. 1991. Epidemiologists, Social Scientists, and the Structure of Medical Research on AIDS in Africa. *Social Science and Medicine*, 33 (7): 771-794.

Pedersen, Marianne Holm. 2005. Flyverdragt og fastelavn: Indvandrefamiliers etablering af skikke og traditioner i børnenes hverdagsliv. In *Lokale liv, fjerne forbindelser. Studier af børn, unge og migration,* ed. L. Gilliam, K. F. Olwig and K. Valentin, 79-94. Copenhagen: Hans Reitzels Forlag.

Schoepf, Brooke. G. 1991. Ethical, Methodological, and Political Issues of AIDS Research in Central Africa. *Social Science and Medicine.* 33 (7): 749-763.

Seeberg, Jens. 1996. *Kulturens sorte kasse: AIDS og Afrika i Danmark.* Ph.d. thesis, Det humanistisk Fakultet, Aarhus University.

Simmel, George. 1950. "The Secret and the Secret Society" and "The Stranger". In *The Sociology of Georg Simmel*, ed. K. H. Wolf, 307-376, 402-208. Glencoe: The Free Press.

Simmel, George. 1971. *On Individuality and Social Forms.* Chicago: The University of Chicago Press.

Statistics Denmark. 2006. *Population by area, marital status age, sex and Citizenship* http://www.statistikbanken.dk/statbank5a/default.asp?w=140, accessed July 6, 2010)

CHAPTER ELEVEN

THE OBLIGATION TO PARTICIPATE: MICRO-INTEGRATIVE PROCESSES OF CIVIL SOCIALITY

SALLY ANDERSON

The present chapter addresses Danish health interventions designed to enhance social cohesion by reducing health inequality. Promoting physical exercise in groups, preferably those run by local voluntary associations, health promotion policies play into and underscore a dominant political truth that participation in civil society produces well-integrated citizens, communities and, by extension, a well-integrated state. Probing this common and rarely contested folk theory of social integration, the chapter draws attention to microprocesses of integration that are intrinsic to the sociality of common civil activity. It also shows how ethnic minorities are doubly obliged to participate in both "society" and "tradition."

The sceptical reader may rightfully ask what health interventions have to do with integration, which is more commonly thought of as how immigrants and refugees fit themselves into (the proper parts of) "Danish society" (Anderson 2006: 62). I suggest that a focus on exercise groups that meet weekly in public clinics and sport facilities affords a broader view of social integration by exposing the fundamental morality of participation in generalized social exchange that is intrinsic to the Danish welfare society. From this perspective, social integration is no mere matter of how foreigners adapt themselves to Danish society. It is more fundamentally about how welfare state policies work to develop and maintain the capacity and moral compulsion among all citizens to "take an active part in society."

In Danish, the concept of "Danish society" is often universalistically configured as *demos*. The Danish welfare state provides benefits to and requires active participation from all co-citizens (*medborgere*). Yet, "Danish society" is also commonly configured as an *ethnos*, a "family" with a common heritage (see Rytter, this volume). The "Danish people" (*folk*) are considered the founding members of present-day Danish society and the country's rightful proprietors, a historical entitlement developed over the last three hundred years (Korsgaard 2004; see also Olwig and Pærregaard, Jöhncke, and Kvale, this volume). As we shall see, this dual configuration of *demos* (all citizens) and *ethnos* (everyone of Danish descent) places the moral obligation to participate in society squarely, yet differently, on the shoulders of both "older" and "newer" members of this society.

The chapter opens with a brief discussion of voluntary association as a historical institution in Denmark, and as a highly valued, moral site of voluntary social integration promoted by current cultural and welfare policies. Next, I present two health promotion projects as examples of transitional sites set up to prepare participants for "integration" into normal venues of physical activity, such as voluntary associations and clubs. Detailed accounts of how participants get to know each other by sharing time, space, activity and small talk show both exercise groups interrelating in ways that create viable, inclusive civil socialities (Anderson 2008). To conclude, I discuss the relationship between social integration and civil society, and how the obligation to participate in the traditions of civil society differs for different categories of co-citizens. Whereas those of Danish and foreign extraction are equally obliged to participate in civil society and, thus, in the generalized exchange of the welfare state, co-citizens of foreign extraction are further obliged to participate in the local traditions of "the Danish people." By paying close attention to the microintegrative processes of sociality in venues of voluntary activity, the chapter affords a deeper understanding of the integrative and segregative aspects of participation in civil society.

Health promotion offers and obligations

Over the last decade, the Danish government has earmarked funds for municipalities to establish affordable health-promotion interventions to improve and maintain the health of patients with "lifestyle diseases."[1] Accordingly, municipalities across Denmark have experimented with a popular health-promotion concept, "Exercise by prescription," which allows primary-care doctors to prescribe participation in exercise groups. These government-endorsed, doctor-prescribed, yet voluntary health interventions have proved efficient in improving the health and life quality of chronically ill citizens (Roessler et al. 2007). In the long term, this intervention is expected to improve Danish life expectancy statistics[2] and benefit the troubled economy of the Danish public health system.

In 2005-2006, I studied two state-subsidized health projects based on this concept, both in the city of Copenhagen. The first project, "Exercise and Diet by Prescription," was established by the municipality in 2004. It allowed primary care doctors to refer patients suffering from overweight, high blood pressure, high cholesterol or type-2 diabetes to exercise and fitness training at physical therapy clinics across the city. The year-long training programme cost participants approximately $130 out of pocket. Exercise sessions at the clinics lasted for four months: twice a week the first two months, and once a week the following two months. At regular intervals participants met with a dietician, who monitored their eating habits and recommended changes. Participants were weighed and tested four times in the course of the year, the majority showing moderate levels of improvement in overall physical fitness (Roessler et al. 2007). Physical therapists instructing the exercise sessions worked to encourage participation in mainstream sports clubs and gymnastics associations when exercise sessions ended.

The second project, "Take Hold: Dialogue, Network and Exercise by Prescription," was organized by Settlement House, a publicly subsidized, not-for-profit organization located in an inner-city neighbourhood. This project differed significantly from other prescribed exercise projects by offering social activities (folk singing, cooking and sewing) and personal counselling, as well as a wide variety of exercise classes and sporting activities organized by the Settlement sports club. In addition to patients with diagnosed lifestyle diseases (see above), "Take Hold" allowed primary-care doctors to refer patients with diffuse physical and psychosocial complaints, such as mild depression, social isolation, and the general malaise known in Danish as *ondt i livet* (literally, life-ache). Providing the first six months for free, the project targeted local patients with limited means: students, the unemployed, welfare recipients and others living on various forms of public pensions. After six months, participants were encouraged to continue as paying members, either in Settlement clubs or in other associations. "Take Hold" participants were not monitored by fitness tests or other quantitative measures, but did report in an evaluative questionnaire that they experienced revitalized "life courage" (*mod på livet*), higher energy levels and a renewed desire to get out among people (Rasmussen 2006). In Denmark, this last – getting out among other people – is the implicit measure of the healthy, active co-citizen (*aktiv medborger*).

I want to draw specific attention to the voluntary and obligatory aspects of these public health interventions. Concerned with increases in the costs of socialized medicine, the Danish government subsidizes the implementation of health promotion projects by local municipalities. Although *not required* to establish projects, municipalities often choose to do so. This shows political good will, secures a local share of carefully disbursed government funding, and provides constituents with affordable health-promoting offers (*tilbud*)[3]. For individual citizens, participation in health promotion projects is also voluntary. Patients given prescriptions for exercise are encouraged, but *not required,* to participate in exercise classes. Those who choose to do so, however, cash in on their right to extensive and affordable health provision, their common endowment as co-citizens of the Danish welfare state.

Although participation in health promotion interventions is not mandatory for municipalities, patients or even doctors, "exercise by prescription" projects are shrouded in moral rhetoric. Municipalities and citizens alike should *feel obliged* to take up the government's offer of subsidized health interventions both for their own sake and for the good of society. Sound offers of health promotion to municipalities and citizens with health issues are offers they ought not to refuse because, by enhancing their own health, they contribute to the overall soundness and common wealth of Danish society. This morality of exchange is not based on any exact cost-benefit measure of direct exchange between partners, but rather on a strong ethic of voluntary participation in a generalized social exchange of all with all.

Social integration in civil society

The health promotion projects presented above are examples of government interventions to establish sheltered exercise venues for citizens with chronic health problems. These are not permanent venues. Deliberately short-term, their goal is to guide and inspire a transition from physically inactive lives (at home) to physically active lives (out among others). Via prescriptions for exercise, it is hoped that patients will experience the beneficial impact that physical activity has on their health and well-being. Instructors work to bolster participants' confidence in their own physical and social resources and to stimulate a desire to "integrate" themselves into ordinary, voluntary venues of physical activity such as associations or clubs. This focus on kinds of physical exercise that involve getting out of the house dovetails neatly with the dominant moral geography of "Danish society." The moral obligation to *take an active part in society* involves symbolic and often very concrete movements *out of the house* and domestic forms of relatedness and *into society* and civil forms of relatedness in public settings. Health interventions, such as exercise groups, that bring people together in spheres of non-domestic civil sociality are thus considered prototypical training sites for social (re)integration. They are trial venues where the marginally healthy may gain (or regain) the capacity and desire to take responsibility for their own health by participating actively in mainstream associations and clubs, archetypal sites of civil society.

Civil society in Denmark dates back to the early 1800s, when rural commoners turned their backs on the state church and established Sunday and evening schools to take their own spiritual enlightenment in hand. In the mid-1800s, voluntary rifle and gymnastic associations established by local groups were endorsed by Denmark's fledgling democracy because they infused the young with national pride and a will to defence at a time of ongoing struggles over the fate of the Danish state (Korsgaard 1997). The flourishing gymnastics movement was particularly integrative in that it brought young people together across entrenched affiliations of family, farm, village and region. Focusing their efforts on the spiritual and physical enlightenment and fitness of "the Danish people," these early grass-roots (*folkelig*) movements laid the foundations for a thriving civil society, presently centred around a wide range of sports and physical activities, enlightenment projects, and social and political activism. Denmark's countless voluntary associations, solidly underwritten by national policy, provide venues where citizens may "take part in society" by joining to cultivate common interests. In this, they are thought to contribute to the creation of a robust, integrated society, both local and national.

Since 1948, Danish voluntary associations and not-for-profit organizations of all kinds have received subsidies from funds generated by the State Betting Service. Referring to the moral obligation such subsidies entail, in the 1980s the Danish government called upon all associations, yet particularly the well-endowed sport and gymnastic associations – prototypical sites of social integration – to take on greater social responsibility for the marginalized sectors of the population. The government pressured sports associations to develop outreach policies and tailor new activities to "resource-weak" citizens, to do their part to provide civil venues where these categories of co-citizens too might voluntarily "take part in society". The present Danish Ministry of Integration promotes civil society as a prime site of social integration. Government policies promote sports associations in particular as sites for integrating into Danish society those immigrants, refugees and ethnic minorities who are considered to have been marginalized by recent immigration, cultural difference and more or less voluntary social isolation. Policy-makers claim that, by joining sports associations, immigrants will learn the workings of Danish democracy and gain useful social networks that cut across conventional ethnic, social, economic and generational divides.

The turgid rhetoric of such policy claims and the seemingly blind faith in the automaticity of integration through participation in voluntary associations both loom as black boxes begging ethnographic examination. The following analysis of sociality in temporary exercise groups set up by health interventions for the good of all is an attempt to prey the lids off of these boxes to explore what happens when strangers meet in civil venues of common activity.

Civil sociality and microprocesses of integration

Exercising regularly in small groups, as prescribed by one's physician, brings persons with no previous relationship or personal knowledge of each other into close physical contact and social relations. It compels them to forge a viable *civil sociality* (Anderson 2008: 14-5), which allows them to get to know each other well enough to get along in the hours they spend together in common activity and space. I argue that the minute physical accommodations and social exchanges of virtual strangers in temporary social venues may be understood as microintegrative processes. Via verbal exchanges and, not least, body language, movement and positioning – what Farnell calls "talking from the body" (2000: 406) – participants create a common socio-corporeal environment for each other. This physical synchrony of *concerted action* is not the specific product of a particular ethnic group, nor does it necessarily hinge on a specific ethnic identity; it is a fundamental aspect of all social interaction (Kendon 1990: 92). While extremely ordinary and mundane, it is a complex exploit, demanding the attendance of all.

> By watching, listening, and perhaps even touching, we continually feel each other's presence in the social environment, at every moment adjusting our movements in response to this ongoing perpetual monitoring. (Ingold 2000: 196)

As Ingold notes, even when people do not take explicit note of each other, they orient themselves towards each other through fine-tuned mutual adjustments. The point here is that microsocial integration achieved through physically orchestrated sociality in civil venues is not inevitably the traditional property of any one ethnic group

Groups of people exercising together in small indoor facilities will inevitably manifest the microintegration of concerted action. By walking or running without bumping into each other or treading on each other's toes, they create a mutual socio-corporeal field. Moving together in a warm-up circle, waiting in line for a machine, not straddling someone else's mat or hanging one's clothes on someone else's chair are simple examples of how participants coordinate their actions in mutual space, adjusting to each other's movements and respecting each other's times and places. Successful social interaction also requires that participants recognize and are capable of bodying forth a social repertoire suitable for an "exercise group." A certain amount of collusion is required by everyone to avoid drawing explicit attention to what must not be noticed in this type of activity setting (Kendon 1990:1; McDermott and Tylbor 1995). For example, in both exercise groups, people noticed each other's lack of physical ability and heard each other's farts, yet paid no explicit social attention to these displays of inability or breaches of etiquette.

In sum, being (and exercising) together with strangers requires that all those present act together to create and maintain a viable civil sociality. Microintegrative processes intrinsic to the ordinary collaborative work of being together in civil venues is thus always improvised, always uncertain, and always carried out by all those present.

Logics of incorporation

During fieldwork, I participated in two different groups, exercising alongside the other participants for the entire season. Toward season end, I interviewed instructors and a selection of participants from each group. One group met at 8 a.m. in a physical therapy clinic located in *Nordvest*, an outlying working-class neighbourhood. The other group met at 2 p.m. in a sports facility in *Vesterbro*, an inner-city neighbourhood. Although both neighbourhoods are socio-economically and ethnically mixed, the health projects targeted lower-income sectors of the population in their aim to alleviate health inequality. The *Nordvest* group, organized by the municipal project, was of mixed gender and was comprised mainly of Danes, both unskilled labourers and health and education professionals. The Vesterbro group, organized by the Settlement project, was gender-segregated and was comprised mainly of unemployed first-generation immigrant women, either with little education or with an education that is not readily viable in the Danish labour market. Here, there were also chronically ill Danes in various stages of rehabilitation designed to bring them back into the work force.

Roughly speaking, these groups were representative of "Danes" and "immigrants," classificatory categories currently used to partition

Denmark's population into ascribed insiders or "those who have always been here" and ascribed outsiders or "incomers of all kinds", a delineation with little regard for the actual facts of residence. According to common ascriptive practices, a white baby, ascribed as a Dane, will have *always* been here, whereas a person with brown skin, ascribed as an immigrant, will still be an incomer after thirty years of residence in the country. From a national perspective (the logic of *ethnos*), all immigrants are foreigners in need of integration into society, a place where all ethnic Danes, regardless of age, already naturally find themselves (cf. Anderson 2005; 2008: xiii-xv). Yet seen from a civil perspective (the logic of *demos*), all co-citizens, whether Danes or immigrants, when they join exercise groups with prescriptions in hand, are at once both co-citizens and strangers to each other.[4] The first logic of integration – being of Danish descent – requires intermarriage and centuries of stable residence. The second logic of integration – taking part in society requires concrete participation in the work force and venues of civil society.

The following accounts reflect the logics of incorporation and microintegrative processes I encountered in the socialities of the two exercise groups. Although premises for interaction were not the same, mainly due to different levels of fluency in Danish, I argue that both groups succeeded in forging viable civil socialities.

Civil sociality among "Danes"

I joined the Nordvest exercise group on their third day of training[5] in a small room on the first floor of a physical therapy clinic. The group included eight people between the ages of 40 and 68, two men and six women. When a younger ethnic minority woman dropped out, no one took her place, as this was a closed group,

All but two of the participants had been born and raised in Denmark; one woman was from the Faeroe Islands, while the country of origin of the woman who dropped out remained unknown. Most had grown up in the working-class neighbourhoods of Nordvest and Nørrebro. One, however, had grown up in an upper-class neighbourhood of Frederiksberg, one in the countryside on the island of Funen (Denmark's third-largest island) and one in Tórshavn, the capital of the Faeroe Islands. Although several had lived elsewhere for longer periods of time – for example, on the Danish island of Møn, in Greenland and in the Faeroe Islands – at present, they all lived in middle- and working-class neighbourhoods of Nordvest. Three had gone to work directly after comprehensive school (after grade nine), one was trained as a home health aid, three had professions (nurse, pedagogue, teacher), and one a university degree. Only two, the men, still held jobs. Of the women, two were on early retirement (*efterløn*), one was retired, one received unemployment benefits, and one an invalid pension.

This information, stemming from interviews, was not immediately available in the training room itself. Visual signs of participants' height, girth, ways of moving and bodily attitudes were, on the other hand, immediately accessible to all. I noted various kinds of movement difficulties, which participants exercised wholeheartedly and which displayed more minimalistic approaches to physical exertion. Bodily attitudes, which changed from session to session, invoked comments from the physical therapist, generally comforting words: "You must be tired today," or encouragement: "You've done a great job!" Verbal signs indexed chatterboxes and more silent souls, and revealed participants' linguistic roots as archetypal Copenhageners, singing Fynbos (inhabitants of Funen), and those of other Nordic extraction than Danish.

In small training rooms, where people are intensely bodily present, there arises a moral imperative to participate in some form of social exchange. As Lévi-Strauss argues, strangers who enter into close proximity – either on a narrow forest path or at a small restaurant table – often feel a need to confirm each other's presence by means of etiquettes of reciprocity (1969: 58-67). In the exercise groups I studied, participants confirmed each other's presence via physical synchrony and the social exchange of small talk. Through small talk, participants offered each other otherwise inaccessible personal information with which to create more composite pictures of those who were standing (and sometimes lying) alongside.

Anthropologist Ghassan Hage calls this mutual implication and affirmation "the gift of commonality," an elementary form of social indebtedness that arises when a collectivity bequeaths social life to individuals (2003: 90-1). The social debt incurred when receiving the "gift of social life" is paid back via engagement and reliable participation in the collective of family, community or "whichever communal group individuals feel have provided them with the gift of commonality" (Hage 2003: 90). These may be already-existing groups one was born into or groups one chooses later in life (ibid.). I contend that they may also be more ephemeral collectives, like temporary exercise groups, in which all the participants are implicated in giving the gift of social life, in breathing life and form into the group at hand through acts of social exchange. Following Lévi-Strauss and Hage, common activities such as exercise, taking place in small groups (and small rooms), may be said to exact reliable participation, etiquettes of exchange and a certain degree of social indebtedness. In my experience, participants in the Nordvest exercise group met these obligations. They participated regularly, exchanged small talk and acted as though socially implicated by the group at hand – not all to the same degree or with the same intensity, but sufficiently to establish a friendly atmosphere, to get to know each other to a certain degree and to make the sociality at hand work for all, as the following account reveals.

In this group, social exchange was kick-started by the physical therapist, who at the first meeting encouraged everyone to talk about their health problems so he could make allowances for these during training. Through this, the participants learned each other's names and obtained information of each other's ailments, information they could build on in later sessions. When I showed up at the third session, a group of women seemed to be already at work on this social project.

> The atmosphere in the clinic is informal, with people greeting each other good-naturedly. From my seat in the reception, I hear the chatter and laughter of women riding exercise bikes in the next room. They are talking amicably about blood sugar counts and the difference between real food and candy. The instructor encourages them, telling them that they are working well and that he can already see an improvement. The familiar atmosphere surprises me, because I know these women met each other for the first time just two weeks ago. I note that the jovial small talk here stands in strong contrast to the silence I experienced the week before at Vesterbro's women's exercise group. (Field notes, September 2005)

My first impression of the Nordvest group's sociality held true. Just before 8 a.m., twice a week, three or four women could be found seated in reception, chatting familiarly like old acquaintances.

> Betty shouts to the physical therapist: "Karsten, my neck hurts! I woke up last night with a terrible pain in my neck!" Undaunted by the interruption, Gerda continues her story about the discomfort of wearing a bra after her breast was removed. "I hate the ones with wires. The doctor suggested that I drop wearing a bra and just wear loose clothes." Together they continue to talk about how "doctors in Denmark aren't as good as the ones in America and England," because their education is always being cut back by the government. "My husband was lucky to get a really good doctor when he had his brain surgery. Now he's back at work!" Gerda reports happily. Suddenly Betty asks how old I am. "56," I answer. "Mere child! I'm 68!" Bente is 60, Gerda 63. Suddenly Annette dances up in front of us in her new exercise tights for "only 100 crowns down in Føtex!"[6]

The social exchange of small talk continues during the training session, consisting of warm-up exercises followed by strength and fitness exercises.

Jens tells Karsten that he's happy to be back after his shoulder injury. "This prescription is the only way to get me to exercise. My work's sedentary, and I'm not the kind who jogs round the marsh."[7] Bent, who has to be at work at nine, reminds us that it's already five minutes past eight. When Karsten keeps talking with Annette about her latest knee injury, Jens and Bent start directing warm-up exercises, hesitantly at first, but with an increasing feel for the game: "Run!", "Hands in the air!", "Stretch!", "UP on your toes!" As everyone joins in, the impossible tempo of the commands brings smiles, while Karsten dryly observes: "It's really great to have so many instructors!" Turning on the music, Karsten takes over at a more suitable tempo. The music gives rise to small dance steps that conjure up a youthfulness that is not usually visible. With a cry, "My legs are tingling", Betty withdraws to a stool along the wall. Curious on everyone's behalf, she asks Karsten how old he is: "Thirty," he answers. "The same as my boy! Do you have children?" Betty asks, whereupon Karsten answers: "No, not yet, but I have girlfriend." "Yeah, yeah, we were already in full swing at your age!" she retorts. Karsten counters that he often baby-sits his nephew, to which Betty rejoins: "Yeah, and you're probably just as hard on him as you are on us!" At this Karsten grabs Betty's hand, pulling her along on the last few rounds of "run," an attention she appears to enjoy.

Next, we get out mats for stomach and back exercises. Lying on our backs, we fall silent, perhaps out of concentration (the exercises are difficult for most) or with a reticence caused by lying on mats close together in compromising positions with almost total strangers. Later, riding exercise bikes, small talk flows freely. Bente informs us proudly that she has lost nine kilos. "Braggart!" Betty snaps, and it stops there. Then Betty admits not getting up until eleven on days when she doesn't come to training. "I don't have anyone to have coffee with," she explains. "Invite the neighbour lady," suggests Bente, "Call over and tell her: Coffee's served!" (Field notes, September-October 2005)

These brief composites give the reader some of the pieces of common information circulating in the small room. We are given some (but not exhaustive) information about Jens' and Annette's injuries, Jens' aversion to jogging and Bent's desire to start on time. We see that the instructor runs some conventional warm-up exercises, and that certain participants venture to play with existing hierarchies by ironically taking over the role of instructor. The playful atmosphere[8] is continued by Betty, who, with blunt questions and plucky rejoinders, establishes common knowledge of the instructor's age, family status and tolerance for teasing. We see that everyone participates willingly in warm-up and mat exercises, albeit at different levels of ability and intensity. During a common bike exercise, we exchange bits of personal information and learn how others receive these gifts. Even when Betty's levelling retort cuts short Bente's pride in having lost weight, Bente responds empathetically to Betty's sigh of loneliness.

Small talk, in general, is about daily routines, weight, jobs, knees, food, bargains, vacations and being alone. Some give more personal information than others. Betty relates that her mother died when she was small, after which her father remarried a woman who sent her out to work at the tender age of thirteen. Of other participants' lives we learn only that they have two children and a bad back, that they have chronic high blood pressure, or that they often visit a sister in Jutland. Most speak eagerly of their exercise habits: Nordic walking every morning, lovely walks in the marsh, working weekends at a collectively owned cottage in Sweden, washing windows, and cleaning apartments and allotment garden cabins (also exercise!). Participants joke about cravings for pastries, for a glass (or two) of red wine at the day's end, for ice-cold aquavit, so hard to do without when in the allotment garden or vacationing at a country inn.

In the course of the first two months, participants in this group forged a viable sociality. In close physical contact, although not close acquaintances, all worked to accommodate each other, feeling out the limits of talk, silence, nearness and distance, so as not to come too close, or inadvertently offend or rebuff. Avoiding both physical and social collision, the group achieved a jovial, microintegrated civil sociality, as long as it lasted.

Civil sociality among "immigrants" and "Danes"

In September 2005, I joined "Gymnastics for women," an exercise class sponsored by "Take Hold" and the Settlement Sport Club to accommodate women who did not want to exercise with men. In contrast to the municipality's short-term offer for patients only, this health promotion venue was open to all (women) and would continue as long as the club could muster an instructor[9] and enough participants to make it worthwhile. Approximately half the participants came with prescriptions for exercise from their doctors. The rest found their way to the exercise class through other channels. For those with prescriptions, club membership for the first six months was free. After this a half-year's membership cost 250 crowns (ca. $40-45). Participants in "Gymnastics for women" were between the ages of 25 and 72. As far as I could ascertain, none held regular jobs, and they all had only limited means. Some were on sick leave, others on unemployment benefits, some received retirement or invalid pensions, two received integration benefits, and a few were "just" housewives. Most participants lived in the local Vesterbro neighbourhood, several in a nearby middle-class neighbourhood, and one in an upper-class neighbourhood. While a few had grown up in Danish cities and towns (Copenhagen, Frederiksberg, Holbæk), the majority had come of age in foreign countries: Brazil, India, Iraq, Macedonia, Morocco, Pakistan and Turkey. Those born elsewhere had come to Denmark as immigrants, refugees, reunited family members (*familiesammenførte*) or the spouses of Danes. One refugee had a part time job washing stairs in apartment buildings, but most of those of foreign background did not work outside the home. Several of the younger women attended school to learn Danish in order to acquire an education. Among those already educated were a tailor, a speech therapist, two kindergarten teachers and a circus artist.[10]

As with the Nordvest group, socioeconomic and demographic information of this kind was not immediately accessible in the training room.[11] Yet here there was no common round of introductions that afforded participants a minimum of information about each other. Thus, participants had very little concrete information on which to build relationships. Most knew that some had been referred by their doctors, but they did not know which ones or why.[12] Visual signs revealed a few women to be obese; several were of normal weight, and the rest somewhere in between. Body types, ways of moving and clothing indicated something about participants' histories, as well as their exercise habits and attitudes toward exercise. Some showed delight in moving their bodies, while others moved with visible effort, though none displayed outright resistance. Pointed toes, good balance and rhythm hinted at earlier experiences with dance, gymnastics or similar traditions of movement. Uncertain movements, awkward coordination and cumbersome training clothes hinted at a lack of experience with movement genres such as exercise classes. Appearances and accents indicated that the majority were foreign-born. The participants' mastery of Danish, their only common language, ranged from almost non-existent to fluent. A handful of women participated regularly, but most others showed up at irregular intervals. More participated at the beginning and end of the season than in the middle – around Ramadan and Christmas.

Language difficulties, a lack of knowledge of each other and the instructor's thoughtful attention framed this group's interaction. At the beginning of the season, most exchanges took place between individual participants and the instructor, not among the participants themselves.

> Women change into training clothes in their preferred corners of the room, some speaking quietly together in a common foreign language. Then they all take an orange ball and begin to massage their backs and shoulders. The instructor, Lene, notes approvingly that quite a few have come today.[13] We warm up with various pulse and stretching exercises to somewhat outdated popular Danish and American music.[14] Next we pull out mats for stomach and back exercises. I learn the women's names from Lene's corrections: "Neena – use your right leg!", or "Turn the other way, Barbara." When Pernille and Lone fall into a longer conversation, Lene asks them to be quiet and concentrate. We move rapidly through a series of exercises that are more functional and effective than aesthetic or fun, and many of the positions we take on the mats are far from attractive. I try to imagine what we must look like, lying on our backs with our legs in air, dressed in training clothes that, besides the ordinary black tights and extra large T-shirts, include a pale lilac nightgown, a bright green salwar kameez,[15] old-fashioned pink silk panties pulled over bright turquoise tights, multicolored hand-knit slippers, thick woollen-knit tights and knee-socks, a thin blue slip with lace edges, tightly-tied hijabs, loose scarves, henna-decorated fingers and tattooed overarms. (Field notes, September 2005)

Although everyone displayed a friendly demeanour, there were few traces of small talk. Compared to the Nordvest group, it was difficult to fall into conversation here. Quiet talk among those who spoke the same language was never public or common for the simple reason that not everyone could understand. The relative silence among the participants afforded Lene much communicative space. She greeted us, led the exercises, corrected us and listened to individual stories of injuries, pains, children, events, experiences and worries. Small talk among the women themselves was made difficult by their limited fluency in Danish, by Lene's calls for concentration, and perhaps also by a sense of modesty with regard to each other's lives and potential health problems, about which the women had very little information. The silence itself could be daunting, as it placed a greater focus on those who did speak. It was hard to know how to break the silence, where to begin and what to talk or ask about. The following example shows the vulnerable and uncertain character of exchanges between strangers.

> There are only five women today, as Ramadan has begun. A new woman, Danish, about sixty years of age, hesitates at the door, asking in a small voice whether she's come to the right place for gymnastics. Lene immediately invites her in and makes her feel welcome. We learn later that

> her name is Anna, but that is all we know. Another woman, Amina, who usually exercises with the Thursday group, joins us. When Lene greets her warmly, asking how she's doing, Amina declares emphatically that without gymnastics she'd be dead, but gives no further explanation as to why this might be so. When I notice that Amina is one of the very few who does all the exercises without difficulty, I ask her curiously, during a short water break, whether she or her family has a history of gymnastics or sports. She answers promptly and directly that her father died when she was 21, her mother when she was 16. Her mother had enjoyed dancing, but hadn't danced after her son, Amina's brother, died. (Field notes, October 2005)

Amina accepted my offer of small talk, yet her own offer, fragments of a tragic life story, left me uncertain about how to respond. Her return opened a chance to learn more about her life, but it also moved us beyond the safety of small talk, a communicative genre requiring appropriately small repartees with appropriately mundane content, a genre suitable for strangers and the time constraints of brief water breaks. Not knowing Amina at all, I was unsure whether her response was an invitation to more intimate conversation about her deceased family members or a way of making me back off and leave her alone. Before we had a chance to go further, Lene called us back to the floor.

Despite a variety of communicative difficulties and uncertainties, the women in this group did not remain silent. During the third training session, I noted the first tenuous attempts to joke and make fun.

> During mat exercises, Lene instructs us to "roll up into a little ball." At this, a hefty woman lying on a mat beside me gasps: "Did she say little?" and giggles can be heard throughout the room. Later, when Sabine's cell phone rings twice during the final quiet relaxation exercise, Lene warns us: "The owner of the next cell phone that rings buys a round!" (Field notes, October 2005)

This kind of joking paved the way for new exchanges that gradually changed the character of the group's sociality.

> Leading the way, Asima is teaching the other women how to – and that it is all right to – tease Lene. Asima enjoys counting the more difficult exercises faster than Lene, in order to be done more quickly: "25, 26, 29, 30, done!" she shouts gleefully. Soon, in Asima's absence, other women take up this practice, giggling and enjoying their own audacity. Others find new ways to make fun. During an exercise, where we all stand with elbows tucked tightly to our sides, underarms held forward, palms upward, an elderly Turkish woman, Seher, smiles broadly, calling out: "Waiter! Waiter!" Suddenly everyone can see that we look like a flock of waiters

carrying heavy, invisible trays. During an exercise where we sit on balls (*boldstik*), everyone has a good laugh when Anna suddenly rolls off with a bump, arms and legs sprawling. Later, there are giggles all round when Seher's ball pops out from under the back of her skirt, as though she just laid an egg. (Field notes, November 2005)

Perhaps encouraged by joking and fun-making, the women seem increasingly relaxed in each other's company. They gradually begin to exchange more talk and more information about each other's lives.

Anna tells the group that she's begun to go to flamenco; she's even bought a new skirt, though, she admits, perhaps in vain, because she finds it hard to coordinate her arms and legs, and sometimes feels a bit alone among all the younger women who already know the dance. When Lene corrects Barbara, a smiling Brazilian with an extremely energetic and idiosyncratic way of moving, Amina tells Lene that she's being too hard on Barbara. After training, Barbara announces in broken Danish that she was at a gospel rally all weekend because she's very fond of Jesus. During a break, an extremely plump woman, Samina, does a perfect split, apparently just for the fun of it, while others watch, impressed by her limberness. As we change into our street clothes, Neena tells us about Diwali,[16] an Indian festival, with "lots of oil lamps" soon to take place in the temple in Skovlunde. "Many Danes will be there; many, many Danes", she assures us, and invites all to come. The following week, Neena brings us sweets, small green balls dripping with syrup, and again invites all to come to the "tempeli in Skovlundi," where everyone is welcome, everyone speaks Danish and there's free food. Women with less fluent Danish communicate via body language. One lifts her shirt to show us a long strip of thick scar tissue from a heart operation that still causes great pain. (Field notes, October-November 2005)

Through these and similar exchanges, we came to know each other better, and soon pairs and clusters of women spoke together regularly before and after training. By exchanging fragments of life history and anecdotes about their daily lives, women offered information upon which each one in the group might potentially build. They also put forth common topics to which all might add. In this way, we learned about each other's families, that Amina had four children, that Seher had grandchildren and that Shadije was pregnant again, although it did not yet show. Catching up on the week's events during training, Lone and Pernille's private conversations made it possible for others to jump in with their own experiences of buying cars, work accidents, male jealousy, and so forth. In the course of the season, exchanges among the women increased despite language difficulties, modesty, shyness toward strangers and Lene's demands for concentration. September's silence was gradually transformed into May's small talk and fun.

The sociality of the Vesterbro group was never as easy or as free-flowing as that of the Nordvest group, as language and communication problems left everyone more socially vulnerable. Yet, over time, and encouraged by Lene's friendly and supportive manner, the Vesterbro group's many immigrants and few Danes engaged each other as equals,[17] despite halting language and the many unknowns of mutual foreignness. Participants created a friendly and lively civil sociality in which, during the course of the season, new members could join.

Moralities of participation

The above accounts reveal how participants in exercise groups collaborate week after week to forge socialities that sustain common social exchange. Although this "integration work" is clearly more complicated in groups with little common language, it is still perfectly feasible, particularly when humour is employed to bridge the communication gap. By attending closely to the microprocesses of social exchange in these exercise groups, I have argued that both groups successfully achieved a socially inclusive environment. I will now explore how moralities of participation and logics of incorporation intrinsic to Danish society impinge on ephemeral groups such as these. To illustrate, I focus on the state the exercise groups were in when my fieldwork came to an end.

The main goal of "Exercise by prescription" projects was to inspire participants to continue to take exercise. I have suggested that project-supported exercise groups acted as sheltered venues for both social and physical training. By exercising in small groups in which it is imperative to interact *as if* equal, participants practised the kind of inclusive civil sociality inherent in "being out in society among others." One question remaining is whether such practice led participants, as hoped, to continue to take part in society by voluntarily seeking out venues offering physical activity, or by exercising together with family or friends.

Members of the Nordvest group did not continue to exercise, at least not together, despite a well-organized plan to do so. As the first two months of training came to an end, one of the men gathered information about and organized visits to local venues where we could continue to train as a group. We visited a fitness centre and an exercise association, and physical education students dropped by the clinic to inform us of new, fun exercise groups and associations they were starting for "people like us." When it came time to leave the clinic, the group had agreed to train together at the same time twice a week at a local fitness centre so as not to interrupt our established routine. Yet even with this timely planning and the professed willingness of everyone to continue, after four months in the clinic and five months in the fitness centre, only one participant still trained regularly. One fell away with no explanation, one ended up in the hospital, one was forced to take a job (*aktivering*),[18] two left on longer trips, one was too busy with all kinds of other activities, and one could not stand the music at the fitness centre. The last person quit during the summer because it was too hot. Interestingly, there was nothing remarkable about this gradual falling away. It was relatively easy for everyone who had been involved to leave behind the common sociality, relationships and mutual knowledge they had built up together over the last many months. Our commonality, contingent on the framework of a public exercise programme, proved temporary, and the group gradually disbanded.

Ephemeral groups such as this one are not fiascos; their demise is a perfectly ordinary and common phenomenon. None of the participants, and no one from the clinic or municipal health authorities, appeared particularly upset about the collapse of the collective we had forged together. No one ever argued that Betty, Annette, Gerda, and Bent were poorly integrated into "Danish society" because they did not continue to socialize with one another beyond the time and space of the exercise class. There were, however, rumblings among policy-makers that people like Betty, Annette and the rest were not participating energetically or voluntarily enough in the state's project to improve their health. Liberal policies based on the idea that health is a person's own responsibility and that poor health and thus health inequality can be remedied through voluntary measures were coming under political attack. Indeed, the government is currently considering more coercive measures, such as higher excise taxes on foods high in sugar and fat, stricter prohibitions on alcohol and tobacco, and a higher degree of intervention in the private lives of "the most vulnerable" to induce their "voluntary" participation in projects. The morality of participation presented in these arguments draws on the logic of *demos*. Voluntary participation in health promotion projects to reduce health inequality and the cost of public medicine and improve Denmark's ranking in the global longevity competition is necessary for the common good of society. The commonality to which Betty, Annette, and Gerda should feel indebted is thus the Danish welfare state.

Things were different in the Vesterbro group. At season's end, "Gymnastics for women" was at the height of its existence, with more participants than ever.

> Walking up the stairs, I hear the hum of female voices. "It's a bazaar!" says Neena with a big smile. A table, piled high with knitted goods of all sizes and colours, is ringed by participants discussing preferences of style and colour, and naming potential recipients. Slippers crocheted in strong colours and complicated patterns are popular. At precisely two o'clock the table is cleared, and training begins. There are 12 today, but soon more old and new faces appear until the small exercise room is filled to the brim. Women, who earlier in the season had worn rather unusual outfits, are now almost all dressed in tights and oversized T-shirts, a standardization that seems to have happened automatically. (Field notes, May 2006)

The Vesterbro group was still going strong, with a core group of regular participants surrounded by many new faces. During the season, the group's sociality was transformed from friendly, modest silence to lively chatter, fun-making and even a bazaar. From having talked almost exclusively with Lene, participants gradually engaged each other through microintegrative processes: the concerted action of exercise, and the social exchange of small talk, joking, outfits and homemade slippers. This may be seen as a giant feat of social integration for women who in various ways were strangers to each other, the Danish language, foreign-sounding names, gymnastics, and perhaps to the very idea of exercise. Yet despite their having created a common sociality across distances of social difference, the logic of incorporation based on *ethnos* apparently required more.

> At the beginning of May, Lene invites everyone to an end-of-season luncheon to be held at Valdemar's Hunting Lodge, a local pub. "It costs only 125-175 crowns[19] for a luncheon platter with herring, meat and cheese," she announces, encouraging us to sign our names to the list. Several Danish participants accept the invitation with enthusiasm. After training, over a cup of hot chocolate provided by the club, these women search the menu provided by Lene for things that *they* can eat. "Maybe fish? Or what about the cheese? There's bound to be something they can eat." Pernille remarks: "There are only Danish names on the list," and Barbara (herself a foreigner) responds: "They never put their names on." Not finding much on the menu "for them," Pernille still insists: "They must come anyway!" (Field notes, May 2006)

To encourage all the women to sign up for the luncheon, Danish women took it upon themselves to find something on the menu that "they" – the foreigners – can eat. This course of action is based on an unreflective assumption that not signing up for the luncheon is solely a matter of foreign (Muslim) food traditions and restrictions. It did not seem to occur to them that pregnant Shadije, Neena who was often in great pain, Aylia with the many children and high-culture Anna may all have had other reasons for not signing up for the luncheon.

Having experienced the women coming together over the course of the season, I was surprised that Lene did not ask the women as a group what kind of end-of-season celebration they might enjoy. Her invitation to Valdemar's Hunting Lodge generated an immediate, explicit differentiation between "Danes" and "immigrants" (Muslims), categories that had not been made explicitly relevant while exercising, nor when small-talking as women in equal need of exercise. The traditional luncheon did not refer specifically to this particular group of women. Instead, it indexed other collectivities: Lene's Thursday's group comprised of Danish retirees who customarily ended their season with a traditional luncheon, and civil groups in general that ritually mark the season's end by eating and drinking together. The practice also indexed an abstract collectivity of Danes, who, solely by virtue of an ascribed ethnicity, automatically value and understand the social import of end-of-season rituals such as traditional pub luncheons.

With the invitation to Valdemar's Hunting Lodge, the commonality forged by the exercise group shifted. It no longer belonged to all of the women in the group, but rather to all those categorized as Danes, the rightful proprietors of Danish society with the power to grant (or not grant) newcomers the gift of social life, as well as the right in return to expect foreigners to participate in Danish custom. Even though all of the women present had contributed to the group's microintegration, signing up for the luncheon became the ultimate mark of the willingness of newcomers (to Denmark, not to the exercise group) to fulfil their moral obligation to participate in Danish tradition. While the logic of *demos* allows the understanding that civil sociality is rightfully owned or hosted by all those who contribute through participation, the luncheon invitation reinaugurated Danes as the rightful hosts of the exercise group, as well as the rightful proprietors of public space, local tradition and Danish society. This inevitably left immigrants "who never put their names on the list" in debt to their hosts, the Danes, "who always sign up." The incorporative logic of *ethnos* being drawn on here does not invoke the commonality of all co-citizens who live in and contribute to the Danish welfare state, but rather the more exclusive commonality of "the Danish people". The obligation compelling "immigrants" to participate in traditional end-of-season luncheons is informed by an understanding of social indebtedness incurred when the gift of commonality is seen as bestowed by the categorical collective of Danes.

Ethnos trumps

A classic question regarding social integration is whether temporary bonds between strangers may form the basis for more permanent bonds that serve to "integrate" ethnic minorities and other socially marginalized sectors into social contexts that improve their positions in society. In the analysis I have presented, I argue that the incorporative logic of *demos* obliges all co-citizens to participate in the generalized exchange of the welfare state, while the incorporative logic of *ethnos* obliges co-citizens belonging to "ethnic minorities" to participate in asymmetric exchange with their Danish hosts. The logic of *ethnos* thus acts as a joker or permanently valid trump card that may be pulled at any time to convert an equivalent relationship of fellow participants into an asymmetrical relationship of proprietors (first-comers) and guests (newcomers).

The demise of the Nordvest group illustrates that, when all the participants are Danes, the logic of *demos* reigns. When none may install themselves as rightful owners of the commonality built up through regular participation, the group is allowed to crumble in peace. The Vesterbro group's end-of-season luncheon illustrates how easy it is – when most participants are not considered "Danes" – to play the trump card of Danish proprietorship. Although it is possible to demonstrate in the finest detail that all participants contribute to the creation of a common environment and thus to the microintegration of the socio-corporeal field (Kendon 1990, Varenne and McDermott 1999, Ingold 2000), the contribution that immigrants make to such successful civil sociality is apparently not enough. Like other co-citizens with lifestyle diseases, immigrant women in the same situation owe the welfare state their voluntary participation in tailor-made health promotion programmes. Yet, it appears that they also owe their self-appointed exercise group hosts participation in traditional end-of season luncheons, a Danish custom which, if truth be told, not all Danes necessarily appreciate.[20]

One question for the future is what changes further processes of globalization will bring to the two current – sometimes competing, sometimes merging – configurations of Danish commonality: the *demos* of the welfare society and the *ethnos* of the Danish people. History has shown the inhabitants of Denmark to be quite capable of incorporating a wide range of foreign persons, words, social forms, products, ideas, sports and even whole cosmologies into local culture and national genealogy and, in the process, appropriating them as "Danish". Whimsical advertisements for "our beer," created by the Carlsberg brewery, draw on this appropriative propensity, as did the more serious evacuation of "Danish"

Jews to Sweden during the German occupation of Denmark in World War II.

As long as the world is comfortably configured by laws that underwrite the *ours* and *theirs* of ethnicized nationalities, we might expect historical processes of "Danish" appropriation to continue to work. Over time, they may even whittle out a category of "our Muslims" around which the hosting arms of "Danish" commonality may reach. Yet national configurations that allocate rights, duties and identities while guarding the illusion of unambiguous boundaries and membership have never been comfortable, not even in the little homogenous country that Denmark is commonly imagined to be. This discomfort has become all the more insistent in the present situation of global migration, flight and transnational lives. Yet, rather than dismantling the "nation" or the "state" of Denmark, one might expect a reconfiguration to take place carved by ongoing tensions between *demos* and *ethnos,* by political partiality towards welfare for all, and a cultural penchant for autochthonous myth. One should not, however, underestimate the impact of the microintegrative processes that take place in numerous, diverse venues of voluntary activity. These do not necessarily follow the overarching, obligatory logics of either *ethnos* or *demos* as claimed and hoped for by policy-makers. They are perhaps more likely to draw on a logic of *topos* – of the commonplace and of a familiarity born out of sharing time, space and sociality in venues of local social life. Of interest to any study of social integration is thus how various forms of local social life become appropriated or rejected by national logics and political programmes established to promote social integration.

Notes

1. "Lifestyle disease" is a term frequently used to designate a range of diseases such as cardiovascular disease, type-2 diabetes, cancer and chronic obstructive lung disease. Lifestyle refers to behaviour regarding diet, exercise, alcohol and tobacco, which are thought to affect health. The idea of a lifestyle disease is based on two assumptions: 1) that behavioural factors are critical in contracting a disease; and 2) that individuals choose their own lifestyle independently of others. Neither of these assumptions is necessarily valid (Vallgårda 2005).
2. Life expectancy in Denmark (76.3 years for men, 80.8 years for women) is lower than that of other Nordic countries (Denmark Statistical Profile, no.10 compiled by Julie A. Norstrand, august 2009. Accessed 27/06/10. http://agingandwork.bc.edu/documents/CP10_Workforce_Denmark.pdf).
3. The Danish word *tilbud*, used to connote the voluntary aspect of various welfare provisions and projects, is also used by retailers to denote a bargain or special offer.

4. They are perhaps also strangers unto themselves in these unfamiliar collective venues of strenuous physical activity.
5. Participants were asked at the first training session if they would agree to an anthropologist following their group. They chose to allow me to join them, despite not knowing what to expect. Only later, when participants told me how surprised they were to find that I "kept coming back" and how they "hardly noticed my being there," did I realize that they had expected my presence to be obtrusive and short-lived.
6. Føtex is the Danish equivalent of Walmart.
7. This refers to a popular jogging area, Utterslev Mose, a large marsh on the outskirts of Copenhagen.
8. See Anderson (2000: 118-23; 2003: 193) for other examples of this playful, ironic genre.
9. The Take Hold project operated with a mixture of volunteer and paid instructors, most of who were trained in gymnastics and sports.
10. I lack information about some of the women's education, partly because they did not speak of education during training, and partly because I did not have the opportunity to interview the many women who participated on an irregular basis.
11. Nor was it immediately accessible in the interviews, as arranged interviews fell through due to irregular attendance.
12. Through interviews I learned that women in this group had been prescribed exercise for mild depression, chronic pain, rehabilitation, diffuse psychosocial complaints and a desire for exercise venues where men were not allowed.
13. We are fourteen in all, with the instructor, Lene, and two small boys, the sons of participants: two Pakistanis, two Arabs (one with a son), a Brazilian, two Turks, a Macedonian, an American and three Danes (one with a son).
14. I was apparently the only one struck by the irony of doing exercises with a group of immigrants to Woody Guthrie's song, "Deportee."
15. The salwar kameez is a traditional dress in various parts of Southeast Asia. The salwar is a pair of loose-fitting trousers; the kameez is a long tunic worn over the trousers.
16. Diwali (Deepavali), or the Festival of Light, is a popular festival celebrated everywhere in the Indian diaspora. Taking place in October-November, Diwali symbolizes the victory of good over evil. Large numbers of oil lamps, candles, neon lights and fireworks belong to this celebration of the renewal of life. Diwali is a time when people strengthen relations with family, friends and acquaintances through mutual visits and gift exchange (Lal 2008).
17. Simmel understood sociability as the play form of sociation, a "pure social form" in which those present focus solely on the immediate success of the sociable moment. According to Simmel, this is done by down-toning individual presences, interests and moods. Simmel characterized sociability as playing at democratic interaction, where individuals "do as if" they were equal. Simmel did not see this as social deception, but rather as an aesthetic form, an art (Simmel 1950[1910]:45-9).
18. Aktivering or "activation" is a work project policy designed to help the long-term unemployed back into the labour market.

19. Approximately $25.
20. Research shows that immigrants' efforts to "do as Danes" are either overlooked or not accepted; they are never "quite right" or "quite enough" (Pedersen 2005).

References

Anderson, Sally. 2000. *I en klasse for sig.* Copenhagen: Gyldendal.
—. 2005. "Vi kender hinanden alle sammen, hvor vi så end er fra": At leve lokalt gennem global sport i København. In *Lokale liv, fjerne forbindelser: Studier af børn, unge og migration,* ed. L. Gilliam, K. F. Olwig and K. Valentin, 153-174. Copenhagen: Hans Reitzel.
—. 2006. Storbymennesker: Tilflyttere og lokale i københavnske kampsportsklubber. In *Den Stille Integration. Nye fortællinger om at høre til i Danmark,* ed. M. H. Pedersen and M. Rytter, 62-90. Copenhagen: C. A. Reitzel.
—. 2008. *Civil Sociality: Children, sport and cultural policy in Denmark,* Charlotte, NC: Information Age Press.
Farnell, Brenda. 2000. Getting out of the *habitus*: An alternative model of dynamically embodied social action. *The Royal Anthropological Association* 6 (3): 397-418.
Hage, Ghassan. 2003. The Differential Intensities of Social Reality. Migration, Participation and Guilt. In *Being there: New Perspectives on Phenomenology and the Analysis of Culture,* ed. Jonas Frykman and Nils Gilje, 79-93. Lund: Nordic Academic Press.
Ingold, Tim. 2000. *The Perception of the Environment. Essays in Livelihood, Dwelling and Skill.* London: Routledge.
Kendon, Adam. 1990. *Conducting interaction: Patterns of behavior in focused encounters.* Cambridge: Cambridge University Press.
Korsgaard, Ove. 1997. *Kampen om Kroppen. Dansk idrætshistorie gennem 200 år.* Copenhagen: Gyldendal.
—. 2004. *Kampen om folket. Et dannelsesperspektiv på dansk historie gennem 500 år.* Copenhagen: Gyldendal.
Lal, Vinay. 2008. Indian festivals: Diwali. On website: *Manas. India and Its neighbors,* (http://www.sscnet.ucla.edu/southasia/Culture/Festivals/Diwali.html. Accessed June 30, 2010).
Lévi-Strauss, Claude. 1969[1949]. *The Elementary Structures of Kinship.* Boston: Beacon Press.
McDermott, Ray and Henry Tylbor. 1995. On the necessity of collusion in conversation. In *The Dialogic emergence of culture,* ed. D. Tedlock and B. Mannheim, 218-236. Chicago: University of Chicago Press.

Norstrand, Julie A. 2009. Denmark. Statistical Profile. The Sloan Center on Aging and Work, Boston College. Statistical Profile no. 10. (http://agingandwork.bc.edu/documents/CP10_Workforce_Denmark.pdf. Accessed June 27, 2010).

Pedersen, Marianne Holm. 2005. Flyverdragt og Fastelavn: Indvandrerfamiliers etablering af skikke og traditioner i børnenes hverdagsliv. In *Lokale liv, fjerne forbindelser: Studier af børn, unge og migration*, ed. L. Gilliam, K. F. Olwig and K. Valentin, 79-94. Copenhagen: Hans Reitzel.

Rasmussen, Pernille Vibe. 2006. *Evalueringen af "Ta'Fat. Netværk, Samtale og Motion på Recept.* Center for Forskning i Idræt, Sundhed og Civil Samfund. Odense: Syddansk Universitet.

Roessler, Kirsten Kaya, Bjarne Ibsen, Bengt Saltin and Jan Sørensen. 2007. *Motion og Kost på Recept i Københavns Kommune Evalueringens Resultater*. Odense: Syddansk Universitetsforlag.

Simmel, Georg. 1950[1910]. Sociability: An Example of Pure or Formal Sociology. In *The Sociology of George Simmel*, ed. and transl. Kurt H. Wolff, 40-57. Glencoe: The Free Press.

Vallgårda, Signild. 2005. Livsstilssygdomme - en misvisende betegnelse. *Ugeskrift for Læger* 167 (04): 422.

Varenne, Herve and Ray McDermott. 1999. *Successful Failure: The School America Builds*. Boulder: Westview Press.

Part III

Epilogues

INTEGRATION, OF THE *FOLK* AND BY THE *FOLK*...

RICHARD JENKINS

During the second half of the twentieth-century Danes took pride in their social and cultural homogeneity, on the one hand, and the example of liberal tolerance that they set to the rest of the world, on the other. As Fog Olwig and Paerregaard insist in their introduction to this collection the first of these collective self-images was never accurate. The second was only sustainable as long as it never had to face a serious test. But pride goes before a fall, and Denmark is now coming to terms, uneasily and amid a public chorus of resentment and worse, with diversity and intolerance. "Integration", or more accurately the *problem* of "integration", is now one of the most public of public issues, and in everyday life it appears to be experienced as such by many Danes.

"Integration" is, however, a contested concept, which can be defined in different ways in political debate, practical policy and service delivery, everyday speech, and the social sciences. Its meanings vary across a broad spectrum, from crude visions of normative, even coercive, assimilation to more nuanced visions of "culturally-strange" immigrants learning the skills that they need to function in a new society. This semantic stretch and the concept's role in debate in the public sphere – in which people use the same word but frequently talk past each other, about very different things – raise significant doubts, at least, about whether "integration" can ever be a useful analytical concept (see also the critiques of the concept by Fog Olwig and Paerregaard and by Sjørslev).

One of the core objectives of this collection is to problematise the Danish notion of "integration", to expose it as cultural and ideological, rooted in local notions of equality and belonging. Seen from within this cultural and ideological framework the "integration problem" in Denmark is primarily an issue of and for immigrants. Not *all* immigrants, however: Norwegian or British or French immigrants, for example – and probably most other European immigrants, too – may well find it difficult to "fit in" in Denmark sometimes, but they do not have, nor are they seen to create, an "integration problem". That "problem" is the presence of visibly different, religiously challenging (mainly Muslim) migrants, who mostly arrived in Denmark from the mid-1980s onwards, and who are, or who find it, difficult to "integrate".

The Danish popular consensus that "integration" is a problem created by "immigrants", and by *particular* immigrants at that, necessarily shapes the substantive focus of this collection. The empirical chapters reflect the taken-for-granted assumptions of Danish political rhetoric, welfare and educational policy, media coverage and everyday popular understandings. These strands of Danish culture are the backdrop and context of the situations that the contributors are seeking to understand, and they also inform patterns of funding for applied research. Nor are these assumptions peculiarly Danish. Internationally, particularly in Europe, talking about "integration" has become a convenient shorthand way to talk about "the immigrant problem", or, even more pointedly, "the Muslim problem".

And, of course, in Denmark, as elsewhere, "integration" – or, rather, integrat*ing* – is, indeed, a challenge *for* immigrants. That much is obvious, and non-controversial. In what follows, however, I shall argue, as indeed do some of the contributors to this collection, that integration is not just, or even *mainly*, either an "immigrant problem" or a problem for immigrants. Organised socio-cultural integration is, like taxation, a routine aspect of the relationship between modern nation-states and their settled inhabitants. What's more, this is spectacularly true in Denmark, of all places. This argument proceeds by way of a number of steps.

The first, and perhaps the most fundamental, is that in order to "get by" in any society, to function adequately and relatively independently in one's own eyes and in the eyes of others, certain basic competences are necessary. In a modern industrial society such as Denmark, these include the ability to communicate comprehensibly in the primary language of everyday life (in this case, Danish; although, as an initial point of departure, the global *lingua franca*, English, is a great deal more helpful than, say, Arabic), some knowledge of the local formal and informal mores and expectations (such as legal requirements, gender norms, and the customs and practices of interpersonal interaction), a set of practical public skills (such how to catch a bus, to shop, or to find one's way around), and a related set of cognitive competences (such as literacy and numeracy).

This list isn't intended to be exhaustive, or of universal application in its details, but it should strike a chord with anyone, not least any anthropologist or foreign exchange student, who has ever had to fit in and function, even if only temporarily and superficially, in a strange and new social setting. It is, however, important to recognise that excellence is not necessary in order to navigate successfully in unfamiliar social waters.

Everyday competence is just that, a matter of practical adequacy and of "showing willing", it does not require the kind of virtuoso performance that might show up some of the locals.

The second point is that, although the locals that one encounters in a strange and new place appear to know, and to be able to do, all of this local stuff, and much more, as "second nature" (Elias 2000: 117), they too had to learn it once upon a time. In that it now fits them like their own skin, the locals may give every impression of having forgotten that they did, in fact, once have to learn how to be locals, and how to do local competence. They may thus be able to dismiss the relative incompetence of immigrant others as a deviation from local taken-for-granted normality.

However, and this is the third step in the argument, we can be absolutely sure that, as children, the locals did once learn this local stuff, because when children come into the world they do so uncultured and poorly provided with instinctive behaviours. At first this doesn't matter, because other people look after them, but very soon they start learning; in other words, they begin to be integrated, and to integrate themselves, into the cultural world in which they find themselves. They begin to comprehend what others are doing and saying, to communicate their wishes and needs clearly to others, to produce the normal behaviours that others expect of them, and to influence others' behaviours. This socialisation process takes place, first, within the family or other domestic care settings, and subsequently within whatever institutions of organised child-care and education might be available, and within non-kin peer groups. An important aspect of this process is what Schiffauer and his collaborators call "civil enculturation", initiation into the local "civil culture":

> competence in relation to the workings of a country's civil society, competence with regard to its nationally specific conventions...and norms of civility, and some familiarity...with its dominant national self-representation (Schiffauer *et al.* 2004: 4).

The integration into a nation – state of its infants and children during primary socialisation, is a routine and necessary process, which affects everyone, not just immigrants or culturally – strange sojourners.

So the making of young Danes and, more broadly, the ongoing (re)production of the Danish *folk* depends on routine, taken-for-granted, institutionalised processes of integration (see Jenkins 2011, for a full discussion of the detail in this and the following paragraphs). This integration begins within the family, where Danish children begin to learn to speak Danish, where ideally they will learn some manners and social etiquette, and where they will quickly learn about local vernacular rituals of the nation, such as the close association between the Danish flag, Dannebrog, and festivities and celebrations, notable birthdays.

The fourth link in my argumentative chain is to observe that the integration of young Danes into wider society is left neither to chance nor to their families or immediate carers. Most Danish children – and it really is most – spend their earliest years, from about eighteen months (and sometimes earlier) to six or seven years, in publicly funded childcare. Here, *ideally*, they learn to be social human beings, along stereotypical Danish lines: a normative mixture of cherished individuality and highly valued co-operation in small groups (with the flag still being waved on birthdays, of which there can be many in a busy kindergarten). As Bundgaard says in her chapter, day care is the most significant institution of social integration in Denmark, for all children.

At school, secondary socialisation starts, and so do lessons in everything from Danish to mathematics to sport. In the last fifteen or so years, the politics of immigration and integration, and of national-cultural angst, have made their way into the school system and the curriculum. Since 1994 Danish municipal schools, which teach children from six or seven to sixteen years old, have had a legal obligation to teach Danish culture to all-comers, ethnic Danes[1] and immigrants alike. Since 2006 schools have been required to teach a centrally proscribed cultural canon, which is nothing less than a portfolio of compulsory, authorised Danishness. Not all the new measures are self-evidently addressed to the whole spectrum of pupils, however. Also in 2006, *kristendomskundskab* – religious education, which, although it makes concessions to comparative religion and philosophy, is centred firmly on Christianity and the national Lutheran church – was re-emphasised and reconfigured as a leaving examination subject. Non-Christians may elect to opt out of these classes.

Recent curricular policy is not the only potentially non-integrative aspect of religion in Danish schools. When they reach fourteen, Christian Danes are faced with the option of confirmation; most of them take it, not least for the festivities and presents that generally mark the event. The upshot is that the class group, a small cohort of children who may well have been together since they entered school, prepares for confirmation together; this preparation, religious instruction by the parish priest, very often takes place in school. In a system which values and emphasises the inclusive solidarity of the class group as the keystone of personal socialisation and communal sociality within the school, the *de facto* exclusion embodied in *kristendomskundskab* and confirmation preparation sends a very powerful message about the role of Christianity in Danishness, and of non-Christians in Denmark[2].

So far, I have argued that national socio-cultural integration is a characteristic and objective – a necessary function, if you like – of modern nation-states, exemplified perhaps most obviously in their formal childcare and education systems. To say this is, of course, no more than to nod respectfully in the direction of Gellner's thesis about nationalism (1983). In Denmark the national system of integration is a powerful interlocking network of institutions, which come into play early and focus on personal socialisation and civil enculturation, the social and individual shaping of Danish citizens who can function in Danish society without having to ask what to do and without disrupting the axiomatic behavioural norms of everyday life.

The fifth element in my argument is implicit in much that I have already said: integration, the gradual induction of individuals into a new, and strange, socio-cultural world, is a two-way process: something that is done *to* people (children) and *by* people (children) themselves. Not too much needs to be said about this, perhaps, other than to insist, on the one hand, that people cannot be integrated if they do not want to be, and, on the other, that it is not enough to want to be integrated, to make that effort, if the significant others in the social world do not accept you. Integration is two-way, a reciprocal process, and this is as true for children as for adults.

The sixth piece in the jigsaw is a robust rejection of any hint of mechanical social and cultural reproduction that might have crept into the discussion so far. The Danish national system of integration, for example, does not simply churn out well-socialised, properly-enculturated teenage Danes, who happily develop into adult Danes, in the same mould as their parents and their parents before them. Nostalgic cultural protectionism may occasionally appear to be what some Danish politicians and commentators want – although that they also want a nation that is fully up-to-speed with modern technology and international marketing is an entertaining paradox – but, if serious, it is a forlorn ambition[3]. Integration can never be a one-way street, in Denmark or anywhere else; it is, rather, a complex tangle of ongoing interactions and transactions, large and small. Incrementally and not always obviously, but very definitely, the process of integrating others, whether they are little Danes or immigrants, changes the national cultural landscape and everyone's knowledge and preferences. The defence of culture against change is impossible, innovation is inevitable: what was an imported novelty to one generation becomes as local, or as national, as hot dogs, or pizza and Diet Coke, to the next.

To sum up so far, every modern nation-state invests significant resources and effort to integrate its inhabitants – whether newborn or newly arrived from elsewhere – into its distinctive local social and cultural world(s) and to inculcate the competences that are necessary for that integration to be effective. This is a routine and necessary aspect of how modern polities work: integration – of the people and by the people, and I do mean *all* the people – is at the heart of every nation-state.

If this is so, what, then, is the "integration problem" that, if political opinion from left to right is to be believed, blights the Danish body politic and civil society? That there is no single or simple answer to that question is one of the key themes of this collection of papers. The problem is a complex interaction of many long-, medium- and short-term factors, including the following:

- the collision between diversity and a society that liked to think of itself as homogeneous;
- the threat to long and dearly held national self-representations as a liberal beacon of tolerance in an intolerant world;
- increases in refugee and asylum-seeking population movements due to conflicts elsewhere;
- successive enlargements of the European Union;
- the increasing economic strains put on the Danish welfare state by an ageing population;
- Danish racism, because there *is* undoubtedly racism;
- the encouragement and exploitation of angst about immigration by the media, particularly certain newspapers, political parties and individual politicians;
- post-9/11 Islamophobia and the radicalisation of relationships between Muslims and Christians;
- undoubted cultural "gaps", in particular the incongruity between Danish gender norms and those of some immigrants; and
- a widespread Danish perception that integration is an immigrant issue, and that the perceived failure of integration is the immigrants' fault.

These are some of the causes of the perceived "integration problem" in Denmark. If nothing else, I hope that I have at least outlined a distinctive perspective from which to think about it, locating integration and any "integration problems" firmly within the routine business of the nation-state and its relations with all sections of its population, rather than identifying them with a subset of troublesome Others.

In closing, drawing on the argument I have outlined so far I shall briefly explore some possible future scenarios (ignoring some completely impossible ones, such as "sending them all back"). The first of these is integration on the current Danish model: here immigrants start doing things in Danish ways, learn Danish, and moderate their customs and habits in order to fit in with the Danes, whose taxes pay for the integration process. This is not a caricature: that it is immigrants who should change in order to fit in is a reasonable summary of the established Danish cross-party consensus on this issue.

This is an unrealistic vision, however, for a number of reasons. First, what "final" integration might look like has not really been considered: when does "integration" stop and ordinary "integrated" life eventually begin? In truth, of course, integration is always a work in progress: a routine, ongoing, open-ended process. Second, as I have already argued, interaction between human beings is mutual and reciprocal, not unilateral, and change is never one-sided. "Ethnic Danish" culture has already been affected by immigration – if truth be told over hundreds, even thousands of years – and this will only continue. Third, there is the inter-ethnic political context. On one side of the debate there are those for whom no amount of "integration" will ever be enough: for these people a Muslim with a brown skin can't become a Dane. On the other side, the experience of being "integrated" may encourage fundamentalism and rejectionism. Although neither ethnic Danish nor Islamic fundamentalists are in the majority yet, there is a real possibility that misguided integration policies will be counterproductive.

This prospect leads on to the second possible future, in which gathering hostilities between a strident, unrealistic and nostalgic cultural Danishness and radical, fundamentalist Islam lead to a widening gap between "us" and "them". At best, this would create a perpetual underclass of guest workers, refugees and their children, subsisting as resentful and resented clients of the Danish welfare state. At worst, there might be widespread violence on the streets.

There are, however, some reasons to think, and realistically to hope, that this vision of the future, in either of its manifestations, won't happen. The dull, but worthy, pragmatism of Danish politics, locally and nationally, probably militates against social conflict of this kind. What's more, despite recent political meddling, the municipal kindergarten and school systems don't really permit large-scale segregation or exclusion[4]. Finally, the everyday business of "being Danish", for everyone, has been globalised. Being Danish is, increasingly, as much a matter of ordering Vietnamese take-away food as it is opening a jar of pickled herring (which might well be curried herring, anyway).

The third possibility is multiculturalism, perhaps along the lines of Britain or Canada. This, too, is unlikely, once again for several reasons. The last two centuries of Danish history have been a story of a forced retreat from pluralism and diversity, as the Danish northern European empire shrank in the face of military disasters and nationalism. In the little land of Denmark too much social and cultural capital was invested in a post-imperial process of "Danification", and the painful construction of a plausible, if not entirely accurate, national self-image of social and cultural homogeneity, for it to be easily dissolved into modern multiculturalism. Multiculturalism would require the abandonment of too much that is too basic to Danish everyday life: flags of all nations *might* work on the birthday cake, for example, but it's unlikely. Finally, the taken-for-granted centrality of Christianity to Danishness for many people, as discussed by Rubow, is another barrier. A confrontation between two monolithic monotheisms, Lutheran Christianity and Islam, does not look like fertile soil for the growth of multiculturalism.

My last scenario, the recasting of Danishness, draws on the previous three options, and depends on the participation in good faith of at least some representatives of all sections of the population. It will be a long process, involving many state-level and everyday negotiations, centring on the school system and employment, obstructed by rearguard resistance and with inevitable conflicts of different kinds. The outcome will be uncertain, as a more inclusive notion of Danishness – not axiomatically Christian, less prescriptive, and accommodating of diversity, whether visual or cultural – evolves in its own good time. A less authoritarian official model of integration, and a more relaxed state approach to the management of Danishness and Danish culture, will be necessary. Who knows what the end product might look like, but there is sufficient evidence of tolerance and moderation, in my own research and the work of others (e.g. Gundelach 2002: 119-25; Larsen 2008; Lassen 2009; Mørck 1998; Togeby 1998), to suggest that this is not a completely implausible future.

It is, however, *at least* in the balance. There is an impressive array of reasons to be less than cheerful about the future. Danish electoral politics and state policies have gradually shifted to the right over the last two decades. Recent history suggests a likely decline into mutual hostility. Internationally, we have witnessed 9/11 and subsequent attacks, there is failure to resolve the problems of Palestine and Iran, and the invasions and occupation of Iraq and Afghanistan continue to be problems rather than solutions. Nationally, within Denmark, the rise of the right-wing Danish People's Party (*Dansk Folkeparti*), ever tighter immigration restrictions, naïve and clumsy integration policies, Danish participation in the so-called "war on terror", the Mohammed cartoons, and the new cultural politics of education all point in discouraging directions. Positions have hardened and the gap between "us" and "them" appears to be wider than ever. In this context, the renegotiation of Danishness might seem to be a utopian suggestion, doomed to failure.

The good news, however, is that change – even some integration – is already happening. Danes in their everyday lives, without making any fuss about it, are redefining *their* Danishness. What's more, although relations between "ethnic Danes" and immigrant strangers – *de fremmede* – may generally be distant, there are bridges, on which people meet and communicate in something other than raised voices: at school, in private homes, at work, and occasionally in the arms of lovers. There are also those who strive for more pluralist and reciprocal accommodations.

Whether politicians, media commentators and the cultural elite approve of the directions in which their fellow citizens are heading, or whether they have even noticed, isn't the point. "Danish culture" and Danishness are not endangered species, in need of government protection; they are moving, ever-changing and complex ways of life. "Integration" is, thank goodness, not the prerogative of the state. Ordinary everyday cultural development will take its course, despite the best (or worst) efforts of the politicians and other managers of the public sphere, and it isn't stoppable. The day-to-day realities are as they are, and left to their own devices people will get on with their lives. In the process everyday life will move on; but it will still be Denmark, and it will still be Danish everyday life, in all of its different hues and moods. I shall give the last word to one of those lives, a teacher from the Jutland town of Skive, where I did my field research: "I do not think we are going to lose our language or our culture. I do not believe that will happen. If it can happen so easily, you have to ask whether it is worth keeping." Yes, indeed: well said.

Acknowledgement

This is a much better contribution to the debate as a result of the comments of Karen Fog Olwig and Karsten Paerregaard. I am grateful to them.

Notes

1. By "ethnic Danes" I mean "white" Danes, who are axiomatically accepted by their neighbours as authentically Danish, whether by descent or upbringing; this is, however, not an expression that all ethnic Danes are happy to accept.
2. This is also a conflict between what Anderson, in her chapter, calls "the obligation to participate" that is so central to the Danish welfare state, and the "traditional model" of the relationship between Lutheran Christianity and Danish identity – i.e. that the latter presupposes the former – which Rubow discusses in her chapter.
3. And it is another paradox, among many, that nostalgic cultural protectionism necessarily depends on the "historical amnesia" identified by Fog Olwig and Paerregaard.
4. Although the mooted move towards larger schools, away from the small-scale intimacies of the current *folkeskole* system is likely to have implications in this respect.

References

Elias, N. 2000. *The Civilizing Process: Sociogenetic and Psychogenetic Investigations*, revised edition. Oxford: Blackwell.
Gellner, E. 1983. *Nations and Nationalism*, Oxford: Basil Blackwell.
Gundelach, P. 2002. *Det er Dansk*. Copenhagen: Hans Reitzels Forlag.
Jenkins, R. 2011. *Being Danish: Paradoxes of Identity in Everyday Life*. Copenhagen: Museum Tusculanum Press.
Larsen, C. A. 2008. *Nationale forestillinger*. Aalborg: Aalborg Universitetsforlag.
Lassen, H. 2009. *Den Anden Virkelighed: Tanker og tal om integration i Danmark*. Copenhagen: Informations Forlag.
Mørck, Y. 1998. *Bindestregsdanskere: Fortællinger om køn, generationer og etnicitet*. Copenhagen: Forlaget Sociologi.
Schiffauer, W., Baumann, G., Kastoryano, R. and Vertovec, S., eds. 2004. *Civil Enculturation: Nation-State, School and Ethnic Difference in The Netherlands, Britain, Germany and France*. New York: Berghahn.
Togeby, L. 1998. Prejudice and tolerance in a period of increasing ethnic diversity and growing unemployment: Denmark since 1970. *Ethnic and Racial Studies*, 21: 1137-54.

DANES AND OTHERS

RALPH GRILLO

The editors asked for an "epilogue" to the English language edition of the present book reflecting on how the contributors, as local anthropologists, have approached the question of integration in Denmark, and how their writing about the topic looks from a comparative, international perspective.

For whatever reason the title of the introduction to the English edition is somewhat different from the original ("Integration: Antropologiske perspektiver"), and indicates a changing emphasis. A key figure, cited by several of the contributors is the German sociologist, Georg Simmel, but the title also has echoes of John Higham's classic book *Strangers in the Land* (1988), on American nativism. *Strangers* also conjures up Camus' novel *L'Étranger*, the title of which is rendered in English as *The Outsider*. Camus, of course, referred not to a "foreigner" (the usual translation of *étranger*), but to someone who is apart from, alienated from society in a philosopher's sense. That refugees, migrants, and their descendants continue to be treated as outsiders (strangers or foreigners), no matter their length of stay, or that they were born and brought up in the country, is telling. Many, of course, would argue that they have brought this on themselves by maintaining their otherness, and living "parallel lives". Their own "excess of alterity", as Giovanni Sartori would put it (2002), is the cause of their alienation, and their continuing perception and reception as "strangers in the nation". But this puts the cart before the horse. What is it about their otherness which generates this perception of them by the "indigenous" populations, and what is it about the present context which has seemingly intensified, if not created, that perception? These are key questions which are testing social scientists across Europe and beyond, and a strength of the present volume is that it provides us with some answers, so far as Denmark is concerned, through its account of Danish policies and practices of "integration".

Integration

Like many ideas which anthropologists explore, integration is a "fuzzy concept" (Grillo 2007b): opaque, elusive, with multiple contested meanings, which are frequently unclear, not least to the people who use it (sometimes those who use it most often), its field of reference changes, often dramatically. It appears in deceptively similar verbal form in various European languages (integration, *integrazione*, *intégration* etc), but when examined closely differences are more apparent than similarities, e.g. between Britain and France (Favell 1998). Sometimes it is taken to mean, simply, assimilation, with immigrants "expected to discard their culture, traditions and language" (Castles et al 2003: 3.1.1), sometimes the emphasis is on "inclusion" (ibid 3.1.3). An exhaustive IMISCOE survey takes that tack, defining integration as

> a generations lasting process of inclusion and acceptance of migrants in the core institutions, relations and statuses of the receiving society. For the migrants integration refers to a process of learning a new culture, an acquisition of rights, access to positions and statuses, a building of personal relations to members of the receiving society and a formation of feelings of belonging and identification towards the immigration society (Heckmann ed. 2006: 5.5.1).

Although Heckman goes on to stress that "the receiving society has to learn new ways of interacting with the newcomers and adapt its institutions to their needs", in fact much European official policy places the burden of integration on immigrants and their descendants, increasingly so; Denmark is not alone in this.

Like "multiculturalism" (another fuzzy concept), integration is best thought of as a spectrum of ideas and practices concerned with governing diversity, a social and political project, involving strategies, institutions, discourses, practices, addressing what is often seen as the "problem" of people of migrant or minority ethnic background who insist on living transnationally and/or abiding by norms, values, moral orders, beliefs which place them at odds with fellow residents. Until recently, and perhaps more widely than is commonly supposed, a relatively liberal view of this "problem" was generally predominant in Europe along the lines advocated for the UK in the 1960s by the then Labour Home Secretary, Roy Jenkins. This was the so-called "Jenkins formula" (Rex 1995):

> Integration is perhaps a rather loose word. I do not regard it as meaning the loss, by immigrants, of their own national characteristics and culture. I do not think we need in this country a "melting pot", which will turn everybody out in a common mould, as one of a series of carbon copies of someone's misplaced vision of the stereotyped Englishman ... I define integration, therefore, not as a flattening process of assimilation but as

equal opportunity, coupled with cultural diversity, in an atmosphere of mutual tolerance (Jenkins 1967: 267).

This urbane concept characterized British policy and practice for many years, notwithstanding changes of government (Grillo 2010a). It was developed towards the end of Britain's role as a colonial/imperial power, and in light of the emergence on the global stage of the idea of a "multiracial commonwealth", which in some respects it echoed. The key phrase was "coupled with cultural diversity": the future for immigrants and the next generation was within a common public sphere of shared norms and values with equal opportunity in employment, housing, education, health and welfare, equality before the law, and protection from racism, with distinctive beliefs, values, practices, religion, language, in private. Minorities would be "here but different", the motif of multicultural policy in Canada and Australia, and across much of Europe, including, albeit to lesser degree, countries like France grounded in Republican ideals of "One and Indivisible" with (officially) no space for difference. Philosophies may be dissimilar; reality is closer than many would believe.

At least, that is how it was, but across Europe there has been growing scepticism about this kind of integration (Vertovec and Wessendorf eds 2010). Far from making space for minority social, cultural and religious difference, receiving societies have increasingly insisted on conformity with existing values and practices, and striven to reassert national homogeneity. From a comparative perspective, therefore, a key question is what, if anything, is specific about the Danish integration project and diversity debate? And, what does this volume, and the anthropological approach it adopts, add to our understanding?

What *The Question of Integration* does is locate the response to the immigrant presence in the context of the socio-cultural history of Denmark, and the changes that have taken place over the last century. As such it goes more deeply into the issues than an earlier book on "multiculturalism Italian-style" (Grillo and Pratt 2002), though Pratt's chapter (2002) has similar intent. First and foremost, the contributors locate the (changing) policy and practice of integration Danish-style within the constellation of values which inform Danish public and private lives: an emphasis on "individual freedom, personal choice and social engagement", as the editors put it, a belief that there is a link between equality and sameness of a kind which the late Marianne Gullestad (2001) identified as a "central organizing concept" for Norway, an "historical amnesia" regarding Denmark's past (a myth of pre-lapsarian cultural homogeneity), and the idea that Danes are a family or "tribe". These values, along with the Protestant faith, have underpinned the evolution of Denmark as a social-democratic society with a strong welfare state and liberal social policies, often represented as the Nordic model. This is the ideological and institutional framework within which "others" have to adapt, and in terms of which Danish policies of integration have to be understood. But the fit is not an easy one.

The recent era has been one in which refugees and economic migrants have been entering Europe in unprecedented numbers, at a time when, across the globe, and not just in Denmark, welfare systems of the Nordic kind have come under great pressure from the so-called "Washington consensus" of the 1970s, which shaped the contemporary neo-liberal ecumene. In this conjuncture, says Jöhncke,

> Danes are confronted with the downside of their ideals. The values they once held dear seem less obviously suited to handling and maintaining a multiethnic and multicultural everyday reality. What is a stake is not just a matter of mere "attitudes to foreigners." The fate of the welfare state has become a matter of what Denmark is all about.

This in turn has led Danes to question the entitlement of outsiders to the welfare benefits which they, the Danes, traditionally enjoyed and which are now seemingly under threat. Mikkel Rytter cites a statement by Bertel Haarder, then Minister of Integration – a title with an Orwellian ring – which pulls together many of these themes:

> We [the Danes] have a job, because we care about what our family and neighbors think about us, and because we want to set a good example for our children. But foreigners do not feel these inhibitions in the same way. They live in a subculture outside the Danish tribe. That is why they so quickly learn about the possibilities for getting money [out of the welfare system] without making an effort (In *Berlingske Tidende*, September 20, 2003).

The Comparative Dimension

This detailed picture of Danish integration is extremely valuable, but the chapters are inevitably heavily focused on the Danish situation, and are concerned with what are largely seen as internal cultural debates (Parkin 1978). This introspection brings out the particularly and peculiarly Danish ideas of self and society and their implications for others, but what is happening in Denmark is not unique, and rewarding though the Danish focus is it misses the opportunity to place the Danish integration debate in a wider context.

There is one important exception to this, which is the comparison with other Scandinavian countries (see also Hedetoft 2010). It is no coincidence that one of the authors most frequently cited by the contributors is Marianne Gullestad who demonstrated the importance of the link between ideas about equality and sameness in Norway, a link found in other Scandinavian countries, giving substance to the notion of a specifically Nordic socio-cultural and socio-economic milieu. One example of the interchange within Nordic countries concerning the position of immigrants and refugees (especially Muslims) is provided by Bertel Haarder, who commended Unni Wikan's *Generous Betrayal* (http://www.socialrdg.dk/ Default.aspx?ID=3540, accessed 22 June, 2010), and who is included among those to whom Wikan herself was "deeply indebted" (2002: xii).

There is now, however, a vast body of multidisciplinary research on immigration and integration in Europe against which Danish (or Nordic) particularism can be tested. It is difficult briefly to sketch the lines along which Denmark's changing diversity regime (Grillo 2010b) may be compared with what is happening elsewhere. State formation and ideology would certainly come into it, as would religious history, colonial past and neo-colonial present, patterns of immigration and settlement, the so-called "white backlash", and the global growth of anti-immigrant, anti-Islamic politics. There is also the matter of scale (Hedetoft 2010). Denmark is small and relatively less differentiated than Britain, France, Germany, Italy or Spain, where there is considerable internal variation with many types of small and large cities and rural areas with different social, cultural, political and industrial histories and institutional complexes. In Italy, for example, there are significant differences between the national and the regional picture, and between different localities within the same region (Riccio 2001). These have many implications for the management of diversity which needs to be investigated at a number of levels. Internal differences of this kind do not appear to be important in what seems be a relatively homogeneous Denmark. Or rather, they are not explored in the present volume in which the contributors focus on the one hand on the national picture, and on the other on micro-institutions and personal relations. This omits the meso-level which often mediates between the two. A worthwhile comparison might be with the Netherlands, another relatively small and relatively homogeneous country, outside but adjacent to the Nordic bloc, which has had a comparable experience of rapidly deteriorating in relations with its largely Muslim immigrant population.

While the Danish focus has the advantage of looking in depth at one nation-state, integration debates and practices cannot be fully comprehended without taking into account the relationship with the wider international context, including that of a converging Europe. There is, among much else, a cross-national interweaving of political, academic and popular discourse, embracing a skein of vocabulary, sources, tropes, ideas, instances, paradigms, and this transnational intertextuality, as it might be called, needs to be addressed. The value of broadening the discussion to incorporate a strong international (and comparative) dimension becomes apparent from an examination of the Cartoons Affair, which seems to have been the *fons et origo* of the present volume (discussed in detail by Heiko Henkel, but clearly of concern to other contributors).

In recent years there have been similar episodes elsewhere apparently involving confrontations between artistic freedom and religious sensitivities, and they have been occurring with seemingly increasing frequency since the Rushdie Affair of 1989. Looking comparatively at these various episodes (see Grillo 2007a for a fuller account) several points stand out. First, many have, albeit to a variable degree, an international and transnational character, and demonstrate "the creation of a modern, unified field of world politics" (Halliday 2006). Some events barely make national headlines, but others become international *causes célèbres*, and the crucial role of the press and TV and of the Internet in all its manifestations in conveying and nourishing these affairs is significant. Secondly, if these episodes are globalized or internationalized, they are also caught up in local issues in the countries where they originate and those to which they spread, and may rapidly become political footballs at and between each level. Governments are sometimes squeezed by this global/local nexus, anxious about their international contacts, but concerned with the effect of such events on public order back home, and on minority populations, especially when they live in areas represented by the ruling party.

Thirdly, these episodes say something about global and local rapports de force, and the social capital on which protagonists can draw. Danish Imams could call on the assistance of several Middle Eastern ambassadors to intervene with the Danish Prime Minister but, when that intervention was rebuffed, toured Muslim countries and secured an impressive array of international supporters. It may well have been in the interests of their supporters to exploit the issue (as in the Rushdie Affair), though exploitation is often mutual. The Sikh diaspora, for example, is much weaker, given the powerful position of India and its importance for intergovernmental relations and for relations with other minority ethnic population. On the other hand, in Britain Muslims and Sikhs are able to draw on the support of local councillors and MPs in constituencies with significant minority electorates, and, through interfaith networks, other religions.

Fourthly, in all these episodes there is a similarly wide spectrum of opinion including fundamentalists of all hues whose views are frequently Orientalist or Occidentalist (Carrier 1995), at times plainly xenophobic. A telling example was the way in which the van Gogh murder in 2004 was widely described in the international media through the trope "ritual slaughter". This is related to a tendency for these episodes to be construed as confrontations between two sides, "them" and "us", and it is striking how often what is said and done feeds and in turn feeds upon each parties' fantasies and nightmares of the Other, how rapidly dehumanized and essentialized the imagery becomes, and how these episodes escalate in word and deed, in action and reaction. As Henkel rightly points out, the cartoons fed Western fantasies of Islam, and at the same time Muslims' own fantasies of where the West stands in relation to their religion. One consequence is that those in the middle find themselves caught. Thus one self-styled "moderate" Danish Muslim (Tabish Kahir, *Guardian*, February 7, 2006) recorded that his silence was not through lack of an opinion, but because there was no room available for him to voice it, neither in Denmark, nor in Muslim countries.

The Anthropological Contribution

The editors ask a fundamental question of wide import:

> how to preserve, and further develop, a social welfare society, based on a system of social solidarity that is closely connected with shared cultural values, in a globalizing world of increasingly interconnectivity and mobility.

The book does not come up with an answer, and perhaps one cannot be expected from anthropologists. We do not do normative questions, but are much better at describing what actually happens, on the ground. This has numerous advantages. The emphasis on concepts and values is shared with other disciplines, but the distinctiveness of the anthropological approach is that it explores such concepts and their effect on practice in the everyday world. It is the "lived experience" of such concepts which is central to anthropological analysis, and in this volume there is a series of chapters which explores that lived experience within the worlds of Muslim converts, programmes for asylum seekers, nursery schools, psychiatric wards, networks of HIV-positive African women, and exercise classes.

This micro approach has limitations, but also strengths. A case in point is Sally Anderson's account of *microintegration*, the ways in which a group of people undertaking a common small-scale activity (an exercise class) creates a mutual socio-corporeal field. Microintegration is both a process and result of the ordinary collaborative work of being together in civil venues. A similar orientation towards actually existing, low intensity, quotidien integration is to be found in the idea of "quiet integration" (Pedersen and Rytter 2006) which several contributors cite. This approach uncovers "street-level diversity practices" (Hedetoft 2010: 111), seemingly at odds with national rhetoric. It also uncovers what may be called the anthropological "uncertainty principle" (Grillo 2010b). Earlier anthropologists often wrote as if there was only one voice (and one truth) in the communities they studied. Under the influence of postmodernism voices have multiplied. We now routinely observe that those voices speak with different powers, but many, perhaps most, speak hesitantly and uncertainly. Some actors have a clear-cut vision; many more will, consciously or not, be sifting through alternatives, shifting from one to another as circumstances, personal and collective, change. Much of the time most actors are working more or less in the dark, and sometimes the decisions they make will be highly idiosyncratic. Tina Gudrun Jensen's chapter illustrates this through the narrative of Aisha and her husband and the moves they make to try and find a place in which she can feel comfortable in her particular version of Islam. It is also apparent in Heiko Henkel's account of the cartoon debates. Not infrequently there is confusion all round, with often enough the right hand not knowing what the left hand is doing. At the same time, through compromise and negotiation people inch their way, painfully, towards a modus vivendi.

Conclusion

In the 1990s it was commonly argued that we now live in a "post-national" era, that globalization and transnationalism undermine, or as some would see it, transcend, the national entity, with important implications for citizenship and human rights in contemporary nation-states (e.g. Bauböck 1994, Soysal 1994). But that belief now seems prematurely optimistic. Indeed, if anything, things are moving in the opposite direction. Across Europe there has been a reassertion of the hegemony of "core" values and national cohesion, and a return to the classic view of "one nation, one culture, one language, one state, one citizenship", and immigration has provided a major justification for this.

Although opposition to immigrants comes from many sources, including conflict over scarce resources, it is often articulated through a discourse which contrasts the (imagined) immigrant with the (equally imagined) national subject, a point which the Danish debate illustrates well. Sometimes this is couched in terms of a generalized "Western" or "European" (perhaps Christian) subject and his/her values which are in danger being overwhelmed by the incoming tide of immigrants and asylum-seekers. Often, however, as with movements of the political right and governments which co-opt their rhetoric, it is the imagined national (native) citizen ("We Danes") who is threatened. There is a specific Danish take on this, as the present volume shows, a specific "tone" in the public debate in Denmark, as Inger Sjørslev puts it, but the theme is a general one; there is no Danish exceptionalism.

There is a paradox: globalization and transnationalism both undermine and strengthen nationalist feelings. So far from withering away in an era of globalization and transnationalism, the nation-state appears to be strengthening. Contemporary globalization is, however, neo-liberal globalization, and we are living through a period of great economic and political change and uncertainty. Whether or not we have seen the end of the hegemony of the Washington consensus, and are now in a post-neo-liberal ecumene remains unclear, but the present conjuncture manifestly threatens ways of life and livelihood, and the order of things, and poses difficult questions about identity. Although globalization and transnationalism are often celebrated as liberating us from essentialism, by challenging the idea that "we" are national cultural subjects, bearers of a culture, they actually do the opposite. There is thus no real paradox, counter-nationalism responds to the threat posed by globalization and transnationalism, and the disrupting, disembedding character of the contemporary conjuncture.

References

Bauböck, Rainer. 1994. *From Aliens to Citizens: Redefining the Legal Status of Immigrants*. Aldershot: Avebury.

Carrier, James. 1995. *Occidentalism: Images of the West*. Oxford: Clarendon Press.

Castles, Stephen, *et al.* 2003. *Integration: Mapping the Field*. London: Home Office

Favell, Adrian. 1998. *Philosophies of Integration: Immigration and the Idea of Citizenship in France and Britain*. London: Macmillan.

Grillo, Ralph. 2007a. Artistic Licence, Free Speech and Religious Sensibilities in a Multicultural Society. In *Law and Ethnic Plurality: Socio-Legal Perspectives*, ed. Prakash Shah, 107-125. Leiden: Brill/Martinus Nijhoff.
—. 2007b. An Excess of Alterity? Debating Difference in a Multicultural Society. *Ethnic and Racial Studies* 30 (6): 979-998.
—. 2010a. British and Others: From "Race" to "Faith". In *The Multiculturalism Backlash: European Discourses, Policies and Practices*, ed. Steven Vertovec & Susanne Wessendorf, 50-71. London: Routledge.
—. 2010b. *Contesting Diversity in Europe: Alternative Regimes and Moral Orders, MMG Working Paper 10-02*. Göttingen: Max Planck Institute for the Study of Religious and Ethnic Diversity.
Grillo, R.D. and Pratt, J.C., eds. 2002. *The Politics of Recognizing Difference: Multiculturalism Italian Style*. Basingstoke: Ashgate.
Gullestad, Marianne. 2001. Imagined Sameness: Shifting Notions of "Us" and "Them" in Norway. In *Forestillinger Om Den Andre. Images of Otherness*, ed. Line Alice Ytrehus, 32-58. Kristiansand: Høyskoleforlaget.
Halliday, Fred. 2006. Blasphemy and Power. *OpenDemocracy*, http://www.opendemocracy.net/globalization/blasphemy_3262.jsp. Accessed 22 June, 2010].
Heckmann, Friedrich, et al. 2006. *Integration and Integration Policies: IMISCOE Network Feasibility Study*. Bamberg: EFMS INTPOL Team.
Hedetoft, Ulf. 2010. Denmark versus Multiculturalism. In *The Multiculturalism Backlash: European Discourses, Policies and Practices*, ed. Steven Vertovec & Susanne Wessendorf, 111-129. London: Routledge.
Higham, John. 1988. *Strangers in the Land: Patterns of American Nativism, 1860-1925*. New Brunswick: Rutgers University Press.
Jenkins, Roy. 1967. *Essays and Speeches*. London: Collins.
Parkin, David. 1978. *The Cultural Definition of Political Response: Lineal Destiny among the Luo*. London: Academic Press.
Pedersen, Marianne Holm & Mikkel Rytter 2006. *Den stille integration*. Copenhagen: C.A. Reitzel.
Pratt, Jeff. 2002. Italy: Political Unity and Cultural Diversity. In *The Politics of Recognizing Difference: Multiculturalism Italian-style*, ed. Ralph Grillo & Jeff Pratt, 25-40. Aldershot: Ashgate.
Rex, John. 1995. The Political Sociology of a Multicultural Society. In *Citizenship and Rights in Multicultural Societies*, ed. Michael Dunne & Tiziano Bonazzi, 79-94. Keele: Keele University Press.

Riccio, Bruno. 2001. From "Ethnic Group" to "Transnational Community"? Senegalese Migrants' Ambivalent Experiences and Multiple Trajectories. *Journal of Ethnic and Migration Studies* 27 (4): 583-599.

Sartori, Giovanni. 2002. *Pluralismo, Multiculturalismo e Estranei*, 2nd Edition. Milan: Rizzoli.

Soysal, Yasmin. 1994. *Limits of Citizenship: Migrants and Post-national Membership in Europe*. Chicago: Chicago University Press.

Vertovec, Steven & Susanne Wessendorf, eds. 2010. *The Multiculturalism Backlash: European Discourses, Policies and Practices*. London: Routledge.

Wikan, Unni. 2002. *Generous Betrayal: Politics of Culture in the New Europe*. Chicago: University of Chicago Press.

THE MULTIPLE REGISTERS OF IMMIGRANT RECEPTION: COMPARATIVE MYTHOLOGIES

VERED AMIT

There are many significant differences between Canada, the country in which I reside, and Denmark, the focus of this volume, particularly with respect to their respective histories and discourses of immigration. If contemporary immigration has discursively been treated in Denmark as introducing a foreign element into an otherwise culturally homogenous society, in Canada immigration is more usually represented as a historically iconic medium for building a diverse society. Yet aspects of the rhetorics associated with immigrant integration in Denmark that are reported in this volume are by no means altogether unfamiliar in Canada.

The Immigrant Other

Thus in 2007, the municipal council of Hérouxville, a small rural town in the Mauricie region of Quebec adopted a code of practice "to indicate to newcomers which 'Quebecois' values must be respected. They went out of their way to note that stoning and female circumcision are formally prohibited in town." (Dubuc 2007). One might have expected that the adoption of these measures in a town that had no resident immigrants would be consigned to a contentious but highly localized eccentricity. But in the lead up to a provincial election, the Hérouxville measures quickly became a political hot potato and the ground was set for their infusion into a broader debate about the "reasonable accommodation" of newcomers to Quebec. Later, an editorial in a Toronto newspaper opined that the opposition to cultural and religious accommodation of new immigrants and other minority groups, which had appeared in a poll administered in Quebec, was likely also felt "to a greater or lesser extent" in the neighbouring province of Ontario (October 15, 2007). Nonetheless, Alain Dubuc, a Quebec journalist, argued that immigrants were probably not the main target of the anger and unhappiness expressed in the Hérouxville measures.

> It isn't women wearing veils that is threatening their identity, but rather the urban world in general, which, with its multiethnic culture, its departure from religion, its various elites and intellectuals, its gay villages, its artists and its movers and shakers, represents a challenge to their more traditional way of life. As Montreal resembles less and less places like Hérouxville, it's becoming for rural Quebecers a foreign land. This same split between the rural communities and urban centres, which have been profoundly transformed by immigration, is found across the western world. (Dubuc 2007).

Like many of the contributions to this volume, Dubuc's comments underscore the manner in which the topic of immigration or immigrant integration serves as a cipher for anxieties about a much wider range of social cleavages and historical transformations. Hanne Mogensen (Chapter 10, this volume) argues that while the challenges experienced by the HIV positive African women she interviewed in Denmark were usually presented in ethnic terms, they serve as a "reminder of more general problems of exclusion and loneliness within the encompassing welfare state". And a globalized and increasingly mobile world, Mogensen argues, poses challenges to the endurance of a Danish welfare state based on presumptions of cultural homogeneity and long-term relationships.

But if globalizing connections can be the catalysts for systemic transformations, they can also serve as the basis for the ramification of particular representations of and debates over these changes. As Karen Olwig and Karsten Paerregaard note in their introduction to this volume, a Danish newspaper's publication of satirical cartoons depicting the prophet Muhammad provoked a global reaction: headlines in media across the world; anger and protest by Muslims in many countries; and the republication of the cartoons in newspapers elsewhere. While in Canada only one newspaper, the *Western Standard*, reprinted the cartoons, this does not mean that the country has been entirely spared the Islamophobia that has diffused through other regions and countries. The phantasm of the menacing Muslim "other", which wafted through the Hérouxville "code of living", was not home grown; it didn't reflect local histories, relationships or cleavages in this exclusively white, francophone Quebec town. But as an internationally disseminated set of prejudices, it was readily available to be imported and grafted onto more familiar resentments. In some important ways, therefore, the Hérouxville and the Danish cartoon controversies are telling illustrations of both the intensely rapid dissemination of certain images and discourses as well as the disjunctures that, as Appadurai (1990:11) noted, occur between the flow of people, images and ideas.

But while non-isomorphic, there is a dynamic feedback loop between these differential flows. As the case studies featured in the second half of this volume illustrate, general distinctions between Danes and immigrants serve as convenient categorical fall backs for explaining away difficulties in accommodating certain clients in various Danish welfare institutions. The invocation of these categorical distinctions do not, in themselves, account for the particular difficulties that certain people experience when accessing services in Danish daycares, clinics, psychiatric institutions, rehabilitation centres, but they do serve to legitimate the marginalization and exclusion of certain people. The various case studies featured in part two of this volume report variants of "it's not what we, the service providers, *do* but who they, the immigrant clients *are* that is the problem". This kind of representation is then used to defer responsibility respectively for the difficulties a child may be experiencing in adjusting to a daycare; or of a psychiatric patient in accessing appropriate treatment; of a refugee being "rehabilitated" as a torture victim without acknowledgement of the political resistance implicated in his/her wounds; or of a desperately lonely woman receiving a professional but arm's length treatment for HIV. So, the disjuncture between the movement of certain kinds of representations and the mobility of people across borders and between institutions does not occlude the dialectic between them. Hence the construction of the immigrant, and these days especially of the *Muslim* immigrant, is at once thoroughly transnational and also intensely localized, as localized as a mother who cannot convince her anxious child to move from the front lobby of a daycare to join her assigned group.

Danish and other Paradigms of National Identity

As much or perhaps even more than categorical constructions of the "immigrant", this volume is concerned with the ways in which debates about immigration are used to construct Danishness. And here again, there is a familiar resonance in this representation of liberal society that extends well beyond the borders of Denmark. The first half of this volume is dedicated to deconstructing dominant ideas of Danish society. The various chapters in this section thus respectively underscore the unexamined nature of Danish ideals of cultural homogeneity and the ways in which this paradigm draws on and in turn informs readings of other national orthodoxies: the centrality of the welfare state, the kinship of the "family of Denmark", the consensus driven National Church, and so on.

Valorization of Danish cultural homogeneity is by no means automatic. As Steffen Jöhncke (this volume) points out, one kind of depiction is likely to represent it as being associated with a prejudiced and parochial "mindset". But another more dominant version of Danish cultural homogeneity imbues it with "individual freedom, personal choice and social engagement" (Olwig and Paerregaard, this volume). As Inger Sjørslev (this volume) notes, the Danish notion of democracy – associated with the work of Hal Koch – as a substantive set of common values rather than a procedural set of rules is a classic version of democratic liberalism. And as such, it is likely to resonate, to a greater or lesser extent, with renderings of democracy in many other Western countries. In many ways, therefore, constructions of Danishness appear to be drawing on claims to a broader Western Enlightenment tradition. And the tendency to assume that Muslim immigrants hold values that are incommensurable with this tradition could similarly be interpreted as an instance of a much more widespread, venerable Western tradition of Orientalism (Said 2003) as well as more recent versions of European cultural fundamentalism (Stolcke 1999). In other words, part of the reason that the trope of "Danish values" can escape examination is that it presumes and draws on a very familiar, widespread orthodoxy or "ideoscape" of Western or European particularity.

In their introduction to this volume, Olwig and Paerregaard contrast the heroic status of immigrants and refugees historically enjoyed in North America with their representation as marginal and problematic populations in Demark and most other Western European countries. But as the debate over "reasonable accommodation" in Quebec illustrates, the distinction between these two mythic stances can at times be painfully thin.

> Regrettably, these two political leaders may just be tapping into a deep well of unease among Quebecers, as well as many in Ontario and elsewhere across Canada, who question whether this country has become too tolerant, has welcomed too many immigrants who don't share *Canadian values* and is naïve to believe multiculturalism works. (emphasis added, Editorial, Toronto Star, October 15, 2007).

Employing Different Registers of Analysis

Given the overlaps between these discourses and their employment of familiar tropes of Enlightenment values and Orientalism, it would be temptingly easy to dismiss the Danish "question of integration" as simply another instance of an enduring Western "mindset". But to give in to this temptation would be to replace Orientalism with Occidentalism. Hence in accounting for immigrant reception in Denmark or Canada, for that matter, the challenge for analysts is to consider the dynamic interplay between the different registers shaping attendant attitudes and practices: global connections, transnational philosophical traditions, more particular regional or national mythic ideals (immigrant society, cultural homogeneity), state and institutional histories, political campaigns and rivalries, cleavages and inequalities, social transformations or the "microintegration" dynamics (Anderson, this volume) of face-to-face encounters and daily practices.

The efforts, in this volume, by a group of Danish scholars to examine the "question of integration" in their own country at many if not all of these levels reminds us of the scope of the analytical challenge this field of inquiry poses. But it also serves as a telling testament of the importance of thoroughly grounding our analysis of the movement of people, ideas and images in particular relationships, institutions, places and regimes. For as Steffen Jöhncke notes (this volume), without this kind of multi-level grounding, scholarly analyses run the risk of entrenching rather than deconstructing the essentialism that so often characterizes popular debates about immigration reception. Fortunately that is far from being the case with this volume.

References

Appadurai, Arjun. 1990. Disjuncture and Difference in the Global Cultural Economy. *Public Culture* 2 (2): 1-24.
Dubuc, Alain. 2007. Fear and ignorance: A rural revolt. *The Vancouver Sun*, March 1 (www.canada.com/story_print.html?id=2d10e22f-1e874faf-a6dc-15ffebaa8ab7&sponsor=, accessed June 19, 2010).
Editorial. 2007. Canadian reality is multicultural. *The Toronto Star*, October 15. (www.thestar.com/printarticle/266436, accessed June 19, 2010).
Said, Edward W. 2003. *Orientalism*. London: Penguin Books.
Stolcke, Verena. 1999. New rhetorics of exclusion in Europe. *International Social Science Journal* 51 (159): 25-35.

CONTRIBUTORS

Vered Amit, Professor of Anthropology, Concordia University. Her research has focused on a range of circumstances and locales including intra- and interethnic boundaries among Armenians in London; youth cultures; ethnic lobbying; expatriacy in the Cayman Islands; transnational consultants and international student travel and an ongoing study of inherited dual citizenship. Running through all of these different projects has been an ongoing preoccupation with the workings of and intersections between different forms of transnational mobility. She is the author or editor of ten books with an eleventh in press, including *Going First Class? New Approaches to Privileged Travel and Movement* (Berghahn, 2007), and the forthcoming *Young Men in Uncertain Times* (with Noel Dyck).

Sally Anderson, Associate Professor, Department of Education, Aarhus University. Her research interests include children, education, religion, and movement culture with specific focus on the forms of sociality intrinsic to processes of civil enculturation and social incorporation. She is the author of numerous articles and *Civil Sociality: Children, Sport and Cultural Policy in Denmark* (2008, Information Age Publishing).

Helle Bundgaard, Associate Professor, Department of Anthropology, University of Copenhagen. She is concerned with cultural identity, childhood, institutionalisation and processes of learning. Among her recent publications are "Targeting immigrant children: Disciplinary rationales in Danish Pre-schools" (with E. Gulløv), in *Exploring Regimes of Discipline: The Dynamics of Restraint*, ed. N. Dyck (Oxford, 2008) and "Children of different Categories: educational Practice and the production of difference in Danish Day-care Institutions" (with E. Gulløv) *Journal of Ethnic and Migration Studies* 32 (1): 145-155, 2006.

Sofie Danneskiold-Samsoe, Assistant Professor, Institute for Society and Globalisation, Roskilde University. Her Ph.D. in anthropology from the University of Copenhagen was entitled *The Moral Economy of Suffering: Social Exchange among Iraqi Refugees in the Danish Welfare State* (2006). Her research focuses on social suffering and gendered violence among Middle Eastern families in the context of the welfare state.

Ralph Grillo, Emeritus Professor of Social Anthropology, the University of Sussex. Although he has written previously on the anthropology of development, and the anthropology of language, his principal concern is now with transnational migration and multiculturalism in Europe, and contemporary debates about managing diversity in France, Italy, the Scandinavian countries, and the UK. Through the Sussex Centre for Migration Research he has been actively involved in the IMISCOE network, and has most recently been collaborating with anthropologists, lawyers and political scientists on issues relating to legal practice and cultural diversity in Europe and North America. Recent publications include R. Grillo, ed., *The Family in Question: Immigrant and Ethnic Minorities in Multicultural Europe* (Amsterdam University Press, 2008), and R. Grillo et al., eds., *Legal Practice and Cultural Diversity* (Ashgate, 2009).

Heiko Henkel, Associate Professor, Department of Anthropology, University of Copenhagen. His current research interests focus on the encounter of European liberal publics with Muslim minorities and among his publications are "Turkish Islam in Germany: A Problematic Tradition or the Fifth Project of Constitutional Patriotism?" *Journal of Muslim Minority Affairs* 28 (1), 2008; "The Location of Islam: Inhabiting Istanbul in a Muslim way", *American Ethnologist* 34(1), 2007, and "Are Muslim women in Europe threatening the secular public sphere? Debate with Thijl Sunier", *Social Anthropology* 17 (4), 2009.

Richard Jenkins, Professor of Sociology, the University of Sheffield. Trained as an anthropologist at the Queen's University of Belfast and the University of Cambridge, he has undertaken field research in Northern Ireland, England, Wales and Denmark. Among his recent publications are *Foundations of Sociology* (Palgrave, 2002), *Social Identity* (3rd edition, Routledge, 2008), *Rethinking Ethnicity* (2nd edition, Sage, 2008) and *Being Danish* (Museum Tusculanum Press, 2011).

Tina Gudrun Jensen, Researcher at the Danish National Centre for Social Research. She has done fieldwork in Brazil and Denmark, and her main areas of interest are religion, cultural complexity, inter-ethnic relations and social integration. Her publications include *Nye muslimer i Danmark – møder og omvendelser* (with K. Østergaard) (2007); "To be 'Danish', becoming 'Muslim': Contestations of National Identity?", *Journal of Ethnic and Migration Studies* (2008); "'Making Room´: Encompassing

Diversity in Denmark", in A. Silj (ed.) *European Multiculturalism Revisited* (2010).

Katrine Schepelern Johansen, Post Doc., Department of Anthropology, University of Copenhagen. Her research areas are transcultural psychiatry, medical anthropology, dual diagnosis, drug use, heroin assisted treatment and her major publications include "Dual diagnosis and psychosocial interventions – Introduction and Commentary" (Co-authored with B. Tylstrup) *Nordic Journal of Psychiatry* 63 (3), 2009; *Dobbelt diagnose – Dobbelt behandling*. Glostrup: KABS-VIDEN (2009); *Kultur og psykiatri – en antropologi om transkulturel psykiatri på danske hospitaler*, PhD thesis, Department of Anthropology, University of Copenhagen (2006).

Steffen Jöhncke, Senior Advisor, Department of Anthropology, University of Copenhagen. He is head of AnthroAnalysis, the department's research unit on applied anthropology and co-operative projects. He has worked as an anthropologist in policy and practice in Denmark since 1988 and his publications include "Treatmentality and the governing of drug use" in *Drugs and Alcohol Today* 9 (4), 2009, and "Culture in the Clinic: Danish Service Providers' View of Immigrants with HIV", in M. Haour-Knipe and R. Rector (eds): *Crossing Borders. Migration, Ethnicity and AIDS,* London: Taylor and Francis (1996).

Hanne O. Mogensen, Associate Professor, Department of Anthropology, University of Copenhagen. She specializes in medical anthropology and has followed the arrival of antiretroviral treatment in African countries. Among her publications are: "New Hopes and New Dilemmas. Disclosure and Recognition in the Time of Antiretroviral Treatment", in H. Dilger og U. Luig (eds): *Morality, Hope and Grief. Anthropologies of AIDS in Africa,* Oxford: Berghahn, 2010; "Surviving AIDS? The Uncertainty of Antiretroviral Treatment", in L. Haram og C. B. Yamba (eds): *Dealing with Uncertainty in Contemporary African Lives*, Nordic Africa Institute, 2009, and *AIDS is a kind of kahungo that kills*, Scandinavia University Press, 1995.

Karen Fog Olwig, Professor, Department of Anthropology, University of Copenhagen. She has published extensively on Caribbean migration with particular focus on the significance of family networks in migration processes. In recent years she has also done research on the social incorporation of migrants and refugees in Danish society. Recent publications include *Caribbean Journeys: An Ethnography of Migration* *and Home in Three Family Networks* (Duke University Press, 2007),*"Integration" - Migrants and Refugees between Scandinavian Welfare Societies and Family Relations*, special issue of *Journal of Ethnic and Migration Studies*, 2011, edited with B.R. Larsen and M. Rytter, and *Mobile Bodies, Mobile Souls: Family, Religion and Migration* (Aarhus University Press, 2011) edited with M. Rytter.

Karsten Paerregaard, Associate Professor, Department of Anthropology, University of Copenhagen. In the past twenty years his research has been focused on migration inside and outside Peru and recently he has engaged in a project studying climate change in Peru. His publications include *Linking Separate Worlds. Urban Migrants and Rural Lives in Peru* (Berg, 1997); *Peruvians Dispersed. A Global Ethnography of Migration* (Lexington Books, 2008), *El Quinto Suyo. Transnacionalidad y formaciones diaspóricas en la migración peruana* (Instituto de Estudios Peruanos, Lima, 2005) edited with U. Berg, and *Peruvian Migration*, special issue of *Latin American Perspectives*, 2011, edited with A. Takenaka and U. Berg.

Cecilie Rubow, Associate Professor, Department of Anthropology, University of Copenhagen. Her research interests are religion, ritual, death, transcendence, environmental ethics and climate change. She has worked primarily in Denmark, but is now engaged in studies in Cook Islands, Polynesia. Her publications include "Making Pastors. Making Christians. Secular and religious transcendences in Danish ordination rituals" *Journal of Ritual Studies*, 23 (2), 2009, and "Metaphysical Aspects of Resilience: South Pacific Responses to Climate Change," in *The Question of Resilience* (The Royal Danish Academy of Sciences and Letters, 2009).

Mikkel Rytter, Assistant Professor, Department of Anthropology, Archaeology and Linguistics, Aarhus University. He is currently involved in the cross-disciplinary research project on "Sufism and Transnational Spirituality". Recent publications include "In-laws and Outlaws. Black magic among Pakistani migrants in Denmark", *The Journal of Royal Anthropological Institute*, 16(1); *"Integration" - Migrants and Refugees between Scandinavian Welfare Societies and Family Relations*, special issue of *Journal of Ethnic and Migration Studies*, 2011, edited with B.R. Larsen and M. Rytter, and *Mobile Bodies, Mobile Souls: Family, Religion and Migration* (Aarhus University Press, 2011) edited with K. F. Olwig.

Inger Sjørslev, Associate Professor, Department of Anthropology, Copenhagen University. She has carried out fieldwork in Denmark on politics, sociality and materiality, and in Brazil on ritual. She has published numerous articles and a monograph in Danish, *Gudernes Rum – en beretning om ritualer og tro i Brasilien,* 1995, and in German translation as *Glaube und Bessessenheit. Ein Bericht über die Candomblé-Religion in Brasilien*, Gifkendorf, Merlin Verlag, 1999.

INDEX

Afghanistan 133, 263
Africa 3, 5, 173, 207-229, 272, 278
al-Jazeera 132, 147
alienation 115, 266
Allah 114, 124
Americas 8
Americans 8-10, 31, 40, 61-63, 79, 91, 94-95, 104, 136, 140, 142, 145-146, 181-182, 187, 198-199, 203, 243, 252, 266
Amit, Vered 23, 224
andelsforeninger (cooperatives) 139
Anderson, Sally 21, 224-26, 252, 265, 273
Annan, Kofi 81
antiretroviral treatment 207-208, 210-212 215, 219, 226
Apparurai, Arjun 138
Arab 120, 122, 123, 191, 252
Arabic 114, 121, 132, 147, 157-158, 162-164, 188, 197, 257
assimilation 8, 9, 136, 138, 145, 256, 267
asylum 19, 63, 66, 80, 81, 85, 89, 90, 187, 261, 272, 274
Australia 268
authenticity 88, 122, 265

Balkan 3
Baumann, Gerd 83, 90
Bornholm 4, 5, 24
Bourdieu, Pierre 107, 189
Brazil 88, 91, 242, 245, 252
Britain 14-15, 23, 38, 61, 136, 147, 256, 263, 267-68, 270-71, 283
Brown, Wendy 140, 141, 147
Bundgaard, Helle 20, 166, 259

Canada 263, 268, 272, 277, 278, 280, 281
cartoons, see Muhammad cartoons
categories 16, 22, 62, 64, 70, 84-85, 96, 112-13, 123, 126, 156, 169, 172-73, 175-77, 179-80, 182, 183, 231, 234, 251
commonsense 20
cultural 15, 164
ethnic 85, 122, 172
categorization 113, 115, 116, 119, 121, 123, 124, 168-186, 193, 217
church 18, 94-111, 142, 234
class 4, 5, 22, 38, 39, 40-50, 106, 139, 152, 173, 236, 237, 242, 262
Chicago School of Sociology 8, 24
children 3, 7, 9, 11, 13, 19-20, 22, 32, 37, 39, 40, 42, 48, 56, 58, 60-62, 65, 67, 69, 84, 86, 102, 121, 123-26, 145, 150-167, 173, 190, 195, 199, 201, 212, 213, 218, 223-24, 226, 240, 241, 243, 245, 249, 258-260, 262, 269, 279
Christianity 37, 87, 94-111, 118, 120-125, 139, 180, 259, 260, 261, 263, 265
Christmas 125, 218, 242
citizenship 45, 55, 57, 59, 63, 64, 68-69, 72, 91, 100, 129, 141, 143, 145-46, 273
civil society 101, 143, 144, 224, 230-32, 234, 237, 258, 261
civility 129, 130, 137, 145, 147, 258
coherence 24-26, 61, 127, 189

cohesion 2, 8, 10, 22, 34-36, 41, 47, 94, 109, 112, 137-38, 145, 208, 221, 230, 273
constructions, 10, 12, 40, 46, 60, 99, 108, 144, 263, 280
   categorical 279
   cultural 16, 18, 32, 36, 39, 49
   social 42
conversion, religious 18, 112-28
Copenhagen 6, 12, 37, 67, 99, 100, 113, 120-21, 124-25, 127, 171, 188, 203, 208, 212, 215, 218, 221, 228, 232, 238, 242
cosiness (*hygge*) 61, 86, 125
cultural anxiety 1
cultural diversity 4, 6, 9, 22, 127, 268
cultural difference 4, 12, 14-15, 18, 22, 38, 60, 122, 181, 222, 242
cultural homogeneity 5, 7, 18, 117, 256, 263, 268, 278-81
cultural formulation, DSM-IV 181-82
cultural fundamentalism 67, 85, 280
cultural models 79, 83, 87, 157
cultural pluralism 9, 112, 143
cultural traditions 4, 8, 13, 114, 137-39, 144-45, 221

Danish Evangelical Lutheran Church 18, 94-111, 114, 131, 138-139, 142-143, 259, 280
Danish Institute for Human Rights 58, 71, 72
Danish People's Party (*Dansk Folkeparti*) 24, 32, 57, 80-82, 89, 98, 137-38, 142-43, 264
Danishness 16, 18, 80, 103, 112-13, 115, 117-18, 126, 130, 136-37, 139, 143-44, 146, 220, 223, 259-60, 262-64, 279-80
Danneskiold-Samsoe, Sofie 20
day-care 19, 150-167, 225, 259, 279

democracy 13, 21, 86-87, 91, 98, 112, 180, 198, 234-35, 280
diagnosing 202
diagnosis 169-171, 175, 182-83, 188, 194
discourse 22, 42, 61, 64-65, 69-70, 72, 77-81, 83, 85, 88, 106, 112-13, 115, 117-18, 123, 126-27, 138, 140, 144, 182, 203-04, 267, 271, 274, 277, 279-80
discrimination 14, 77, 90, 146, 216
disintegration 34, 137
distinction 35, 55, 64, 144, 172, 175-77, 280
distinctions, categorical 6, 12, 30, 87, 279
drug use 139, 169, 175-76
Dubuc, Alain 277-78
Durkheim, Émile 33, 34, 49, 94, 105, 107, 109, 208

Einhorn, Eric S. 31, 50
education 7, 13, 16, 21, 30, 35, 40, 50, 68, 100, 152, 173, 190, 210, 236, 239, 242, 246, 252, 258-60, 264
emancipation 152, 153, 165
Emerek, Ruth 30
emic 88
empire, imperial power 5, 6, 221, 263, 268
Englishman 267
Enlightenment 280
equality 2, 17, 22, 23, 31, 40, 43-44, 46, 72, 79, 86, 96, 98, 109, 159, 162, 180, 210, 256, 268, 270
Esping-Andersen, Gösta 38-39, 43, 47
ethnic boundaries 21-22, 122
ethnic diversity 1
ethnic group 13, 114, 122, 137, 172, 212-13, 235
ethnic minorities 30-32, 44-45, 48-49, 82, 150, 153, 165, 172, 180-83, 231, 234, 237, 250

ethnic organizations 7
ethnic stereotypes 20
ethnic terms 227, 278
ethnicity 44, 47, 110, 119, 169, 172, 179, 182-83, 189, 249
ethno-nationalism 138
ethnos 230-31, 237, 248-51
exchange 21, 35, 125, 144, 163, 189, 190, 197-99, 235, 238, 243-246, 250, 252
  generalized 231, 250
  morality of 233
  social 21, 35, 187-90, 197-99, 202, 230, 235, 238-41, 244-46, 248
  theory of 189
exclusion 2, 12, 18-19, 35, 45, 77, 79-80, 83-84, 88, 117, 208, 214, 217, 227, 259, 262, 278-79

family reunification 14, 54-55, 58-59, 61, 63-64, 66-71
Farnell, Brenda 235
Faroe Islands 5, 6, 24, 71
feelings 23, 35, 70, 105-06, 151, 171-72, 222, 267, 274
fieldwork 24, 106, 113, 117-18, 150, 160, 165, 171, 176, 180, 191, 195, 204-5, 209, 216, 218, 222-23, 236, 246
folk 110, 231-32, 257-58
folkekirke 94-95, 110, 131, 138-39, 142-43
folketing (parliament) 54, 64, 70, 98
Foner, Nancy 8, 10
Foucault, Michel 83, 140
France, French 41, 61, 66, 264, 267-68
French Huguenots 12
Funen (Fyn) 120, 127, 237-38

Geertz, Clifford 103
Gellner, Ernest 260
gender 119, 122, 159-60, 175, 182, 189, 236, 257, 261

generation 2, 3, 5, 9, 16, 22, 37, 54, 63, 66, 69, 98, 139, 189, 235-36, 260, 267-68
Germany 5, 6, 12, 18, 38-39, 67, 78, 79, 88, 130, 140, 251, 270
Gingrich, André 83-84, 90-91, 137
globalization 2, 145, 22, 23, 57, 70, 108, 137, 250, 273-74
Graeber, David 199, 204
grammar, structural 83-84, 90
Greece 187
Greenland 5-6, 24, 71, 237
Grillo, Ralph 14, 23
Grundtvig, N.F.S. 139
guest workers 12, 13, 61, 262
Gullestad, Marianne 25, 42, 86, 210, 268, 270
Gulløv, Eva 165, 225

Haarder, Bertel 56, 66, 80, 269-70
Habermas, Jürgen 129, 144, 147
Hage, Ghassan 238
halal (allowed) 116, 121, 125
Hamburger, Charlotte 30
haram (forbidden) 116, 121, 125
health 2, 20-21, 31, 39-40, 42, 49-50, 89, 99, 104, 169, 179-80, 187, 190, 192, 194-97, 200, 202, 211-12, 219, 222-23, 230-37, 239, 241, 243, 247, 250-51, 268
Henkel, Heiko 19, 272-73
heritage 4, 63, 151, 221
Hérouxville 277-78
heterogeneity 22, 34, 39, 118, 127, 278
Higham, John 266
hijab (veil) 115, 119, 124, 127, 243
HIV/AIDS 21, 207-12, 214-19, 222-27, 272, 278-79
Hizb ut-Tarir 141
Hlayhel, Raed 132
Holstein 5, 57
homogeneity 38-39, 45, 95, 117, 221, 222, 227, 268
  cultural 5, 7, 18, 256, 263, 268, 278-79, 280-81

Honneth, Axel 129-30, 143-44, 147
Hornbech, Birthe Rønn 142
Howell, Signe 65, 67
hygge, see cosiness

ideals 30, 40, 46, 211, 268-69, 279, 281
Iceland 5, 71
identity 9, 17, 19, 32, 40-42, 55, 57, 65, 69-70, 79, 82-83, 88, 90-91, 105-6, 112-13, 115-121, 123-24, 126-27, 130, 134, 136-138, 143, 146, 172, 174, 182, 208, 217, 220, 226, 228, 235, 265, 274, 278-79
  cultural 182
  Danish 82, 112, 115-18, 123, 126, 208, 217, 265
  ethnic 9, 123, 172-73, 235
  Muslim 116, 118-19, 124, 136
  religious 118, 120, 123-24, 134
  social 113
identification 35, 96, 113, 115-16, 123, 172, 191, 267
ideology 22, 32, 35, 80, 84-86, 88-89, 99, 103, 153, 165, 270
iftar (break-fast) 125
imam 114, 121, 132-35, 191, 196, 271
inclusion 83, 86, 88, 117, 149, 267
India 5, 71, 90, 242, 245, 252, 271
individualization 165
inequality 7, 18, 43-44, 162, 230, 236, 247
Ingold, Tim 235, 250
integration 2, 8-13, 15, 18-19, 22-23, 31-32, 35-36, 38, 46, 49, 54-56, 64-65, 71, 77-91, 95-96, 99, 102, 109, 112-13, 117, 127, 138-39, 150, 187-88, 190, 192-98, 203-4, 208, 210-11, 222, 230-31, 233-35, 237, 242, 246, 248, 250-51, 256-60, 267-70, 273, 277-78, 280
  cultural 30, 257, 260
  debate 14, 208, 210, 270-71
  definition 14, 30, 267
  micro- 19, 21, 230, 235, 249-50, 273, 281
  Ministry of 11, 23, 34, 56, 66, 80, 142, 193, 205, 234, 269
  process 12, 19, 69, 85, 108, 138-39, 258
  problem 22-23, 35, 37, 46, 80, 261
  policy 13, 36, 70, 82, 262, 264, 269
  social 30, 33, 35-36, 150, 192, 193, 198, 203, 230-31, 233-35, 248, 250-51, 25
interpreter 156, 162, 170, 177-79
Iran 3, 119, 146, 191, 203, 263
Iraq 3, 20, 133, 187-92, 195-96, 198, 200-1, 203, 242, 263
Islam 1, 7, 18, 80, 96-97, 99, 102, 112-128, 129-48, 180, 184, 190-1, 197, 205, 262-63, 270, 272-73
Islamisk Trossamfund 141-42
Islamophobia 18, 81-82, 90, 261, 278
Italy 268, 270,

Jehovah's Witnesses 102, 124
Jenkins, Richard 22
Jenkins, Roy 267-68
Jensen, Tina Gudrun 18, 61, 273
Jews 12, 78, 102, 251
jilbab (dress) 115, 119
Jöhncke, Steffen 17, 171, 174, 193, 210, 269, 280
Johansen, Katrine Schepelern 20, 184
Jutland (Jylland) 4, 119-21, 124-25, 127, 195, 241, 264
Juul, Jesper 152
Jyllands-Posten 81-82, 129, 131-34, 136, 140, 147

kindergarten 151-52, 218, 224-25, 242, 259, 262
kinship 55-56, 60, 62-64, 68-70, 122, 160, 280, 281
Kirk, Hans 4
Klemperer, Victor 78-79, 81, 89
Koch, Hal 86-87, 280
Koran 121

labour 3-6, 10, 34, 49, 70, 236, 267
  market 13, 31, 35, 39, 45, 49, 58, 80-81, 90, 152, 193, 236, 252
  migration 3, 12-13, 45, 63
  union 6
language 11, 17-18, 24, 31, 50, 56-57, 60, 68, 70, 78-79, 81-82, 84, 88, 91, 109, 112-13, 115, 132, 135, 147, 151, 153, 155, 160-65, 178-79, 181, 193, 235, 242-43, 245-46, 248, 257, 264, 267-68, 273
Larsen, Rune Engelbrecht 81-82, 90
Lebanon 3, 120, 132 238
Lévi-Strauss, Claude
likeness, see sameness
Luckmann, Thomas 105-06, 109
Luhmann, Niklas 35
Lutheranism 4, 96, 100, 104
Lykkeberg, Rune 47

marginalization 44, 134, 137, 234, 250, 279
marriage 2, 3, 7, 13, 17, 48, 54-55, 58-59, 62, 64-66, 68-70, 72, 78, 114-15, 119-20, 122, 127, 161, 213, 228, 237, 241
martyrdom 191, 202
Mauss, Marcel 189, 197, 204
McDermott, Ray 156
Mecca 121
media 1, 11-14, 18, 57, 64, 77-78, 80, 89, 106, 107, 131, 133, 135-36, 144, 147, 182, 257, 261, 264, 272, 278

"melting pot" 10, 267
Mexico 10
Middle East 1, 3, 45, 97, 122, 132-35, 142, 147, 179, 271
Ministry of Integration and Church Affairs 11, 34, 56, 66, 80, 142, 193, 205, 234, 269
minorities 14, 20, 30-32, 44-45, 48-49, 55, 61-62, 81-82, 96-97, 104, 102, 108, 115, 129-31, 134, 137, 140, 144-46, 150, 153, 155-56, 159-60, 164-65, 169-75, 179-83, 230, 234, 237, 250, 267-68, 271-72, 277
mobility 16, 225, 227, 272, 279
  international, transnational 31, 68
  social and economic 8-9, 34, 44
Mogensen, Hanne Overgaard 21, 278
monarchy 5, 50, 96, 98
Montreal 278
mosques 99, 113, 120-25
Muhammad cartoons 1-2, 14, 19, 22, 25, 77, 81-82, 90, 96-97, 100, 129-148, 191, 264, 271-73, 278
multicultural discourse 182
multicultural empire 5, 221
multicultural everyday reality 40, 269
multicultural identity 9
multicultural perspective 104
multicultural politics 140-41, 268
multicultural society 9, 23, 37, 102, 113, 182
multiculturalism 23, 114, 263, 267-68, 280
multiethnic society 9
multiethnic population 182
multiracial commonwealth 268
Muslims 1-2, 7, 14, 18-19, 22, 34, 55, 77, 79-82, 89, 96, 99, 102, 108, 112-128, 129-37, 140-47, 177-81, 183, 190-91, 218, 248-

49, 251, 257, 261-62, 270-72, 278-80

Nader, Laura 35-36, 46
nation state 5-6, 8, 23, 35, 56-57, 59, 63, 65, 94, 129, 137, 221, 257, 260, 261, 271, 273-274
national attachment 55-60, 64-65, 67-68, 70-72
national characteristics 267
national community 7, 8, 17, 55-57, 60-64, 66, 69-70, 98
national culture 112, 137, 139
national history 57
national identity 17, 32, 40-41, 65, 118, 137, 279
national order 56-57, 59, 63
national policy 70, 234
nationalism 32, 59-60, 63-64, 70, 106, 117, 138, 260, 263
nationalist discourse 138
nationalist feelings 23, 46, 137, 274
nationalist imaginary 38
nationalist politics 24, 32, 81, 98, 130, 137, 141
Nexø, Martin Andersen 4
norms 1, 2, 5, 13, 15, 30, 47, 81, 108, 139, 146, 151, 154-55, 172, 173, 221, 257-58, 260-61, 267-68
North America 8-10, 62, 132, 135, 280
Nørrebro 125, 237
Norway 5, 25, 42, 57, 59, 65, 86, 256, 268, 270

Occidentalism 281
Olsen, Lars 47
Olwig, Karen Fog 39, 221, 256, 265, 278, 280
Ontario 278, 280
orientalism 90, 280-81

Paerregaard, Karsten 39, 221, 256, 265, 278, 280

Pakistan 3, 16, 23, 54, 57, 59, 67, 69, 72, 242, 252
Parsons, Talcott 33
patients 20, 61, 168-186, 196, 198, 201, 215, 219, 222, 231-33, 241, 279
pedagogy 11, 152, 165
Pedersen, Marianne Holm 218
play, children's 150-53, 159, 164, 189, 197, 199
Poland 5, 24
Politiken 81, 90, 100, 147
population
  Danish 4-7, 10, 13-17, 24, 31, 39, 42, 47, 49, 57, 81, 82, 95-96, 107, 109, 114, 170, 180, 225, 237, 261
  immigrant 1-3, 10, 24, 45, 49, 54, 57, 66, 168, 170, 181-82, 261
  indigenous/native 21, 180, 266, 274
  movement 3, 6, 10, 70, 261
prejudice 37, 121, 278, 280
pre-school 11, 20, 21, 150-51, 225
psychiatry 167-171, 182-184
public debate 2, 14, 17-18, 78-80, 90, 91, 102-103, 127, 136-137, 180, 274

Quebec 23, 277-278, 280

racism 14-15, 45, 50, 78, 81-82, 163-164, 219, 261, 268
Ramadan 119, 125, 242-43
Rasmussen, Anders Fogh 89, 100, 132-133, 137-138, 140, 203
reciprocity 189, 198-199, 203-204, 238
religion 4, 38-39, 60, 63, 94-97, 99-109, 112, 116, 118, 122-124, 127, 170, 180, 259, 268, 272, 278
rights 9, 17, 31, 36, 42, 48, 56-58, 60, 66-67, 82, 98, 103, 133,

143-144, 147, 155, 174, 182-183, 196, 251, 267, 273
Rubow, Cecilie 18, 263, 265
Rytter, Mikkel 17, 25, 269
Ross, Alf 87
Rushdie Affair 271

salah (prayer) 119
sameness 31, 79, 86, 210-211, 220, 225-227, 268, 270
Sartori, Giovanni 267
Scandinavia 23-25, 31-32, 38-42, 46-47, 50, 61, 79, 86, 94, 96, 210, 270
Schierup, Carl-Ulrik 25, 30, 45
Schiffauer, Werner 258
Schimmelmann, Ernst 24
schismogenesis 135
schizophrenia 171, 176-177, 179, 183
Schleswig 5, 6, 24, 57
Schneider, David 62-64, 69
Schwartz, Jonathan 8, 10, 12, 15, 61
secularism 112, 142
Seidenfaden, Tøger 81, 90
shahada (profession of faith in Islam) 114, 121
Sikhs 271
Simmel, Georg 208-209, 217, 220-222, 252, 267
Sjørslev, Inger 17, 18, 91, 274, 280
social debt 238
social drama 132, 145
social gift 197, 204
social networks 122, 136, 224, 235
social technology 171-72, 174-177, 179, 183, 193-194
sociality 86, 207-209, 211, 224-26, 231, 234-37, 239, 241, 244, 246-251, 259
socialization 22, 114, 150
Somalia 3, 45, 66
Søvndal, Villy 141-43, 146
Spain 270
Spencer, Herbert 34

Sri Lanka 3, 45
Srole, Leo 9
Steincke, K.K. 37
stigma 17, 42, 116, 134, 212
Sweden 6, 41, 57, 65, 67-68, 84-85, 89, 94, 138, 241, 251

Taylor, Charles 11, 129, 147
terrorism 112
terrorist 2, 146
therapy 169, 196, 201, 232, 236-37
Thomas, W.I. 24
Tilly, Charles 8
tolerance 82, 137, 140-41, 145, 241, 256, 261, 263, 268
transcendence 105, 106
transnational family 69
transnational marriage 54, 58, 64-65, 67, 68
transnational belonging 66
transnationalism 23, 134, 251, 267, 271, 273-74
trauma 170, 187, 188, 193-95
Turkey 23, 55, 136, 242, 252
Turner, Victor 130, 145
Tylbor, Stephen 26

Uganda 21, 207-13, 215, 218, 220-23, 228
United Kingdom/UK see Britain
United Nations 81
United States/USA 9, 10, 24, 38, 57, 72, 95, 104, 109, 181-3, 194, 198

values 7, 8, 13, 18, 23, 31, 40, 46, 47, 49, 61, 79, 82-83, 87-88, 98, 101, 126, 137, 139, 151-52, 189, 193, 203-04, 259, 267-69, 272-74, 278, 280
Canadian 280
cultural 2, 15-16, 78-79, 99, 151, 172-73, 180-81, 272
Danish 8, 80, 112, 140, 165, 280
egalitarian 80
moral 151

Muslim 81
national 137
symbolic 189
van Gogh 272
Varenne, Hervé 250
Venstre/Liberal Party of Denmark 24, 54, 56, 79-80, 84, 89, 91, 133, 137
Vietnam 3, 91, 194
Vietnamese 16, 263
violence 132, 135, 144, 188, 194, 196, 262
voluntary association 86, 230, 234, 235

Warner, W. Lloyd 9
welfare 11, 17, 19, 22, 31, 38, 40-42, 46, 48, 98, 112, 151, 196, 225, 251, 257, 268
 benefits 20, 49, 169, 202, 269
 bureaucracy 45
 institutions 11, 18, 20, 170, 188-89, 195, 198, 200, 203-5, 227, 279
 officers 198-99
 offices 188
 policies 38, 41
 professionals 188
 programs 38, 42
 provisions 47-49, 251
 recipients 232
 scrounges 42
 schemes 43, 47
 services 7

society 2, 6-8, 11, 15-17, 22, 25, 104, 151-52, 230, 250, 272
state 6, 17, 19, 30-31, 32, 34-42, 44-50, 56-57, 60-61, 64, 69-70, 89, 98, 100, 110, 139, 165, 168-69, 180, 190, 194-97, 202-5, 208, 210-11, 222, 226-27, 230-31, 233, 247, 249-50, 261-62, 265, 269, 280
system 7, 8, 15-16, 20-22, 32, 41, 45-49, 56, 61, 64, 109, 188, 195-97, 211, 219, 221, 269
technologies 204
West Indies 5
Wikan, Unni 25, 270
Willerslev, Richard 24
Wirth, Lewis 24
women 7, 21, 48, 55, 84, 114, 115, 119, 120, 122, 124, 125, 152, 188, 209, 211, 212, 214, 222, 223, 224, 227, 228, 236, 237, 238, 239, 241, 242, 243, 244, 245, 247, 248, 249, 250, 251, 252, 272, 278
Wren, Karen 15

xenophobia 83, 115

Yugoslavia 23

Zealand (Sjælland) 121, 127, 150
Znaniecki, F. 24
Zuckerman, Phil 94, 104-5, 109